The State of the Parties

The State of the Parties:
The Changing Role of Contemporary
American Parties

EDITED BY

Daniel M. Shea
John C. Green

ROWMAN & LITTLEFIELD PUBLISHERS, INC.

ROWMAN & LITTLEFIELD PUBLISHERS, INC.

Published in the United States of America
by Rowman & Littlefield Publishers, Inc.
4720 Boston Way, Lanham, Maryland 20706

3 Henrietta Street
London WC2E 8LU, England

Copyright © 1994 by the Ray C. Bliss Institute of Applied Politics

All rights reserved. No part of this publication may be reproduced,
stored in a retrieval system, or transmitted in any form or by any
means, electronic, mechanical, photocopying, recording, or otherwise,
without the prior permission of the publisher.

British Cataloging in Publication Information Available

Library of Congress Cataloging-in-Publication Data

The state of the parties : the changing role of contemporary American parties / edited by
Daniel W. Shea and John C. Green.
p. cm.
Includes bibliographical references and index.
1. Political parties—United States. I. Shea, Daniel M. II. Green, John Clifford
JK2261.S824 1994 94-2297 324.273—dc20 CIP

ISBN 0-8476-7979-9 (cloth : alk. paper)
ISBN 0-8476-7980-2 (pbk. : alk. paper)

Printed in the United States of America

⊖™ The paper used in this publication meets the minimum requirements of
American National Standard for Information Sciences—Permanence of
Paper for Printed Library Materials, ANSI Z39.48–1964.

Dedicated to

*Dennis and Rosemary Shea
and
John and June Green*

Contents

Preface   xi

1. Paths and Crossroads: The State of the Parties and Party Scholarship, *Daniel M. Shea and John C. Green*   1

PART ONE
The Two-Party System Under Stress

2. The Future of the American Two-Party System, *A. James Reichley*   13

3. Who Speaks for the Political Parties? Or Martin Van Buren, Where Are You When We Need You? *Ralph M. Goldman*   27

4. Toward a Responsible Three-Party System, *Theodore J. Lowi*   45

PART TWO
Party Activities in 1992

5. The Politics of Cohesion: The Role of the National Party Committees in the 1992 Election, *Anthony Corrado*   61

6. Party Strategy and Campaign Activities in the 1992 Congressional Elections, *Paul S. Herrnson*   83

7. Hard Facts and Soft Money: State Party Finance in the 1992 Federal Elections, *Robert Biersack*   107

8. Local Political Parties and Legislative Races in 1992, *John Frendreis, Alan R. Gitelson, Gregory Flemming, and Anne Layzell*   133

9. Sources of Activism in the 1992 Perot Campaign, *Randall W. Partin, Lori M. Weber, Ronald B. Rapoport, and Walter J. Stone*   147

PART THREE
Party Activities: A Closer Look

10 Women's Political Leadership and the State of the Parties, *Barbara C. Burrell* — 165

11 Partry Strategy and Political Reality: The Distribution of Congressional Campaign Committee Resources, *Diana Dwyre* — 175

12 Party Resources Allocation: The Timing of Contributions and Coordinated Expenditures, *Janet M. Box-Steffensmeier* — 191

13 Explaining Party Leadership Activity among House Freshman: The Class of 1980–1988, *Stephen A. Borrelli and Kevin M. Leyden* — 201

14. State Legislative Campaign Committees: New Partners or New Competitors?, *Daniel M. Shea* — 219

PART FOUR
Party Policy, Culture, and Values

15 A Tale of Two Parties: National Committee Policy Initiatives, *Laura Berkowitz and Steve Lilienthal* — 237

16 The Democratic Leadership Council: Institutionalizing Party Faction, *Jon F. Hale* — 249

17 Proclaiming Party Identity: A View from the Platforms, *Terri Susan Fine* — 265

18 Party Culture and Party Behavior, *Philip Klinker* — 275

19 Responsible Political Parties and the Decentering of American Metropolitan Areas, *Michael Margolis and David Resnick* — 289

PART FIVE
Reconceptualizing Parties: 1992 and Beyond

20 The Resurgence of Party Organization? A Dissent from the New Orthodoxy, *John J. Coleman* — 311

21 Confusions in the Analysis of American Political Parties, *Tim Hames* — 329

22 Voters, Government Officials, and Party Organizations:
    Connections and Distinctions, *John Frendreis*   339

23 Understanding Organizational Innovations and Party-Building,
    Andrew M. Appleton and Daniel S. Ward   349

References   365
Index   383
About the Contributors   393

Preface

This volume originated in a conference entitled "State of the Parties: 1992 and Beyond" held at the University of Akron September 23-24, 1993. Early versions of most of the papers included here were presented at the conference, although some were added later. Many people deserve special thanks for helping organize the conference and preparing this volume, including John Bibby, Robert Huckshorn, John Kessel, Lawrence Longley, Joel Liske, John White, James Nathanson, Kent Marcus, Ed Rollins, Sam Barone, Alex Lamis, James Ruvolo, Rex Elsass, David Menefee-Libey, L. Sandy Maisel, Herbert Waltzer, Paul Beck, Jesse Marquette, and Steve Brooks.

Holly Harris-Bane, Assistant Director of the Bliss Institute, deserves special credit for organizing the original conference, while Shannon Little and Kimberly Haverkamp did yeoman service at the conference and in the preparation of the manuscript. Deirdre Mullervy, Julie Kirsch, and Jon Sisk of Rowman & Littlefield are owed special thanks for their help and patience.

Danield M. Shea
John C. Green, Director
Bliss Institute

1

Paths and Crossroads: The State of the Parties and Party Scholarship

Daniel M. Shea
John C. Green

The 1992 election raises daunting questions about the state of American political parties. The rise of Ross Perot, deep divisions within governing coalitions, and the continued decline of voter partisanship all point to a weakened state of the parties. These patterns are confused, however, by countertrends suggesting a strengthened state: the return of party government at the national level, evidence of increased party unity, and the continued expansion of party organizations. Overall, the parties appear to be in a state of flux. This situation would be challenge enough for scholars, but there is the added burden that party scholarship is in flux as well.

Political scientists trained in the paradigms of the 1950s and 1960s increasingly find themselves questioning the ability of political parties to link the governed with the government, and, perhaps, in their quieter moments, the desirability of such linkages. Meanwhile, scholars trained in the 1970s and 1980s find it difficult to teach the old virtues of party government. But even those who view party decline as the norm are confronted by the increased vitality of many party organizations. Indeed, the enterprise that many of us have chosen, learning and teaching about parties, seems increasingly alienated from real-world politics. The question of how best to think about parties is being raised precisely when the parties have provided a lot to think about.

At one level, this book does little to resolve the situation. It is only honest to admit that the state of contradiction and paradox that bedevils the study of parties is amply displayed here, and the value of these essays stems as much from the portrait of work in progress as from the picture of the parties presented. Yet, taken as a whole these essays outline new understandings of parties and new directions for party scholarship. The parties themselves confront divergent paths and it is unclear which direction they will follow. And not coincidentally, party scholarship also stands at a crossroads, uncertain of what should be studied and how. The good news is that there is no shortage of effort on either front. These efforts can be usefully organized around three broad topics: party systems, party activities, and party values.

The focus on party systems involves crucial questions regarding the role of parties in the political system, including their relationship to citizens, public officials, and social processes, and what should it be? Also, what elements of the larger political environment affect parties? Attention to the party activities raises narrower, but no less important queries: what do the parties actually do, and what difference does it make? And a focus on party values highlights parallel concerns namely, what do parties care about and how do these concerns matter? These are not new questions, of course, and a brief review of the path of previous scholarship will help set the present dilemmas in context.

Past Paths: The Tripod and Responsible Party Models

Much of the puzzlement surrounding parties comes from the confrontation of time-honored postulates with present realities. Chief among these is the "tripod" view of parties, which conceives of parties as party-in-the-electorate, party-in-government, and party-as-organization. This distinction has been used skillfully by students and teachers for better than half a century. When combined with another venerable concept, the "responsible" party model, the results offer a set of empirical and normative expectations about the operation of parties which once gave persuasive answers to the questions now posed.

Party was seen as the most important link between voters and government officials. Voter preferences, the raw material for public policy in a democracy, were assumed to be the core source of partisan affections. Party organizations, in turn, sought to use these affections in order to mobilize votes on behalf of their candidates. If successful at the polls, the preferences of voters would then be extended to the government. As such, the activities and values of party organizations bore a direct relationship to the party's linkage role in the political system. The engine of this process was electoral competition and the American constitutional arrangements imposed a two-party structure, which was regarded as at least adequate, if not especially well-suited, for the task.

For advocates of responsible parties, this linkage was accomplished when a party's candidates offered clear policy stands to the voters, carried out their promises when elected, and faced the wrath or reward of the voters in the next election. Alliances of copartisans in government could overcome the separation of powers and federalism. Accordingly, policy formulation was the key feature of well-functioning parties. Other scholars doubted the practically and/or wisdom of strict policy responsibility and assumed that parties had narrower goals, namely winning elections, and that public policy was only one means of appealing to voters. But this "conventional," "rational-efficient," or "pluralist-organizational" view of parties still largely accepted the tripod model. Of course, party organizations often failed to perform as expected, but there was reason to expect they could do better. The "state of the parties" thus took on great significance and proposals for improving the major party organizations became a staple of the literature.

The debate over party responsibility aside, the elements of the tripod were once well-supported by large bodies of research. In many areas this is no longer the case. For example, studies of the electorate once showed that partisanship was the dominant influence on vote choice. When tied to generational change and dramatic events, scholars identified critical elections, the "mainsprings" of American politics, that marked the transition from one period of stable partisanship and public policy to another. However, recent research suggests a sharp decline in partisanship and the theory of critical elections is under serious reconsideration. A similar pattern occurred for party-in-government: partisanship was once the dominant factor in legislative and executive behavior, but divided government and candidate-centered politics has reduced its importance. Changes of a different sort have occurred for party organizations. Once-potent local parties have atrophied and been replaced by stronger state and national organizations, which are more active, capable, and sophisticated than ever before, yet more distant from the citizenry.

The net effect of these changes has been to simultaneously cast doubt on the usefulness of the tripod and to intensify the debate over party responsibility. Indeed, advocates and critics of responsible parties have attacked the tripod, including some in this volume (chapters 21 and 22). The crucial problem is the ruptures of the link between partisans in the electorate and government, which some critics lay at the feet of the tripod itself by identifying separate spheres of party activity. Other critics point to the vitality of party organizations, and argue that the tripod misspecified parties by the inclusion of voters and candidates. A renewed demand for responsible parties has become a potent cross current in these disputes. Other scholars still find the tripod useful in descriptive terms at least, and others wait with increasing frustration for the development of an alternative.

It is these considerations that produce the new focus on party systems, activities, and values. In some respects these topics represent an extension and abstraction of the tripod, but in other respects they are a narrowing of concerns and a return to basic questions. And chief among these is the role that parties can and should play in the democratic process.

Divergent Paths: The Party System Under Stress

The first section of this book confronts the role of parties in the political system. All three authors agree that the state of the parties is poor, but each offers a different understanding of the problem and possible sources of improvement. In order, they find the problems outside the party system, outside of the parties, and within the parties themselves, and argue, respectively, for renewed partisanship, better partisanship, and a new kind of partisanship in the electorate and elsewhere. James Reichley (chapter 2) argues that the American two-party system is likely to weather its current woes, but there is no guarantee that the present parties will survive, or if they do, that they will maintain recognizable coalitions. He suggests that the party system operates on 60 to 70 year "super cycles," and that we are nearing the end of the present one. Parties are performing poorly because the polity is confused by the massive societal transformations of our era. As in the past, these changes may conclude with political settlements of which strengthened parties and renewed partisanship will be a part.

In partial contrast, Ralph Goldman (chapter 3) finds that the weakened state of the parties comes from within the political system itself. He argues that the vital functions parties perform have been misunderstood and deprecated by political elites. Unless public opinion toward parties is improved, the major parties will continue to decline, even if the political situation changes or new reforms are instituted. Goldman proposes a thoroughgoing public relations campaign and a "bill of rights" for the parties. All told, the broader linkage role of parties requires the creation of better partisans, committed to party organizations as instruments of democracy.

Theodore Lowi (chapter 4) departs sharply from the previous essays by arguing that the two-party system has outlived its usefulness and that modern America needs a "responsible three-party system." The parties are performing poorly because they are old, entrenched institutions unwilling and unable to confront the problems of the day, to the detriment of the government and the disgust of the governed. He argues that it is unlikely that societal transformations will renew the party system (as Reichley suggests) or that the system can be salvaged from within (as Goldman proposes). Thus, a new system is required with a genuine "third" party as its centerpiece. Lowi details how such a new party might arise and how this new kind of partisanship would improve the performance of the system.

A Well-Traveled Path: Party Activities

Whether or not the present party system can be renewed from the outside or from within, or must be replaced, there remains the crucial question of what parties actually do and what impact these activities have. The ten essays in the second and third sections of this book address this topic with a close eye on the 1992 elections. Overall, these essays suggest a more positive state of the parties than the essays in the previous section: parties are shown to be active organizations and poor performance is certainly not due to lack of effort. Most of these chapters draw inspiration from the party organizational studies of the last decade, which have proved to be one of the most productive research paths in the field.

Anthony Corrado (chapter 5) provides a detailed portrait of the activities of the Democratic and Republican National Committees in the 1992 election. Even jaded observers will be impressed by the efforts of the national organizations to encourage strong candidacies, develop party unity, and deploy resources effectively. In fact, the success of Bill Clinton owes much to the efforts of national Democratic leaders, while George Bush suffered from confusion among the Republicans. The national committees may be catching up with their congressional counterparts, the efforts of which are detailed by Paul Herrnson (chapter 6). In 1992, "hill committees" were challenged by scandals, retirements, and redistricting. Although facing more demands than they could meet, both parties were able to effectively deploy a vast array of resources. In contrast to the presidential campaign, the Republicans appear to have been somewhat more effective in these efforts. Overall, the much discussed growth of the national organizations continues unabated.

Such efforts also included extensive financial links between the national, state and local party organizations, which are reported on by Robert Biersack (chapter 7). Using newly available data on "soft money," Biersack argues that the strategic deployment of these resources may represent an important step toward the integration of national, state and local party committees. John Frendreis, Alan Gitelson, Gregory Flemming, and Anne Layzell (chapter 8) report on the activities of county party committees in state legislative races and find a similarly high degree of activity. Local parties displayed considerable structural capacity and assistance to local campaign, particularly traditional grassroots activities such as recruiting campaign volunteers and get-out-the-vote efforts.

Grassroots activities were not limited to the major parties in 1992, as Randall Partin, Lori Weber, Ronald Rapoport, and Walter Stone (chapter 9) report in their analysis of Ross Perot activists. As one might expect, the Perot following was characterized by a combination of disgust with the major parties and attraction to Perot, but, surprisingly, many of his followers had been previously involved in party and interest group activities. Perot drew substantially from the existing activist corps, but also expanded that group for future campaigns. These activists could serve as a foundation for a new party or as an impetus for the renewal of the existing ones.

Taken together, these essays reveal extensive electoral activities by the major party—and protoparty—organizations. The range of efforts is impressive and they appear to have had positive impact on electoral outcomes. The chapters in the next section focus more narrowly on the question of electoral success and collectively conclude that party organizations are geared almost exclusively to winning elections.

The 1992 election was widely billed as the "year of the woman" and Barbara Burrell (chapter 10) takes a careful look at how parties aided female candidates. She reports that while women have made considerable gains as activists and leaders, women candidates have often had to bypass the party to gain nominations and elected office. Now that it has become clear that women are strong candidates, the party organizations are more supportive. This emphasis on electoral success is echoed by Diana Dwyre (chapter 11) in her study of a decade of campaign support by the congressional campaign committees. She finds that these organizations by and large distribute funds so as to maximize the number of seats won. Janet Box-Steffensmeier (chapter 12) finds much the same pattern for the timing of party allocations within individual congressional campaigns using an innovative statistical approach.

This emphasis on electoral success also figures prominently in Stephen Borrelli and Kevin Leyden's (chapter 13) work on leadership activity among new members of Congress. They find previous campaign support by the congressional parties as well as factors that are associated with party support, such as previous elective or party experience, figure prominently in the ascension to the leadership. Finally, Daniel Shea (chapter 14) examines the emergence of state legislative campaign committees, the organizational counterparts of the congressional campaign committees, now operating in forty states. He finds that, like the national party organizations, these committees are largely driven by electoral concerns and the desire to maximize seats. Overall, the "electoral connection" seems to dominate the activities of contemporary party organizations.

The Path Less Traveled: Party Values

Professor Shea ends his analysis of legislative campaign committees with a cautionary note: these new organizations may actually be a threat to traditional parties rather than an example of organizational adaptation and revival. What is strikingly absent in legislative campaign committees is concern for public policy. In fact, all the research mentioned above notes a similar lacunae to one degree or another: the extensive activities of party organizations are removed from the substantive values that gives party politics meaning.

Of course, the lack of party values is an ancient complaint. After all, the responsible party model demanded that parties develop and proclaim distinct values, particularly in the form of detailed legislative programs. Such parties have been rare in the United States—the disappointment with party programs has taken on a legendary quality. The lack of progress on policy making, paralleling the expansion of other kinds of programmatic activities, has surely made the situation worse. Perhaps as a consequence, there has been relatively little research on the policy-oriented qualities of party organizations that fall short of the responsible ideal.

The chapters in Part Four deal with party values in a number of provocative ways. First, Laura Berkowitz and Steve Lilienthal (chapter 15) describe the recent policy-making initiatives of the Democratic and Republican National Committees. Perplexed by the results of the 1992 election, both parties set about encouraging the development of new ideas. These initiatives are unprecedented in their use of modern communications technology but, as the authors point out, the interests of office holders and candidates may eventually limit them.

On the other hand, Jon Hale's (chapter 16) work on the Democratic Leadership Council (DLC) reveals a novel approach to party policy making: the institutionalization of a party faction. Born out of the desire of moderate Democratic office holders to change the policy direction of their party, the DLC developed a new agenda, which Bill Clinton used to capture the White House. A similar organization, Empower America, has been recently formed in the GOP, suggesting that this strategy may become common.

Terri Susan Fine's (chapter 17) essay on symbolism in the 1992 party platforms offers a novel look at party values. Given the well-known limitations of the electorate, it may well be that symbols communicate values more effectively than detailed policy proposals. Philip Klinkner's (chapter 18) essay on party cultures offers another interesting way of looking at party values. He finds striking differences in the basic assumptions of major party elites, and usefully links them to their customary modes of operation and responses to crises. Finally, Michael Margolis and David Resnick (chapter 19) present a telling description of the lack of interest of local political parties in the problems of contemporary metropolitan areas.

Party Concepts at a Crossroads

One might conclude from the foregoing chapters that the poor state of the party system results from the disjunction between new party activities and weakened party values. This situation has produced a debate on the focus of party scholarship, which closely resembles the original debate over the responsible parties. The watchwords of this disagreement are party "decline" versus "revival." Not surprisingly, scholars most interested in party values and impressed by the apparent rupture between voters and elected officials find parties in decline, while those most interested in party activities and impressed by the recent growth of party organizations find them undergoing revival.

John Coleman (chapter 20) offers a critique of the party revival camp and organizational studies in particular. What difference does it make, he asks, if party organizations are stronger and more complex, if voters disdain them and elected officials ignore them? He argues for integrating the various party components to changes in the economy, echoing in many respects Reichley's arguments about cycles in the party system (chapter 2). Tim Hames (chapter 21) complements this argument with a broad critique of the tripod model of parties. Like Coleman, he argues for further integrative work on "party-as-an-institution."

John Frendreis (chapter 22) offers a rebuttal to the critique of Coleman and Hames. Writing at the request of the editors of this volume, he produces a concise response to the issues raised. While also arguing that the tripod model of parties should be abandoned, he offers a model of parties using firms in the marketplace as a metaphor, in language reminiscent of Lowi (chapter 4). Frendreis points out, for instance, that party voters and party organizations are as separate as customers and the firms selling them products; there is a similar distinction between parties and elected officials. The behavior of voters and officials should not be seen *as* the behavior of parties, but as a *function* of the behavior of parties.

Frendreis concludes his essay with a call for a more systematic effort to gather data on party organizations, and our final chapter (23) by Andrew Appleton and Daniel Ward describes an innovative data collection project. The "State Party Archive Project" will collect observed data on party organization and behavior from the records of state parties. In this chapter, the authors present some preliminary results from this project on organizational innovation in Texas and Arkansas. Both these new data and their conceptual apparatus will surely prove interesting to party scholars.

New Directions in Party Scholarship

Just as the parties are in a state of flux, party scholarship is in a state of transition. It is unclear at this juncture whether a new paradigm lies over the horizon or if a slow accumulation of research will gradually fill the present void. Improving upon the tripod and responsible party models is by no means a simple task. But clearly these essays raise important questions worthy of more attention.

Concerning party systems, the connections between parties and their environment is open to new scrutiny. Does economic change underlie the party system? And if so, what other equally dynamic aspects of social life, such as demographic transitions, value shifts, and technological transformations shape party dynamics? Conceivably, "the state of the parties" is a reflection of the state of American society. In this regard, the "privileged position" of the two-party system in scholarly discourse is increasingly open to question. Is it inevitable in the American context, and is it desirable under present circumstances? These questions lie at the foundation of party scholarship.

Party activities are clearly central to such an understanding, and there is much more to learn about them. Scholars are now in a position to move beyond documenting the activities of parties, which generally implies that more is better, to exploring their quality and impact. A broad array of data and techniques are likely to be valuable here, from intensive interviews with party leaders to archival data to time-series analysis. Overall, what impact do party activities have on elections, the quality of government, and the party system itself?

Along similar lines, organizational innovation and change are important research topics. Whether it is the creation of new organizations, adoption of new techniques, absorption of new interests and constituencies, or adaption to political circumstances, the dynamic context of party activities must be better understood.

Party values are also certainly pivotal to understanding party change. What is the connection of party cultures and norms to party activities on the one hand, and the party system on the other? Will new mechanisms develop for making party policy? These questions lead us back to basic questions: do organizational adjustment and growth produce more effective and/or responsible parties?

These topics are sufficient, of course, to fill a generation of research and occupy the attention of countless teachers and students for longer than that. But all should rejoice, however, that efforts to answer these and other questions are well underway; the state of the parties is in flux, inspiring new directions in scholarship.

PART ONE

The Two-Party System Under Stress

2

The Future of the American Two-Party System

A. James Reichley

Predicting the future of the American two-party system requires answers to two initial questions: Will parties of any kind continue to play an important role in structuring American politics? And, if so, will we continue to have a predominantly two-party system, which of course is unusual in most democratic polities? If the answer to both of these questions is affirmative, there remain the questions, with which this chapter will principally deal, of whether the two major parties will be the Republicans and the Democrats, as they have been since the Civil War, and whether one party or the other will normally be dominant, as has sometimes occurred (though not recently) in our history.

On the question of the survival of any kind of party system, I have elsewhere argued that the parties are in trouble (Reichley 1992:411–33) but that nevertheless it is difficult to imagine democratic politics completely without parties, and that given effective leadership and some changes in laws regulating parties and the ways they function, it is possible and even likely that before the end of this decade parties will achieve at least modest revival. Some thoughtful analysts disagree. They have concluded that the current phenomenon of dealignment, in which more and more Americans feel little or no connection to either major party, will continue to the point that parties will be almost irrelevant to either politics or government (Phillips 1993:233).

There is much evidence on their side. About one-third of those interviewed by pollsters now say they regard themselves as independents. Analysis has shown that about two-thirds of those calling themselves independents are about as regular in their support of one party in national elections as the so-called weak party identifiers (Keith et al. 1992). But the true lesson of this finding seems to me to be not that most declared independents are closet partisans, but rather that many who nominally identify with a party are in fact behavioral independents. Certainly the remarkable 19 percent showing of the independent candidate Ross Perot in the 1992 presidential elections shows that there are a great many voters in the national electorate who are quite prepared to cast their presidential ballots for someone other than the Republican or Democratic candidate.

The old patronage-based state and local machines that used to provide foot soldiers for the parties are almost everywhere in ruins. The media perform much of the role of screening candidates that used to be carried out by the party organizations. Presidential nominees are chosen through state primaries and caucuses in which party organizations play little part. Candidates for state, congressional, and local offices rely more on personal organizations and backing from interest groups than on party organizations. Many voters think nothing of splitting their tickets between parties in voting for president and members of Congress.

We are not going back to the times in the late nineteenth and early twentieth centuries when the major parties were like great popular armies, almost churches, which fought in well-drilled and enthusiastic ranks in each campaign. Other forces—the media, interest groups, citizen watchdog organizations, professional campaign consultants—will continue to rival the parties for influence in our politics. There is little reason for complacency among those of us who believe that strong parties make an essential contribution to democracy. But parties are likely to continue playing a major role in national politics for the foreseeable future. Actually, during the 1980s there were some signs of party revival. National party organizations, including the congressional campaign committees, which used to be relatively weak, raised more money and were more active than ever before in our history. Party unity in Congress trended upward. The major parties were more ideologically distinct than at any time since the early 1930s. All of these trends have continued into the 1990s.

A Durable System

Will the United States, however, continue to maintain a predominantly two-party system? Most democratic polities, even in relatively homogeneous countries like Sweden and the Netherlands, have tended to divide into three or more parties. Maurice Duverger pointed out long ago (in his formulation known as Duverger's law) that polities which maintain single-member, first-past-the-post systems of election, principally the United States and the British dominions, tend to foster the development of two major parties. Systems including two rounds of elections or using some form of proportional representation tend to produce a multiplicity of parties (Duverger 1954:217).

Even polities like Britain, Canada, and Australia, however, which like the United States, use the first-past-the-post system, have generally had at least one significant minor party represented in parliament alongside two major ones. Why have enduring minor parties with significant impact been so rare in the United States?

I have argued that American politics has usually been formed, at least loosely, around two great ideological traditions, which I have called the republican tradition and the liberal tradition. These are, roughly, the tradition descended from Alexander Hamilton and represented since the Civil War by the Republican Party on the one side, and the competing tradition descended from Thomas Jefferson and represented since the time of Andrew Jackson by the Democratic Party on the other (Reichley 1992:3–6). A two-party system has thus been in a sense natural to our politics.

I do not doubt, however, that without the shaping influence of electoral institutions the political system of a nation so large and economically and culturally diverse as the United States would long since have produced a substantial number of competing parties. The first-past-the-post system helps push us toward a two-party system. But the thing that has really kept this system locked in place has been the institution of the electoral college for selecting presidents.

Quite contrary to the Founders' intention, the electoral college, so long as most states retain the at-large system for choosing electors (not required by the Constitution), effectively limits the presidential candidates with a real chance of winning to the nominees of the two major parties (or at least has done so since 1860). Ross Perot won 19 percent of the popular vote but did not receive a single vote in the electoral college. It even makes it unlikely that a minor party can hold the balance of power between the two major parties, as has sometimes occurred in Britain and Canada. Strom Thurmond in 1948 and George Wallace in 1968, running as candidates of states' rights parties opposing racial integration, were able to win the electoral votes of several southern states. But the tendency of the electoral college to magnify the margin of the major party candidate with the larger popular vote usually produces a safe electoral vote majority for the popular vote winner. Constitutional change to eliminate the electoral college, which a majority of voters tell pollsters they favor, would entail a political effort that is unlikely to be forthcoming—at least until the winner in the popular vote loses in the electoral college, as occurred several times in the nineteenth century and almost happened in 1976.

Thus the high visibility of presidential elections shapes our entire political system. So long as the institution of the electoral college confines the real presidential competition to the candidates of the two major parties, the United States will continue to have a two-party system in most congressional and state elections.

Support for Change

Of course we live in changing times. Two states, Maine and Nebraska, now elect some of their presidential electors at the congressional district level.

If this trend were to continue, minor party candidates could pick up electoral votes from specialized constituencies here and there across the country, preventing either major party candidate from winning the required absolute majority in the electoral college and throwing the presidential election into the House of Representatives.

Even if the electoral college remains with little change, modern communications and transportation technology enables independent or minor party candidates to assemble formidable national followings for a single election. If party ties continue to weaken, Perot or some successor might cross the threshold at which he or she would have a realistic chance of winning, overcoming the objection that voting for an independent is "throwing your vote away." Significantly, when asked by a Lou Harris poll in 1952 whether "the two-party system is serving this country well," 59 percent of the participants answered "No." Nevertheless, the institutional supports provided by the electoral college as now constituted and the first-past-the-post system make the emergence of a multi-party system, as both called for and predicted by Theodore Lowi and other political scientists and commentators, improbable any time soon (see chapter 4).

This does not, however, necessarily mean that the two major parties will continue to be the Republicans and the Democrats. Even in countries with institutionally fortified two-party systems, new parties have at times displaced one of the major existing parties, as the Republicans did the Whigs in the United States in the 1850s, and the Labor did the Liberals in Britain in the 1920s.

It has seemed anomalous to many observers that the United States has never had a true left-wing party in the European sense, and some have predicted that the Democrats will eventually break up and give way to a socialist successor. The worldwide decline of socialism in recent years has perhaps made this less likely, but there is still the possibility that intraparty revolt against an unpopular centrist Democratic president might produce a significant break-away party on the left. On the other side, at low ebbs of the Republican Party, such as 1964 and 1976, some conservatives have proposed abandonment of the Republican label and creation of a new national conservative party. And there is recurring sentiment among the electorate that what we really need is a new centrist party, divorced from the extremes of the Republicans and Democrats, which Perot to some extent tapped in 1992.

The difficulties of forming a new major party, nevertheless, are formidable—as Perot himself discovered. It is no accident that no enduring new major party has emerged in American politics for more than 130 years. The existing major parties have proven adept at picking up the issues attracting support to new parties, as did the Democrats with the Populists in the 1890s, the Republicans and the Democrats with the Progressives in the

1910s, the Democrats with various liberal and socialist minor parties, and the Republicans with various states' rights parties.

The representatives of the two major parties have taken pains to enact election laws that strongly favor major party candidates. Public financing of presidential election campaigns heavily advantages the Republican and Democratic nominees. At the state level, barriers against third-party candidates are even more severe. In Pennsylvania, for example, Republican or Democratic candidates for the state senate need only 1,000 signatures on petitions to get their names on the ballot while minor party candidates require 29,000 (reduced from 56,000 by court order).

A major national disaster or conflict might lead to the creation of a new major party, as the struggle over slavery gave birth to the Republicans in the 1850s. Barring such a catastrophe, it is probable not only that we will continue to have a two-party system, but also that the Republicans and the Democrats will be the main competitors. After all, even the Great Depression of the 1930s failed to put enduring cracks in the existing two-part system, though for a time it spawned some successful third parties at the state level, such as the Farmer-Labor party in Minnesota and the Progressives in Wisconsin.

Throwing the Rascals Out

Let us, then, concentrate on the two-party system as we know it and consider what appear to be its electoral characteristics, particularly those that may give some clue to our likely political future. We still really do not have very extensive spans of experience for studying the long-range behavior of party systems (two-party or otherwise): about two centuries in the United States and Britain; somewhat less in France, some countries of northwestern Europe, and the British dominions; only since the Second World War in most of the other democracies; and only two or three years in Eastern Europe and the countries of the former Soviet Union.

Nevertheless, some characteristics of the electoral effects of party competition seem to appear. First, there seems to be a tendency for voters to grow disenchanted with a party in power, even if no major disasters occur, after about ten years. The normal result is for the incumbent party to be voted out, often by a large majority, and the former opposition installed. This tendency may be countered or outweighed by special circumstances, as when the fear of including communist parties in government in France and Italy kept conservative parties in power for extended periods; or when voters' distrust of the opposition or lack of a fully developed party system produced long-lasting dominance by one party, such as the Socialists in Sweden from the 1930s to the 1970s, Labor in Israel from independence to the early 1970s, the

Congress Party in India from the 1940s to the 1970s, and the Liberal-Democrats in Japan from the 1950s to 1993. Even in these instances, however, accumulation of voter discontent and stagnation or corruption within the old majority party eventually led to change of party control.

The operation of the ten-year cycle appears particularly pronounced in countries with two-party systems, probably because this system inhibits formation of new coalitions through which incumbent parties sometimes are able to hold onto power under multi-party systems. In the United States, the ten-year cycle translates into two or three presidential terms. Since the early 1950s, the Republicans and Democrats have regularly alternated in control of the White House, with three two-term cycles, one three-term (the Reagan-Bush years), and one that was confined to a single term (the Carter administration).

Going back somewhat further, since the present party system was formed in the 1850s, the average duration of party control of the White House has been 11 years. The only markedly longer periods of party dominance were the 24-year tenure of the Republicans during and after the Civil War, and the 20-year period of Democratic supremacy during and after the Great Depression.

Similar cycles appear to operate for the governorship in states with competitive two-party systems. In the seven most populated states with truly competitive systems, the average period of party control of the governorship from 1950 to 1990 was 8.5 years. This average conceals some extended periods when one party or the other was dominant in New York and Michigan, and some long stretches of uninterrupted control by the Republicans in Illinois and the Democrats in New Jersey. But in Pennsylvania, Ohio, and California, the two parties exchanged control of the governor's office with almost rhythmic regularity. Cyclical party turnover now seems to be developing in some of the Southern states where the Democrats used to enjoy one-party dominance, such as Texas and North Carolina.

The impulse of voters to "throw the rascals out" by changing party control at regular intervals is both understandable and rational. After two or three terms of one party in control of a nation or state, enough things are likely to have gone wrong to give voters a taste for change. This may sometimes be unjust to the party in power, but it at least keeps incumbent parties on their toes, seeking to come up with policies and solutions that will cause voters to relent and give them "four more years." Moreover, under conditions of modern government, a party team that has held office for two terms or more is likely to be rundown, reduced to petty bickering and bereft of new ideas. Henry Kissinger used to say that an administration begins to use up its intellectual capital from the day it takes office.

Since the 1950s, regular shifts in party control have not occurred in Congress. From the Civil War to the Eisenhower administration, control of Congress normally accompanied, or slightly preceded, the presidential cycle.

In only three two-year periods did the President's party not control at least one house of Congress (under Hayes 1879-80; Cleveland 1895-96; and Wilson 1919-20.) Since 1954, however, the Democrats have controlled the House of Representatives without interruption, and have held the Senate except for a six-year stretch from 1981 through 1986. As a result, Republican presidents during this 40-year span have regularly confronted Congresses controlled by their partisan opposition, producing the famous deadlock that has wreaked havoc with the policy-making process. David Mayhew has offered evidence to show that the effects of divided control have not been so bad (Mayhew 1991). This may be true in some policy areas, but in crucial areas of budget making and foreign policy the liabilities seem clear.

The breakdown in cyclical change of party control of Congress resulted in part from the fact that the Democrats happened to be in control at the time when advantages of incumbency began to rise (or perhaps happened is not the right word—Democratic majorities after all legislated many of the advantages such as expanded staffs and campaign finance laws swelling the influence of political action committees that give mainly to incumbents.) Democrats also, however, have been helped by the reluctance of many voters to give the Republicans complete control of the federal government. Such voters, as Byron Shafer has argued, have normally seemed to prefer Republicans in charge of the executive branch functions, but have relied on the Democrats in Congress, particularly the House, to preserve the flow of welfare state benefits (Shafer 1991). I suspect this may reflect something deeper transpiring in our politics, which may now be in the process of working itself out, and which I will get to shortly.

In any case, the failure of cyclical turnover in Congress seems to have had damaging effects on the entire political system. Even apart from the policy results of deadlock, the long dominance of Congress by the Democrats has contributed to the impression among many voters that the system is impervious to electoral change, and this impression probably plays a part in the long-term decline in voter participation. (The level of voter participation was up slightly in 1992, but remained far below that of the 1960s). It also has probably been bad for the congressional Democrats themselves (as a political force, though not of course in terms of individual members). The effects of long duration in power by one party that special circumstances have produced in the politics of, for example, Japan, Italy, and Mexico have been all too evident in recent years in Congress: arrogance, preoccupation with "perks," outright corruption, and stagnation of ideas.

Cyclical Theories

Beyond the normal two- or three-term cycle in party control of the presidency, the existence of party cycles (or ideological cycles) in national politics becomes speculative. Such cycles, if they exist, however, are important and require inclusion in any overall consideration of parties. Probably the best known of the theories of long-term political cycles is that of the historian Arthur Schlesinger, Jr. (1986:32–33) carrying on work begun by his father. Schlesinger's theory is more closely related to ideology than to party, but also has party manifestations.

According to Schlesinger, there have been throughout American history regular alterations between cycles of liberalism and conservatism, each lasting about sixteen years or four presidential terms. Liberalism is defined as commitment to "public purpose," and conservatism as defense of "private interest." The most recent cycles have been the liberal one launched by John Kennedy in 1960, and its conservative successor that began in the late 1970s. Right on time, a new liberal cycle began with the inauguration of Bill Clinton in 1993.

This theory—like almost all cyclical theories—requires some nimble tucking. The Civil War Republicans, "liberal" under Lincoln, somehow become "conservative" under Grant (though in many cases they were the same people) and hang on long beyond their allotted cycle; Theodore Roosevelt, Taft, and Wilson are lumped together in a liberal cycle, despite the bitter interparty and intraparty battles of the time; Nixon and Ford become part of the liberal cycle that began in 1960; and Carter becomes the harbinger of a return to conservatism. The primary identifications of conservatism with private interest and liberalism with public purpose are somewhat suspect, given conservatism's commitment to publicly maintained moral standards and liberalism's defense of private choice on questions of personal behavior. Still, the theory has sufficient resonance in history to suggest the presence of a real phenomenon. What Schlesinger is on to, I think, is the succession of phases in a much longer cycle, which I will describe below.

The most widely discussed cyclical theory developed in political science was introduced by V. O. Key (1955), linking cycles to "realigning" or "critical" elections which, it is claimed, have periodically purged American politics and government of accumulated detritus and opened the way to new growth. Key's work has been carried on in recent years by, among others, Walter Dean Burnham (1970), James Sundquist (1983), Gerald Pomper (1970), and Paul Allen Beck (1974:199–21). In most versions of this theory, realigning elections, ending the dominance of one political party and ushering in normal majority control by another, have occurred every 28 to 36 years. The root of these cycles appears to be policy upheaval, coupled with generational change.

There is some dispute over which were the actual realigning elections, but general agreement places realignments at or just before the elections of Thomas Jefferson in 1800, Andrew Jackson in 1828, Abraham Lincoln in 1860, William McKinley in 1896, and Franklin Roosevelt in 1932. (Some theorists drop the elections of Jefferson and Jackson, on the ground that the party system did not achieve mature development until the 1830s.)

A puzzle for believers in the theory of realigning elections is the apparent failure of one to occur on schedule in the 1960s. Burnham deals with this problem by arguing that a realignment *did* occur with the election of Richard Nixon as President in 1968 and the creation of a new Republican majority in presidential politics. Certainly the shift of the South away from the Democrats at the presidential level after 1968 was a major change in national politics. But if this was a realignment, why did it not produce a change in control of Congress or of most of the major states, as previous realignments had done? Everett Carl Ladd (1991) and Byron Shafer (1991), among others, have argued that realignment theory, whatever utility it may once have had for political science, has been made obsolete by technological and social change.

Super-Cycles

The elections usually identified as critical to realignments—1800, 1828, 1860, 1896, and 1932—were clearly times when something important happened in American politics. But were all of these major realignments in the sense of changing one majority party for another? The victories of the (Jeffersonian) Republicans in 1800, the Republicans in 1860, and the Democrats in 1932 certainly were. But what of the 1828 and 1896 elections, which are needed to maintain the 36 year cycle?

Jackson won in 1828 after a period of about ten years in which national politics had been in flux and the old hegemony of Jefferson's party appeared shaken. But Jackson was clearly in the line of the Jeffersonians, and was so recognized at the time. Martin Van Buren, one of Jackson's principal lieutenants and his successor as president, wrote: "The two great parties of this country, with occasional changes in their names only, have, for the principal part of a century, occupied antagonistic positions upon all important political questions. They have maintained an unbroken succession . . ." (Van Buren 1967:2). Jackson carried every state Jefferson carried in 1800 and lost every state Jefferson lost. Jefferson's narrow victory over John Adams in 1800 was converted into Jackson's landslide triumph over John Quincy Adams in 1828 by the addition of new western states in which the Democrats were strong. So the 1828 election *restored* the dominance of the Democrats (under their new name) instead of bringing in a new majority party.

Similarly, McKinley's victory in 1896 followed a period in which Republicans and Democrats had taken turns controlling the federal government, or dividing control, and in which there had been no clear majority party. The 1896 election represented a rallying of the forces, temporarily in eclipse, that had made the Republicans the clear majority party from 1860 to 1876. McKinley won through renewal of the coalition of northeastern and midwestern states on which the Republican Party had been founded. William Jennings Bryan, his Democratic opponent, swept the South, the Democrats' principal stronghold since the end of Reconstruction. Bryan also tapped the farmers' revolt and the silver issue in the West to win some of the normally Republican western states that had been admitted to the Union since the Civil War. But within a few years most of these were back in the Republican column where they normally remained until the Great Depression of the 1930s. The 1896 election, therefore, did not displace the former majority party, but renewed and strengthened the party that became dominant after the last major realignment—a point also made by Pomper (1970).

What, then, do we have? Not five or six major realigning elections but three: 1800, 1860, and 1932. Each of these began a cycle in which one party was generally dominant, lasting not 36 years, but *60 to 70 years*. The climactic elections won by Jackson and McKinley, which I identify as 1832 (rather than 1828) and 1896, were in this scheme elections in which the dominant force of the cycle that had begun about 30 years before met and decisively defeated a force trying to turn back the clock to the prevailing ethos of the preceding cycle (the conservative opposition directed by Nicholas Biddle in 1832 and the populist crusade championed by Bryan in 1896).

The mystery of why no true realignment occurred in the 1960s is thus explained: it was not due. What actually happened in the 1960s was the climax of the cycle dominated by liberalism and the Democratic Party that had begun in the 1930s. In 1964, Lyndon Johnson decisively defeated Barry Goldwater, representing a radical version of the laissez-faire economic doctrine that had prevailed during the preceding cycle. The movement of the South away from the Democrats at the end of the 1960s was an early sign of the breakup of the New Deal cycle—similar to the move of the Northeast away from the Democrats in the 1840s and the swing of major northern cities away from the Republicans in the era of Woodrow Wilson.

As shown schematically in Figure 2.1, each of the 60 to 70 year long cycles moved through roughly similar phases: 1. a breakthrough election in which the new majority gained power under a charismatic leader (Jefferson, Lincoln, F. D. Roosevelt), followed by an extended period during which the new majority party changed the direction of government and enacted much of its program; 2. a period of pause in which the new majority lost some of its dynamism and the forces that dominated the preceding cycle staged a minor comeback (J. Q. Adams, Cleveland, Eisenhower); 3. a climactic victory by the majority party over a more radical expression of the ethos of the preceding cycle (Jackson over Biddle, McKinley over Bryan, Johnson over Goldwater), followed by enactment of remaining items in the majority party's program; and, finally, 4. the gradual decline and ultimate collapse of the majority party, opening the way for a new realignment and a new majority. There have been only three such fully developed cycles in our national history, though, as Figure 2.1 shows, the outline of an earlier cycle can be seen in the nation-

Figure 2.1 American Political Cycles

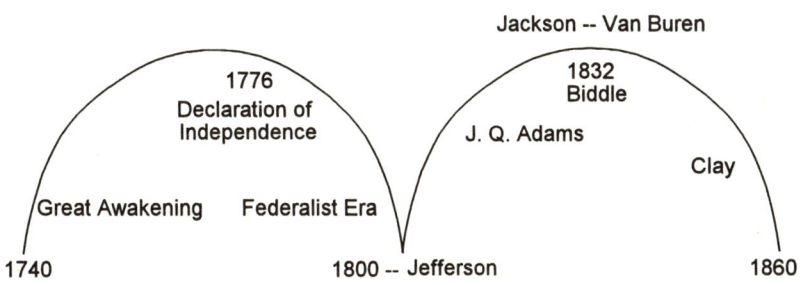

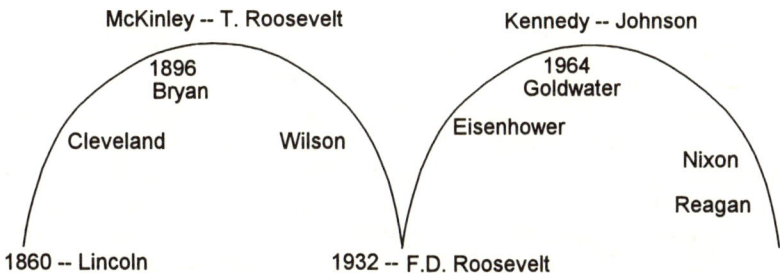

building process that reached its climax with the American Revolution, and went through its declining, though still fruitful, phase during the Federalist era.

The phases in the 60- to 70-year-long cycle correspond roughly to some of Schlesinger's sixteen-year cycles. The long-cycle theory, however, explains why the Jeffersonians after 1800, the Republicans after 1860, and the Democrats after 1932 held onto power for longer than Schlesinger's theory would predict. Those were all periods covered by the initial phase of the long cycle, during which the new majority is fresh and holds the support of the public through an extended series of elections. The separate cycles posited in the 28- to 36-year theory correspond neatly to the rise and decline segments of the long cycle.

The Next Major Change

The possibility of a 60- to 70-year cycle has occasionally been glimpsed by political scientists and historians, and was first discussed, to my knowledge, by the political scientist Quincy Wright in 1942 (1942:143–145). In recent years, William Riker (1982:214–16) and Jerome Mileur (1989:1–3) have suggested the possibility of a 60- to 70-year cycle. Political scientists have generally been reluctant to consider the possibility of 60- to 70-year party dominance cycles, largely, I think, because the limited time over which democracies have so far extended gives us little material against which to test such a hypothesis. Such skepticism is understandable and even reasonable. But the long-cycle theory fits the evidence we have better than any of the other cyclical schemes. There is also some indication that long cycles have been at work in Britain and France, although this requires further study.

If such long cycles exist, what comes then? Perhaps to some extent it reflects cycles in the underlying economic system, such as the "long wave" cycles suggested in the 1920s by the Russian economist Nikolai Kondratieff (1984:32 ff) and discussed often since by futurist economists. Kondratieff and his followers have claimed to detect cycles lasting about 50 years in which market economies swing between booms and major depressions caused by "overbuilding of the capital sector." Kondratieff long waves correspond roughly with the long party dominance cycles in American history. The economic expansion that started in the 1790s petered out through the 1840s and 1850s, and the expansion that began in the 1860s, though interrupted by several pauses, did not truly collapse until the depression of the 1930s. According to Kondratieff theorists, we are now in the down swing of the expansion that began in the 1940s. For more than a decade, many of them have been predicting that a new economic collapse is just around the corner.

Political cycles are also probably rooted to some extent in generational change. Schlesinger argues that his sixteen-year cycles reflect the succession of political generations. Members of the political generation of John Kennedy, for example, were putting into effect values and attitudes acquired during their youths in the liberal environment of the 1930s. The Reaganites of the 1980s were applying views they had developed during the relatively conservative 1950s (though many of the Reaganites regarded themselves as revolting *against* Eisenhower moderate Republicanism). Members of the generation of the 1990s, in this theory, are prepared to reintroduce the liberal values with which Kennedy inspired them during their college years in the 1960s (Schlesinger 1986:33–34).

Schlesinger's analysis, like his larger cyclical theory, captures at least part of the truth. Truly major changes in political direction, however, seem to occur only after persons whose political values and party loyalties were formed by a major realignment, including many who were in childhood at the time, have largely passed from the political scene. So long as generations whose party ties were shaped by the Civil War remained politically active, even voting in substantial numbers, the normal Republican majority in national elections was hard to shake. Similarly, party loyalties formed by the Great Depression and the New Deal have been exceptionally durable. In the 1990s, the generations whose attitudes were most deeply marked by the Depression and the New Deal, roughly those born from 1905 to 1930, will inevitably become a sharply declining share of the total electorate—already less than 15 percent. This, I think, is a major reason for the increasing share of voters who feel no particular loyalty to either major party.

The last two major realignments, in the 1860s and 1930s, came at the time of massive traumas within the larger social system, respectively the Civil War and the Great Depression. The first realignment, in the 1800s, coincided with huge territorial growth and migration of population. Probably a major realignment requires *both* extraordinary social upheaval *and* an electorate in which ties to the existing party system have grown weak. We certainly now have the latter. If the Kondratieff theorists are correct, we will probably soon encounter severe economic turmoil. But the causes of social upheaval need not be primarily economic—those of the 1800s and 1860s were not. Possibly an ecological crisis could trigger the next political realignment. Or continuation of current trends toward moral and social disorder and decay could bring it on. The point is that the political system is now open, as it was not in the 1960s when the hold of the New Deal alignment remained strong, for transformation by a major economic or social shock. If the precedent of earlier long cycles holds, the 1990s may correspond not to the 1960s, but to the 1850s and late 1920s. Bill Clinton, then, could turn out to be not John Kennedy, but James Buchanan or Herbert Hoover.

Another factor holding up major realignment during most of the 1970s and 1980s was divided government. While one party controlled the White House and the other Congress, the voters found it difficult to fix responsibility for the conduct of government and therefore to take out discontent on one party or the other. After one term of united government under the Democrats at the end of the 1970s, the Republicans won the White House and the Senate and made substantial gains in the House in 1980. Having failed to gain complete control of Congress at the time of Ronald Reagan's first election, however, it was unlikely they would do so thereafter during the Reagan or Bush administrations—the voters tending to take out resentments against the party controlling the White House by voting for the opposition in congressional elections.

It is possible that 1992 will turn out to have been a critical election. Though Clinton won with a popular vote plurality of only 43 percent, this was actually more than Lincoln's plurality of 40 percent, in a four-candidate race, in the realigning election of 1860. If the economy flourishes and the Clinton administration deals successfully with public needs in areas like health care, crime, and education, the Democrats might settle down to extended control of both branches of the federal government.

If, however, the Clinton administration is perceived to have failed, the Republicans should before the end of this decade have an opportunity to regain the normal majority party status that they lost in 1932 and begin a new political cycle. This does not of course mean they will do so. Even if the Republicans win the presidency in 1996 or the year 2000, they will have to provide creative solutions to the nation's outstanding problems and opportunities—as Jefferson, Lincoln, and Roosevelt did after their parties took control of government at the start of three earlier cycles. That is why it is important that Republicans who aim to achieve a lasting political turnaround should be working now to develop just and effective social, economic, and international policies to implement when their party next holds the reins of national power.

If the Democrats fail to make good on their current opportunity, and the Republicans on their next one, the continued dealignment predicted by many analysts may well take place. National politics will then increasingly be built around personalities, campaign cosmetics, and interest group pressures.

There is another possibility. Public disaffection with both major parties and the entire party system is now so great that a new political force promising to transcend all parties and return to something like the nonpartisan system the Founders intended, might be able to break through the barriers protecting the existing party system and get control of the national government, at least for a term or two. The floodgates to major constitutional change might then be opened, leading to—who knows what? A parliamentary system? Government by electronic referenda? Or a truly imperial presidency?

The *most* likely next major change in national politics, probably in a term or two, is a strong swing to the Republicans, potentially for an extended period. But the imponderables of politics make this prospect uncertain. No doubt history still has many surprises up its sleeve.

3

Who Speaks for the Political Parties Or, Martin Van Buren, Where Are You When We Need You?

Ralph M. Goldman

Congress and the Clinton administration have committed themselves to major electoral reform. In the past, reforms have been little more than tinkerings with one of the nation's most vital institutions, namely, its party system. The most usual changes include new but circumventable limits on campaign contributions, a modicum of public financing, and slightly more demanding disclosure requirements. Amidst all the current interest in reform, *little mention is made regarding the principals themselves*, namely, the executives of the nation's political parties. Their failure to make a serious contribution to the public debate is perceived by many citizens as an admission of guilt for unnamed sins.

Institutional rationalization of the American, party system is certainly long overdue, but is difficult to achieve in a suspect and hostile attitudinal environment. After two centuries of wear and tear, it should be reasonable to discuss change to the party system. Components of the system need to be better connected structurally. Desirable functions need to be better protected and nurtured. Essential activities need to be explained and conducted more openly. Total system effort needs to be subject to rules and practices that make the effort more effective and efficient, with full organizational accountability for management and outcomes. These are significant and legitimate matters for citizens, legislators, media, and party executives to examine. The political parties are, after all, legitimate associations whose service to the community includes such profoundly important duties as the implementation of popular sovereignty, the formulation of the public agenda, and the advancement of a democratic way of life.

The Parties' Systematic and Persistent Bad Rap

Unfortunately, a strong, and sometimes justifiable, antiparty tradition has taken hold in the United States, making a candid and constructive approach to party organization, management, and accountability difficult beyond the ordinary. Anti-partyism, especially as articulated by the media, by practicing politicians who should know better, and by competitors for political influence, has produced a collection of dubious assumptions and unfriendly attitudes that is brought into play upon revelation of occasional political horror stories involving bribes, excessive campaign contributions, or unethical use of public resources. Such revelations are usually accompanied by righteous calls for harnessing party "monsters" or, at least, cutting off one or another of their functional limbs.

This bad rap started a long time ago. The British party system, the first modern party system, was barely a century old when Viscount Henry St. John Bolingbroke (1782) pronounced parties *obsolete*. As a Tory leader during the early decades of the eighteenth century, Bolingbroke wrote the best contemporary analysis of party as an institution. Almost always in the opposition and himself a master of machination, Bolingbroke vented his frustrations in his analysis, decrying parties as "corrupt," Parliament as "enslaved" by the parties, and party debate generally "nasty." Bolingbroke failed to understand that the British party system was the institutional alternative to English civil wars of the preceding millennia, hence, by definition, the arena for non-military political nastiness (Goldman 1990:ch. 3).[1]

A half century later, another notable, President George Washington, added his antiparty commentary. In his message to the Third Congress of the United States on November 19, 1794, the president specifically condemned the activities of "certain self-created societies." His reference was to the highly partisan county and city political associations that, at that time, provided support to the Jeffersonian Democratic-Republican party. Washington's statement led to a resolution offered by the Federalists in Congress strongly supporting the denunciation. James Madison, the Democratic-Republican leader in the House of Representatives, worked diligently to water down the resolution and succeeded only when the Speaker broke the tie vote.

Ironically, the Federalists refused to acknowledge that they were a political party. One Federalist—Alexander Hamilton—knew better. In 1802, soon after the Jeffersonians captured the presidency, Hamilton offered his colleagues a plan to establish a national Federalist association to be called "The Christian Constitutional Society." This society was to be headed by a president and a twelve-member national council. There would be "sub-directing Councils" of thirteen members for each state and as many local branches as possible. Financed by a five dollar annual fee, this association would diffuse information about "fit" men and promote their election. The association would also pursue "charitable and useful" activities, particularly in the growing cities, through relief societies for immigrants and vocational schools for workers (Hamilton 1851:540–43). These were precisely the activities that political parties performed at that time. Hamilton's Federalist colleagues would have none of it. The Federalists disappeared as a party during the next decade.

The nineteenth century was a time of flux, factionalism, and failure in the party system. Factions came and went with ease and frequency. Party failure to deal with the slavery issue led to the Civil War and radical Republicanism produced a vindictive Reconstruction Era. Tammany Hall and Boss Tweed became the model for urban machines, whose dominance was contested from time to time by wealthy merchants and other civic-minded citizen. State machines became prominent toward the latter part of the century, their alliances influencing national politics and the distribution of national patronage. The press was sharp-tongued and partisan. Protest movements arose, sometimes became "third" parties, then disappeared. Corruption made its appearance at state legislatures. Paradoxically, despite a high level of voter loyalty to their own party at election time, by the end of the century citizens in general had little confidence in the party system.

The opening of the twentieth century brought in muckrakers and progressives, the former to expose partisan evil and the latter to reconstruct the party system with the direct primary, nonpartisan elections, an expanding civil service, and a host of other antiparty measures. The credibility of the parties was further undermined by the emergence of a racist one-party South, presidential nominations engineered in "smoke-filled rooms," corporate bribery scandals, and the like. At times, if newspapers and commentary journals were to be believed, logic demanded the outlawing of parties.

In the reality beyond the media, however, party organizations somehow managed to nominate and elect distinguished citizens to public offices, welcome and Americanize millions of immigrants, keep voter participation at a high level, distribute jobs and assistance to the needy, transform street gangs into civic safety patrols, and maintain a close watch and an open ear for signs of popular discontent. In general, Americans seemed willing to pay for these positive civic functions by tolerating urban and state party machines, various forms of patronage, and the winner-take-all principle. At the turn of the century, however, the aforementioned excesses and corruption, together with the perennial bad rap, brought constraints to the party process.

Deprecating Assumptions and Tongue-Tied Defenders

Progressive factions in both major parties, defectors to third parties, massive immigration and virulent nativism, the one-party South, and the antiparty predispositions of newly admitted Western states kept the parties in stress during the first third of the twentieth century. The stress was aggravated by the enduring antiparty assumptions. Some are quite familiar. Money in politics is presumed to be either intrinsically evil or a source of evil.

Party executives are presumed to be power-hungry, self-aggrandizing "slickers" and "bosses." Corruption, rather than public service, is considered the principal product of party activism. Contributions to political campaigns are invariably deemed excessive. Money or patronage for maintenance of party organizations is thought to be wasteful, if not immoral. These are the more prominent hostile assumptions.

Those who agree with these assumptions rarely, if ever, acknowledge parties as the principal instruments of several fundamental extra-electoral functions: the implementers of popular sovereignty in a democracy; the institutional alternative to civil war; the principal recruiters of public servants; the nation's most influential civic educator; the nation's most important political agenda maker. These critics, perhaps for lack of knowledge about the history of political institutions, are the last to recognize that failure to nourish these vital functions could cost a nation its democracy. The case for these profoundly important extra-electoral functions can be readily and briefly made.

Popular Sovereignty

Mass participation in the election of national leaders and the making of public policies was, for the most part, a nineteenth-century development spurred by theories of popular sovereignty and representative government. Various election systems were designed to give an authoritative "voice" to the people, but it was political parties and the many organized interest groups that coalesced within and around the parties that formulated the arguments about political issues, legislated the rules of popular participation, and mobilized voters to exercise their sovereignty at the polls. In the twentieth century, whether in totalitarian or democratic states, popular sovereignty, as manifest in election outcomes, has been assumed and has been the event that legitimizes the holding of government office. In dictatorships as in competitive party systems, under conditions of duress or in free and fair elections, party organizations have turned out the votes that give leaders their mandate from the popular sovereigns.

Alternative to War

England's centuries of civil war ended when a viable party system emerged in the seventeenth century. The United States' Civil War began when its party system collapsed in the late 1850s—Whigs disappearing, Republicans trying to take their place, and Democrats splitting asunder. Recently, El Salvador, Nicaragua, South Africa, the Philippines, the Russian Federation, and a host of other nations have struggled to establish competitive party systems to replace defunct dictatorships and inconclusive civil wars. The process that makes these critical transitions possible is observable: the principal architects are party leaders, and the end product is an enduring party system (Goldman 1990).

Recruiters of Public Servants

In one way or another, the parties are principal recruiters of citizens willing to render public service. Through nomination for election and job patronage in victory, early U.S. parties found and "pre-selected" the persons to fill the offices of government. Jefferson and Madison actively sought out candidates for Congress in order to challenge the Federalist hold on that institution, and national party leaders continue to do so. Despite occasional excesses and corruption, early urban and rural bosses and party machines played a major role in electing or appointing "their people" to the local and state jobs that performed the operations of government. With the adoption of nonpartisan elections by many communities, party labels have been made opaque for the election day occasion, but fool hardly anyone. In recent times, with the diminution of party patronage, much recruitment flows through lobbying and legislative channels, but almost always with a partisan orientation.[2]

Civic Educators

Totalitarian parties are determinative in matters of ideological and civic education. They organize thoroughly for this purpose and teach aggressively. In the American context, civic education can be described as casual, negligible, and indirect. Family and religious sources transmit basic values, many of them indirectly political and partisan in consequence. Schools deal lightly with political history, symbols, rituals, and broad structures of government, usually evading discussion of parties and partisanship. Most information about politics and government comes to the citizenry, again indirectly, by way of the contests between the parties and the reports about this competition by the media. That this information is grossly inadequate is confirmed by survey after survey. Lack of information is perhaps the major reason for the low esteem in which U.S. political institutions are held.

Agenda Makers

Gaining public attention, getting onto the policy-making agenda, moving up to the top of the agenda, and coming off the agenda with a favorable policy decision in hand is difficult and extremely competitive work. Largely, this is the work of the parties at different stages and levels of government. For the most part, the national public policy agenda is found in the often invisible agenda decisions of party leaders in Congress, the rhetoric of candidates for office in the heat of an election contest, the unread platforms of the parties, and the headlines and pictures of the media. Whereas organized interests and the media have been increasingly influential at the early stages of gaining public attention and setting up popular attitudes, in the last analysis it is party leaders who must negotiate the subject-matter and the priorities of the agenda.

By ignoring these many significant extra-electoral functions, the several negative assumptions about parties have led to faulty questions about real pathologies of the party system and its functions. In a Gresham's Law of analysis, these poorly framed questions drive out the significant ones. This in turn tends to produce legislation that often puts into place unworkable panaceas that cause unintended and unfortunate consequences. In such an environment, it becomes unthinkable, for example, to argue that money, when given in a public manner and disclosed on the public record, is a legitimate source of political influence in competitive politics. Limitations on campaign contributions do not limit; they merely challenge campaigners' ingenuity to invent new circumventions and subterfuges for giving.

Where is the party executive who will take the time and effort to explain that political parties are organizations which, like other organizations, must have staff and funds if they are to render public service? Let us suppose that the parties were perceived and structured as ordinary stock-issuing corporations (not that they could or should be). How differently the party organization, management, financing, and other operational and management needs would be treated! The party name and symbols would undoubtedly be legally protected for their good-will value, a protection currently reserved for corporate names and trademarks in the commercial arena. The party's nominations would probably take on the character of an explicit contract, with the nominee making a binding promise to represent the party's program and constituencies in exchange for acquiring the legitimacy and good will inherent in the party's name and the promotional effort of the party's organization. The party's financial operations and records would become public accounts subject to periodic professional audit and publication. In other words, if the parties were treated as public utility corporations, perceptions, assumptions, issues, attitudes, and solutions would be radically altered, and for the good of American democracy (Epstein 1989:239).

However, these are *not* the perspectives from which the ills of the U.S. party system are diagnosed. Consequently, those who are dedicated to party renewal and party development rush in with suggestions for fixing *the parties*: a reorganization here, a reform there, a panacea elsewhere. Yet, the problem may have more to do with political culture than political organization. The approach should be *to fix the political and attitudinal context in which the parties must live.*

There are examples in the world of business. When poisoned capsules were found in Tylenol™ containers, what did executives of that corporation do to recover the reputation of their company and product? They explained in detail the circumstances of the problem, they countered accusations of production negligence, and they proclaimed once again the wonders of their products. PepsiCola™ executives acted similarly when people claimed that they were finding medical syringes in soda cans.

These comparisons may be somewhat overdrawn, but they make the point that corporate executives have a responsibility to explain problems and defend their enterprise. Political party executives have exactly the same responsibility: explaining party functions in general; in particular instances, exposing the details of a bad rap; countering the validity of charges; and proclaiming the wonders of their organization and the party system. When was the last time a national party chairman performed such civic education? Jim Farley and Ray Bliss come to mind.

The independent presidential candidacy of Ross Perot in 1992 brought into sharp focus serious questions about the viability of the U.S. party system. A *Washington Post*-ABC News Poll conducted June 24–28, 1992, asked: "Do you agree or disagree with the following statement: Both political parties are pretty much out of touch with the American people." The responses were 82 percent agree 15 percent disagree and 3 percent didn't know. A second question asked: "Thinking about both the Republican and Democratic parties, do you generally think that political parties are playing a bigger role or a smaller role in people's lives today than they did in the past?" A total of 41 percent chose "bigger role," 50 percent thought a "smaller role," 4 percent the same role, and 5 percent didn't know.

Although these data suggest overwhelming disappointment in the two major parties, total disenchantment with parties in general was not evident. Sixty-six percent thought it would be good for the country if there were a new major party to compete with the Democrats and Republicans; only 24 percent thought adding a new party would be bad. Although the situation seemed ripe for a Ross Perot third-party effort, there was an even 44 to 44 percent split on the question of whether Perot should be the one to start his own independent political party. The most intense anger against the two major parties appeared among the Perot supporters who, when asked what the term "political party" meant to them, responded with such phrases as "corruption," "rich, wealthy," "self-serving," "good-old-boy networks," "liars," and the like (Morin and Dionne 1992).

David S. Broder, one of the few pundits who is a serious student of parties, has more than once issued a call for "the rediscovery of political parties." But Broder acknowledges that "[I]t will not be easy to persuade people that this [the need for parties] is the case" (1993). He continues:

> ... Parties are almost invisible in the public dialogue today—especially on television. On the tube, conflicts are always personal, not institutional—Clarence Thomas v.

Anita Hill, not a Republican president against a Democratic Senate. Individualistic office-seekers ignore or camouflage their party labels. Federal and state laws impede the parties' operations.

Broder concludes with a note of urgency and an assignment of responsibility for "the rediscovery of parties."

> ... One reason that people don't vote along party lines any longer is that the media on which they depend don't tell them that parties make a difference.
> But this is not a task for the press alone. The men and women of learning—especially the historians and political scientists—need to be heard on these issues. Our experiment in republican government is faltering today. Quack remedies such as term limits are being successfully hawked to the public.[3] Scholarly detachment, at such a moment, is a crime. Either we will begin the rescue of responsible politics and effective government this year or hasten their disappearance.

The Functional Competitors to Parties

Over the past half century, institutional competitors have emerged and have arrogated to themselves many of the functions traditionally performed by the political parties. These competitors include the bureaucracies that administer the welfare state, the political entrepreneurs who become Members of Congress, community service groups, campaign consultants, organized interests, and the mass media.

Bureaucracies

It was no coincidence that urban and rural political machines began to disintegrate soon after the New Deal brought in the welfare state. Federal civil servants were assigned many of the functions previously handled by party personnel. The job-finding work of precinct and ward captains was taken over by the United States Employment Service, thus diminishing job patronage, which, like profit for a business enterprise, is among the major motivations for seeking party victory. The Social Security Administration provided benefits to the destitute, the unemployed, and the elderly to a far greater extent and more reliably than any party organization ever did. Additional government agencies took over other party activities.

Members of Congress

Rich or poor, citizens used to turn to their local party leaders for guidance and help in dealing with government agencies. The modest "fee" for such assistance was usually party loyalty during election campaigns and at the ballot box. The past half century has seen individual members of Congress increasingly rendering the constituent services formerly provided by party executives. Today, about 50 percent of congressional staff effort is devoted to constituency service. This transfer of function is undoubtedly correlated with the decline in the role of the parties in the nomination and election of members of Congress and senators. In previous times, local party leaders, meeting in caucus or committees, played the leading role in placing nominees for Congress on the ballot. In recent decades, running for Congress has been a personal entrepreneurial exercise. Candidates are self-selected. Nominations are made in primary elections, with or without party endorsement. Campaigns are self-directed, with little party support and little obligation to adhere to party platforms (Center for Party Development 1993). This disengagement of members of Congress from party has been facilitated in part by congressional appropriation of funds for maintaining members' district offices. Why should a constituent go to local party headquarters for help when he or she can go directly to the district office of the more influential member of Congress for faster and better service?

Community Service Groups

For a century and a half the parties provided the energy that kept the melting pot warm and welcoming. The Americanization of millions of immigrants, the political management of ethnic ghettos and enclaves, and the ladder of upward mobility for many of the new citizens were the work of party organizations. Today, however, local party figures no longer welcome arrivals at the dock or the airport. Today, these activities are conducted by community groups, organized principally by ethnic leaders, educators, social workers, or the staffs of candidates for office.

Campaign Consultants

Ever since public opinion polling became a relatively exact science in the 1930s, voters have been asked about their party affiliation, social characteristics, eligibility to vote, probability of voting, attitudes toward different ideological labels and current political issues, perceptions of candidates, responses to different messages, and so on. As polling technology improved, so has the precision and marketability of findings. In the course of this evolution, opinion pollsters have displaced precinct captains as the principal empiricists in matters of local demography, political issues, partisan attitudes, voting preferences, and other information about the party-in-the-electorate. Moreover, with this technology have come the experts; traditional party intelligence operations have become the merchandise of public relations consultants.

Organized Interests

Freedom of association and the right of petition under the Constitution have given rise to thousands of organized interest groups, many of which have spawned "political action committees" (PACs). In order to maximize their influence, interest groups and PACs give major attention to party nominations, platforms, and election campaigns. They exercise influence in several ways: informationally, by testimony during legislative and party platform hearings; organizationally, by supporting voter registration and turnout campaigns; and, financially, by contributing funds principally to candidate campaigns.

Financial contributions have increased in recent decades in part because election campaigns have become increasingly competitive and expensive. The average cost of a campaign for a member of Congress is $600,000 and for Senator $7,000,000. Almost everyone agrees that campaign costs and contributions have become exorbitant, but few suggest meaningful alternatives. Whenever this apparent excess reaches the "outrageous" level, Congress passes legislation placing new constraints on contributions. Within one or two elections thereafter, however, it becomes clear that money, like water, finds its way through unnoticed cracks, with party organizations the least benefited. Major contributors would rather give to individual candidates than to a party agency. The PACs pay attention to candidates' official status, incumbency record, and issue commitments, regardless of party affiliation. This practice confounds the fundraising efforts of the parties.

Media

Another class of functional competitors of the parties is the mass media: newspapers, news and commentary magazines, radio, and, above all, television. Prior to the 1960s, a candidate for public office usually needed to convince party peers of his political skills and electability. For example, in the 1960 Humphrey-Kennedy contest for the Democratic presidential nomination, Jack Kennedy challenged Hubert Humphrey in the West Virginia primary, thought to be "Humphrey country." Kennedy won, and the party's leaders, particularly Mayor Richard Daley and other urban bosses, were convinced that their national nominating convention delegations should vote for Kennedy.

With the arrival of radio and television into nearly every American home, it became possible for a candidate, particularly a rich one, to circumvent the assessments of party peers. A self-selected candidate can win a party's nomination without a word of endorsement from the leadership or rank-and-file of the party. Several candidates for the Senate were soon doing just this. In the striking case of Ross Perot, his wealth permitted him to run for the presidency without a party. A couple of million dollars worth of television exposure coupled with perhaps excessive "free" media coverage made his name a household word within a few weeks.[4]

But the media are more than a technology and a campaign tool. They are also publishers, editors, pundits, and reporters with a special opportunity to determine the perceptions and attitudes of their audiences, the content and strategy of political campaigns, and, often enough, the outcome of elections. For example, in presidential election campaigns it is common for television and newspaper commentators to complain that the candidates are failing to address substantive issues. Yet, each party has a platform and each candidate's headquarters distributes elaborate policy statements on almost every issue. The campaigns are "issueless" mainly because the media fail to report and analyze these policy statements, preferring to report campaigns as horse races.

As these competitors take over traditional party functions, what is left for the parties to do? There are, of course, those "invisible functions" for which parties were created in the first place: the implementation of the concept of popular sovereignty; the search for social and governing consensus; the recruitment and experiential training of political leaders; the articulation of dissent; and the harnessing of conflict to nonviolent methods of disagreement. These are hardly small tasks. Political philosophers would probably applaud these invisible functions and argue that they are worth everything a democratic community can contribute to their sustenance. How, then, should party executives and devotees of the party system attack the problem of fixing the political and attitudinal context in which the parties must operate?

A Public Relations Campaign for the Parties

We are dealing with an antiparty ethic, that is, a long-time, deeply ingrained attitudinal pattern. This pattern is debilitating, if not destructive, of a precious political institution. How may we go about fixing the political and attitudinal context in which the parties must live? Behavioral scientists will warn how difficult it is to change attitudes. Advertising executives are much more optimistic and bet their livelihoods on public relations campaigns. The public relations campaigns defending Tylenol™ and PepsiCola™ were brief, reasonable, and successful. But a PR campaign on behalf of the party system? Sounds gimmicky. We may expect that the concept of a public relations campaign on behalf of the party system will evoke ridicule and controversy.

By separating out the principal negative beliefs in the pattern of attitudes about parties, the pro-party themes of a public relations program may be reasonably constructed. Each of the negative beliefs requires exposure, rebuttal, or reformulation, tasks that are common in public relations campaigns. The following is a short list of negative beliefs that would need to be targeted.

- Money and related resources are always a negative influence in public affairs.
- Limits on campaign contributions and expenditures will prevent corruption and the exercise of undue influence.
- Party activity should be voluntary rather than a normal cost of democracy.
- Party reform or change of any kind is likely to benefit one side in the competition between parties and also destabilize the work of incumbents.
- It is a good thing that functional competitors—bureaucrats, members of Congress, community groups, political consultants, organized interest groups, candidates' personal organizations, and the media—have benefited from the disablement of party function and influence.

What would be some of the elements of a continuing public relations campaign on behalf of the U.S. party system? Some suggestions follow.

Revive Civic Education

Survey after survey during the last several decades reports that most parents would *not* want their children to make a career of politics, that is, party politics. We also know that children from ages as young as 10 and 11 begin to be aware of and interested in political phenomena. Half of all young adults 18–24 years of age voted for president in the early 1970s; only a third participated in the most recent elections. At some period between childhood and parenthood, civic education in the United States is failing miserably.

Elementary and secondary schools are in great need of civic education programs that are realistic, exciting, informative, and legitimating of our communal lives as a democratic nation. Textbooks and lectures alone will not do it. Simulations, field trips, internships, computer-assisted games and simulations, charismatic party leaders, and inventive teachers have roles to play. The disagreements and self-interests that manifest themselves in our party system and other political institutions should be characterized as legitimate and, if conducted in keeping with the "rules of the game," honorable. The nature of professionalism in public service should be fully and fairly described. Above all, skepticism and inquiry should replace cynicism and condemnation in what we teach our young and our new citizens about our party system.

Political Parties Day

Americans commemorate innumerable occasions and causes, from Ground Hog Day in February to Sadie Hawkins Day in November. A Political Parties Day[5] celebrated annually in an enlightening fashion on an appropriate day could become a salutary ritual. Perhaps the day chosen should be the one traditionally associated with the parties, namely, July 4, a day for patriotic feelings. Name the day and the rest of the celebratory arrangements can be left to American ingenuity.

Monitor the Media

"Except as a way to hand out patronage, 'the political party' went out with the icebox and the running board." This is the view of the executive producer of CBS's highly influential *60 Minutes* (Hewitt 1992). A distinguished political commentator (Drew 1993) stated the following: "The need to reform the system by which politicians raise money for their campaigns is by now pretty well understood. The current system is one of legalized corruption." George Will, in support of term limits, offers these words on the idea of public funding of campaigns: "True, public finance would eliminate fundraising, the most tiresome aspect of careers devoted to politics. But there should not be such careers. And until the political class will accede to term limits . . . nothing should be done to make the life of the political class less disagreeable" (1993).

Such antiparty punditry is pervasive and hardly helps improve a precious institution that is in trouble. Most media references to the parties, unfortunately, are loaded with innuendos and unsupported charges. Politicians portrayed on television dramatizations tend to be purchasable, sexist, slick, and/or dim-witted. Print media seem unable to describe campaign activities, expenditures, and financial contributions without implying theft, corruption, and other evils. Party leaders attending party fund-raisers are almost invariably reported as guilty-by-association, implicitly auctioning off their less-than-sacred honor. And the White House aide who accepts a gift watch had better pack his bags the next day. The targets of these ad hoc media-generated ethical standards are consistently party leaders. The standards are applied by the media "guardians."

Unquestionably, the media set the perceptions, the attitudes, and the tone with which the people of the United States see and respond to their political parties. It does not require a First Amendment scholar to recognize that the media serve a vital function in our politics. The performance of this function should be of the highest quality and accountability, particularly as it relates to the operations of our party system and the work of its leaders. The situation calls for creation of a commission, a professional group, an ombudsman, or some other body to monitor, call to account, and promote the objectivity and fairness with which the media in specific instances treat the parties and the party system. We should never censor the media, but we need not acquiesce to their perceptions and behavior, particularly if these are tearing down our party system.

The State of the Parties

A Bill of Rights Statute

All bills of rights are agendas for focusing attention, provoking debate, and legitimizing reinterpretation of concepts and principles. Consider the two centuries of attention, debate, and reinterpretation of each of the first ten amendments to the United States Constitution. There could hardly have been invented a better device to keep such fundamental principles as free speech, freedom of association, and right of petition close to the lives and minds of Americans. A legislated Bill of Rights for Political Parties may render similar sociopsychological as well as political purposes.

A good model for setting forth the mutuality of rights *and* responsibilities of parties is the U.S. Bill of Rights. The provisions, which would be applicable to all party systems, might include the following:

1. Political parties shall be protected from violence and the threat of violence and shall themselves refrain from acts of and incitements to violence and harassment.
2. Political parties shall share in the rights of freedom of association and shall accordingly abide by the constitutional and statutory rules of association.
3. Political parties shall enjoy the rights of free speech and be assured fair communication access to the entire citizenry. The parties, in turn, shall refrain from disruption of communication channels and presentation of false information.
4. The name of a political party, its symbols, its declarations, and its endorsements shall be protected under the laws of copyright and parties shall abide by these same laws and their own published regulations regarding these matters.
5. The nominating prerogatives of legally established parties and the opportunity for new parties to enter the nomination and election processes shall be protected under the law. For their part, political parties shall refrain from frivolous nominations, secret nominating procedures, and disruption of nonpartisan nominating and election activities.
6. In recognition of the public services rendered by political parties, selected organizational, campaign, nomination, and election functions of duly established parties shall be financed from public revenues. In order to remain qualified for public funding, the parties must adhere to the laws governing ethical uses of private as well as public funds and related resources and abide by rules of public disclosure of all private and public receipts and expenditures of funds.
7. In order that parties may pursue their nomination, campaign, and election functions with maximum safety, they shall be assured secrecy of the ballot, security of voting places and ballots cast, and opportunity for their chosen

agents to observe the administration of the election laws and procedures. The parties shall respect the security of all polling places, election officials, and authorized observers.
8. Military personnel on active duty and practicing clergy of any denomination may not be nominated by political parties for any elective public office. The parties shall refrain from employing clergy or military personnel in election campaigns and other activities related to the pursuit of elective office.
9. Political parties may organize in an overt and legally prescribed manner across geographical and political boundaries whether within a nation or transnationally among nations. These transcommunal party associations shall abide by the laws of the subnational or national entities among which they operate or associate, and they shall refrain from subversion, violence, or secret organizing activity that may jeopardize the host community.
10. The elections and other legal outcomes of party effort shall be acknowledged by the prompt and peaceful installation of elected party nominees into the public offices won. The parties shall submit disputed nominations and elections to an independent judiciary or a nonpartisan third-party agency for resolution.

Although most of these provisions seem to be already in place and respected here and in other democracies, closer inspection, the United States still has a distance to go to meet some of the standards. With respect to Provision 2, for example, do U.S. parties really share all the rights of freedom of association? From time to time, this question comes before the courts. As recently as 1986, the Supreme Court, on appeal, affirmed that the state of Connecticut could not prevent unaffiliated voters from voting in certain Republican primary elections when the Republican party invited them to do so (*Tashjian v. Republican Party of Connecticut* 1986). Connecticut argued that it was protecting the two-party system by confining registered party voters to their own party's primary. The Court declared Connecticut's attempt to prevent participation to be an infringement of freedom of association. In this and other cases, the courts have had to be called upon in order to clarify freedom of association as it applies to political parties.

Provision 6 concerns the public funding of parties. This would probably be the most loudly debated provision. Is it proper to ask U.S. citizens to pay the parties a "fee" for rendering public services? It costs money to open and maintain party headquarters. Minimal communication with the citizenry—more during campaign periods—requires funds or free access to public channels. If nominating procedures must be conducted in a public manner, as in primary elections, parties must expend funds and other resources. The presentation of programs of public policy cannot be done without financial cost. Participation in election administration is expensive.

The principle of public funding of party functions is already established for such activities as the conduct of national nominating conventions, primary elections, and general elections. Yet, the decline in one-dollar check-offs for the parties told us that the citizens would rather not pay for these services. Surprisingly, politicians themselves share this attitude.[6] Is the problem one of ethics, ignorance, or institutional procedure?

Provision 9 alludes to cross-boundary party collaborations. Americans know of such collaborations from their experience with federalism and the coalition of state parties into national parties. However, they know very little about transnational party collaborations such as those of the Christian Democratic, Socialist, Liberal, Conservative, and Green internationals. If anything, many Americans continue to believe that the defunct Communist International is still among us, largely because the Comintern received heightened press coverage in the years when it seemed to threaten American security. Transnational parties are likely to have a substantial role in U.S. and global politics in the not-too-distant future, but few are prepared to deal with the emerging challenge to the concept of national sovereignty that transnational parties pose. In sum, the citizens and leaders of the United States could profit from a thoughtful debate generated by a proposed bill of rights and responsibilities for the parties.

A statement of institutional rights and responsibilities such as a Bill of Rights for Political Parties could reformulate public consideration of the parties and their problems, emphasizing positive goals and change rather than negative attributions and constraints. Talk of improvement would replace condemnation as the content of public discussion about the debilities of the parties.

These suggestions for a continuing public relations campaign on behalf of the party system are just that, suggestions rather than panaceas. Any response to the bad rap needs popular involvement and creative thought. We need to hear again the words of a somewhat forgotten president of the United States, Martin VanBuren (1967):

> But knowing, as all men of sense know, that political parties are inseparable from free governments, and that in many and material respects they are highly useful to the country, I never could bring myself for my part to deprecate their existence. . . The disposition to abuse power, so deeply planted in the human heart, can by no other means be more effectively checked; and it has always struck me as more honorable and manly and more in harmony with the character of our People and of our Institutions to deal with the subject of Political Parties in a sincere and wiser spirit.

Notes

1. Two hundred and sixty years later, E. J. Dionne (1993) asked, "Why has [party] politics become such a nasty and often inhumane business?" Dionne offers several possible explanations, among them the inclination of politicians to "pound each other, often viciously"

when they are mandated to but cannot find real answers to real crises. "Name-calling is especially widespread on emotive issues," particularly since adversaries feel that they must demonize each other. What Dionne—and Bolingbroke—did not recall is the historical fact that party systems often take the place of more violent, hence even nastier, forms of political controversy.

2. There is an ample political science literature describing the motivations of persons choosing a career in politics and public service and the avenues of their entry into the system.

3. Apropos term limits, a recent survey of former members of Congress (Center for Party Development (1993:17) asked whether term limits would, in their opinion, increase or decrease the influence of the political parties in the recruitment of [candidates for Congress]. Party influence would increase according to 45.3 percent of the former members, decrease in the view of 12.6 percent, and make no difference in the opinion of 37.9 percent. Comparisons were made to term-limit practices in Latin America, where party leaders frequently play musical chairs in high offices, but, as a group, maintain control. Term limit legislation may well become a panacea with unintended consequences, such as strengthening rather than weakening the role of the parties.

4. Bertram Gross has speculated how a totalitarian future may emerge in the United States (1980). Some of the tendencies identified by him appear in the Perot "phenomenon."

5. The implication of this title is that Americans would prefer to celebrate their respective parties, major and minor, rather than a party *system*.

6. The survey of former members of Congress (Center for Party Development 1993) found that 75-80 percent of the former members, as do most of their fellow-citizens, oppose public funding of organizational units of the parties.

4

Toward a Responsible Three-Party System

Theodore J. Lowi

One of the best kept secrets in American politics is that the two-party system has long been brain dead—kept alive by support systems like state electoral laws that protect the established parties from rivals and by public subsidies and so-called campaign reform. The two-party system would collapse in an instant if the tubes were pulled and the IVs were cut. The current parties will not, and cannot, reform a system that drastically needs overhauling. The extraordinary rise of Ross Perot in the 1992 election and the remarkable outburst of enthusiasm for his ill-defined alternative to the established parties removed all doubt about the viability of a broad-based third party. It now falls to others to make a breakthrough to a responsible three-party system.[1]

At the same time, any suggestion of the possibility of a genuine third party receives the cold shoulder from the press and bored ridicule from academics. This reaction should surprise no one. Like the established parties themselves, social scientists are rarely given to innovation; they are almost always on the side of conventional wisdom, proven methodology, and the prevailing canon of their disciplines. Political scientists may call two-party doctrine a paradigm rather than canon, but they are no less loyal to it. With almost religious zeal, the high priests of the two-party system have preached the established faith, and their students who became leading journalists have perpetuated the two-party dogma. Thus, impetus for reform is about as unlikely to come from professors as from precinct captains.

To be sure, a great deal of scholarly "analysis" has been advanced to explain why third parties quickly disappear and why the two-party system is both natural and virtuous. Political scientists who believe this hold that the traditional Anglo-Saxon electoral system—based on first-past-the-post, single member districts—produces the two-party system by routinely discouraging new parties. They reason that since there can be only one victor in each district, even voters who strongly favor the candidate of a third or fourth party will ultimately vote for one of the two major candidates to avoid wasting their vote and also to avoid contributing to the victory of the least preferred of the major candidates. A two-party system is the best of all possible worlds, they hold, because it produces automatic majorities, enabling the victorious party to govern effectively for its full term of office.

Interestingly enough, although many scholars present the two-party system as being inevitable, it has never been left to accomplish its wonders alone. It has been supplemented by primary laws, nomination laws, campaign-finance laws, and electoral rules that are heavily biased against the formation and maintenance of anything other than the two-party system. And even with all that nourishment, two-party systems have prevailed in only a minority of all electoral districts in the United States since 1896. Most of the districts, from those that elect members of state legislatures up to the state as a whole in presidential elections, have in fact been dominated by one-party systems. During the past century, most of our larger cities and many counties, especially those governed by political machines, were admired by social scientists for their ability to overcome governmental fragmentation and to integrate immigrants into electoral politics even as they preached the gospel of the two-party system. While crusading reformers attacked the machines, most political scientists continued to defend them, even while they criticized specific abuses. Although academics are often aware of the deficiencies and strengths of parties, their commitment to the present system prevents them from considering a new one.

It is now time for a frank, realistic discussion of alternatives. No amount of tinkering, adjustment, reorganization, or aggressive public relations campaigns can bring back to life a party system that on its own devices would surely have crumbled a long time ago and that remains vibrant only in the hearts of party practioners and political scientists. It is becoming increasingly clear that the usual scapegoats—divided government, campaign practices, scandals—are not the problem. The problem is, and always was, to be found within the two-party system itself.

The Constituent Function of American Parties

Much of the reluctance on the part of scholars to jettison myths surrounding the two-party system stems from a fundamental misconception regarding the true function of American parties. As I have argued elsewhere and at some length,[2] parties perform a *constituent* or *constitutional* role in the American polity. Because this notion bears directly on my argument concerning the need for a responsible three-party system, a brief summary is in order.

By stating that parties perform constituent functions, I am not suggesting simply that they represent certain groups or individuals—all parties at least try to represent some segment of the public. Instead, I am using the term in a much broader sense, meaning "necessary in the formation of the whole;

forming; composing; making as an essential part." Constituent means that which constitutes. Constitution is the setting up of the way in which a political regime is organized and the laws that govern its organization. Parties have played a crucial role—intended or not—in "constituting" the American political regime by providing much of the organization and rules by which it is structured, staffed, and operated.

This view of party rests upon the distinction between constituent processes on the one hand and policy processes on the other. Political parties may perform both constituent and policy functions; such parties have been labeled as "responsible." American parties have almost never been responsible, policy-making parties, and most reform efforts to make them so have failed. On the other hand, political parties may perform only constituent functions; such parties have been variously called "pragmatic" or "rational-efficient." American parties have nearly always been constituent-based, and attempts to improve their organizational capacity in this regard have often succeeded. Indeed, the genius of the American party system, if genius is the right word, is that it has split the regime from policy, keeping the legitimacy of the government separate from the consequences of governing.

One important effect of constituent parties has been the lack of development of American political institutions, even as the society grew and modernized dramatically. A careful review of American history reveals several important regularities of the two-party system. First, the formation of new parties (or the dissolution or reorganization of existing ones) produces changes in the nature of the regime, while the functioning of established parties does not. In fact, the shift from new to established parties has been accompanied by a parallel shift in the effects of party, from liberal to conservative, from innovation to consolidation, or from change to resistance to change.

Second, new ideas and issues develop or redevelop parties, but parties, particularly established ones, rarely develop ideas or present new issues on their own. Party organizations are thus vehicles for changes in policy originating in other places, but they are not often incubators of policy alternatives. Once a system of parties is established, the range and scope of policy discussion is set, until and unless some disturbance arises from other quarters. Third, the key feature of the functioning of constituent parties has been the existence of competition and not so much what the competition was about. The more dynamic and intense the level of competition, the more democratic parties become, often in spite of themselves. But the more regularized and diffuse the competition, the more conservative the parties become. The key to understanding the two-party system, and the current necessity of a genuine third party, lies in understanding these regularities.

During the first party period, roughly from 1789 to 1840, parties served a liberating, democratic role. To begin with, the new parties helped democratize the presidency. The first great organized effort to carry an opposition candidate, Thomas Jefferson, into office in the campaign of 1800 was a giant step toward the plebiscitary presidency—namely, the pledging of electors. By such means the election of the President was decentralized and popularized by the parties. The growth of parties directly checked or reversed tendencies towards a "fusion of powers" at the national level, mainly through the influence that the new parties exerted upon recruitment and succession of leaders.

The new parties also helped disperse national power by encouraging the formation of local organizations. The election of Andrew Jackson, the first rank "outsider," and the nominating, organizing, and campaigning of professional politicians around Martin Van Buren increased participation in the regime. The existence of vibrant organizations dedicated to the pursuit of many offices provided the raw material for opposition and debate. Grand alliances of these organizations made it possible to coordinate the activities of office holders in a fragmented governmental system. Finally, the new parties helped democratize the electorate. This effect is easiest to document by the sheer expansion of political activity at local levels. As a result of the expansion of organized political activity, individual involvement also spread greatly and mass participation in nominations and elections became highly visible at all levels of public office. The spread of political activity helped increase the size of the electorate and produced increasingly large turnout. None of these consequences of the emerging parties were particularly policy oriented, of course, but the process of party development linked elites to masses around the key issues of the day.

By the 1840s, however, the national party system seemed to pause in its development. Parties would henceforth monopolize all important elections and party machinery would dominate, if not monopolize, all nominations. Parties would also monopolize the procedures and administration of Congress as well as virtually all of the state legislatures. The schemes of party organization and procedure were to remain about the same for decades to come. Parties no longer served a liberating or democratic role, but rather a constricting, conservative one. With a few exceptions, the two-party system has functioned this way ever since.

The tendencies of established parties were as nearly opposite to those of new parties as is possible in a dynamic, modernizing society. For one thing, the established parties contributed to the status quo in government structure. For example, they helped maintain the centrality of federalism, even as the national government and the Constitution expanded to meet the problems of a nationally integrated country. Political leaders, including members of Congress, developed a fundamental stake in the integrity of the state boundary because it was the largest unit for electoral office. This force has had a powerful impact on the substance of much important national legislation throughout the last century, from social insurance to environmental protection. Parties have participated in a silent conspiracy to prevent policy innovations from departing too far from eighteenth-century constitutional structure.

The established parties also made elective offices less democratic by resisting leadership change and policy innovation. From the courthouse to the White House, the parties have not of their own accord brought new elites to the fore or offered powerful checks on existing elites. Neither do they regularly bring new issues to the fore. It has been rare for the two major parties to take opposite stands on new controversies; it is much more common for new cleavages to develop within the existing parties, providing incentives to avoid addressing these controversies.

Finally, there is little evidence to suggest partisan competition has any real impact on electoral mobilization. In many instances closely balanced parties appear to have actively resisted further democratization of the electorate. Expanding the franchise to new voters and mobilizing existing ones often threatens existing party coalitions, and thus established parties have reasons to ignore or actively oppose such expansions. Along these lines, established parties have an investment in existing social cleavages and no real interest in building a consensus across the myriad of ethnic, religious and regional groupings that characterize American society.

Of course, there have been a few important instances since the 1840s when the established parties have been programmatic and innovative. At such times—most clearly in 1856-60, 1896-1900, 1912-14, and 1933-35—significant differences appeared between the parties and they became innovative rather than conservative. Each period was ushered in by the "redevelopment" of one of the established parties after an earlier political disaster. Such reorganization made the party oligarchies more susceptible to direction from interest groups with strong policy commitments. Party leaders also became more susceptible to mass opinion, partly as the result of the mobilization of new social movements, but also due to increased competition from rivals. And in these periods, the appearance of a third party was a powerful force in implementing these changes. Of course, these third parties eventually faded, once the major parties stole their message and followers, and reestablished a new, conservative equilibrium.

The Two-Party Impasse

Back when the federal government was smaller and less important, the two-party system could carry out its constituent functions without much regard to ideology or policy. Its unresponsiveness produced major political blunders from time to time, but the system was able to right itself after a brief period of reorganization. But with the New Deal and the rise of the welfare state, the federal government became increasingly vulnerable to ideological battles over policy. Even then, such problems were not particularly noticeable while the government and the economy were expanding, but in the early 1970s class and ideological conflicts began to emerge more starkly, and the two-party system was increasingly unable to offer productive competition.

Thus were born the familiar "wedge" issues—crime, welfare, prayer, economic regulation, social regulation, taxes, deficits, and anticommunism. No matter what position party leaders took on such issues, they were bound to alienate a substantial segment of their constituency. While the Democrats were the first to feel the cut of wedge issues, particularly concerning race, Republicans are now having their own agonies over abortion, crime, foreign policy, and budget deficits. Wedge issues immobilize party leadership, and once parties are immobilized the government is itself immobilized.

Party leaders have responded to this gridlock not with renewed efforts to mobilize the electorate but with the strategy of scandal. An occasional exposure of genuine corruption is a healthy thing for a democracy, but when scandal becomes an alternative to issues, leaving the status quo basically unaltered, it is almost certain that all the lights at the crossroads are stuck on red. In fact, the use of scandal as a political strategy has been so effective that politicians have undermined themselves by demonstrating to the American people that the system itself is corrupt.

The established parties have atrophied because both have been in power too long. In theory, a defeated party becomes vulnerable to new interests because it is weaker and therefore more willing to take risks. But for nearly forty years, both parties have in effect been majority parties. Since each party has controlled a branch of government for much of that time, neither is eager to settle major policy issues in the voting booth. Voters find it difficult to assess blame or praise, making accountability judgments and partisan affiliation difficult. A very important aspect of the corruption of leadership is the tacit contract between the two parties to avoid taking important issues to the voters and in general to avoid taking risks.

Even a brief look at the two established parties reveals the urgency of the need for fundamental reform, and any remaining doubt will be removed before the end of the Clinton Administration. The established parties do not lack for leadership, and with briefing books a foot thick and plenty of economists-for-rent, they certainly do not lack for programs. Here Ross Perot certainly was right: Washington is full of plans, good plans, which the two parties turn into useless parchment. The Republican and Democratic parties are immobilized by having to promise too many things to too many people.

Republicans say that they consider government to be the problem, not the solution, particularly in economic matters. Yet, to attract enough voters to win elections, they have also pushed measures designed to make moral choices for all citizens; for example, restrictions on abortions are hardly the mark of a party that distrusts government action.

The Democrats like government action: the commitment of government to new programs with grandiose goals and generous budgets is, for them, tantamount to solving problems. President Clinton, for example, took bold stands on a multitude of issues during the campaign, but he conveyed no sense of priority among them. Once in office, Clinton quickly conceded the impossibility of the task he had defined. As *The New York Times* put it in a headline on its front page: "Clinton, after raising hope, tries to lower expectations."

As in the past, the present two-party system functions to keep leadership, succession, and governmental structure separate from the actual settlement of issues. The tendencies of the established parties to preserve institutional structure, avoid issues, and stifle competition are too far advanced for easy reversal. It is time for a new party organization, championing new ideas, to make the party system more competitive, as the original American parties did. A genuine third party would shatter this conservative alliance, jump-start the development process, and once again make parties agents of liberation, democracy, and innovation.

The Impact of a Genuine Third Party

Predictably, defenders of the two-party system have devoted considerable energy to shooting down any suggestion that the status quo can be improved upon. They have produced all sorts of scenarios about how a third party could throw presidential elections into the Congress, with the House of Representatives choosing the president and the Senate choosing the vice president. Worse yet, if it survived to future elections, a third party would hold the balance of power and, as a result, wield an influence far out of proportion to its electoral size. It might, by its example, produce a fourth or a fifth party. And if it elected members to Congress, it might even inconvenience congressional leaders in their allocation of committee assignments. There is a great deal of truth in these scenarios: a genuine third party might well cause such things and as a consequence help reconstitute the American regime.

With three parties, no party needs to seek a majority or pretend that it is a majority. What a liberating effect this would have on party leaders and candidates, to go after constituencies composed of 34 percent rather than 51 percent of the voters. When 51 percent is needed, a party or candidate has to be all things to all people—going after about 80 percent of the voters to get the required 51 percent. A three-party system would be driven more by issues, precisely because parties fighting for pluralities can be clearer in their positions. Third parties have often presented constructive and imaginative programs, which have then been ridiculed by leaders of the two major parties, who point out that third-party candidates can afford to be intelligent and bold since they cannot possibly win. But that is the point. In a three-party system, even the two major parties would have stronger incentives to be more clearly programmatic, because their goal would be more realistic and their constituency base would be simpler. Thus, each party could be a responsible party.

Two factors would help prevent the fragmentation that multi-party systems sometimes cause abroad, as in Israel. First, the American electoral system is not based on pure proportional representation. That system, allowing a party garnering a small number of votes to send at least one representative to the legislature, benefits the smallest of parties. Second, the fact that voters formally elect the chief executive provides incentives for splinter parties to coalesce behind one candidate. In a classic parliamentary system, even a party that has elected only a few representatives can exert a disproportionate influence on the selection of a premier.

Flowing directly from three-party competition, voting would increase, as would other forms of participation. Virtually our entire political experience tells us that more organized party competition produces more participation. And we already know that genuine three-party competition draws people into politics—not merely as voters but as petition gatherers, door knockers, envelope lickers, and $5 contributors—making the three-party system an antidote to the mass politics that virtually everybody complains about nowadays.

Even defenders of the two-party system criticize the candidates' reliance on television, computerized voter lists, mass mailings, and phone banks—which dehumanize politics, discourage participation, replace discourse with ten-second sound bites, and reduce substantive alternatives to subliminal imagery and pictorial allusion. And the inordinate expense of this mass politics has led to a reliance on corporate money, particularly through political action committees, destroying any hope of collective party responsibility.

These practices and their consequences cannot be eliminated by new laws—even if the laws did not violate the First Amendment. A multi-party system would not immediately wipe out capital-intensive mass politics, but it would eliminate many of the pressures and incentives that produce its extremes, because third parties tend to rely on labor-intensive politics. Third parties simply do not have access to the kind of financing that capital-intensive politics requires. But more than that, there is an enthusiasm about an emerging party that inspires people to come out from their private lives and to convert their civic activity to political activity.

Finally, the existence of a genuine third party would parliamentarize the presidency. As noted above, once a third party proves that it has staying power, it would increase the probability of presidential elections being settled in the House of Representatives, immediately making Congress the primary constituency of the presidency. Congress would not suddenly "have power over" the presidency. It has such power already, in that the Constitution allows it complete discretion in choosing from among the top three candidates. But if Congress were the constituency of the president, the president would have to engage Congress in constant discourse. The president might under those circumstances have even more power than now, but he would have far less incentive to go over the head of Congress to build a mass following. Even now, with two parties based loosely on mythical majorities, a president cannot depend on his party to provide a consistent congressional majority. The whole idea of an electoral mandate is something a victorious president claims but few members of Congress accept, even for the length of the reputed honeymoon. Thus, current reality already forces the president to bargain with members of the opposition party.

Confronting three parties in Congress, each of whose members elected on the basis of clear policy positions, the president's opportunities for bargaining for majority support would be more fluid and frequent. In our two-party environment, issues are bargained out within the ranks of each party and often never see the light of day, particularly during the session prior to a presidential election. A third party with a small contingent of members of Congress would insure a more open and substantive atmosphere for bargaining to take place—after the election.

A genuine third party would play the role of honest broker and policy manager, because it would hold a balance of power in many important and divisive issues. There would be little fear of the tail wagging the dog, because, unlike European parties, Democrats and Republicans are not ideologically very far apart—they have simply not been cooperating with each other. The presence of a third-party delegation gives the president an alternative for bargaining, but if the new party raised its price too high it would simply give the president a greater incentive to bargain with the other major party. Another important myth in the United States is that policy making is a matter of debate between the affirmative and the negative. But simple yea versus nay on clearly defined alternatives is a very late stage in any policy-making process.

Over time, a three-party system would alter the constitution of the American regime. Very quickly and directly, the entire pattern of recruitment and succession would change. The separation of powers would begin to recede until the presidency and both houses of Congress had become a single institution. The function of the cabinet and the very purpose of cabinet officers would change. These patterns would develop whether the lead issues were crime, economic development, health care, or foreign affairs. The parties would inevitably be more policy-oriented and responsive to the public will.

The point here is that the third party is a liberating rather than a confining force, a force for open debate on policies. Just as the rise of the two-party system fundamentally altered the constitutional structure of our government appropriately for the nineteenth century, so a three-party system would alter the structure appropriately for the twenty first century.

Toward a Genuine Third Party

Immediately, one must add an important proviso: A genuine third party must be built from the bottom up. It must be an opportunistic party, oriented toward the winning of elections. It must nominate and campaign for its own candidates at all levels and not simply run someone for president. Of course, building such a party will be difficult. It will require mobilizing a large number of people and resources. And it must attract regular Democrats and Republicans by nominating some of them to run as candidates with the third-party nomination as well as that of their own party. Joint sponsorship has been practiced by the Liberal and Conservative parties in New York for decades. Being listed on two lines on the ballot is a powerful incentive for regular Democrats and Republicans to cooperate with a new party, if not to switch over. About forty states have laws preventing or discouraging this practice, but their provisions will probably not stand up to serious litigation.

Although a genuine third party will not be able to elect a president, it must elect enough legislators to make a difference. This was a big error for Ross Perot when he ran for president. Not only did he mistakenly assume he could win, but even if he had won, he would not have had a majority in Congress; in fact, he would have faced a very hostile Congress. Perot would have been able to carry out none of his programs. Thus, a third party may present voters a clear set of policy alternatives but it must be clear on what it can accomplish. It is not a governing party; it must pursue means other than taking over the government in order to implement programs.

Here history provides some good examples. While genuine third parties have been infrequent in the United States, whenever they have organized from the bottom up they have had significant and generally positive effects on the regime. One of these is providing a halfway house for groups "wedged" out of the two larger parties. In 1924, the progressive movement succeeded in forming the Progressive Party in Wisconsin and other midwestern states, which nominated Robert M. La Follette for president. In the 1930s, the Farmer-Labor Party flourished in Minnesota, where it eventually fused with an invigorated Democratic Party. In the process, both of these third parties provided the channel through which many dissident and alienated groups found their way back into politics, and their influence lingered long after the parties themselves. Similarly, wherever the Dixiecrats organized as a party, that state was later transformed to a genuinely competitive two-party state.

Of course, many third parties in American history have not built from the bottom up, including left- and right-wing splinter factions, protest movements, candidate caucuses, and single-issue interest groups, most of which sought merely to use a presidential campaign to advance their substantive message. Few of these groups have wanted or tried to play a continuing role in the American political system. Here again, Ross Perot provides an instructive example and a warning. After the election, he chose not to institutionalize his campaign by building a genuine third party, but chose instead to found a "citizens lobby," United We Stand America. Our system hardly needs another sophisticated lobby stirring up the grassroots to pressure the established parties, particularly one that is dominated by its celebrity founder. The resources available in the Perot campaign—plentiful money, a dynamic leader, thousands of committed volunteers, and millions of disenchanted citizens—are wasted on such an effort. Just imagine where a third party would be today if a fraction of Perot's expenditures had gone to organizing efforts at the grassroots level to field candidates from municipal elections on up.

There are, however, numerous efforts under way to exploit the opportunity Perot has apparently abandoned. A national Independence Party was founded in 1992, drawing on many former Perot activists but operating on a party principle rather than a group principle. In 1993, the party's name was changed to the Federation of Independent Parties to accommodate the several affiliated state parties operating under different names. Some pre-dated our national effort, and others were operating in states which do not permit the use of party labels, such as Independent, that have been used before or might tend to misrepresent the size or character of the membership. But as with most such efforts, the national party began to founder in 1994, when at its organizing convention it was split apart by integration with the New Alliance Party. The party changed its name to the Patriot Party and the leaders of the New Alliance Party dropped their name and separate identity in an effort to indicate that they are no longer a fringe party. Although the future of the national party was left very much in doubt, the elements of a real national candidacy were in place. And meanwhile, genuine centrist were forming in more than twenty states, some affiliated with the national party and some not. Candidates for governor and Congress and other offices were nominated in 1994, and there was the beginning of real progress toward three-way electoral contests—and also two-way contests where the third party candidate offered at least some opposition to an otherwise uncontested incumbent.

Such efforts that produce few if any electoral victories confirm to mainstream observers the futility of efforts to form a new electoral party. However, if the leaders, organizers, and activists within the new party maintain awareness that victory comes in more than one form—politics is not a game—the chance of persistence and growth is enhanced. So is the ultimate goal of transformation of American politics by turning the two-party system into a three-party system. The results of such a three-party system would be immediate, unlike the long and unintended developments of party reform within the context of the two-party system. The first definite possibility is that the two major parties would, in this three-party context, be able to realize more of their own virtues. The programs and goals of the established two parties are not inherently evil; it is their duopoly that is evil. Both operate as majority parties, both enjoy much of the satisfactions of majority parties and have for a long time. Because of that, they are decadent parties. If power, according to the philosopher, does corrupt, it is usually from having a lot of it for too long a time. The duopoly has to go.

A second consequence, again an immediate consequence flowing from the permanent establishment of a three-party system, is improvement in the legitimacy of political action and public objects. It is no figment of the imagination that the public is receptive to a new third party organization. The results of the 1992 election reveal that millions of Americans are willing to vote for someone and some party other than the Democratic or Republican. Polls conducted during the most partisan season, the spring and summer of 1992, confirmed that nearly 60 percent of the American people were favorably disposed toward the creation of a new political party.

Meanwhile, personal commitment to the major parties continues to decline and public distrust of politicians continues to increase unabated. The high priests of the two-party system are looking for the explanation everywhere except where the explanation truly resides—in the present party itself. Since the two parties are a duopoly and operate as a duopoly, they have no incentive or will to break open and look publicly at the hundreds of thousands of established coalitions and networks that support the programs that give rise to the deficit and the impossibility of reducing it. There is no way these party leaders can reduce the deficit by screaming at the deficit figure itself and by passing legislation like Gramm-Rudman or constitutional amendments to promise some kind of ceiling on the aggregate figure itself. That is akin to howling at the moon. The gridlock over the deficit and the growing national debt was never attributed to divided government. It was attributed to the two-party duopoly and its primordial stake in the maintenance of the networks of support for existing programs, whether they are still useful or completely outmoded. A third party with no stake in those networks will not immediately bring honesty and integrity to government and will not immediately bring the budget into balance. But it will contribute to honesty in budgeting, because it will have every incentive, every selfish incentive, to do so.

Finally, if this new effort to create a genuine third party in a new three-party system accomplishes nothing else, it will at least make a great contribution to political pedagogy and public education. It should be considered a great success if it jolts entrenched political journalism and academic political science toward a reconsideration of their myth-ridden conception of the prerequisite of democracy in general and American democracy in particular. And it can be considered a great success already to the extent that textbooks and classrooms are raising fresh and new curiosities about what really works in a democratic political system. We end as we begin, with the proposition that there is nothing in the universe that demands a two-party system, and therefore it is not sacrilegious to advocate an alternative.

Notes

1. This essay parallels arguments I have made elsewhere, including Lowi 1992a, 1992b, and 1994.

2. See Lowi 1975.

PART TWO

Party Activities in 1992

5

The Politics of Cohesion: The Role of the National Party Committees in the 1992 Election

Anthony Corrado

The last two decades have witnessed a resurgence of national party activity in electoral politics. Once cast as institutions of "politics without power" (Cotter and Hennessey 1964) in an increasingly candidate-centered political culture, the national party committees have responded to changes in their environment by expanding their institutional capacities and restructuring their operations to provide the services and resources candidates need in modern elections. They have improved their fundraising abilities, stabilized their staffs, and enhanced their technological capabilities, which, in turn, has revitalized their role in political campaigns and their relations with state and local parties.[1] As a result, the national party organizations have been able to recapture some of their former influence in the political process, especially in congressional elections, where they play a major role in providing campaign services and financial support to candidates (Herrnson 1988, 1989).

The extent to which this renewed level of national party activity has influenced presidential elections has been a more open question. Beginning in the late 1960s and early 1970s, the national party committees became more active and asserted their authority to formulate delegate selection rules and procedures for national nominating conventions (Ranney 1975; Shafer 1983; Price 1984; Wekkin 1984). But these rules changes have had the largely unintended effect of undermining the role of party organizations in the presidential nomination process (Crotty 1978; Ceasar 1982; Polsby 1983). Most importantly, the new rules opened up the selection process, which ended party control of the presidential nomination and produced more competitive, even divisive, primaries. Competition was also encouraged by other reforms, especially the limitations and public funding provisions of the campaign finance reforms of the 1970s (H. Alexander 1992; Corrado 1993).

Consequently, presidential elections have become candidate-based contests in which contenders, relying on their own organizations and fundraising abilities, attempt to mobilize issue activists and other constituencies behind their individual candidacies. The national party organizations generally exercise little influence in this process. Yet, despite their declining influence, the party committees are still expected to carry out the difficult task of trying to unify partisan factions divided by the nomination contest. Their success in fulfilling this role constitutes an increasingly important electoral objective. As Martin Wattenberg has shown, the candidate with the most unified party has won every election since 1964, which has led him to conclude that "unified party support has become more crucial than ever to a presidential election victory" (1991b:40) as the role of partisanship as a general determinant of voting behavior has declined (Stone 1984; Buell 1986).

This chapter examines some of the ways in which the revitalized national party organizations have tried to promote partisan cohesiveness in national elections.[2] In particular, it discusses the role of the Democratic National Committee (DNC) and Republican National Committee (RNC) in the 1992 presidential race, and the use of resources designed to promote party integration and organizational strength in the general election campaign.

An Overview

Since the advent of the modern party reform movement, the national party committees have participated in the presidential selection process only to a limited extent. They are responsible for the rules that govern delegate selection. They organize the national conventions, which are technically part of the nominating process, and assist in the selection of members to the convention standing committees, which have the formal responsibility for drafting convention rules and writing the party's platform. They also provide indirect assistance to the party nominee through such activities as generic party advertising and the financing of voter registration and mobilization programs in the general election.

The DNC and RNC have generally taken a hands-off approach in the presidential nomination campaign and have eschewed expressing a candidate preference due to the prospect of an endorsed candidate losing the race. As Paul Herrnson has noted, such an outcome "would be disastrous . . . because the successful, unsupported candidate would become the head of the party's ticket and its titular leader" (1994a:58). The parties have therefore, for political purposes, usually served as no more than honest brokers, allowing candidates to make their own decisions and form their own organizations in seeking the nomination.

The presidential race thus presents the party committees with two challenges that must be addressed in advance of the general election. First, nomination contests encourage party factionalism, particularly when the nomination is hotly contested, as in the 1976 Republican selection or the Democratic contests of the 1980s. But even in races in which the choice of a nominee is apparent relatively early, such as the 1988 Republican and 1992 Democratic contests, party divisions may result. Because the party platform and the convention are often used as vehicles for promoting party unification, unsuccessful candidates or issue activists within the party may continue to challenge the nomination in hopes of influencing the party's platform or being invited to address the convention (Polsby and Wildavsky 1984; Davis 1983; Shafer 1988). These efforts, regardless of their success, can serve to intensify splits within the party.

The incentive for candidates or issue activists to continue to mount a challenge for the party's standard is especially strong in the Democratic Party. The Democrats' rules mandate the proportional allocation of delegates based on voter preferences and a fairly open selection process for delegates and convention committee members, which tend to foster more prolonged contests or at least provide certain groups within the party an opportunity to realize voting strength sufficient to have an effect on the platform or other convention decisions (Kirkpatrick 1979; Sullivan, Pressman, and Arterton 1976; Kamarck 1990; Corrado 1991). The Republicans suffer less from long, divisive primary campaigns due to their greater reliance on winner-take-all delegate systems (Wattenberg 1991b:41). Despite this, the party has experienced in-fighting between candidate partisans and different wings of the party, as in the 1976 contest between President Ford and Ronald Reagan or the more recent struggles between party moderates and conservative activists.

The second problem the national party organizations must confront is how to conduct a unified campaign effort. How are the activities of the two organizational structures, the party committees (national, state, and local) and the nominee's campaign, to be combined and coordinated? Usually this issue is resolved in a way that fails to promote party integration or organizational development; the nominee's campaign committee takes central responsibility for the general election and often seeks either to control the party organizations or to bypass them altogether.

In recent elections, presidential campaigns have increasingly relied on their own personnel to conduct state campaigns and often attempt to co-opt the party structure by shifting key campaign staff members to the party payroll. In 1984, Democratic nominee Walter Mondale even attempted to replace Charles Manatt as party chair during the Democratic National Convention, only to be rebuffed by members of the national committee (Germond and Witcover 1985:381-85). Such actions diminish the value of party organizations and heighten tensions between party officials and the presidential nominee. Indeed, concern among party officials about their role in national elections had become so pronounced by the beginning of the 1992 cycle that one of the Democratic presidential aspirants sought their support by promising that his campaign staff would not be sent into their states to manage the general election if he won the nomination.[3] So, despite their supposed revitalization, national party committees were not considered to be a vital institutional partner in the conduct of presidential campaigns through the 1980s.

Conventional wisdom argues that the party of the president has an advantage in resolving these problems and achieving party unity when the incumbent is seeking reelection. The national party chair is usually the hand-picked choice of the president and the national committee functions as an extended political arm of the White House. The incumbent president normally lacks a serious challenger from within the party for the nomination. If he is challenged, the nomination is often decided early and his challenger concedes well before the convention, so there is plenty of time to ensure a harmonious convention. This is especially true if a Republican holds the Oval Office, since the Republicans tend to be more cohesive and less likely to divide over issue concerns (Wattenberg 1991b).

In accordance with this view, George Bush was considered to have a substantial advantage entering the 1992 election cycle. Besides having the "traditional" edge presumed of an incumbent, Bush enjoyed an extraordinary level of public popularity in 1991 as a result of the end of the Cold War and the victory in the Gulf War. Many political observers thought that Bush could simply sit back and watch the Democrats "tear themselves up" in a primary campaign before undertaking a general election victory tour. Many Democratic party leaders subscribed to this view as well, and some party officials and putative presidential candidates shifted their focus from 1992 to the possibilities in 1996. One Democrat who did not follow the pack was DNC Chair Ron Brown, who instead of conceding the election or shifting attention to the congressional and state races, took advantage of the Democrats' adverse position to harness the potential of a revitalized DNC and unite the party behind a common goal--recapturing the White House in 1992.

The Prenomination Campaign

The Democrats

When Ron Brown was elected chairman of the DNC, he took over a party organization in disarray. The Democrats had lost five of the past six presidential elections, including a humiliating loss in 1988 to George Bush. These elections had highlighted the Republican Party's superiority in resources and campaign planning. The Democrats' relative organizational weakness was made particularly clear in 1988, since the party seemed incapable of halting Michael Dukakis's descent from a double-digit lead in early August to a resounding defeat at the polls in November.

More importantly, the 1988 experience threatened to divide the Democratic coalition since it rekindled the internal party debate concerning its strategy in national elections. In the aftermath of the election, some party leaders claimed that the key to future electoral success was to maintain the party's traditional liberal ideology and focus on strategies designed to register and mobilize strongly partisan voting blocs, especially minorities and the poor. Others, especially the leaders of the Democratic Leadership Council (DLC), an institutionalized faction within the party, argued vehemently against this view (see chapter 16). Instead, they advocated the need to recast the party's themes and programs to enhance their appeal to moderate, middle-class, and independent voters. Specifically, they advanced the need for a more populist, "progressive economic message" based on the values of upward mobility, individual responsibility, and equal opportunity that would recognize the interests of the middle class and the "moral sentiments of average Americans" rather than the liberal social views of the party elite (Galston and Kamarck 1989:17).

The 1988 contest thus left the party confused as to its future, and the selection of Brown, a member of the party's liberal wing who had formerly assisted Senator Edward Kennedy and supported the Reverend Jesse Jackson, did not initially allay many concerns. But Brown quickly articulated a set of objectives that he hoped would bring the party together. First, he wanted to strengthen the DNC as a party institution and transform it "into a tough, aggressive, professional campaign organization" (Brown quoted in Ifill 1992b). Second, he wanted to strengthen relations between the national committee and state party affiliates, and assist in the modernization of state party organizations. Third, he felt the DNC should be devoted to one central goal: winning elections, especially the 1992 presidential election.

Brown's conception of the DNC and its electoral role was modeled on the RNC. As he saw it, the Democrats' problems in presidential races stemmed from an over-emphasis on the nomination process; the party and its candidates had focused on party rules and divisive primary contests at the expense of general election planning (Ifill 1992b; Nagourney 1991). This left the party unprepared for the general election, forcing it to "reinvent the wheel" after each national convention. Conversely, the Republicans paid most attention to general election campaigns and applied strategies, which enabled them to provide substantial assistance to their nominee as soon as their convention was over. "There has been a mindset in the Democratic Party that you worry about the general election after you get past the nomination," Brown said. "We have to reverse that thinking" (Nagourney 1991). To achieve this purpose, Brown felt the party had to concentrate on the development of a political organization and a general election strategy that could be delivered to the party's nominee right after the convention. The role of the DNC would be to serve as the "designated agent" for general election planning (Germond and Witcover 1993:87). While the presidential challengers competed in the primaries, the national committee would engage in such tasks as targeting, polling, issues research, and other activities geared towards the presidential election. Such an approach would highlight the party's objective of winning elections, as well as help secure an influential role for the party organization in the conduct of the general election campaign, since the DNC would be responsible for services that the presidential candidate would value.

As early as 1989, Brown set about the task of reorienting the party to his objectives. He began by strengthening the DNC institutionally. Although the general effect of recent party rules reforms has been to weaken the party's role in presidential campaigns, the DNC adopted two rules changes shortly after the 1988 election that served to enhance its role. The DNC overturned a rule adopted by the 1988 national convention and reinstated the members of the national committee as automatic, unpledged convention delegates (Corrado 1991). The committee also changed the term of the party chair to run from election to election, rather than convention to convention (Longley 1992). This change eliminated the prospect of a potentially disruptive leadership struggle or major turnover in the party hierarchy in the midst of the nominating convention.

Brown's primary institutional concern was the RNC's sizeable advantage in staff and resources (Longley 1992). The DNC embarked on an effort to enhance its organizational capacity and gave priority to the improvement of its fundraising, media communications, and research staffs. Robert Farmer, who had directed Dukakis's successful 1988 fundraising effort and was chosen to serve as DNC treasurer in 1989, restructured the finance staff and developed programs for soliciting large gifts and soft money that could be used on party-building activities. The party developed new press operations, enhanced its capacity to tape "actualities" that could be transmitted to radio stations with the party's response to an issue of the day, and increased its ability to reach key constituencies through specialized publications such as minority and union newspapers (Barnes 1989b). The research staff, which in 1988 essentially consisted of two individuals largely responsible for speech writing, was enlarged to a staff of six. This group was responsible for polls and focus groups, targeting analysis, issues research, and opposition candidate research. In addition, the DNC spent more than $30,000 to hire outside companies to investigate various activities of Bush and his family (Isikoff 1992). These investments in personnel and resources significantly improved the DNC's capabilities. Yet they still failed to compare to the RNC. For example, the RNC continued to raise significantly more money than the DNC (Federal Election Commission 1993b), and even after expanding the communications division, the DNC staff was still seven times smaller than its Republican counterpart (Barnes 1989b).

The DNC also focused on its relationship with the state party organizations. During the 1980s, the national committee had begun an effort to modernize some state party organizations by providing them with funds, usually raised in the form of "soft money" not subject to federal contribution limits, to build voter files and develop voter mobilization programs. Brown and Paul Tully, the DNC political director, dramatically expanded such efforts in order to strengthen the party's organizational ties and enhance its political efficacy. The vehicle for fulfilling this purpose was the "coordinated campaign." The DNC encouraged state party organizations to work with both the national committee and individual candidates to construct and finance a central political operation, independent of any particular candidate, that was responsible for building voter files, registering voters, and mobilizing the Democratic vote in each state (Longley 1992). These coordinated campaigns promoted cooperation between party organizations and candidates, and thus spurred working relationships between these actors, as well as the coordination of common organizational tasks. Party leaders felt that such efforts would create a "web of relationships" that would serve as an infrastructure designed to mobilize the vote in a presidential race (Barnes 1989b:1104). The party would thus be able to offer the nominee a pre-existing party organizational network that could be included as part of an overall general election campaign structure.

To demonstrate the potential benefit of coordinated campaign operations, the DNC initiated model programs in special congressional elections in 1989 and went on to establish coordinated programs in over 30 states in 1990 (Barnes 1989b; Longley 1992). Then, in 1991, Tully developed a presentation, which he delivered at a series of party meetings, designed to sell the concept to party officials and fundraisers and convince them to raise the funds needed for a more extensive coordinated campaign operation in 1992 (Germond and Witcover 1993:87; Daley 1991a, 1991b; Edsall and Balz 1991).

In addition, the DNC research operation initiated a series of polls, focus groups, and targeting analyses designed to determine a national political strategy that would form the broader context of the DNC's electoral efforts and serve as a game plan for the presidential campaign. The DNC thus generated an approach that "would target key coastal, Midwestern and southern border states; revive efforts to mobilize black voters, who were generally neglected in 1988; and concentrate extraordinary resources in California, which, with 54 electoral votes, is assured of a pivotal role in any close presidential contest" (Edsall and Balz 1991). The party considered California, which would also be the site of two U.S. Senate races and 52 House contests, so important to its electoral success that the DNC held a meeting in the state in April 1992 where Brown asked party officials to sign an agreement to stage an $8 million effort to enhance research on state and local Republican candidates, voter registration, and get-out-the-vote programs (Ifill 1992b).

Besides these technical considerations, Brown sought to advance a message and issue agenda that could unify various groups within the party and serve as the foundation of a general election theme. Rather than have party officials debate such contentious issues as the death penalty, abortion, and budget policy, Brown attempted to focus the party on domestic concerns, including the economy, health care, and education. For example, even at the height of Bush's post-Gulf War popularity, Brown was arguing that the election would hinge on domestic concerns and that Democrats would benefit from a weak economy (Dillin 1991). He even encouraged the party leadership to draft policy resolutions on health care and trade to heighten attention to these areas (Shogan 1991).

Brown's efforts as chair to set an issue agenda for the party helped to increase the prospects for party unity. By increasing the salience of domestic concerns, the party highlighted Bush's weaknesses and steered away from the social issues and liberal policies that had become a source of tension within the party elite. It also linked the party to issues that appealed to the more populist, moderate Southern Democrats and middle-class voters, two groups the party was hoping to recapture in 1992 (see Edsall and Balz 1991; Germond and Witcover 1993:87–89). Brown personally assisted in establishing these links by conducting a special meeting of Southern Democrats and by recognizing the DLC as an important group within the party (May and Drape 1991; see chapter 16). On one occasion he even left a DNC conference so that he could attend a simultaneous meeting of the DLC. Interestingly, Brown's actions drew little response from the party's liberal wing; instead, he seemed to benefit from a general sense of pragmatism that permeated the party leadership, who were apparently willing to suppress ideological differences for the sake of winning an election.

One of the unique aspects of Brown's chairmanship was that he adopted a more interventionist approach to the presidential election than previous party leaders. He wanted the party in effect to nominate a candidate early in the primary campaign with minimal infighting so that the Democrats would not start the general election contest at a relative disadvantage. As the field of candidates began to emerge in late 1991, he intervened on a number of occasions to try to determine the field. One of his first actions in this regard was to approach Reverend Jesse Jackson and urge him not to enter the race so that the party could be relieved of the internal tensions it had experienced in the previous two elections (Ayres 1992). Instead, he ultimately persuaded Jackson to work with the party and play a leading role in the DNC's minority registration and mobilization programs (Broder 1992; Ifill 1992a; Wickham 1992). He also publicly prodded Governor Mario Cuomo of New York to make a decision concerning a presidential bid by late December so that the spectre of a Cuomo candidacy would not dominate the race and shift attention away from other candidates (Cook 1991).

As the campaign unfolded, Brown exerted his authority in an attempt to prevent bitter partisan bickering. He used his position as party spokesperson to warn presidential contenders to keep the debate civil, and specifically rebuked former California governor Jerry Brown in late March for personal attacks on Bill Clinton (apparently with relatively little effect—Brown continued to contest the nomination through to the convention) (Berke 1992; Ifill 1992b). Once it was clear that Clinton would be the nominee, Brown asked party leaders to unite behind him. Brown also ensured that representatives of key Democratic constituencies, such as labor, minority groups, and elected officials, would be included in the deliberations leading up to the convention. This latter goal was achieved in part through the 25 party leader and elected official positions (PLEOs) he controlled on each convention committee (platform, rules, and credentials), which are appointed by the party chair in accordance with national party rules.

The Republicans

The Republicans entered the 1992 election cycle with high hopes of another presidential victory. By March of 1991, President Bush's approval rating was soaring as a result of the Gulf War, as was support for his party. According to a Times-Mirror survey conducted at the time, 36 percent of the public identified themselves as Republicans, while only 29 percent identified themselves as Democrats. The survey also found that 50 percent of respondents wanted to see a Republican win in their congressional district, as opposed to 40 percent who hoped for a Democrat (Toner 1991b). The RNC planned to capitalize on this renewed level of support to expand its influence in elections at all levels.

Institutionally, the RNC was well-positioned to pursue this goal. Unlike the DNC, the Republicans had been engaged in party-building activities for more than a decade and had well-established candidate recruitment, campaign services, and political outreach operations (Conway 1983). They also had a more secure financial base. In 1990, the RNC raised over $68 million in federal funds alone, as opposed to only $14 million for the Democrats. During the first six months of 1991, the RNC raised over $23 million (in both federal and nonfederal funds), compared to slightly more than $5 million for the DNC. This financial base, when combined with the RNC's larger staff and greater technological capabilities, suggested that the Republicans had achieved a level of organizational development that would allow the party to play a major role in national and state legislative elections.

Despite their success in presidential elections throughout the 1980s, the Republicans had been plagued by continuing Democratic majorities in Congress and most state legislatures. In an effort to reverse this trend, the party emphasized the importance of "down-ticket" programs; that is, party programs designed to assist state and local candidates. These programs, which included voter registration and mobilization efforts similar to those being developed by the Democrats, encompassed a wide array of activities, all of which were designed to increase Republican voting strength at all levels of government.

The RNC therefore devoted significant resources to activities designed to strengthen the party in non-presidential elections. For example, the RNC considered the redistricting process to be an important vehicle for improving Republican prospects in 1992 and beyond. Party officials, however, could not rely on state legislative committees to protect Republican interests, since the majority of state legislatures were controlled by Democrats. The RNC leaders also considered the opportunity to gain seats through this process to be so important that the task could not be left to some other organ, as the Democrats had done.[4] The party therefore spent substantial amounts, primarily from soft money accounts, on redistricting battles in selected states. In 1991 and 1992, the RNC spent over $2.2 million in at least twelve states on redistricting efforts.[5] In most cases, according to Federal Election Commission (FEC) reports, the RNC sent soft money funds to data analysis and computer graphics firms to research and design various redistricting models. In other instances, the RNC simply transferred funds to ad hoc committees organized for the purpose of coordinating redistricting efforts, such as the Massachusetts Redistricting Task Force. The national party thus provided the funds needed for what has become a highly sophisticated, technologically advanced process. It thereby provided valuable assistance to state parties and state legislative committees, most of which would not have been able to finance such services on their own.

Many political observers expected that the RNC would also exploit the favorable political environment of 1991 to prepare for the presidential race. By getting an early start on fundraising and strategic planning, the party organization could help lock up Bush's renomination and provide him with a substantial head start in the election. The party did begin to plan a strategy along these lines. In late summer and early fall, members of the RNC staff began to develop an aggressive financial strategy based on a series of fundraising events designed to raise millions of dollars before the election year. The plan, however, was never implemented because the party had problems securing commitments from the White House for scheduling the President's appearance at these events.[6] This experience exemplified one of the major problems the RNC faced throughout the 1992 cycle—fragmented party leadership.

As the party in control of the White House, the Republicans had to operate within a more complicated organizational context than the Democrats. Because the president is the *de facto* leader, although not the titular head, of the party, the party in power has to coordinate its activities with the White House (Davis 1992). This can benefit the party since it provides the organization with access to the government and the perquisites that accompany the Oval Office. But it also limits the national party organization's efficacy, since policy is largely dictated by the White House and political operations are split between the White House political staff and the party apparatus, which can produce internal tensions and lack of coordination (Barnes 1989a).

This coordination problem might have been resolved if Lee Atwater, Bush's hand-picked chair, had not fallen ill. At the time of Atwater's selection, "it seemed likely that Bush would run his reelection out of the RNC, thus placing the party apparatus at the center of presidential politics to a degree unseen for years" (Ceasar and Busch 1993:36-37; see also Barnes 1989a). After Atwater's death and the selection of Clayton Yeutter, a former CEO of the Chicago Mercantile Exchange and Secretary of Agriculture in the Bush administration, as his replacement, this plan was never fully put into effect. Instead, party decision making was further complicated as the election year approached, since the creation of Bush's campaign committee established yet another organization with responsibility for electoral and political activities. This organizational disarray continued into the election year and, in February 1992, Yeutter, who was criticized for being an ineffective party manager, was replaced with Rich Bond, a former deputy chair of the RNC and Bush's 1988 deputy campaign chair.

Despite these obstacles, the RNC did take some steps during the primaries to assist President Bush. First, the RNC and some state party organizations undertook "a concerted effort" to keep David Duke, the former Ku Klux Klan leader, off Republican primary ballots (Smith 1991). Duke, who declared his candidacy for the Republican nomination on December 4, 1991, hoped to enter 28 primaries, but his ballot access efforts were opposed by Republican officials in a number of states, which often forced his campaign to pursue non-party-related means to make the ballot, such as court challenges and ballot petitions (Smith 1991; Cook 1991). In some states, such as Georgia and Florida, where the party controlled the ballot access process, the party successfully kept him off (Cook 1992). The chief objective of these efforts was not to deny Duke the nomination (no party leaders thought he had a realistic chance of beating the president), but to ensure that he and his followers would not be represented at the national convention, where they might gain the sort of media exposure that would link Duke to the Republican Party (Smith 1991).

The national party organization was less successful in stifling the insurgent candidacy of former Nixon speech writer and conservative television commentator Pat Buchanan. Buchanan entered the race in December on a platform designed to mobilize conservative activists. He attacked Bush for violating his tax pledge and advanced a policy agenda based on trade protectionism, immigration restrictions, and foreign policy isolationism. Buchanan's candidacy thus highlighted conservative dissatisfaction with Bush and asked right-wing activists to abandon the president for the sake of ideology. Buchanan's challenge also demonstrated the limits of party influence in nomination contests. Even with the Republicans' renewed institutional strength and party-oriented delegate selection rules, any individual with resources and adequate levels of personal support can enter a bid for the nomination. What is most interesting about the Buchanan challenge is that the national party leadership did not take a hands-off approach towards the race or even present a public image of neutrality. Instead the party leadership actively sought to discourage this challenge. Buchanan charged that the party hierarchy was treating him like Duke, noting that he was denied access to party contributor lists, denied opposition research on Democrats, and given no assistance in his efforts to qualify for the ballot in certain states (Cook 1991:3736). Chairman Bond did little to disavow this perception; in fact, in a nationally televised interview, he claimed that one purpose of Buchanan's campaign was to "basically highjack David Duke's message on race and religious tolerance and put a jacket and tie on it and try to clean it up" (Bond quoted in Jehl 1992). This and other statements from Bond calling for Buchanan to end his campaign and support the president led Buchanan, at one point, to call for Bond's resignation and urge his supporters to withhold contributions to the RNC until Bond was removed (Jehl 1992; Dionne and Devroy 1992; *The Washington Post* 1992). Bond remained, but so did Buchanan, who had no chance at gaining the nomination yet stayed in the race in hopes of having some influence on the party platform and convention.

The Conventions

Although the national party organizations have the formal responsibility for the presidential nominating conventions, in practice the nominee's campaign operation exercises the greatest influence over these quadrennial spectacles. The party committees oversee site selection and logistics, and are technically responsible for enacting the nomination, passing a party platform, and managing the convention program. But in recent decades these activities have been overshadowed by the convention's role as a public relations vehicle for promoting the presidential ticket and general election themes and strategies (Davis 1983; Shafer 1988; Smith and Nimmo 1991). The orchestration of the convention has therefore become of crucial concern to presidential candidates. Consequently, campaign operatives and political consultants have usurped many of the functions formerly carried out by party officials. The party leadership still participates in these functions, but they are usually relegated to the role of assisting in the implementation of candidate strategies and providing less visible media services for the party's nonpresidential candidates (Herrnson 1994:59). One of the functions the party leaders do perform is to help broker relations between competing candidates or between the nominees and various groups within the party. This often takes the form of assisting campaign staff in the development of

The Politics of Cohesion

platform concessions or convention speaking opportunities that can be used to satisfy reticent groups or former opponents. A party chair's effectiveness in fulfilling this role, however, depends on a number of factors, especially the chair's internal party political relationships and ability to influence convention decision-making. The varying levels of success the party chair may achieve are suggested by the experiences of the party leaders in 1992.

Given his actions prior to the convention, it is not surprising that Ron Brown actively sought to ensure the event's success and produce a united party for the fall campaign. He supported the position that only those who had endorsed Clinton would be allowed to speak and served as Clinton's liaison to Reverend Jackson in the period prior to the convention (Ayres 1992). Brown also relied on his personal relationship with Cuomo, perhaps the party's most prominent liberal spokesman, to encourage him to deliver the speech nominating Clinton (Germond and Witcover 1993:344–345).

Brown further helped to guarantee a unified party and convention by using his authority over the platform committee to ensure that the platform would reflect the positions of the party's nominee, Bill Clinton, which were essentially the positions staked out by the DLC. The DNC chair has the potential to influence platform deliberations because he holds significant authority with respect to the composition of the platform committee. Under party rules, most of the 161 committee members are selected at the state level, but the chair appoints the cochairs of the committee, the vice chairs, and 25 party leaders and elected officials who serve as committee members (Maisel 1994). In addition, the DNC head is responsible for selecting the membership of the Drafting Committee, which in practice is the most influential group in the platform-writing process because it develops the draft that becomes the working document for committee deliberations.

In 1992, Brown selected the Drafting Committee with two goals in mind: to assure the domination of Clinton supporters so that the platform would reflect the positions Clinton would run on in the fall, and to include representatives of groups considered critical to a winning coalition in the general election. As L. Sandy Maisel has noted in his study of the 1992 process:

> Chairman Brown named New Mexico Congressman Bill Richardson as chair of the Drafting Committee early in the process, but he did not name the other members until early June, well after the nomination of Bill Clinton was assured. The appointment of Drafting Committee members reflected Brown's desire that the convention be run in such a way as to enhance the nominee's chances in November. Thus, Brown permitted the Clinton staff to dictate roughly half of the members of the committee. He in turn used the remaining committee slots to guarantee representation by those groups, important to the party, that he did not want to slight (1994:676).

The document produced by this group met Brown's expectations; it reflected the central themes and issues that formed the basis of Clinton's candidacy. Although the draft did go through some changes when considered by the full committee, this body was clearly controlled by the Clinton forces and few substantive changes were made (Maisel 1994). In the spirit of party unity, the committee, with the Clinton campaign's support, even approved four minority planks put forth by the Tsongas camp for full convention consideration. These planks, however, were not a source of major controversy, and eventually the Tsongas forces withdrew all but one of the proposals.

Since DNC rules mandate the proportional allocation of convention committee positions based on each candidate's vote share in caucuses and primaries, Clinton supporters would have formed the majority even without Brown's assistance. However, Brown's actions minimized the potential for internal party divisions surrounding the platform deliberations and thus guarded against the showcasing of intraparty squabbles at the convention. Brown's effectiveness was also in large part a function of the fact that he was working to assist the nominee, who already had control of the convention. Moreover, he benefited from a general sense of pragmatism that permeated the party by the time of the convention. After enduring so many presidential losses, potential critics of the platform, particularly party liberals, were in no mood to weaken the party by engaging in a divisive platform debate. Although Jerry Brown was still contesting the nomination at the convention, the delegates were not interested in a fight and the Democrats enjoyed their most unified convention of the postreform era.

In sharp contrast to the Democrats, the Republicans faced serious internal party divisions in advance of their convention. Buchanan's challenge had served to heighten conservatives' dissatisfaction with Bush's economic policy and the Christian Right had been active throughout the primaries to guarantee that they would have a voice in convention proceedings (Oldfield 1992). These activists succeeded in gaining representation on convention committees in part because RNC rules are less candidate-oriented than the Democratic guidelines. Although the RNC chair is responsible for selecting the chair and cochairs of the platform committee (which is technically called the Committee on Resolutions), the 107 members of the committee are appointed by state party organizations in a manner largely determined by the individual states. Moreover, while Bond appointed the chair and cochairs, these selections were "in fact dictated by the president's reelection committee" (Maisel 1994:681).

The selection of Senator Don Nickles of Oklahoma to chair the Republican platform deliberations represented an effort by the Bush-Quayle committee to provide the conservative wing of the party with a candidate with whom it could be comfortable. This selection also reflected the GOP's broader convention strategy. In June, campaign officials developed a plan designed to use the convention as a vehicle for reassuring the conservative wing of the party about Bush's candidacy in order to form a conservative coalition they felt would be the key to victory in a prospective three-way presidential race with Clinton and Perot (Wines 1992; Duffy and Goodgame 1992:272). To mobilize this constituency, Bush strategists returned to the theme of "cultural warfare" that had worked well in previous elections (Dionne 1991; Baer et al. 1992). By emphasizing "traditional family values," the Republicans hoped to assuage the rightwing, especially Buchanan and his supporters (Goldman and Matthews 1992:68–69), and distinguish Bush from Clinton, while at the same time elevating the concerns of the plurality of the electorate who did not trust Clinton and had an unfavorable view of his personal life (Kelly 1992).

This focus on family values fueled a debate within the party over the campaign's message. Some party leaders, including Buchanan, Vice President Quayle, and officials of Christian Right organizations, accepted this approach, arguing that the party should position the Democrats as out of touch with average Americans due to their advocacy of such issues as abortion and gay rights. Others, including Representative Vin Weber of Minnesota, argued that "values issues" had to be linked to an economic agenda (Baer et al. 1992). Bush and the RNC leadership appeared uncertain about the direction the campaign should take. Thus, in the weeks leading up to the convention, the party leadership failed to set a clear course. During this period the Republicans also displayed other signs of dissension, including forcing Bush to reject the advice of some party leaders "to drop Quayle from the ticket, to fire his economic team as a sign that he would now address the economy, and even to step aside and let another candidate carry the Republican banner" (Quirk and Dalager 1993:69; see also Goldman and Mathews 1992a:65–69).

The issues debate might not have been so prominent if the Republican platform committee members had been as submissive to the wishes of the party chair and nominee as their Democratic counterparts. But the Republicans were not so fortunate. Since it became clear early on that Bush would win the party's nomination, issue activists devoted their attention to being selected as delegates and convention committee members. This was especially true of members of the Christian Coalition, who wanted a party platform that reflected their preferences on such core issues as abortion, gay rights, and religion. As a result, the platform committee included a significant number of conservative activists. In fact, according to one estimate, 20 of the 107 members selected at the state level were members of the Christian Coalition (Oldfield 1992). The rules and dynamics of the Republican nomination process thus allowed the sorts of "issue amateurs" who are normally associated with the Democratic party to exert an influence on the Republican proceedings. This phenomenon was also observed by Maisel, who concluded that "in an ironic twist, issue activists whose prime concern was not with winning the election but rather for specific policies came to play a key role in a Republican convention because of lack of candidate competition, the exact opposite circumstance under which issue purists gained prominence in the Democratic party" (1994:682).

Accordingly, the party platform became a focal point of party and media attention in the weeks prior to the convention. Conservatives upset with Bush's economic policy, led by Weber and Congressman Robert Walker of Pennsylvania, pushed for a return to Reagan-era economic principles and, at one point, adopted proposed platform language stating that Bush had made a mistake in agreeing to the 1990 budget compromise, which included a major tax increase. Christian activists, hoping to protect the antiabortion language of past platforms, defeated a weak effort to change the party's position and went on to add provisions on a host of preferred policies, including a paragraph lauding the two-parent family, new passages on home schooling and pornography, and a specific reference to the country's "Judeo-Christian tradition." The committee also adopted a number of antigay and lesbian provisions, apparently with little input from the Bush campaign (Oldfield 1992:27–28). In the end, the party produced a document the President could stand by, but not before Bush campaign officials had entered into some relatively public arm-twisting, including the need for Charles Black, a Bush consultant, to convince an economic subcommittee to reconvene and eliminate the reference to Bush's tax "mistake" (Maisel 1994:689).

Bond also did his part to unite the conservative coalition at this time. He launched a bitter attack against Hillary Clinton in a speech before the RNC, and joined Quayle in an attack on the news media (Germond and Witcover 1993:408). He thus assisted in the overall implementation of the Republican "cultural warfare" strategy. Ultimately, the Republican right was appeased by the platform that emerged, as well as by the attention given to the values issues by the speakers, primarily conservatives, selected to address the convention. But this party cohesion was achieved at a significant cost: The Republican convention left a distinct impression on the public of a party that had gone too far to the right. According to polls taken after the event, a majority of the electorate felt that the president had spent more time attacking the Democrats than explaining what he would do; they disapproved of the emphasis placed on homosexual issues; and 76 percent felt that the criticism of Hillary Clinton had gone too far (Frankovic 1993). Or, as Mary Matalin, a former RNC official and top Bush campaign advisor, frankly observed: "We were in a deep, deep hole after the convention" (Wines 1992).

The General Election

Both national party committees played a significant role in the general election campaign. Although the presidential campaigns were managed by the respective candidate organizations, and the parties' activities were limited by the provisions of federal campaign finance law, the RNC and DNC still mounted extensive political operations designed to assist their presidential nominee as well as other federal and non-federal candidates running under their party's banner. Both party organizations provided their candidates with the kinds of campaign services and assistance that had become commonplace in the 1980s. For example, they established communications outreach programs for distributing daily messages to media outlets and partisan opinion leaders; they made their media facilities available to candidates to develop television advertisements and videotaped messages; they made coordinated expenditures on behalf of their federal candidates; and they made direct campaign contributions to selected federal and nonfederal candidates. In addition, they conducted a range of programs designed to improve voter turnout and party support.

Major party candidates who accept public funding for their general election campaigns are prohibited from accepting private contributions from other sources, including political parties. Federal law does, however, allow party committees to raise and spend funds on party-building and other generic activities, such as voter registration drives and mobilization programs, that are designed to benefit all party candidates and thus indirectly benefit the presidential nominee. Because these programs, which are known as "joint activities," help both federal and nonfederal candidates, they may be financed through a combination of federally limited and nonlimited funding. The latter type of funding is popularly known as "soft money," since it is not subject to the more stringent limits of federal law. In 1992, both parties relied heavily on soft money to influence the outcome of the elections.

While the RNC has been conducting extensive soft money efforts for some time, the DNC has usually been hampered by its failure to match Republican fundraising efforts. In 1992, however, the Democrats effectively competed with the Republicans due to the fundraising generated by the favorable political circumstances following their national convention. Relying on a fundraising effort managed by Rahm Emmanuel, who had served as Clinton's chief fundraiser during the prenomination campaign, the Democrats capitalized on Clinton's popularity and promising electoral prospects to raise about $20.1 million in nonfederal funds from July 1 to election day, as compared to an estimated $12.8 million for the Republicans. This success allowed the Democrats to narrow the resource gap that had developed over the first 18 months of the election cycle, when the Republicans had surpassed the Democrats by a margin of about $11 million.[7]

The DNC's financial success in the months after the convention was a crucial factor in the 1992 race because it allowed the party to implement the electoral strategy it had been developing since 1988. The cornerstone of this strategy was the coordinated campaign operation, which served as the main vehicle for registering and mobilizing Democratic voters. The DNC targeting plan and coordinated campaign program were implemented in almost every state, with heavy concentration on states the DNC political operation had identified as essential to a presidential victory. The program encouraged the state party organization, with DNC support, to serve as a coordinating agent for various federal and state and local campaigns, and carry out a joint program of voter identification and turnout on behalf of all participating Democratic candidates. The party and campaign organizations worked together to conduct extensive phone bank and canvassing operations to identify and mobilize the Democratic vote, usually in shared headquarters, relying on computerized voter lists and targeting information developed by the party.

To finance these efforts, the DNC transferred approximately $9.5 million in soft money funds to 47 states, much of which was used to develop voter files, conduct registration drives, and cover overhead expenses. The DNC also spent at least $1.9 million on telephone bank equipment that was sent to 34 state parties. The Democrats thus conducted an extensive party-based voter identification effort similar to those carried out by the RNC in past elections. The RNC, as well, also sponsored registration and mobilization efforts in 1992, as it continued to provide the services that have become almost a standard part of the party's operations in national election campaigns. The RNC transferred approximately $5.4 million in soft money funds to 42 states, and provided at least 25 state party organizations with telephone bank equipment, at a cost of over $1.5 million.

The RNC and DNC also spent significant sums from their soft money accounts to assist party campaign organizations and candidates. The RNC emphasized direct contributions to party committees and candidates. The party transferred funds to state legislative campaign committees, as well as state party committees, in at least 15 states. The RNC also contributed a total of $1.2 million in nonfederal funds to candidates seeking office at the state level, including about $800,000 to candidates in 23 states during the general election period. These efforts were conducted as part of the RNC's "down-ticket" programs to help build Republican support in state legislatures and capitols around the country, and thus reverse the pattern of recent elections in which the party wins the presidential race but fails to capture a majority of the nation's state houses.

The Democrats spent none of their soft money during the 1992 general election on direct contributions to candidates. The contributions that were reported were actually "in-kind" contributions of polling information. The DNC hired the firm of Stanley Greenberg, Clinton's campaign pollster, and five other Washington-based polling organizations to conduct surveys in 31 states. In 27 of these states, all of which were targeted by the coordinated campaign operation, polls were conducted at least two or three times during the course of the campaign. The results were shared with the state party committees, the presidential campaign, and other candidates in an effort to help them target their appeals and voter canvassing efforts. Soft money thus allowed the Democrats to provide a valuable resource, statewide polling data, to state parties and candidates.

The RNC also did some polling, although apparently on a more modest scale. The Republicans report spending some $220,000 on polls and surveys in 39 states that were shared with state parties and candidates. This DNC and RNC activity benefitted affiliated party committees and candidates in a number of ways. It provided high-quality survey research to a substantial number of committees and candidates. Such information helps promote effective communication with voters and enhances the ability to target resources more efficiently. In addition, in most cases, this service facilitated access to information that the recipient committee might not have been able to afford on its own, or at least reduced the cost incurred by the recipient for polling services since it helped defray the amount the candidate had to spend on polling services. This is especially true with respect to the presidential campaign, in that the party polling allowed the campaign to assess its support in targeted states without having to conduct polls of its own on a regular basis in each state.

The national party organizations also invested heavily in generic advertising, especially television advertising, that encouraged the electorate to "Vote Democratic" or "Vote Republican." The DNC and RNC both used a combination of federal and nonfederal monies to pay for the production and broadcast of ads. Overall, the Democrats spent about $14.2 million on advertising and the Republicans spent about $10 million (Frisby 1992). The Republicans basically followed the strategy employed in the past few elections, in which they spent substantial amounts of soft money on generic advertising. The scope of the DNC's efforts, however, vastly exceeded those of the past. While the party did broadcast some ads in 1988, the total amount spent was only about $1 million (Labaton 1992). The resources available to the party in 1992 allowed it to dramatically increase this aspect of its electoral program.

Generic advertising allows the national committees to participate meaningfully in elections and build support for party candidates at all levels. This form of communication can be especially beneficial to the party's presidential ticket, particularly when the ads are designed to reinforce the nominee's message, as they were in 1992. The Democrats, for example, used soft money to finance ads that did not mention Bill Clinton directly (to do so would violate federal contribution laws) but did emphasize the economic message that was the foundation of Clinton's campaign. These ads also helped the presidential campaign to decide where to allocate its resources. During the last week of the campaign, for instance, the Clinton campaign was running tight on money and thus decided to buy a half-hour of national television time as opposed to additional broadcast time in the highly competitive state of Texas. The Democrats, however, did not leave Texas unattended; instead, the DNC broadcast generic ads in the state to spread the party's message. The Republicans adopted a similar strategy. The Bush campaign, facing substantial resource demands because the president was trailing Clinton in a majority of the states, relied on party advertising to strengthen its support in traditional Republican strongholds and in crucial battleground states like Texas and Florida (Frisby 1992).

Conclusion

The 1992 presidential election highlights the organizational revitalization of the RNC and DNC that has been widely noted in recent years. Although the presidential selection process remains a largely candidate-centered system in which the candidate's campaign committees play the leading role, both parties were active participants at each stage of the process. Most importantly, each national party organization provided its presidential ticket with substantial electoral assistance in the general election through party spending designed to benefit the ticket indirectly, either by building support for the party or by identifying and mobilizing partisan supporters.

The major change from past elections is that the Democrats were better prepared to compete with the Republicans as a result of the particular dynamics of the 1992 contest. As Paul Herrnson and David Menefee-Libey (1990) have noted, the organizational development of party organizations is associated with two conditions: a perceived crisis that opens a window of opportunity for change and a political entrepreneur who takes advantage of this opportunity. Both of these conditions existed for the Democrats in 1992. When Ron Brown assumed the leadership of the DNC, the Democrats were demoralized, and emerging factions threatened to divide the party. Brown seized the opportunity created by the Democrats' string of defeats in national elections to establish clear electoral goals for the party. By focusing attention on common electoral goals rather than potentially divisive ideological concerns, Brown was able to minimize intraparty tensions and restructure the national party organization to fulfill his objectives. He then pursued a course of action designed to promote party unity and ensure a meaningful party role in the conduct of the 1992 presidential campaign.

Interestingly, Brown was able to achieve his objectives in part by relying on the limited authority the DNC chair is granted under party rules. Although the rules are generally considered to have undermined the role of the party leadership in the presidential selection process, Brown used his position to broker relations between members of the DNC and the DLC, and to try to moderate the tone of the nomination contest. He also used his authority to influence the platform and convention proceedings in a way that helped unify the party behind Clinton's candidacy. His success, however, was in large part due to the personal relations he enjoyed with key party members such as Cuomo and Jackson, his willingness to implement the Clinton strategy, and the lack of major opposition from issues activists within the party.

In contrast, the Republicans enjoyed few of the conditions that led to the Democrats' success. After the death of Lee Atwater, the party organization lacked strong leadership and eventually, with the support of the White House, a new chair was appointed during the election year. The new leader, Rich Bond, was confronted by divisions among party moderates and conservatives over economic policy and social issues, which rose to the forefront as a result of the nomination bid by Pat Buchanan and the heightened attention to party policy that developed in the absence of a serious challenge to President Bush. In addition, the party rules allowed issues activists to gain access to the platform-writing process, which forced an internal party debate that culminated in a convention that failed to attract wide support among the electorate.

Whether the party organizations will continue to play a prominent role in future presidential elections remains to be seen. The 1992 experience produced no major change in the factors that encourage candidate-centered elections and was shaped more by the particular circumstances that accompanied the election than any institutional changes in the national party organizations. The role of the party organizations in the future, as in the past, is likely to depend on the entrepreneurship of the party leaders, the opportunities for influence available to the party committees, and the particular dynamics of the race. It will also depend on any actions the Congress may take with respect to campaign finance reform, since reform may alter the provisions for soft money financing that were crucial to the financing of party electoral activity in 1992. Whatever the future holds, the 1992 experience clearly shows that national party organizations can play an important role in presidential elections and can have a substantial influence on electoral outcomes.

Notes

1. See Cotter and Bibby 1980; Conway 1983; Schlesinger 1985; Kayden and Mahe 1985; Huckshorn, Gibson, Cotter, and Bibby 1986; Herrnson 1988; Sabato 1988; Frantzich 1989.

2. The author thanks Erik Belenky for his assistance with the research for this chapter and acknowledges the support of the Colby College Social Science Grants Committee.

3. After Michael Dukakis's 1988 defeat in the presidential election, many DNC members expressed dissatisfaction with the campaign staff members from the Northeast who had been sent to manage their states in the general election. Senator Tom Harkin of Iowa, one of the candidates for the 1992 Democratic presidential nomination, thus sought to appeal to these party leaders in September 1991 when he declared at a meeting of the DNC: "If I'm your nominee, you will not see hordes of young Iowans coming into your state to tell you how to run your state" (Toner 1991c).

4. Because of their limited fundraising success from 1989 to 1991, the DNC could not commit sizeable sums to redistricting battles. Most of the funding on the Democratic side was

generated through an independent group, Impact 2000, which was established by major Democratic fundraisers and labor groups to finance redistricting efforts.

5. These states included Illinois, Virginia, California, Massachusetts, New Mexico, Maryland, New Hampshire, Oregon, Ohio, Georgia, North Carolina, and Arkansas. Figures are based on amounts disclosed in reports filed at the Federal Election Commission.

6. Remarks delivered by Margaret Alexander at the Citizens' Research Foundation Presidential Finance Officers conference, Washington, DC, 1992.

7. Unless otherwise noted, the figures reported here and throughout the rest of this section are based on the FEC disclosure reports for nonfederal accounts filed by the DNC and RNC for the 1991-92 election cycle.

6

Party Strategy and Campaign Activities in the 1992 Congressional Elections

Paul S. Herrnson

There was an old woman who lived in a shoe,
She had so many children she didn't know what to do,
She gave them some broth without any bread;
She whipped them all soundly and put them to bed.
—from the *Annotated Mother Goose*,
William S. Baring-Gould and Ceil Baring-Gould, eds.

The 1992 congressional elections posed many challenges and opportunities for political parties. The election cycle was characterized by a record number of congressional retirements, widespread public dissatisfaction with government, and an emphasis on "change" among politicians. Over a decade of organizational modernization enabled national party committees to amass the resources needed to play a significant role in these elections. However, allocating these resources would not be an easy task. Both parties fielded unusually large numbers of highly qualified challengers and open-seat candidates, and many House and Senate incumbents were extremely anxious about their prospects for reelection. The 1992 congressional elections presented party decision makers with an acute case of a familiar ailment. Like the old woman who lived in the shoe, the parties had a severe shortage of resources—in this case campaign money and services—and an abundance of deserving beneficiaries clamoring for them.

This chapter analyzes the strategies and activities of party organizations in the 1992 elections. Interviews with the staffs of the Democratic and Republican national, congressional, and senatorial campaign committees and the managers of over a dozen PACs provide insights into how the political parties selected candidates for support and the kinds of assistance they distributed. Survey data collected from 362 major party congressional candidates and campaign managers, and personal interviews with a smaller group of campaigners, give insights into their perspectives on party campaign activities.[1] Campaign finance data furnished by the Federal Election Commission (FEC) are used to examine the parties' spending patterns.

The 1992 Elections

Some of elements of the political climate that surrounded the 1992 congressional elections were typical of recent election cycles. An incumbent president was gearing up for reelection, the nation was suffering from a weak economy, and Americans were taking pride in their country's most recent display of military force in the Middle East. Following the completion of the census and the reapportionment of House seats, state governments began redrawing congressional districts. George Bush was enjoying record levels of presidential popularity during the Gulf War; only after the war did his levels of support plummet (Frankovic 1993).

Civil rights continued to occupy a place on the political agenda, both in some familiar and some new forms. Racial and gender discrimination and violence were relevant issues in many campaigns due to the highly publicized studies of the unequal salaries and advancement prospects for women and blacks, the beating of black motorist Rodney King by four white police officers, and Anita Hill's testimony against Supreme Court nominee Clarence Thomas. Gay rights found its place on the agenda after the military's longstanding policy against homosexuals serving in the military became a salient issue. The Supreme Court's ruling in *Thornburg v. Gingles*, which declared that states could not draw election districts in ways that diluted minority representation, had a major impact on several House elections.

Perennial issues like health care and education also occupied a space on the political agenda. Moreover, as has been the case in most recent elections, voter dissatisfaction with the political establishment in Washington was high. The savings and loan crisis, government "gridlock," and congressional scandal left many voters frustrated and angry with their elected officials. Much of this hostility was directed toward Congress, and many incumbents were preparing to respond using a strategy that had served them well in the past—running for reelection to Congress by campaigning against the institution itself (Fenno 1975). Nevertheless, all of these issues took a back seat to the economy, which was on almost everyone's mind.

Although no one of the events or conditions that preceded the 1992 election was particularly unusual, collectively these factors created some unique possibilities for congressional candidates, parties, PACs, and other politically active groups. Redistricting, scandal, declining job satisfaction, and a myriad of personal considerations led an unprecedented 66 House members to retire.[2] An additional 19 members of the House lost their primary elections nominations, and another two died before the general election.[3] The result was record numbers of new, redrawn, and open House seats. The retirement of 8 Senators and the defeat of another, Senator Alan Dixon, in the Illinois Democratic primary, also insured that many seats in the upper chamber would be competitive.[4] The sheer number of open-seat contests—91 for the House and 9 for the Senate—gave politicians who had been waiting for the chance to run for Congress on a level playing field the opportunity to do so. It also gave parties and interest groups the opportunity to try to replace some of their old foes in Congress with more sympathetic members. The political conditions that preceded the election insured the appearance of many new faces in the 103rd Congress.

The political climate affected every aspect of the 1992 congressional elections. It affected who ran for office, the strategies they used, the resources at their disposal, and the decisions made by the over 104.4 million citizens who voted on election day (Federal Election Commission 1992). It also influenced the funding decisions of political parties, PACs, and wealthy campaign contributors. The climate created intense competition among congressional candidates both in their election districts and in the nation's capital. Candidates had to compete with opponents in their election districts for votes and with other congressional candidates, including their fellow partisans, in Washington, D.C., for campaign resources.

Political Parties and Contemporary Congressional Elections

The roles that political parties play in congressional campaigns have been shaped by the same forces that fostered the development of the modern, candidate-centered election system (Sorauf 1980; Herrnson 1988). This system emphasizes campaign activities requiring technical expertise and in-depth research, which many candidates lack. Incumbents usually turn to political consultants, PACs, and interest groups for campaign assistance. Nonincumbents, particularly House challengers, have more difficulty assembling the money and expertise needed to wage a competitive bid for Congress.

Party committees in the nation's capital have developed into major repositories of campaign money, services, and political advice. The Democratic and Republican national committees focus most of their efforts on presidential elections, giving some attention to gubernatorial, statehouse, and a small number of mayoral elections. They also undertake considerable efforts to strengthen state and local party organizations. The national committees' involvement in House and Senate elections, however, is relatively limited. It usually involves conducting a few candidate training seminars, furnishing candidates with party manifestos and "talking points," and cooperating with their congressional, senatorial, state, and local campaign committees in a coordinated campaign effort to mobilize voters. Congressional candidates in search of money, election services, or assistance in running their campaigns rarely turn to their national committee for help.

The parties' congressional and senatorial campaign committees, sometimes referred to as the "hill committees,"[5] on the other hand, have developed into major centers of support for House and Senate candidates.

The congressional campaign committees focus the vast majority of their efforts on House races and the two senatorial campaign committees focus on Senate contests, though party committees at all levels cooperate with one another in a variety of areas. In 1992, the Democratic Congressional Campaign Committee (DCCC) amassed a budget in excess $12.8 million, while its rival, the National Republican Congressional Committee (NRCC) raised just under $34.4 million. The two senatorial committees—the Democratic Senatorial Campaign Committee (DSCC) and the National Republican Senatorial Committee (NRSC)—raised $25.4 million and $72.3 million, respectively.[6]

In addition to their members, who are selected by their colleagues in the House or Senate, the hill committees employ highly skilled political professionals. The DCCC and DSCC employed 64 and 35 full-time staff respectively, and their Republican counterparts had 89 and 130 full-time employees during the 1992 election cycle. For the most part, the members function like boards of directors, setting priorities and giving staff the support they need to raise money and recruit candidates. The staffs oversee the committees' daily operations, are very influential in formulating campaign strategies, and play a major role in implementing those strategies, particularly in selecting candidates for and delivering campaign assistance. The campaign committee staffs are divided along functional lines; different divisions are responsible for administration, fundraising, research, communications, and campaign activities. In 1992, both the DCCC and the NRCC added redistricting divisions to focus on the decennial redrawing of House districts. The NRCC also added an in-house polling operation to its political division.

Party Strategy, Decision Making, and Targeting

The hill committees have a common overriding goal of maximizing the number of seats their party holds in Congress (Jacobson 1985–86). They become heavily involved in some elections, giving selected candidates large campaign contributions and making substantial campaign expenditures on their behalf. Many of these candidates also receive assistance with aspects of campaigning requiring technical expertise, in-depth research, or connections with PACs, campaign consultants, and other groups that possess some of the resources needed to conduct a congressional campaign. Finally, the campaign committees participate along with other party committees in generic, party-focused election activities that are designed to help the entire ticket get elected.

The campaign committees focus most of their efforts on competitive House and Senate contests, but protecting incumbents is also a major priority. Pressures from nervous incumbents can skew the distribution of committee resources away from competitive challenger and open-seat candidates and toward members of Congress who hold relatively safe seats. The funds available to a committee and the aspirations of its chair and other members can also affect the way it distributes resources (Herrnson 1989).

National political and economic conditions are additional factors that influence which candidates get campaign resources. When the president is popular and the economy is strong, the campaign committees of the president's party usually invest more resources in competitive challenger and open-seat races. Conversely, the out-party committees use more of their resources to support incumbents. When national conditions do not favor the president's party, the patterns are reversed: the in-party committees take a "protectionist" posture that favors incumbents and the out-party committees go on the offensive, using more of their resources to help nonincumbents (Jacobson and Kernell 1983). The unpredictable nature of national political conditions, economic trends, and events that take place in states and congressional districts means that committee decision making and targeting are necessarily imperfect. As a result, some safe incumbents and uncompetitive nonincumbents inevitably receive committee assistance, while a number of competitive nonincumbents get little or no help.

The conditions surrounding the 1992 election cycle made strategic decision making and targeting very difficult, especially for the two House campaign committees.[7] Redistricting, a process that is always fraught with ambiguities, was complicated by the Supreme Court ruling in *Thornburg v. Gingles*. It caused many states to run behind schedule in redrawing the boundaries of their congressional districts, resulted in many redistricting plans being challenged in court, and delayed primary elections in several states.

Factors besides the huge number of redrawn or newly created seats complicated the committees' tasks. President Bush's popularity seesawed up and down, making it difficult for the committees to decide whether to pursue offensive or defensive strategies. The House banking and post office scandals, and the hostility that voters directed toward Congress, had a similar effect. Bounced checks and other ethical lapses resulted in a large group of incumbents, like Mary Rose Oakar (D-OH), Bill Goodling (R-PA), and Nick Mavroules (D-MA), finding themselves in jeopardy, and gave numerous challengers an unexpected boost. The late retirements of some House members and the primary defeats of others further complicated the committees' efforts.

As a result of the uncertainty surrounding the 1992 elections, the NRCC and DCCC delayed drawing up their "watch" lists of "opportunity" (or competitive) races and had difficulty paring their lists down to size. The lists that committees initially compiled were extensive. Each included roughly 300 elections, more than three times the number listed in a normal election cycle. These lists were revised and shortened over the course of the election cycle, but going into the last week of the election both committees listed over 150 races as top priorities—more than three times the number they had included in the 1990 election.

Individual candidates are selected for placement on the committees' watch lists on the basis of several criteria. The competitiveness of the district and incumbency are the first two considerations. Candidates running in districts that were decided by close margins in the last election or competing in open seats are likely to be placed on a committee's watch list and targeted for campaign assistance. In 1992, House members running in incumbent vs. incumbent contests or who were in jeopardy for other reasons were also considered top priorities.

The strength of the candidate and the quality of his or her campaign organization are considerations for nonincumbents. Those who have had political experience, are well known, or who have celebrity status are also likely to be targeted. Challengers and open-seat contestants who have assembled professional campaign organizations are prime candidates for party support as well (Herrnson 1989). A professional campaign organization assures the committee that the resources they contribute will be properly utilized, especially if campaign committee officials are familiar with the consultants who have been hired.

A variety of idiosyncratic factors may also come into play when the committees select the candidates who will initially be given the most support. An incumbent who is accused of committing an ethical transgression, is perceived to be out of touch with people in the district, or is in trouble for some other reason is a likely candidate for extra committee help. These difficulties also often provoke a response by the other party's campaign committee, resulting in the incumbent's opponent also benefiting from extra party money and campaign services.

Although 1992 was proclaimed to be "The Year of the Woman," and party leaders worked aggressively to recruit women to run for Congress, campaign committee staff maintain that gender was not a criterion used to decide who would be given campaign assistance (Biersack and Herrnson 1994). Women were targeted only to the degree that their races were expected to be competitive.

Finally, ideology is not a stated criterion for targeting candidates. Campaign committee staffs explain that ideology is irrelevant in all of their decisions, except to the degree that it can influence a particular candidate's competitiveness. An extreme right-wing Republican challenger running in very liberal Democratic district, for example, would be evaluated as uncompetitive not because of the candidate's political leanings, but because of being out of step with the district. As Deborah Flavin, Director of Political Education at the NRCC, explains:

> At the NRCC our only ideology is that you have a "big R" by your name. There is no litmus test on any issue. We ask candidates how they feel on "issue X" and "issue Y". Then, we help them articulate what they feel. We are here to help Republicans win.

The staffs of the Democratic committees voice similar sentiments.

The committees' lists of competitive elections are continuously revised throughout the election cycle. Campaign committee field coordinators who are assigned to monitor congressional races within designated regions advise their colleagues in Washington, D.C. about the latest developments in individual elections. As a result, some candidates drop in priority and are cut off from party help, while others gain more committee attention and support. The tremendous uncertainty surrounding the 1992 elections was expected to make targeting very difficult for party committees. Early in the election cycle both House campaign committees decided to distribute their resources broadly. As Tom Cole, Executive Director of the NRCC, stated in December 1991, "We are going hunting with a shotgun instead of a rifle this year." DCCC decision makers confirmed that they, too, would employ the "shotgun" approach.

Campaign Spending

Party spending in congressional elections is severely restricted by the limitations imposed by the Federal Election Campaign Act (FECA). National, congressional, and state party campaign committees can each give $5,000 per primary, runoff, and general election to a House candidate.[8] The parties' national and senatorial campaign committees can give a combined total of $17,500 to a Senate candidate. State committees can contribute an additional $5,000 to Senate candidates.

Parties can, however, spend larger sums of money on behalf of individual candidates. This spending, often referred to as "coordinated expenditures" because they can be made in direct coordination with a candidate's campaign, typically consists of campaign services that a hill committee or some other party organization gives to an individual candidate or purchases from a political consultant on the candidate's behalf. Coordinated expenditures frequently take the form of polls, radio advertisements, television commercials, fundraising events, direct-mail solicitations, or issue research. They differ from campaign contributions in that the party retains some control over them, giving it the ability to influence some aspects of how the campaign is run. Originally set at $10,000 each for a state and national committee, the limits for coordinated expenditures on behalf of House candidates are adjusted for inflation and reached $27,620 per committee in 1992.[9] The limits for coordinated expenditures in Senate elections vary by the size of a state's population and are also indexed to inflation. They ranged from $55,240 per committee in the smallest states to $1,227,322 in California. Although state and national party committees are each authorized to spend the same amount in coordinated expenditures, the committees often create "agency agreements" that allow the parties' congressional or senatorial campaign committee to take over a state party's share of the expenditure in situations when a state party committee does not have the funds to make them (Herrnson 1988).

Coordinated expenditures are the vehicle of choice for most party activity in congressional elections. Their higher limits, possibility for creating agency agreements, and the direct role they afford party committees in individual candidates' campaigns make coordinated expenditures an attractive avenue for party involvement. Not surprisingly, the campaign committees spend greater portions of their money on coordinated expenditures than on contributions (see Table 6.1). Another reason for the attractiveness of coordinated expenditures is that they enable the parties to take advantage of economies of scale when purchasing and distributing campaign services. Because the parties purchase the services of political consultants in large quantities, they pay below-market rates, which enables them to provide candidates with services whose true market value exceed the FECA's coordinated expenditure limits.[10]

Most party spending in congressional elections is done by the four hill committees. In 1992, the NRCC spent over $5.85 million in the campaigns of Republican House candidates, roughly $900,000 more than the DCCC. The RNC and NRSC spent an additional $1.7 million. Total Republican

Table 6.1. National Party Spending in the 1992 Congressional Elections*

	House		Senate	
	Contributions	Coordinated Expenditures	Contributions	Coordinated Expenditures
Democrats				
DNC	$0	$913,935	$0	$195,351
DCCC	818,846	4,132,292	18,682	2,606
DSCC	10,000	2,600	618,450	11,233,120
State and local	366,477	750,451	72,699	487,415
Total	1,195,323	5,799,278	709,831	11,918,492
Republicans				
RNC	$778,503	$832,347	$9,000	$0
NRCC	686,916	5,166,647	3,500	0
NRSC	78,500	0	614,814	16,485,039
State and local	626,057	868,908	127,960	3,617,303
Total	$2,169,976	$6,867,902	$755,274	$20,102,342

* Figures include contributions and coordinated expenditures by the parties' national, congressional, and senatorial campaign committees for all major party candidates in two-party contests, except incumbent vs. incumbent House elections. They do not include soft money expenditures.
Source: Federal Election Commission.

spending in House races reached $9.04 million, over $2 million more than that spent by the Democrats. Although the Democrats were outspent by their Republican counterparts, the spending gap between the two parties has closed considerably over the last six election cycles.[11] This is due both to a fall-off in Republican receipts and improved Democratic fundraising.[12]

Democratic and Republican state and local party committees spent $1.1 million and $1.5 million, respectively, in the 1992 House elections. This accounts for only 16 percent of all party spending made directly in House campaigns. Although House campaigns are waged locally, national parties play a bigger financial role in them than do state and local parties.

National parties also outspent state and local parties in Senate elections. The NRSC was the more active of the senatorial campaign committees, outspending its rival by $6.3 million in 1992. The Republican committee also transferred almost $2 million more to state party committees than did the DSCC.[13] The two senatorial committees accounted for the lion's share of party spending in Senate elections.

As expected, the national parties distributed most of their campaign money to candidates in close elections (see Table 6.2).[14] Turning first to the House, the Republicans' allocation patterns indicate that they pursued a fairly aggressive, offensive strategy. The NRCC, and other Washington-based Republican committees, directed 75 percent of their contributions and coordinated expenditures to challengers and open-seat candidates. The remaining money was committed to incumbents.

GOP money was fairly well targeted. Hopeful challengers (whose elections were decided by margins of 20 percent or less) and open-seat prospects (whose elections were decided by the same margin) got 34 percent and 26 percent of the party's funds. Incumbents in jeopardy (whose elections were decided by 20 percent or less of the vote) got 22 percent. The party gave only 5 percent of its funds to "shoo-ins" (incumbents whose contests were decided by margins greater than 20 percent), 10 percent to "likely losers" (challengers whose races were decided by margins greater than 20 percent), and 5 percent to open-seat candidates running in one-party districts (where the race was also decided by more than 20 percent of the vote).

The Democrats' allocation strategy is more difficult to discern from its spending patterns. This is partially due to the impreciseness of DCCC targeting. Democratic House members, who outnumbered Republican incumbents 267 to 167, received a total of 43 percent of the party's expenditures, with Democratic shoo-ins raking in a full 21 percent.[15] Democratic challengers received 36 percent of the party's money, and the party allocated more money to challengers who were likely to lose than those who had better odds of winning. Democratic spending in open-seat contests was somewhat better targeted, but as has been the case in previous elections, the Democrats continue to spend substantial sums of money on incumbents who do not need it and on nonincumbents who are not likely to benefit from it (Jacobson 1985–1986; Herrnson 1989).

It is relatively easy for the parties to target their money in Senate elections. DSCC and NRSC officials have to assess their candidates' prospects in only 33 to 35 races that take place within borders that do not shift every 10 years because of redistricting. The result is that virtually all of their money is spent in close elections. In 1992, the Democrats spent all but 10 percent of their money in competitive contests, favoring hopeful challengers and open-seat candidates over incumbents in jeopardy, shoo-ins, and likely losers.[16] The Republicans distributed all but 13 percent of their funds to candidates in close elections, but favored incumbents in jeopardy over hopeful challengers and open-seat contestants. Both parties perceived open-seat elections to be contests where some hard fought battles would take place. These spending patterns indicate that the Democrats took a highly aggressive posture, and the Republicans took the complementary defensive position.

From a candidate's point of view, the most important thing is the actual amount of party money in his or her campaign. Republican House candidates in close races benefited from greater national party spending in 1992 than did the Democrats they ran against. GOP committees in Washington spent an average of $34,000 on Republicans in jeopardy, about $12,000 more than the Democrats spent on the challengers who hoped to take away their seats (see Table 6.3). These figures amount to 5 percent of the total spent in the campaign of a typical GOP House member in jeopardy and 11 percent of the funds spent on the average Democratic hopeful. Democratic national party organizations typically spent just $17,000 on their House members who were in close races, which amounts to $16,700 less than the GOP spent on the challengers who hoped to defeat them. These figures represent 2 percent and 10 percent of the money spent in these campaigns. The GOP also outspent the Democrats by better than two-to-one in competitive open-seat contests. Although Republican House candidates benefit from their party's greater wealth and superior targeting, hopeful challengers of both parties, who have the most difficulty in raising money, are the greatest beneficiaries of party spending.

In 1992, Republican Senators in jeopardy benefited from the most national party spending, an average of almost $285,000 more than was spent on the Democratic hopefuls who hoped to take away their jobs. These figures represent 16 percent and 15 percent of these candidates' respective budgets. Republican hopefuls benefited from approximately $508,000 in national party spending, roughly 21 percent of the campaign spending in their races, and about one and one-half times as much money as the Democratic party spent on the incumbents these GOP candidates tried to unseat.

Table 6.2 The Allocation of National Party Funds in the 1992 Congressional Elections

	House Democrats	House Republicans	Senate Democrats	Senate Republicans
Incumbents				
In Jeopardy	22%	20%	18%	39%
	(72)*	(41)	(6)	(6)
Shoo-ins	21	5	5	8
	(121)	(79)	(8)	(6)
Challengers				
Hopefuls	16	34	42	19
	(41)	(72)	(6)	(6)
Likely losers	20	10	5	5
	(79)	(121)	(6)	(8)
Open seats				
Prospects	15	26	29	29
	(50)	(50)	(8)	(8)
One-party areas	5	5	—	—
	(34)	(34)		
Total**	$5,479	$7,074	$10,907	$16,037
	(397)	(397)	(34)	(34)

* Number of races are in parenthesis.
** In thousands of dollars.
Source: Compiled from Federal Election Commission data.

Both parties were important players in Senate open-seat contests, accounting for 11 percent of the money spent in Democratic campaigns and 17 percent in GOP bids for office. Bruce Herschensohn was the greatest beneficiary of national party money. The NRSC spent a total of $2,472,144 million in his race for California's open Senate seat, which comprised 24 percent of the funds spent directly in conjunction with his campaign.[17] The DSCC and DNC invested a total of $1,635,960 in the campaign of Congresswoman Barbara Boxer, the ultimate victor in the race.[18] This accounted for 14 percent of all the funds spent in conjunction with her campaign. Spending by Republican party committees in the nation's capital broke the $1 million mark in five 1992 Senate races and Democratic national party spending exceeded it in three.[19]

Table 6.3. Average National Party Spending in Congressional Elections*

	House		Senate	
	Democrats	Republicans	Democrats	Republicans
Incumbents				
In Jeopardy	$16,860	$34,410	$333,100	$1,052,900
Shoo-ins	9,705	4,227	63,814	208,544
Challengers				
Hopefuls	21,888	33,565	767,910	507,816
Likely losers	13,563	5,906	98,255	91,712
Open seats				
Prospects	16,941	36,466	400,148	585,972
One-party areas	8,093	11,379	—	—
All candidates	13,802	17,818	320,083	471,677

* Figures include contributions and coordinated expenditures by the parties' national, congressional, and senatorial campaign committees for all major party candidates in two-party contests, except incumbent vs. incumbent house elections. They do not include soft money expenditures. The number of races are the same as in Table 6.2.
Source: Compiled from Federal Election Commission data.

Campaign Services

The parties' congressional and senatorial campaign committees provide selected candidates with assistance in specialized campaign activities, such as campaign management, gauging public opinion, issue and opposition research, and campaign communications. They also provide transactional assistance, acting as brokers between candidates, PACs, individual contributors, and political consultants. The DCCC and NRCC typically become closely involved in the campaigns of candidates on their watch lists and have little involvement in others. Their Senate counterparts work with all of their candidates, but are less involved in the details of running their campaigns. All four committees play important roles in congressional elections.

Campaign Management

Candidates and their campaign organizations can get help from their hill committees with hiring and training campaign staff, making strategic and tactical decisions, and other management-related activities. The committees maintain directories of campaign managers, fundraising specialists, media experts, pollsters, voter list vendors, and other political consultants that candidates and managers can use to hire staff and purchase campaign services. Committee officials sometimes recommend particular consultants, especially to House challengers and open-seat candidates.[20]

The campaign committees also train candidates and managers in the latest campaign techniques. The DCCC and the NRCC hold training seminars to introduce campaigners to innovations in targeting, fundraising, and other election activities. Seminars for incumbents, which are held in the committees' headquarters, cover such topics as staying in touch with the district, getting the most political mileage out of congressionally franked mail, defending unpopular votes, and PAC fundraising. Seminars for challengers and open-seat candidates focus on more basic subjects, such as the "stump" speech, filing campaign finance reports with the FEC, and building coalitions. Even long-term members of the House and Senate find the seminars beneficial, if for no other reason than they remind them to do things they already know they ought to be doing (Anderson and Binstein 1993).

In 1992, both committees introduced a number of innovations in their management-related service programs, including the use of precinct-level election results, geodemographic data and polls to help campaigns plan their mailings, electronic media ads, voter mobilization drives, and candidate field trips. Over the course of the election cycle, the NRCC held training schools that were attended by 199 candidates and 76 spouses. The committee also cosponsored, with the RNC, a series of week-long intensive programs in campaign management, communications, and fundraising that were attended by 314 campaign staffers (National Republican Campaign Committee 1992). Although this activity pales next to the six- to twelve-week training programs the committee once conducted under the guise of the Republican Campaign Academy,[21] it is more extensive than the training sessions organized by the Democrats. According to DCCC National Political Director Rob Engel, the Democrats traditionally devote fewer resources to candidate and campaign manager training because they "have a very deep bench [of candidates and consultants], a much deeper bench than the Republicans."

The hill committees also serve as centers of strategic advice. Committee field representatives and staffs in Washington serve as important sources of tactical information. Because they follow congressional elections nationwide and can draw on experiences from previous election cycles, the committees are among the few organizations that have the knowledge and institutional memory to advise candidates and their managers on how to deal with some of the dilemmas they encounter (Hershey 1984).

Gauging Public Opinion

Candidates can also receive significant assistance in gauging public opinion from natural party committees. The DNC and RNC circulate the findings of nationwide polls in newsletters and memoranda they distribute to members of Congress, party activists, and congressional candidates. In 1992, the DNC undertook a major polling effort that included statewide polls designed to furnish information to the Clinton-Gore campaign and to Democratic candidates for governor, state legislature, the House, and the Senate. The RNC focused most of its attention on the presidential race.

The congressional and senatorial campaign committees conduct or commission hundreds of polls and targeting studies in a given election cycle. In 1992, the NRCC hired a director of survey research to conduct polls for 117 Republican candidates and to assist others in purchasing and interpreting surveys from private polling firms. The committee took benchmark polls for incumbents, challengers, and open-seat contestants, recruitment surveys for potential candidates, and tracking polls for a small group of candidates who were running neck and neck with their Democratic opponents at the end of the election. Many of these polls, which had a market value between $8,000 and $10,000, were given to candidates as in-kind contributions or coordinated expenditures of $1,800 to $3,500 using a depreciating option allowed by the FEC.[22] The committee also carried out two national surveys to measure the effects the check-bouncing scandal had on public opinion, to test some anti-Congress and anti-Democratic attack themes, and to examine public response to several defense-related issues.

The DCCC did not hire a director of survey research or conduct "in-house" polls for its candidates in 1992. It explored this possibility after the 1990 election cycle, but chose to continue to rely on private polling firms instead. As it had in the past, the committee gave selected candidates surveys that were purchased from prominent Democratic consultants as in-kind contributions or coordinated expenditures. It also cooperated with the Democratic national and senatorial campaign committees in taking statewide and national polls.

Selected candidates also receive precinct-level targeting studies from the hill committees. In 1992, the DSCC and DCCC used geodemographic data and election returns provided by the National Committee for an Effective Congress (NCEC), a leading liberal PAC, to help Democratic candidates design their voter mobilization strategies, guide their media purchases, and carry out other communications and field activities (Herrnson 1994b). Republican House candidates received similar assistance from the NRCC's redistricting and campaign divisions, and Republican Senate candidates got targeting help from the NRSC's campaign division.

Issue and Opposition Research

During the 1980s, national party organizations became major centers for political research. The DNC and RNC extended their traditional research activities in several new directions, most of which are party-focused rather than candidate-directed. Members of Congress, governors, state legislators, and candidates and activists at all levels are routinely sent issue briefs and talking points on salient national issues.

Candidates for Congress also receive party-focused research materials from the senatorial and congressional campaign committees. The parties write issue booklets that discuss the economy, crime, drugs, health care, and other national concerns to help candidates formulate their positions and prepare for campaign debates. The booklets include footnoted facts, summaries of a party's major achievements, and criticisms of the opposing party's performance and programs. In 1992, the NRCC distributed its issues handbook to 350 Republican primary and general election challengers and open-seat candidates. House Democrats distributed their issues handbook to all of their candidates, and to thousands of Democratic activists.[23]

More important than the issue booklets are the issue packages the hill committees provide to selected candidates. These include information drawn from major newspapers, the Associated Press wire service, the Lexis/Nexis electronic data base, and government publications. The packages present a detailed description of the district, hard facts about issues that are important to local voters, and talking points that help candidates discuss these issues in a thematic and interesting manner. Candidates can access additional information by dialing into the committees' electronic bulletin boards. Many candidates make extensive use of this information when developing their campaign themes and policy positions. Open-seat candidates and challengers, who have none of the congressional perks enjoyed by incumbents, use party research as a substitute for the studies that House members get from their staffs, the Congressional Research Service, or the General Accounting Office.

In 1992, the NRCC conducted opposition research on every Democratic member of the House. Highly detailed opposition research packages were assembled on the 120 most vulnerable Democratic House members (National Republican Congressional Committee 1992). The DCCC had a smaller task to perform since fewer Republicans occupy House seats. Each hill committee also conducted opposition research on many of its own members of Congress so they could "innoculate" themselves against attacks they anticipated would be made by their opponents.

Campaign Communications

The hill committees also give selected candidates assistance with campaign communications. Both the DCCC and NRCC have state-of-the-art television and radio production facilities on their premises and can furnish candidates with technical and editorial assistance in producing TV and radio ads. They also have satellite capabilities that enable candidates to beam their television communications back to their districts instantly and interact "live" with voters. This technology is extremely popular with incumbents from western states.

Each media center produces several "generic" or "doughnut" ads that they customize to meet the specific needs of individual candidates. One generic radio ad that was heard in connection with House campaigns across the country was based on the television show "Lifestyles of the Rich and Famous" and portrayed incumbent Democrats as jet-setters who vacation around the world at taxpayers' expense. Originally developed during the 1990 election, this NRCC ad was also used by many Republican challengers in 1992.

House candidates and their consultants can use the congressional campaign committees' recording and editing suites to produce individualized radio and television commercials.[24] Committee production staff are available to give technical and editorial advice. In a small number of campaigns, the NRCC goes several steps further. A communications division staffer meets with the candidate, his or her pollster, campaign manager, and a party political operative to design a full blown media campaign. The staffer develops advertising themes, writes television and radio scripts, and produces the ads. The staffer may also help design flyers and other printed matter (Herrnson 1988).

In 1992, the NRCC produced 188 television advertisements for 45 House candidates: 23 incumbents and 22 challenger or open-seat candidates. According to Peter Pessel, one of the committee's producers, two-thirds of the ads were specifically designed for individual candidates. The remainders were doughnut ads with visual inserts and voice-overs. The committee also produced radio ads for 45 House members and 44 nonincumbents. The DCCC provided a much larger crop of candidates with less personalized service. Just over 170 House members and 70 nonincumbents used the Democrats' Harriman Communications Center to record and edit their television commercials. Under 20 used the committee's facilities to record their radio advertisements most preferred to tape their radio ads in their campaign headquarters and other sites.

By providing candidates with issue packages and communications assistance, the congressional and senatorial campaign committees have clearly contributed to the nationalization of American politics. Few congressional candidates needed to be told the economy was the major issue in 1992, but the hill committees helped them discuss this issue thematically and frame it in ways that were more meaningful to voters. The committees' opposition research also contributed to many campaigns, but in ways that many voters might not look upon favorably. Just as the hill committees assist candidates in putting a positive spin on some aspects of their campaigns, they help them put a negative spin on others, thereby contributing to the mudslinging that has become commonplace in congressional elections.

Fundraising

In addition to providing contributions, coordinated expenditures, and campaign services, the hill committees also help selected candidates raise money from individuals and PACs. To this end, the committees give the candidates strategic advice and fundraising assistance. They also expend tremendous amounts of time and other resources furnishing PACs and Washington insiders with information that they can use when formulating their contribution strategies and selecting individual candidates for support.

The hill committees help candidates raise money from individuals in a variety of ways. They help candidates design direct-mail fundraising letters and give them tips on how to organize fundraising committees and events. Sometimes the committees host the events or assist in setting them up. In 1992, the NRCC introduced an innovation in fundraising when it employed satellite technology to help candidates raise big contributions from wealthy individuals. The committee arranged for Secretary of Housing and Urban Development Jack Kemp, House Minority Whip Newt Gingrich, and other GOP leaders to address contributors at Republican fundraisers across the country from the party's national convention in Houston. The broadcast "appearances" of these dignitaries helped bring in large sums of money.

The committees also work to steer large contributions from wealthy individuals, PACs, or members of Congress to needy candidates. It is illegal for the parties to "earmark" checks they receive from individuals or PACs for specific candidates, but committee members and staff can suggest to contributors that they consider giving a contribution to one of the candidates on their watch list. The NRSC has led the way in pioneering new ways to broker money to congressional candidates, but all four hill committees have been innovative in brokering contributions to congressional candidates in competitive races. Some of the most successful recent innovations have been introduced by DCCC Chair Vic Fazio. In 1992, Fazio succeeded in getting his House Democratic colleagues to contribute money from their campaign chests and PACs to the DCCC and Democratic candidates in close contests. He raised over $600,000 from House Democrats to help retire the DCCC's 1990 election debt (Democratic Congressional Campaign Committee 1992). Following the death of Republican House Member Sylvio Conte in February 1990, Fazio was able to convince over 50 Democratic House members to "pony up" large contributions to help Democrat John Olver beat Republican Steven Pierce in a special election held in Massachusetts' first district. Fazio and the DCCC also played a critical role in steering over $300,000 in contributions from Washington PACs, lobbyists, and other insiders to Olver's successful campaign (Democratic Congressional Campaign Committee 1992).

The campaign committees assist candidates in raising PAC money in two ways. First, they give candidates the knowledge and tools to raise PAC money. The committees help candidates design PAC kits they can use to introduce themselves to members of the PAC community.[25] Candidates can get lists of PACs that include each committee's address, a contact person, and a mailing label that can be used to send a solicitation. The lists also indicate how much cash each PAC has on hand so candidates will not waste their time soliciting committees that have no money or take "no" for an answer when a PAC manager "claims poverty" but still has funds.

The committees also tutor candidates on how to approach PACs for money. Kristine Wolfe, the NRCC's Director of Coalitions and PACs, explains that most nonincumbents need to be coached on how to fill out the questionnaires that many PACs use to learn about candidates' issue positions. According to Wolfe, giving an answer that is only marginally different from a PAC's stand on a core issue can cost a candidate a contribution. Moreover, answering a question in a misleading way can result in a candidate getting a reputation as a "chameleon" and freeze up prospects for raising PAC money once the managers of different PACs confer with one another.

The hill committees also assist candidates with designing the grassroots part of their PAC fundraising strategies. They instruct candidates on how to win endorsements from state-level branches of federated PACs and how to build coalitions among local PAC donors. As Wolfe's assistant, Matt Niemeyer, explains, "It's difficult for the manager of a national PAC to say no to a request [for a contribution] when it comes from a PAC's state affiliate or local donors."

A second way the parties help candidates raise money from PACs is through the manipulation of the information environment in which PACs make their contribution decisions. This is one of the major activities of the campaign committees' PAC directors and other top party officials. A PAC director's major goals are to channel the flow of PAC money toward their party's most competitive congressional contenders and away from their opponents. This an especially difficult task to perform on behalf of House challengers and open-seat candidates because they are largely unknown to the PAC community and unable to use the powers of incumbency to leverage PAC money. Some junior House members also need to have attention called to their races. The campaign committees often enlist the support of party leaders, committee and subcommittee chairs, or ranking members to attend a candidate's fundraising event or call a PAC manager on a candidate's behalf. Former DCCC chair, Tony Coelho, was legendary for his ability to "fry the fat" out of PACs (Jackson 1988). All four hill committees make meeting rooms and telephones available to facilitate PAC fundraising.[26]

The hill committees use a variety of approaches to circulate information about House and Senate elections to PACs and other potential contributors. The committees' campaign expenditures are one form of information that can have a tremendous impact on the fundraising prospects of nonincumbents. Large party expenditures can help them raise money because they draw the attention of PACs, wealthy individuals, and political journalists who give contributions or write about congressional elections (Herrnson 1988). PAC receptions, often referred to as "meet and greets" serve similar purposes. They give candidates, especially nonincumbents, an opportunity to ask PAC managers for contributions. The hill committees routinely hold meet and greets in their headquarters buildings. In presidential election years, they are also held at the parties' national conventions.

The committees also mail watch lists and information packages that discuss individual candidates' electoral prospects and financial needs to supportive PACs. Other mailings provided details on candidates' races, including poll results, press clippings, endorsements, campaign highlights, and revelations about problems experienced by their opponents. These mailings commonly range from 10 to 20 pages in length and are sent to approximately 1,000 PACs. During the heat of the election season, the campaign committees' PAC directors sent out mailings on a weekly or biweekly basis.

In addition to mailings and meet and greets, the committees' PAC directors hold briefings to discuss their opportunity races and inform PAC managers about their candidates' progress. These briefings provide PAC managers with the opportunity to ask committee staffers questions about specific campaigns and afford PAC managers an opportunity to discuss their contribution strategies with one another. PAC briefings are an important forum for networking among campaign finance elites.

PAC directors and party leaders spend a tremendous amount of time making telephone calls on behalf of their most competitive and financially needy candidates. Some of these calls are made to PAC managers who are recognized leaders of PAC networks. The DCCC and DSCC, for example, work closely with the NCEC and the AFL-CIO's Committee on Political Education (COPE), while their GOP counterparts work closely with the Business-Industry Political Action Committee (BIPAC). The committees encourage these "lead" PACs to endorse their top contestants and communicate their support to other PACs in their networks.

Finally, the hill committees send streams of communications to the editors of the *Cook Political Report*, the *Rothenberg Political Report*, and other political newsletters that are heavily subscribed to by PACs. These newsletters handicap congressional races and provide information on developments in campaigns located across the country. Party officials undertake tremendous efforts to keep the newsletter editors abreast of the latest developments in their candidates' campaigns, speaking with them several times a week. Charlie Cook and Stuart Rothenberg, who edit the newsletters that bear their names, confirm that hill committee officials are major sources of their political information.

By helping candidates understand how the PAC community works and furnishing PACs with information about candidates, the congressional and senatorial campaign committees have become important intermediaries in the fundraising process. They have entered into symbiotic relationships with some PACs that have enabled them to become brokers between candidates and PACs (Sabato 1984; Jackson 1988). The relationship is based largely on honest and reliable exchanges of information about the prospects of individual candidates. In some cases the information exchange is bilateral. The NCEC, BIPAC, and other "lead" PACs have information that they share with the committees (Biersack 1994). Campaign committee officials recognize that any attempt to mislead a PAC manager by providing inaccurate information could harm the committee's credibility, curtail its influence in the PAC community, and undercut its ability to help its candidates (Herrnson 1988).

Hill committee communications to PACs are somewhat controversial because they can have a major impact on the fundraising prospects of individual candidates. Candidates who receive their campaign committee's endorsement derive significant advantages in raising PAC money, while nonincumbents who are not usually unable to collect significant funds from PACs. PAC managers have been known to justify refusing a contribution request because a nonincumbent was not included on a hill committee's watch list. The campaign committees' brokerage activities clearly play to the advantage of some candidates and harm the prospects of others.

The Impact of Party Services

When asked to discuss the importance of campaign assistance from local, state, and national party organizations, PACs, unions, and other groups in aspects of campaigning requiring professional expertise or in-depth research, candidates and campaign aides involved in the 1992 House elections rank their party's hill committee first. About one-third of all House candidates and managers consider their congressional campaign committee to be at least moderately helpful in campaign management. Roughly 40 percent gave similar assessments for hill committee assistance in gauging public opinion. Over half of all the House contestants report that committee issue research plays at least a moderately important role in their campaigns, with 20 percent describing it as very important and another 11 percent asserting that it is extremely important. More than 40 percent of the House candidates, mostly challengers, also rely heavily on their congressional campaign committee for opposition research. About 30 percent of all House campaigns receive significant DCCC or NRCC help in producing their campaign communications. Slightly more candidates and campaign aides find hill committees to be moderately important to their fundraising efforts. However, House candidates report receiving greater fundraising assistance from PACs and other interest groups. The DCCC and NRCC are also rated lower than state and local party organizations and interest groups in grassroots activities, reflecting their lack of direct involvement in these aspects of campaigning.

Most Senate candidates and campaign managers give evaluations of hill committee assistance that are as favorable as those given by House candidates even though the DSCC and NRSC staff tend to be less involved than their House counterparts in formulating or implementing candidates' campaign strategies.[27] Instead, senatorial campaign committee staffs provide candidates with feedback, advice, campaign contributions, and election services purchased from political consultants. They also help candidates collect money from PACs and wealthy contributors. The senatorial campaign committees are rated above any other group in every area of campaigning except for providing information about voters, voter mobilization, and volunteer recruitment, where state and local party organizations and interest groups are ranked higher.

The evaluations of House and Senate candidates and campaign aides indicate that most hill committee help is given to candidates in close races, reflecting the parties' goal of winning as many seats in Congress as possible. As was the case with campaign spending, the NRCC distributes its campaign services more effectively than its Democratic counterpart. Both senatorial campaign committees also concentrate their resources in close races. Hill committee assistance is more important to hopeful challengers and open-seat prospects than it is to incumbents in jeopardy, reflecting the fact that incumbents have problems in getting reelected, but they are rarely due to an inability to raise money, assemble a campaign organization, or communicate with voters.[28]

The hill committees also play bigger roles in the campaigns of Republican House and Senate candidates than in the campaigns of their Democratic opponents. The campaign evaluations, like the distribution of national party money, indicate that the NRCC and the NRSC outperformed the two Democratic hill committees in 1992. The gap between the committees has shrunk in recent years, but a Republican advantage persists.

Party Differences

There are major differences in the parties' performance in House elections. The Republicans spend more money, distribute more services, and target them better than the Democrats. For example, over 80 percent of all national party spending in House contests was done in close races, as opposed to only 54 percent of all national Democratic party spending. The spending differences in open-seat races are especially telling. The Democrats spent, on average, just under $17,000 to help House candidates for open-seats in competitive districts and an average of $8,000 to help open-seat candidates in one-party districts. The Republicans, on the other hand, typically spent over $36,000 and $11,000 to help GOP candidates in these same contests.

The disparities in party targeting merit some explanation. First, Republican party organizations have traditionally taken a more business-like approach to allocating campaign funds. The NRCC's decision-making process is more staff driven and less politicized than that of its Democratic counterpart (Herrnson 1989). The Democrats' control of the House, greater diversity, and the leadership aspirations of DCCC chairmen and members occasionally override the committee's stated goal of maximizing House seats. Second, the NRCC has been one step ahead of the DCCC in gathering campaign information. The Republican committee was the first to have staff observing campaigns in the field. Its new polling division may have given it an advantage over the DCCC in targeting. Third, Rob Engel explains that House Democrats' heavy use of the DCCC's media center, which the committee counts as a contribution or coordinated expenditure, to some degree inflate the figures for party money spent in connection shoo-in incumbent races. Finally, according to Engel, a difference in philosophy might have been at work. His committee tried to "keep more races alive, for a longer period, before bailing out," which led Democratic funds to be distributed more broadly, and less effectively, than Republican money.

Conclusion

The 1992 elections provided political parties with the opportunity to contribute to the sea change that was expected to take place in the U.S. Congress. Democratic and Republican party committees located in the nation's capital were poised to play a role in this election, but were confronted with a barrage of requests for help from an unusually large number of highly talented candidates. Moreover, they had to select candidates for support under conditions of extreme uncertainty. The NRCC was able to cope with the demands of this unusual election cycle better than its Democratic counterpart. The parties' senatorial campaign committees had a less complex task to perform and both committees targeted their resources extremely effectively. Nevertheless, all four hill committees, as well as many other party organizations, made important contributions during the 1992 congressional elections.

Notes

1. The material in this chapter is drawn from chapters 4 and 6 of. A detailed discussion of the survey and the data is presented there. I wish to thank Robert Biersack for assistance with the analysis of campaign finance data; Michael Gusmano, Robert Tennant, and Candace Kahn for assistance with data entry; and students from my Honors Seminar on Campaigning for Congress for assistance with data collection. Financial support for this research was provided by a grant from the Graduate Research Board and the Center for Political Leadership of the University of Maryland.

Party Strategy and Campaign Activities

2. The previous modern (post-1946) record for House retirements was 49, set in 1978 (see Ornstein, Mann, Malbin 1992).

3. The previous modern (post-1946) record for House members defeated was 18, set in 1946 (see Ornstein, Mann, Malbin 1990).

4. The number of Senate retirements in 1992 has only been exceed twice since 1946: 9 Senators retired prior to that election and 10 retired prior to the 1978 election (see Ornstein, Mann, and Malbin 1992).

5. The term "hill committees" to refer to the congressional and senatorial campaign committees probably originates from the fact that they were originally located in congressional office space on Capitol Hill.

6. These figures include only "hard" dollars that can be spent directly in federal campaigns (see Federal Election Commission 1993).

7. The information on committee strategy, decision making, and targeting in 1992 is drawn from personal interviews that were conducted over the course of the election cycle. Interviews were held with several officials at the congressional campaign committees, including Rob Engel, National Political Director, DCCC; Eric Wilson, Deputy Director, DCCC; Marty Stone, Regional Field Coordinator, DCCC; Tom Cole, Executive Director, NRCC; Kris Wolfe, Director of PACs and Coalitions, NRCC; Matt Neimeyer, Deputy PAC Director, Kevin O'Donnell, Director of Survey Research, NRCC. On committee strategy and decision making in previous elections, see Jacobson and Kernell (1983) and Herrnson (1989).

8. These are each considered separate elections under the FECA. Party committees, however, usually only give contributions to general election candidates.

9. Coordinated expenditure limits for states with only one House member are $55,240.

10. Party committees can also give "in-kind" services in lieu of cash contributions, however, they are more likely to use the coordinated expenditure route.

11. In 1982, for example, the NRCC spent just under $7.5 million on House elections and the DCCC spent a total of $761,000 (Sorauf 1992).

12. An NRCC decision to transfer almost $1.9 million to 21 state party committees instead of forming agency agreements with those committees also contributed to the decline in NRCC money that was contributed to or spent on behalf of Republican House candidates. According to Tom Cole, the NRCC negotiated agreements to transfer the funds, much of it "soft" money that could not be spent directly on federal candidates, with the understanding that the state committees that received the funds would spend an equal amount of "hard" money on their House candidates' campaigns. The transfers enabled the NRCC to use its "soft" money, which flows outside of the FECA's contributions and spending limits reporting requirements, to help its House candidates. The DCCC transferred about half as much money to Democratic state committees and most of the money it transferred was hard money that could have been spent legally on federal candidates. On soft money, see Drew (1983); Sorauf (1988). The information on party transfers is from FEC (1993b). The information on NRCC strategy is from a personal interview with Tom Cole on January 11, 1993.

13. The transfers include both hard and soft money.

14. The figures include spending by all three national party organizations because they are subject to a common limit and thus must be made in coordination with one another. Crossover expenditures, such as those made by the senatorial campaign committees in House campaigns, usually consist of polls that are shared among House and Senate candidates. Separating hill committee spending from all national party spending barely affects the figures in Table 6.2. Similarly, the patterns for the distribution of all party money, including state and local committee expenditures, resemble those in the table.

15. Rep. Bernard Sanders, an Independent from Vermont, accounts for the 435th House seat.

16. The Senate candidates are grouped using the same vote margins as are House candidates. All of the open-seat Senate races are classified as competitive.

17. Herschensohn spent a total of $7,859,072, and received $17,500 in contributions from the NRSC, $5,000 from the California Republican Party, and $1,000 from the Republican Club of Leisure World. He also benefited from an additional $2,454,644 in NRSC coordinated expenditures. These figures exclude party soft money expenditures and independent expenditures by PACs and other groups.

18. Boxer spent a total of $10,363,251, and received $17,500 in contributions from the DSCC, $950 from the DNC, $5,000 from the Democratic State Central Committee of California, $1,258 from the Sacramento County Democratic Committee's United Campaign Committee. She also benefited from $16,735 in DNC coordinated expenditures, and $1,600,775 in DSCC coordinated expenditures, and $118,614 in Democratic State Central Committee coordinated expenditures.

19. In addition to the Herschensohn race, the Republicans spent over $1 million in campaigns waged by John Seymour, Alfonse D'Amato, Arlen Spector, and Paul Coverdell. The Democrats spent over $1 million on Boxer's, Dianne Feinstein's and Robert Abrams's campaigns.

20. In some cases, the congressional campaign committees require candidates to use the services of one of their preferred consultants as a precondition for committee support. Although these cases are rare, they can arouse the ire of both candidates and political consultants (Herrnson 1988; Frantzich 1989; Salmore and Salmore 1989).

21. The NRCC closed down its campaign academy because of the difficulty its graduates had in finding employment in nonelection years and because the costs of maintaining the academy became prohibitive. For more information on the academy (see Herrnson 1988:57, 15, 156–157.)

22. The allocable costs of the polls varied by type, size, and when they were released to the candidates. FEC regulations specify that candidates must pay 100 percent of the costs if they receive the poll results within 15 days of when it was completed, 50 percent if they receive them between 16 and 60 days, and 5 percent if the results are received between 61 and 180 days. After 180 days, a poll can be give to a candidate free of charge.

23. The Democrats' issues handbook, *Taking Charge of America's Future*, was written and printed by the House Democratic Caucus with the assistance of staffers from the DCCC, DNC, the Democratic Leadership Conference, and the Clinton campaign.

24. A small number of Senate candidates and other party dignitaries also use the committee's media equipment.

25. PAC kits typically include information about the candidate's personal background, political experience, campaign staff, support in the district, endorsements, issue positions, and campaign strategy.

26. Outside meeting rooms and telephones are necessary because it is illegal to solicit campaign money from the capitol complex.

27. It is difficult to make generalizations about Senate campaigns because of the small number of Senate elections that occur in one election cycle, the tremendous diversity in the size and composition of the states that form U.S. Senate districts, and a different one-third of all Senate seats are up for election every two years. The fact that only 28 (41%) of the Senate campaigns returned completed questionnaires is additional cause for concern. In order to improve the strength of the findings about Senate campaigns, the generalizations in this section are based on observations that span the 1984, 1986, and 1992 election cycles.

28. Incumbents rarely have difficulty raising money; and, as Gary C. Jacobson notes, their fundraising and spending are driven largely by their perception of the threat a challenger poses to their reelection (Jacobson 1980, 1992).

7

Hard Facts and Soft Money: State Party Finance in the 1992 Federal Elections

Robert Biersack

American political parties have been forced to evolve in the face of a changing political environment. Confronted with a world in which neither candidates nor voters are tightly linked to parties, the national Republican and Democratic committees and their state and local counterparts have been forced to redefine their role and develop organizations consistent with their place in the political world.

Party committees now primarily provide services to candidates. Rather than merely delivering votes on election day—although voter mobilization remains an important party activity—they supply polls, issue research, media assistance, direct mail, financial support, and campaign expertise to targeted candidates. They also act as "brokers" between sources of money, service vendors, and candidates (Herrnson 1988). Providing these services efficiently requires a level of financial stability not common for parties in the days when the labor of precinct volunteers represented the currency of party activity. The parties literature has documented this transformation by tracking increasing financial strength and organizational capability and describing how those resources have been translated into specific campaign services (see chapters 5 and 6). How those funds are raised and distributed among national, state, and local organizations is, however, not clearly understood. This chapter describes changes in one element of the federal campaign reporting structure which took place in 1991, its impact on what parties do, and what we know about the parties activities.

The shift from voter-centered activities to campaign services may have also altered relationships among national, state and local organizations. Once described as a stratarchy (Eldersveld 1964)—where each subunits had a significant degree autonomy—today the structure may resemble more closely a centralized hierarchy. This change occurred primarily because of the large-scale fundraising capabilities of the national organizations, particularly with regard to "soft money."[1]

Understanding these and other nuances, and describing the condition of party organizations overall, has been difficult because of the rules under which parties raise and spend money. The wide variety of elective offices at different levels of government, along with the constitutional sovereignty of states in conducting these elections, complicates the process for participants and observers alike.

In 1992, for the first time, the national parties were required to disclose all of their financial activity in one place. Using this data we now see that national party organizations are heavily involved in financing party activities at all levels. One of the assumptions generally made about soft money is that it is simply raised and spent in conjunction with the presidential campaign. That is, big dollar contributions are made to soft-money accounts in order to influence the presidential election. Findings presented here suggest soft-money spending patterns are considerably more complex, influenced by a wide set of variables independent of presidential election dynamics.

While still incomplete, an expanded picture of state party activity is now available as well. These units are financially sound and involved in a variety of activities. Moreover, while state parties are by no means completely dependent on the national organizations for financial support, the soft money linkage is clearly an important new development for both levels of the organization.

The Regulatory System Before 1991

The Federal Election Campaign Act of 1971 (FECA) recognized the paramount role of state and local parties in the conduct of state and local elections. Regulations were thus sought that define the boundaries between federal elections and state and local party activities that might impact federal elections. However, many of the things political parties do during and between campaigns are aimed at helping the full slate of candidates; success in these activities translates into votes for candidates for many offices. It is also clear that the financial resources required to conduct these activities are highly flexible and their impact on specific races can be difficult to ascertain—funds used for one purpose may free resources for another. This combination of externalities inherent in many political activities, along with the fungibility of money, makes regulation of political finance more of an art than a science.

Prior to 1991, the burden of making judgements about how much generic party activity was directed toward federal elections and how much was related to state or local campaigns was largely left to the party organizations themselves. The law required activity having some impact on a federal election be conducted with financing allowable under federal law in the same proportion as the activity's impact. In other words, if party headquarters and staff were devoted to federal campaigns 20 percent of the time, then 20 percent of the funding for those activities must have come from federally allowable sources. (No corporate or labor union funds are eligible, for example, and contributions from individuals to a state party committee could not exceed $5,000 per year.) Any activity related solely to federal candidates, such as direct contributions to the campaign or coordinated expenditures, were limited and must be paid with federal funds. A few other activities related to presidential campaigns, such as the preparation and distribution of yard signs and bumper stickers, were specifically exempted from normal contribution or expenditure limits as a result of the 1979 amendments to the act, but the financing for such activities are restricted to federally allowable sources.

With regard to implementing these rules, parties determined the proportion of their activity that was geared toward federal candidates by using "any reasonable method" to allocate their costs. The definition of "reasonable" was exceedingly broad and parties were only required to support their allocations when specifically questioned. Moreover, parties were required to report to the Federal Election Commission (FEC) only the portion of these "shared" expenses from federal funds. This regulatory and reporting scheme applied to party organizations at all levels. National parties could create nonfederal organizations to support state and local candidates, and they could also allocate administrative and other overhead expenses between federal and nonfederal sides. The only disclosure required was the portion being paid for with federal receipts. As a result, readily available information about party finance was limited and fragmented, and was dependent on the reporting requirements of each states.

The Regulatory System after 1991

Federal court rulings handed down in the late 1980s required the FEC to write new regulations that would identify a more specific standard for allocation among federal and nonfederal elections—as well as insure that the allocation rules were being followed. The long and complex rule-making process that followed resulted in a number of changes in the way party organizations allocate their expenditures. It also modified the disclosure requirements to permit more comprehensive reporting of financial activity of national, state, and local party organizations. In brief, the previous standard of "any reasonable method" to allocate expenses was replaced with specific allocation procedures.

The procedures have two basic elements. First, administrative expenses and the cost of generic activities that indirectly affect all candidates must now be allocated according to specific percentages for national party committees (at least 60 percent federal in nonelection years, 65 percent federal in election years) and according to the composition of the next general election ballot for state and local party organizations. In these cases, each type of race (president, U.S. Senate, U.S. House, governor, other statewide offices, State Senate, State House of Representatives, local offices) receives one point. The allocation ratio is the proportion of federal offices to total offices on the ballot.[2] In the 1991–92 election cycle, this ballot composition ratio ranged from a low of 25 percent federal in Delaware to a high of 75 percent federal in Maryland.

Other types of activity continue to have flexible allocation rules. For example, fundraising costs may be paid on a "funds received" basis, where the cost of the fundraiser is allocated according to the proportion of funds actually received which would be allowable under federal restrictions. Accordingly, if 20 percent of the funds received from an event met FECA requirements, one-fifth of the costs must be paid from federal funds. A similar rule is used for activities which are exempt from contribution or expenditure limits by the 1979 amendments (yard signs, etc.) and for activities that support both federal and nonfederal candidates. These activities must be paid according to a "funds expended" method, where the federal share of the cost is commensurate with the federal portion of the activity.

Second, the method for paying bills and reporting activity was changed to require greater disclosure of party activity and allow for review of compliance with allocation rules. National party organizations are now required to disclose activity of all aspects of the organization—whether federal, nonfederal, or mixed. State and local party organizations are required to pay bills for allocable activity from their federal account and report transfers received from nonfederal accounts to pay the nonfederal portion of these expenses. This change effectively reversed the flow of funds and reporting; prior to this time only transfers out of federal funds for these purposes were disclosed, but now the full value of the activity is reported with the nonfederal portion being transferred into the federal account.

As a result of these changes, information available at the FEC now accounts for all national party financial activity and a significantly greater proportion of state party finance. The only aspect of state party activity that is not reported is that activity which is exclusively devoted to state and local campaigns.

Party Finance in the New Regulatory Era

With these reporting requirements on the books, a new picture of overall party finances emerges. Party committees at all levels reported receipts of about $680 million in 1991–92, up from about $300 million in 1990 and $375 million in 1988. Approximately 25 percent of all activity money but not data reported by the two major parties represented activity disclosed for the first time during the 1992 election cycle.

The national Democratic committees, including the national committee and the senatorial and congressional campaign committees, reported $37 million in nonfederal funds while their counterparts at the state and local level reported $35 million as the nonfederal share of allocable expenses. Republicans at the national level raised $52 million in soft money, while state and local Republican committees reported $29 million as the nonfederal share of their allocable activity. Although complete information about the nonfederal activity of national parties is unavailable for earlier years, it is likely that this activity is much higher during presidential elections. It is generally estimated that the two parties raised $20-$25 million each from these sources during the 1988 campaign (Alexander and Bauer 1991). In 1990, however, the *combined* total for both parties was reported to be about $25 million (Goldstein 1991).

Federally allowable funds raised by the two major parties at all levels also increased in 1992. The national Democratic committees increased their federal fundraising from $91 million in 1988 to $120 million in 1992, while the national Republican committees raised $192 million in 1988 and $211 million in 1992.

State and local Democratic committees raised $58 million in "hard" money acceptable under FECA restrictions during the 1992 cycle, up from $36 million in 1990. Republicans at the state and local level reported $64 million in federal revenue in 1992, compared with $39 million raised from these sources in 1990. While some of this increase may represent greater fundraising success in a competitive election year, including a presidential race, clearly at least part of this growth at the state and local level is the result of mandated ballot composition ratios for federal and nonfederal funds, as described above. Patterns of fundraising over several cycles suggest that the use of the ballot as a guide for allocating activity between federal and state/local races results in a greater need for funds consistent with FECA limits than under the allocation methods previously used.

Figures 7.1 and 7.2 summarize the receipts of the Democratic and Republican National Committees during 1991-92. This represents a full accounting of all monies raised by these committees, including nonfederal accounts. The charts show that at least two-thirds of all funds raised by the national committees were raised within the restrictions and prohibitions of the FECA. Both national committees relied more heavily on contributions from individuals, which fell within the limit of $20,000 per person per year, than any other source of funds—hard or soft. Moreover, the RNC raised more absolute dollars from individuals in increments of less than $200 each than it raised from all soft money sources combined. While Republican organizations have experienced some difficulty with their direct-mail fundraising operations

112   *The State of the Parties*

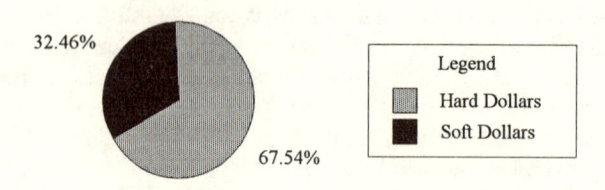

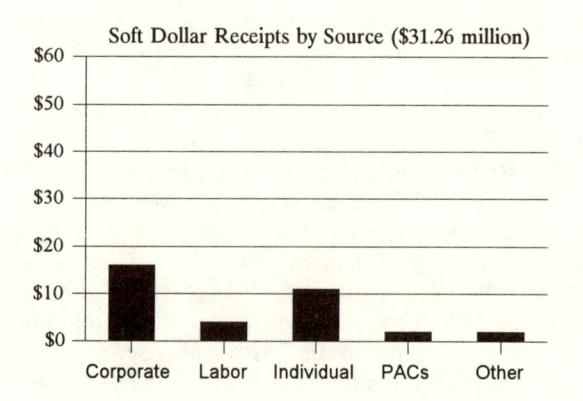

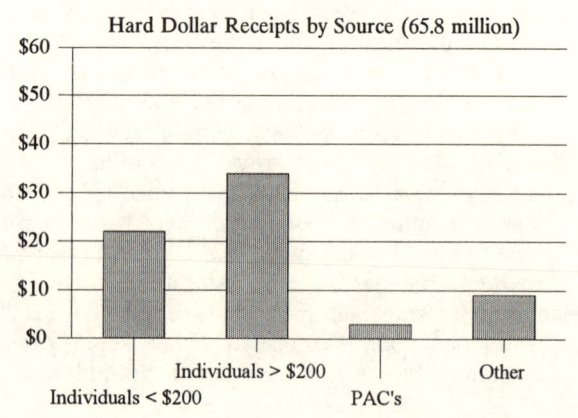

Figure 7.1 DNC National Party Receipts 1991–1992

Total Fundraising ($97.4 million)

32.46%
67.54%

Legend
▨ Hard Dollars
■ Soft Dollars

Soft Dollar Receipts by Source ($31.26 million)

Source	Amount
Corporate	~$16
Labor	~$4
Individual	~$10
PACs	~$2
Other	~$2

Hard Dollar Receipts by Source (65.8 million)

Source	Amount
Individuals < $200	~$22
Individuals > $200	~$34
PAC's	~$3
Other	~$9

Hard Facts and Soft Money 113

Figure 7.2 RNC National Party Receipts 1991–1992

Total Fundraising ($121.66 million)

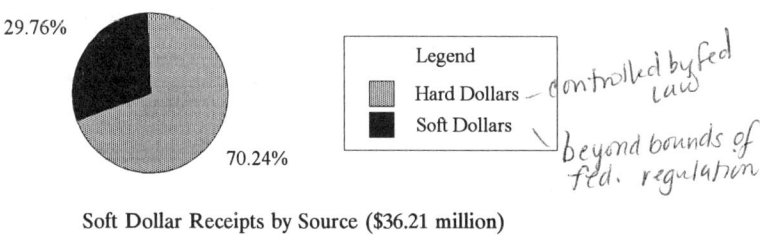

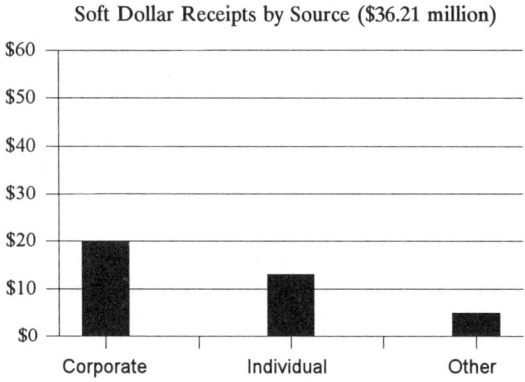

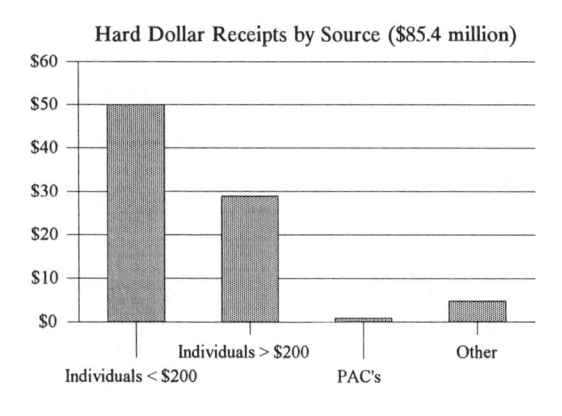

29.76%

70.24%

Legend
- Hard Dollars — *controlled by fed law*
- Soft Dollars — *beyond bounds of fed. regulation*

Soft Dollar Receipts by Source ($36.21 million)

Corporate | Individual | Other

Hard Dollar Receipts by Source ($85.4 million)

Individuals < $200 | Individuals > $200 | PAC's | Other

of late (resulting in declining revenue in several cycles leading up to 1992), that program remains the most formidable part of their fundraising apparatus.

The DNC, by contrast, showed greater reliance on larger contributions and was more dependent on institutional support. It is noteworthy that the DNC received more financial support from corporations in its nonfederal accounts than it received from organized labor. This does not include direct campaign involvement by labor organizations, however, nor does it include union efforts to mobilize their members.

The senatorial and congressional campaign committees are similar to their parent organizations with regard to sources of funds. Republican committees (NRSC and NRCC) have substantial direct-mail donor bases, where small contributions accounted for a vast majority of the "hard" dollars raised. The Democratic units (DSCC and DCCC) raised considerably less than their Republican counterparts, and were more dependent on larger contributions and PACs.

The two senatorial committees diverged in terms of soft money, with the DSCC raising only $600,000 outside federal limits, all intended for support of its facilities. The NRSC, on the other hand, raised about $9 million and transferred about $1.5 million to state party organizations. Totals raised by the nonfederal accounts of the two House campaign committees were similar —$6 million for the Republicans and $5 million for the Democrats. Here again, the Democratic Congressional Campaign Committee used most of its soft money for administrative expenses and facilities, while its Republican counterpart transferred $1.7 million to the states.

Figures 7.3 and 7.4 compare the *spending* of the two national committees in 1991–92. Funds raised and spent under the restrictions of the FECA are examined separately from those raised and spent outside federal law. The data suggest the two parties used somewhat different spending strategies during the campaign. The RNC allocated a larger proportion of its funds on national overhead expenses, including purely federal operating expenses, fundraising, and building funds. They spent comparatively less in direct support of state and local party organizations. For example, while the DNC spent 10 percent of its federal dollars and 31 percent of its nonfederal funds in direct support of state parties, the corresponding percentages for the RNC were one percent in federal and 15 percent for nonfederal funds.

It is important to note that both national committees made a significant portion of their transfers to states in the form of in-kind services. For the DNC, many of the nonfederal transfers were actually regional polling results commissioned by the national committee and distributed to the states. The RNC spent most of the federal dollars in support of state party voter mobilization phone banks, which operated in the last days of the general election. In many cases, these in-kind transfers can have considerably greater

Hard Facts and Soft Money 115

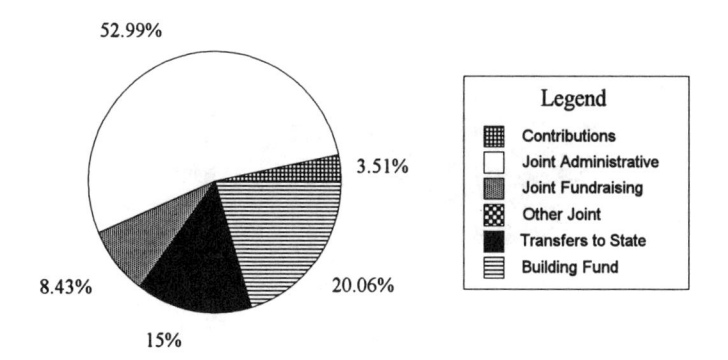

Figure 7.3 RNC National Party Spending 1991–1992

Federal Portion ($81.9 million)

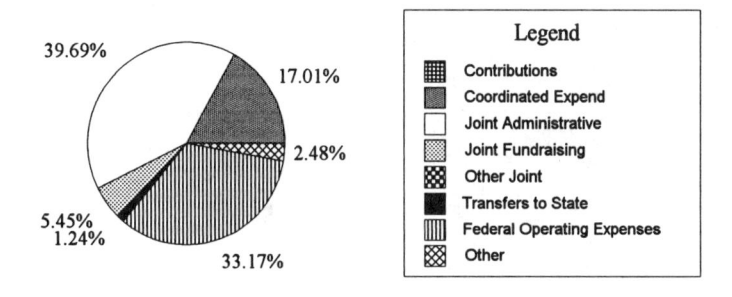

39.69%
17.01%
2.48%
5.45%
1.24%
33.17%

Legend
- Contributions
- Coordinated Expend
- Joint Administrative
- Joint Fundraising
- Other Joint
- Transfers to State
- Federal Operating Expenses
- Other

Non Federal Portion ($35.6 million)

52.99%
3.51%
8.43%
20.06%
15%

Legend
- Contributions
- Joint Administrative
- Joint Fundraising
- Other Joint
- Transfers to State
- Building Fund

Figure 7.4 DNC National Party Spending 1991–1992

Federal Portion ($65 million)

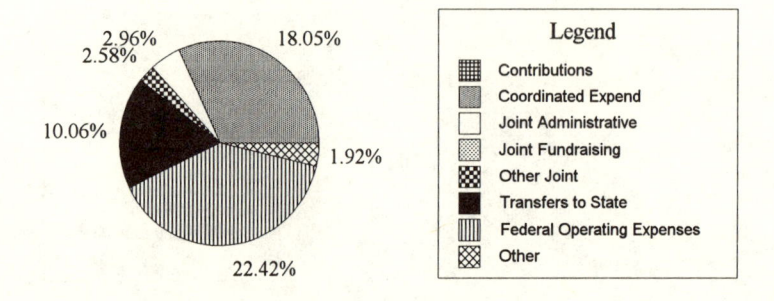

- 2.96%
- 2.58%
- 18.05%
- 10.06%
- 1.92%
- 22.42%

Legend
- Contributions
- Coordinated Expend
- Joint Administrative
- Joint Fundraising
- Other Joint
- Transfers to State
- Federal Operating Expenses
- Other

Non Federal Portion ($30.5 million)

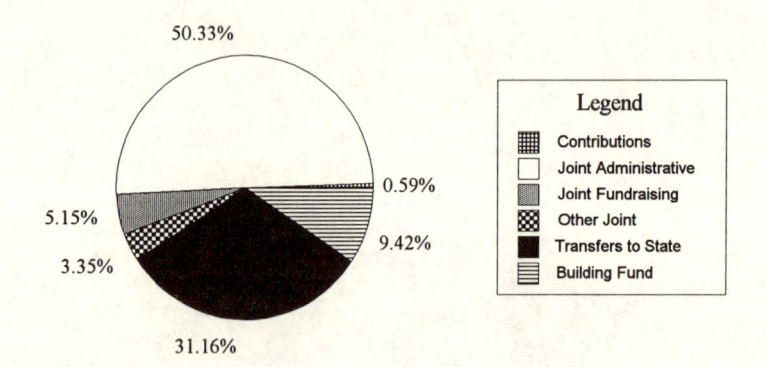

- 50.33%
- 0.59%
- 5.15%
- 9.42%
- 3.35%
- 31.16%

Legend
- Contributions
- Joint Administrative
- Joint Fundraising
- Other Joint
- Transfers to State
- Building Fund

real value than the dollar value attributed to them because the national parties provide these services for considerably less than the private sector might.

State Party Activity in 1992

Table 7.1 summarizes the expanded, but not complete, reporting of 1991-92 financial activity of state party committees under the new reporting rules. It shows these organizations have developed substantial financial resources. In only one-fifth of the states did the Democratic organizations raise less than $500,000 during the election cycle. For Republicans, 28 percent of the states reported receipts under one-half a million dollars. In contrast, about 95 percent of all PACs that reported raising money in 1991-92 compiled less than $500,000. While there are significant differences on a state by state basis between the two parties, overall there was remarkably equal access to financial resources.

Improved disclosure of state party activity does not, however, mean complete disclosure. Any activity related exclusively to state and local elections remains completely within the purview of state law and is only disclosed if required by that state. In some respects, the limited information about state parties included here makes suggests their financial position may be even more impressive than at first glance. Purely state and local activities would only enhance the already strong financial position these organization appear to already have.

On the federal reports one state party organization—the New Jersey Republicans—chose to disclose all of its financial activity. New Jersey is one of only two states which holds state elections in odd numbered years, so it may represent an unusual case. With this in mind, about 25 percent of the total funds spent during the cycle were devoted to direct support of state and local candidates in an election cycle with no gubernatorial campaign ($1.2 million out of $4.6 million). Generalizing from a single case is very hazardous, but it seems likely that in many cases total state party activity would be at least 25 percent more than reported to the federal government.

Table 7.2 provides similar information for local party organizations which have chosen to register and report under federal law. The 1979 amendments were intended in part to free local party organizations from the record-keeping and reporting requirements imposed on other levels of the party organization. Many of the activities local parties participated in that are directly or indirectly related to federal races are specifically exempted from federal rules so long as the amounts spent were relatively modest. Even with this special treatment, several states have many local party committees which reported sizable receipts and disbursements during 1991-92.

Table 7.1 State Party Activity Reported to the FEC, 1991–1992

State	DEMOCRATS Receipts	Disbursements	Disbursements Rank	REPUBLICANS Receipts	Disbursements	Disbursements Rank
Alabama	$1,177,281	$1,104,129	25	$815,113	$813,960	28
Alaska	$286,185	$284,869	48	$174,068	$176,433	48
Arizona	$820,937	$822,909	34	$1,149,610	$1,154,509	22
Arkansas	$2,323,710	$2,122,218	13	$519,287	$538,299	36
California	$12,667,577	$12,632,625	1	$6,275,385	$6,251,173	2
Colorado	$2,224,185	$2,054,502	14	$2,438,076	$2,438,319	11
Connecticut	$1,103,243	$1,074,158	27	$1,054,196	$1,051,007	25
Delaware	$486,292	$472,153	42	$1,001,656	$949,102	27
Florida	$879,375	$1,016,542	29	$4,826,829	$4,750,182	5
Georgia	$4,500,364	$4,492,793	3	$2,506,770	$2,413,472	12
Hawaii	$1,220,291	$1,199,356	23	$272,377	$302,979	43
Idaho	$369,436	$382,924	47	$1,140,922	$1,107,779	23
Illinois	2,988,964	$2,857,360	11	$1,848,656	$1,815,648	20
Indiana	2,423,004	$2,647,955	12	$2,470,944	$2,143,796	15
Iowa	$1,929,723	$1,929,523	15	$2,233,042	$2,223,873	14
Kansas	$397,437	$390,061	46	$670,249	$668,910	33
Kentucky	$1,522,094	$1,526,498	19	$1,073,955	$1,051,156	24
Louisiana	$1,641,666	$1,835,185	16	$350,312	$338,759	42
Maine	$598,369	$543,241	37	$46,722	$48,667	50
Maryland	$1,199,529	$1,286,890	22	4774,432	$773,296	29
Massachusetts	$1,505,330	$1,451,734	21	$1,936,822	$1,994,830	16
Michigan	$3,527,789	$3,549,243	8	$5,568,711	$5,528,094	4
Minnesota	$3,361,370	$3,334,483	9	$2,745,218	$2,661,001	9
Mississippi	$932,973	$896,281	31	$90,638	$104,707	49
Missouri	$1,565,973	$1,563,712	18	$2,057,881	$1,959,781	18

Montana	$910,846	$1,098,643	26	$432,232	$431,425	40
Nebraska	$483,885	$485,017	41	$984,833	$996,567	26
Nevada	$497,638	$516,46	39	$274,563	$278,933	45
New Hampshire	$397,885	$393,813	45	$390,624	$387,573	41
New Jersey	$2,955,715	$3,586,538	7	$4,627,660	$4,652,854	6
New Mexico	$851,855	$807,692	35	$497,638	$524,736	37
New York	$4,325,444	$4,322,320	3	$2,416,776	$2,369,607	13
North Carolina	$4,091,444	$4,085,669	5	$1,938,340	$1,959,998	17
North Dakota	$846,392	$841,235	33	$702,609	$728,970	31
Ohio	$4,146,675	$3,864,038	6	$6,017,237	$6,016,173	3
Oklahoma	$418,417	$413,164	44	$566,999	$558,166	34
Oregon	$1,042,744	$1,015,521	30	$494,365	$492,485	38
Pennsylvania	$3,166,953	$2,901,905	10	$3,530,942	$3,455,392	7
Rhode Island	$129,484	$134,874	50	$301,049	$302,944	44
South Carolina	$518,334	$456,798	43	$543,681	$539,481	35
South Dakota	$856,436	$864,024	32	$675,413	$707,292	32
Tennessee	$1,195,184	$1,109,940	24	$1,425,633	$1,380,925	21
Texas	$4,224,844	$4,233,267	4	$7,024,126	$7,002,858	1
Utah	$562,791	$559,785	36	$772,143	$756,632	30
Vermont	$532,051	$534,611	38	$441,692	$438,556	39
Virginia	$1,076,394	$1,066,432	28	$1,941,375	$1,938,146	19
Washington	$1,455,140	$1,503,530	20	$2,598,902	$2,593,057	10
West Virginia	$561,506	$500,545	40	$199,791	$194,477	47
Wisconsin	$1,879,507	$1,742,400	17	$2,702,669	$2,689,962	8
Wyoming	$233,946	$229,509	49	$274,991	$274,180	46
Total	$89,044,607	$88,739,060		$85,818,154	$84,931,121	

Note: Activity totally related to state and local races is not reported to the FEC.
Source: Federal Election Commission.

Table 7.2 Local Party Activity Reported to the FEC, 1991–1992

State	DEMOCRATS Number of Committees	Receipts	Disbursements	REPUBLICANS Number of Committees	Receipts	Disbursements
Alabama	1	$0	$0	2	$192,441	$191,852
Alaska	1	$0	$0	0	$0	$0
Arizona	0	$0	$0	1	$0	$0
Arkansas	0	$0	$0	1	$0	$0
California	23	$612,332	$556,429	37	$2,454,320	$2,415,853
Colorado	0	$0	$0	0	$0	$0
Connecticut	0	$0	$0	5	$51,419	$59,831
Delaware	0	$0	$0	0	$0	$0
Florida	3	$77,602	$75,309	5	$122,718	$125,000
Georgia	2	$253,118	$280,290	2	$3,700	$3,611
Hawaii	0	$0	$0	1	$0	$0
Idaho	1	$9,483	$27,772	0	$0	$0
Illinois	1	$0	$0	4	$214,336	$215,427
Indiana	1	$31,320	$27,181	4	$152,349	$165,268
Iowa	6	$35,771	$32,255	0	$0	$0
Kansas	0	$0	$0	1	$1,443	$4,053
Kentucky	1	$43,372	$41,707	3	$33,836	$31,517
Louisiana	0	$0	$0	1	$0	$0
Maine	0	$0	$0	0	$0	$0
Maryland	6	$420,343	$384,219	6	$47,286	$46,479
Massachusetts	0	$0	$0	1	$0	$0
Michigan	29	$797,715	$809,393	16	$1,267,222	$1,284,774
Minnesota	4	$23,956	$25,926	1	$0	$0
Mississippi	0	$0	$0	1	$1,623	$1,726
Missouri	1	$50,748	$65,564	2	$15,600	$2,709

State				
Montana	0	$0	2	$750
Nebraska	0	$0	1	$58,939
Nevada	0	$0	1	$29,385
New Hampshire	0	$0	1	$0
New Jersey	1	$1,375	2	$627
New Mexico	0	$0	1	$0
New York	13	$41,049	4	$866,977
North Carolina	4	$37,002	6	$62,961
North Dakota	0	$0	0	$0
Ohio	1	$18,614	7	$256,636
Oklahoma	1	$0	3	$64,063
Oregon	0	$0	4	$17,725
Pennsylvania	4	$36,798	4	$322,029
Rhode Island	0	$0	0	$0
South Carolina	0	$0	0	$0
South Dakota	0	$0	0	$0
Tennessee	3	$324,855	4	$105,1499
Texas	12	$1,285,002	9	$304,089
Utah	0	$0	1	$3,921
Vermont	0	$0	0	$0
Virginia	16	$383,223	18	$419,404
Washington	1	$0	5	$523
West Virginia	0	$0	4	$16,120
Wisconsin	7	$28,005	9	$63,687
Wyoming	0	40	0	$0
Total	143	$4,511,683	180	$7,141,085

	$0	
	$0	
	$0	
	$150	
	$0	
	$37,288	
	$40,038	
	$0	
	$18,950	
	$0	
	$0	
	$33,870	
	$0	
	$0	
	$0	
	$327,454	
	$1,282,151	
	$0	
	$0	
	$367,092	
	$0	
	$0	
	$25,144	
	$0	
	$4,458,182	

	$785
	$59,497
	$27,283
	$0
	$310
	$0
	$822,970
	$64,355
	$0
	$242,997
	$70,515
	$17,094
	$279,908
	$0
	$0
	$0
	$117,520
	$304,644
	$3,880
	$0
	$429,598
	$0
	$18,762
	$68,220
	$0
	$7,086,631

Note: Activity totally related to state and local races is not reported to the FEC.
Source: Federal Election Commission.

Tables 7.3 and 7.4 identify the primary sources of disclosed state party receipts, first for Republican organizations, and then for the Democrats. The fundraising pattern apparent for national parties is again suggested here. Republican state parties are more dependent on contributions from individuals and less dependent on the national organization than the Democrats. It is also noteworthy that the nonfederal share of allocable activities undertaken by the states represents roughly one-third of their overall revenues. This likely reflects the bulk of funds used for overhead and generic activities conducted by state parties (primarily get out the vote efforts) since any activity that indirectly affects federal elections must now be disclosed. It does not include funding for programs and activities directed exclusively toward state and local campaigns.

Party Integration

The regulations and reporting rules now in place permit a fuller examination of the financial relationships between national and state parties. Tables 7.5 and 7.6 list the sum of all national party support for each state, along with several variables which might help explain variations.

The Democratic national organizations provided some monetary or in-kind support to every state organization, with amounts ranging from $10,750 for Alaska to nearly $1.9 million for California. The Republican national organizations provided financial assistance to all states except Hawaii and Nebraska. They provided nearly $1.1 million in funds and services to the Ohio Republican Party alone.

Roughly two-thirds of the support given by national committees came from sources outside the restrictions of the FECA to be used for nonfederal elections. Some funds might have been used as part of the state soft money share of joint activities. They might also have been used for strictly state and local purposes, which would mean its ultimate use could not be isolated in state party filings at the FEC. The full scope of state party activity thus remains out of reach. This limitation affects our ability to fully specify the relationship between national parties and their state counterparts. We know the total amount that the national organizations have provided to the states, but do not have a full picture of how much money the state parties generated on their own. As a result, our conclusions about the dependence of "subordinate" levels of party on national fundraising must be seen as preliminary.

How the national committees choose among the states when allocating financial resources is no doubt a complex calculation. Clearly the size of the state and competitiveness of elections are important factors. It is also reasonable to assume the nature of presidential campaigns will shape national party priorities, as would the existence of competitive state-wide races. Other factors might include the capacity of the state party to use funds efficiently, and the relationship between state party leaders and the national committees. Finally, state campaign finance law may restrict the types of national party support that can be accepted.

For illustrative purposes, indicators of some of these factors are included in Tables 7.5 and 7.6. States are arranged by the number of electoral votes, an indicator of state size, which when combined with the margin of victory in the presidential race would account for national party allocation of soft money if this activity were guided only by the needs of the presidential campaign. The existence of a gubernatorial race, along with the proportion of the ballot in the state made up of federal races, are included as well.

A cursory examination of DNC transfers to state parties suggests that while the demands of the presidential campaign are plainly associated with the distribution of soft dollars, other factors are as work. There are states with large numbers of electoral votes and a close presidential margin, where the state committees received relatively little DNC soft money (Florida, Virginia, and Indiana, for example). On the other hand, some relatively small states received much more soft money than their size and competitiveness would suggest, such as Louisiana. Deviations from a purely presidential strategy are also apparent for RNC transfers as well. Here states like North Dakota, Washington, and South Carolina received far more soft money support from the national party than their place in the presidential campaign would imply. Large, competitive states like Texas, New Jersey, and Florida received less than one might guess. The existence of competitive gubernatorial elections seem to play an important role.

Conclusion

This chapter has described some of the restrictions within which state and national parties raise and spend the "mother's milk of politics." As such, it represents a starting point for further consideration of the role of money in the development of parties at all levels. The information provided reinforces other studies of party organization by demonstrating once again that parties are, for the most part, large and complex financial organizations. How these resources are translated into meaningful political activity is an important question in need of further research.

We have also begun to probe the financial relationships among different levels of party, finding some states that appear quite dependent on their national counterparts, while others are more inclined (or more able) to go it alone. All state parties receive some national financial assistance, however, and the ability of the national committees to control important resources has undoubtedly increased their influence over aspects of state party activity.

Table 7.3 Sources of Receipts for Democratic State Parties

State	Contrib from Individuals	Contrib from PACs	Hard Dollars - National Cmtes	Hard Dollars - ASOC	State Soft Money	Receipts
Alabama	$438,811	$47,500	$36,766	$4,879	$483,980	$1,177,281
Alaska	$139,166	$15,000	$2,750	$14,401	$113,853	$286,185
Arizona	$555,168	$52,540	$61,372	$2,693	$121,090	$820,937
Arkansas	$586,409	$32,500	$402,725	$40,365	$1,001,852	$2,323,710
California	$6,516,234	$362,616	$673,039	$58,300	$4,609,070	$12,667,577
Colorado	$1,391,601	$54,086	$111,909	$10,100	$509,207	$2,224,185
Connecticut	$363,708	$114,230	$102,000	$78,651	$323,319	$1,103,243
Delaware	$98,023	$40,000	$37,316	$35,891	$265,855	$486,292
Florida	$535,042	$29,350	$35,694	$47,500	$308,685	$879,375
Georgia	$856,990	$243,115	$427,171	$63,175	$2,596,958	$4,500,364
Hawaii	$457,973	$8,000	$17,518	$3,972	$708,092	$1,220,291
Idaho	$186,882	$38,800	$11,100	$0	$93,951	$369,436
Illinois	$1,585,338	$152,230	$242,361	$22,168	$911,622	$2,988,964
Indiana	$1,099,285	$32,900	$13,800	$237,881	$1,038,018	$2,423,004
Iowa	$627,173	$103,350	$140,745	$317,609	$630,363	$1,929,723
Kansas	$216,205	$11,750	$12,016	$94,495	$15,180	$397,437
Kentucky	$442,171	$90,000	$34,000	$8,785	$812,836	$1,552,094
Louisiana	$334,897	$71,700	$58,043	$9,843	$992,424	$1,641,666
Maine	$161,328	$22,500	$82,442	$85,596	$223,660	$598,369
Maryland	$442,066	$120,775	$99,023	$144,591	$275,341	$1,199,529
Massachusetts	$382,437	$136,450	$288,244	$74,300	$535,240	$1,505,330
Michigan	$743,300	$152,835	$435,135	$381,439	$1,775,564	$3,527,789
Minnesota	$1,395,073	$50,400	$14,094	$20,700	$1,480,178	$3,361,370
Mississippi	$612,635	$17,500	$2,300	$14,226	$215,350	$932,973
Missouri	$238,613	$115,465	$191,084	$92,645	$849,669	$1,565,973
Montana	$659,742	$96,325	$37,060	$6,900	$16,584	$910,846

Nebraska	$138,263	$11,250	$103,482	$175,041	$483,885
Nevada	$67,859	$23,925	$4,300	$228,687	$497,638
New Hampshire	$54,050	$47,750	$22,300	$187,800	$397,885
New Jersey	$339,683	$100,100	$100,191	$1,298,287	$2,955,715
New Mexico	$168,130	$78,000	$81,034	$454,146	$851,855
New York	$2,905,713	$22,000	$5,001	$938,182	$4,325,444
North Carolina	$1,840,471	$132,650	$12,700	$1,238,918	$4,091,444
North Dakota	$221,341	$92,750	$63,881	$270,193	$846,392
Ohio	$937,153	$108,909	$177,809	$1,725,764	$4,146,675
Oklahoma	$294,739	$21,250	$63,803	$43,392	$418,417
Oregon	$382,158	$94,500	$113,276	$408,589	$1,042,744
Pennsylvania	$1,262,821	$195,075	$600	$1,170,519	$3,166,953
Rhode Island	$19,403	$22,500	$7,107	$39,901	$129,484
South Carolina	$147,192	$40,000	$66,790	$206,861	$518,334
South Dakota	$279,778	$74,270	$0	$255,987	$856,436
Tennessee	$524,887	$112,450	$95,255	$219,608	$1,195,184
Texas	$947,087	$78,600	$430,824	$2,284,825	$4,224,844
Utah	$106,175	$28,800	$80,040	$318,656	$562,791
Vermont	$63,634	$100,600	$70,605	$222,702	$532,051
Virginia	$225,224	$16,000	$353,583	$421,109	$1,076,394
Washington	$919,070	$64,000	$0	$235,281	$1,455,140
West Virginia	$163,698	$18,330	$16,205	$152,332	$561,506
Wisconsin	$304,249	$124,780	$292,138	$837,345	$233,946
Wyoming	$103,864	$5,100	$83,265	$31,552	$233,946
Total	$33,417,912	$3,835,506	$4,115,294	$34,273,618	$89,044,607

Note: Hard dollars meet the limits and restrictions of the FECA. State Soft Money is the nonfederal share of spending that effects all campaigns.
Source: Federal Election Commission.

Table 7.4 Sources of Receipts for Republican State Parties

State	Contrib from Individuals	Contrib from PACs	Hard Dollars - National Cmtes	State Soft Money	Receipts
Alabama	$542,477	$6,000	$35,596	$185,154	$815,113
Alaska	$64,410	$0	$21,450	$88,207	$174,068
Arizona	$683,352	$15,225	$96,800	$115,015	$1,149,610
Arkansas	$347,973	$0	$0	$125,520	$519,287
California	$4,081,837	$33,244	$1,625	$1,881,045	$6,275,385
Colorado	$1,284,155	$5,000	$133,650	$979,741	$2438,076
Connecticut	$372,167	$5,206	$18,500	$146,765	$1,054,196
Delaware	$354,767	$0	$6,250	$619,599	$1,001,656
Florida	$2,459,308	$9,684	$201,519	$1,946,822	$4,826,829
Georgia	$978,609	$31,075	$224,181	$1,101,313	$2,506,770
Hawaii	$183,546	$2,700	$0	$60,000	$272,377
Idaho	$327,271	$15,000	$96,033	$568,292	$1,140,922
Illinois	$911,472	$33,000	$53,334	$530,516	$1,848,656
Indiana	$1,347,571	$1,600	$9,340	$1,091,611	$2,470,944
Iowa	$1,674,725	$8,000	$69,231	$284,976	$2,233,042
Kansas	$489,854	$24,500	$0	$126,772	$670,249
Kentucky	$556,650	$14,625	$6,300	$154,742	$1,073,955
Louisiana	$221,732	$4,500	$90,533	$30,177	$350,312
Maine	$15,755	$0	$585	$20,356	$46,722
Maryland	$696,721	$3,500	$19,000	$44,725	$774,432
Massachusetts	$1,343,356	$14,250	$19,300	$554,216	$1,936,822
Michigan	$2,560,561	$95,340	$306,758	$2,524,396	$5,568,711
Minnesota	$1,563,744	$5,000	$12,939	$1,068,995	$2,745,218
Mississippi	$77,800	$1,000	$14,500	$0	$90,638
Missouri	$966,362	$2,500	$41,853	$950,680	$2,057,881
Montana	$315,554	$2,000	$20,153	$93,668	$432,232

Nebraska	$488,745	$2,530	$490,445	$984,833
Nevada	$170,998	$0	$101,564	$274,563
New Hampshire	$283,919	$1,250	$0	$390,624
New Jersey	$1,185,223	$18,000	$3,125,032	$4,627,660
New Mexico	$198,596	$0	$285,591	$497,638
New York	$807,762	$88,115	$617,332	$2,416,776
North Carolina	$1,575,988	$11,722	$245,599	$1,938,340
North Dakota	$500,833	$0	$127,141	$702,609
Ohio	$2,861,208	$32,479	$2,639,701	$6,017,237
Oklahoma	$463,746	$0	$80,903	$566,999
Oregon	$444,990	$27,000	$24,375	$494,365
Pennsylvania	$2,196,565	$47,950	$655,318	$3,530,942
Rhode Island	$149,315	$0	$147,943	$301,049
South Carolina	$463,571	$35,500	$0	$543,681
South Dakota	$436,439	$1,000	$179,195	$675,413
Tennessee	$1,205,207	$27,900	$45,898	$1,425,633
Texas	$5,253,226	$128,421	$1,334,929	$7,024,126
Utah	$317,424	$6,300	$432,541	$772,143
Vermont	$218,748	$5,000	$189,922	$441,692
Virginia	$1,362,133	$500	$373,458	$1,941,375
Washington	$1,710,132	$2,500	$1,058,522	$2,598,902
West Virginia	$171,820	$0	$0	$199,791
Wisconsin	$1,491,824	$39,730	$470,464	$2,702,669
Wyoming	$172,864	$0	$56,905	$274,991
Total	$48,553,005	$808,846	$27,976,081	$85,818,154

Note: Hard dollars meet the limits and restrictions of the FECA. State Soft Money is the nonfederal share of spending that effects all campaigns.
Source: Federal Election Commission.

Table 7.5 DNC Support of State Parties, 1991-92

State	Electoral Votes	Presidential Margin	Gov Race	Senate Race	Federal % of Ballot	DNC Hard Transfers	DNC Soft Transfers	Total DNC to State Party	State Party Spending-Federal
California	54	14%		2	44%	$668,039	$1,204,814	$1,872,853	$12,632,625
New York	33	16%		x	37%	$243,037	$612,125	$855,162	$4,322,320
Texas	32	3%			29%	$445,786	$1,035,766	$1,481,552	$4,233,267
Florida	25	2%		x	43%	$35,694	$116,896	$152,590	$1,016,542
Pennsylvania	23	9%		2	33%	$364,672	$572,579	$937,251	$2,901,905
Illinois	22	14%		x	50%	$230,608	$463,132	$693,740	$2,857,360
Ohio	21	2%		x	33%	$620,931	$279,043	$899,974	$3,864,038
Michigan	18	8%			29%	$431,073	$330,627	$761,700	$3,549,243
New Jersey	15	2%			33%	$655,027	$243,258	$898,285	$3,586,538
North Carolina	14	1%	X	x	30%	$167,897	$596,300	$764,197	$4,085,669
Virginia	13	4%			40%	$2,306	$25,812	$28,118	$1,066,432
Georgia	13	1%		x	33%	$404,671	$648,497	$1,053,168	$4,492,793
Massachusetts	12	18%			40%	$270,744	$1,500	$272,244	$1,451,734
Indiana	12	6%	X		33%	$13,800	$19,999	$33,799	$2,647,955
Wisconsin	11	3%		x	43%	$225,778	$215,146	$440,924	$1,742,400
Washington	11	11%	X	x	33%	$93,137	$82,492	$175,629	$1,503,530
Tennessee	11	5%		x	33%	$194,223	$260,961	$455,184	$1,109,940
Missouri	11	10%	X	x	30%	$191,084	$337,464	$528,548	$1,563,712
Maryland	10	15%		x	50%	$89,023	$74,300	$163,323	$1,286,890
Minnesota	10	12%			40%	$14,094	$161,020	$175,114	$3,334,483
Alabama	9	7%		x	50%	$16,766	$53,291	$70,057	$1,104,129
Louisiana	9	5%		x	33%	$58,043	$378,432	$436,475	$1,835,185
South Carolina	8	8%		x	43%	$30,288	$52,276	$82,564	$456,798
Connecticut	8	6%		x	43%	$92,000	$135,222	$227,222	$1,074,158
Oklahoma	8	9%		x	37%	$15,263	$0	$15,263	$413,164
Arizona	8	2%		x	34%	$61,372	$52,215	$113,587	$822,909

State							
Colorado	8	4%		33%	$111,909	$88,261	$200,170	$2,054,502
Kentucky	8	3%		33%	$34,000	$106,000	$140,000	$1,526,498
Iowa	7	6%		43%	$120,745	$172,262	$293,007	$1,929,523
Oregon	7	9%		33%	$132,956	$171,540	$304,496	$1,015,521
Mississippi	7	9%		25%	$2,300	$100,000	$102,300	$896,281
Arkansas	6	18%		50%	$402,725	$231,537	$634,262	$2,122,218
Kansas	6	5%	x	50%	$12,016	$12,778	$24,794	$390,061
Nebraska	5	17%	x	40%	$10,600	$14,500	$25,100	$485,017
Utah	5	16%	X	33%	$5,800	$8,000	$13,800	$559,785
New Mexico	5	8%		29%	$99,322	$92,018	$191,340	$807,692
West Virginia	5	13%	X	25%	$117,793	$0	$117,793	$500,545
Idaho	5	14%		50%	$11,100	$20,500	$31,600	$382,924
Hawaii	4	11%	x	43%	$17,518	$30,000	$47,518	$1,199,356
Nevada	4	2%	x	43%	$14,683	$36,101	$50,784	$516,446
New Hampshire	4	1%	X	37%	$26,400	$84,800	$111,200	$393,813
Maine	4	8%		33%	$82,442	$63,232	$145,674	$543,241
Rhode Island	4	18%	X	25%	$40,140	$10,000	$50,140	$134,874
Alaska	3	9%		50%	$2,750	$8,000	$10,750	$284,869
North Dakota	3	12%	X	37%	$9,350	$54,150	$63,500	$841,235
South Dakota	3	4%	x	37%	$10,100	$43,103	$53,203	$864,024
Vermont	3	16%	X	33%	$35,622	$43,420	$79,042	$534,611
Wyoming	3	6%		33%	$3,800	$8,000	$11,800	$229,509
Delaware	3	8%	X	25%	$37,316	$40,431	$77,747	$472,153
Montana	3	2%	X	25%	$24,560	$108,689	$133,249	$1,098,643

Source: Federal Election Commission.

Table 7.6 RNC Support of State Parties, 1991–92

State	Electoral Votes	Presidential Margin	Gov Race	Senate Race	Federal % of Ballot	RNC Hard Transfers	RNC Soft Transfers	Total RNC to State Party	State Party Spending-Federal
California	54	14%		2	44%	$1,625	$489,650	$491,275	$6,251,173
New York	33	16%		x	37%	$20,500	$0	$20,500	$2,369,607
Texas	32	3%			29%	$51,369	$184,377	$235,746	$7,002,858
Florida	25	2%		x	43%	$201,519	$222,432	$423,951	$4,750,182
Pennsylvania	23	9%		2	33%	$7,350	$226,381	$233,731	$3,455,392
Illinois	22	14%		x	50%	$53,334	$175,785	$229,119	$1,815,648
Ohio	21	2%		x	33%	$128,209	$968,891	$1,097,100	$6,016,173
Michigan	18	8%			29%	$306,758	$307,325	$614,083	$5,528,094
New Jersey	15	2%			33%	$113,442	$184,793	$298,235	$4,652,854
North Carolina	14	1%	X	x	30%	$42,479	$325,452	$367,931	$1,959,998
Virginia	13	4%			40%	$211,325	$9,000	$220,325	$1,938,146
Georgia	13	1%		x	33%	$179,181	$292,860	$472,041	$2,413,472
Massachusetts	12	18%			40%	$19,300	$0	$19,300	$1,994,830
Indiana	12	6%	X		33%	$4,000	$90,497	$94,497	$2,143,796
Wisconsin	11	3%		x	43%	$237,210	$20,000	$257,210	$2,689,962
Washington	11	11%	X	x	33%	$5,275	$256,725	$262,000	$2,593,580
Tennessee	11	5%		x	33%	$89,066	$22,522	$111,588	$1,380,925
Missouri	11	10%	X		30%	$41,853	$207,987	$249,840	$1,959,781
Maryland	10	15%		x	50%	$19,000	$0	$19,000	$773,296
Minnesota	10	12%		x	40%	$12,939	$10,850	$23,789	$2,661,001
Alabama	9	7%		x	50%	$35,596	$23,731	$59,327	$813,960
Louisiana	9	5%		x	33%	$90,533	$30,177	$120,710	$338,759
South Carolina	8	8%		x	43%	$0	$239,500	$239,500	$539,481
Connecticut	8	6%			43%	$18,500	$0	$18,500	$1,051,007
Oklahoma	8	9%		x	37%	$10,875	$69,903	$80,778	$558,166
Arizona	8	2%		x	34%	$96,800	$68,400	$165,200	$1,154,509

Hard Facts and Soft Money 131

Colorado	8	4%		x	$50,650	$74,401	$125,051	$2,438,319
Kentucky	8	3%		x	$1,300	$51,059	$52,359	$1,051,156
Iowa	7	6%		x	$69,231	$136,921	$206,152	$2,223,873
Oregon	7	9%		x	$9,766	$20,000	$29,766	$492,485
Mississippi	7	9%			$12,000	$8,500	$20,500	$104,707
Arkansas	6	18%		x	$0	$11,500	$11,500	$538,299
Kansas	6	5%		x	$0	$15,000	$15,000	$668,910
Nebraska	5	17%			$0	$0	$0	$996,567
Utah	5	16%	X		$0	$0	$0	$756,632
New Mexico	5	8%		x	$18,525	$22,627	$41,152	$524,736
West Virginia	5	13%	X		$4,000	$0	$4,000	$194,477
Idaho	4	14%		x	$12,875	$15,625	$28,500	$1,107,779
Hawaii	4	11%		x	$0	$0	$0	$302,979
Nevada	4	2%			$750	$49,366	$50,116	$278,933
New Hampshire	4	1%	X		$40,977	$8,500	$49,477	$387,573
Maine	4	8%			$585	$25,671	$26,256	$48,667
Rhode Island	4	18%	X		$0	$14,000	$14,000	$302,944
Alaska	3	9%		x	$21,450	$13,550	$35,000	$176,433
North Dakota	3	12%	X	x	$61,775	$253,775	$315,550	$728,970
South Dakota	3	4%		x	$0	$25,178	$25,178	$707,292
Vermont	3	16%	X		$6,200	$101,833	$108,033	$438,556
Wyoming	3	6%			$2,500	$7,880	$10,380	$274,180
Delaware	3	8%	X		$6,250	$61,750	$68,000	$949,102
Montana	3	2%	X		$11,153	$54,221	$65,374	$431,425

Source: Federal Election Commission.

National committees enjoy more widespread access to all sources of funds—those controlled by federal law as well as the soft money sources beyond the bounds of federal regulation. Their ability to decide where those funds are used inevitably makes them a powerful force, potentially shaping the agenda at all levels. How these growing financial ties will effect intraparty relationships is another area of inquiry that the information presented here can only partially reveal.

Notes

1. In campaign finance jargon, money that would be permitted in elections for state or local office but would not be permissible in federal elections is described as "soft money." Some states, for example, permit corporations or labor unions to directly contribute to candidates for state and local office. Political parties that are active in all campaigns must therefore find a way to meet the restrictions of both systems. In general, any money allowable under state or local rules that might have even an *indirect* effect on a federal race is soft money.

2. During 1991 the FEC amended the rule to add an additional nonfederal point for each state.

8

Local Political Parties and Legislative Races in 1992

John Frendreis
Alan R. Gitelson
Gregory Flemming
Anne Layzell

Shortly before Speaker Tip O'Neill's retirement from the House of Representatives in 1986, he reminded a group of constituents of the one law of politics that had governed his overall perspective of the American political system: "All politics are local." This often-repeated quote has been used over and over again by textbook authors to remind our students that the nexus of the political system is located at the local level, where politics and government have such a significant impact on public policy.

Ironically, the locus of most contemporary scholarly research and journalistic attention on party organization has focused elsewhere—at the national and state levels. This pattern is at once understandable, valuable, and problematic. It is understandable in that national and state politics are both more dramatic and more accessible to scholars and national columnists. It is valuable in that much has been learned about the new and changing nature of party organizations at the national and state levels;[1] those changes and the subsequent debate on the nature of party transformation over the past thirty years are reflected in several of the chapters in this volume. However, it is also problematic because the past three decades have been marked by a dearth of scholarship on local party organizations in their manifold roles of organization building, fundraising, recruitment, getting-out-the-vote, campaign coordination, and patronage, particularly in subcongressional races. Here we attempt to address this limitation in the extant literature, focusing on the electoral role of contemporary local parties in state legislative races.

Local Political Parties and the Electoral Process

To observe that there has been limited research on local political parties is not to suggest that there has been no research in this area (see, for example, Crotty 1986; Margolis and Green 1992). Indeed, one type of local party organization, the urban machine, has been described as "the most written about, the best recorded, and the most romanticized in U.S. political history" (Crotty 1991a:1155). However, research on political machines has little relevance for an understanding of contemporary local parties. Other research on local parties extended beyond the study of machine politics.[2] The collective scholarship of Cutright and Rossi (1958), Katz and Eldersveld (1961), Wolfinger (1963), Cutright (1963, 1964), and Crotty (1971), seeking to identify the electoral consequences of county, municipal, and precinct-level party activity, found moderate relationships between party activity and electoral outcomes. However, prior to 1980 almost all research on party organizations below the state level were case studies with little generalizeability. In addition, with the exception of Crotty's 1971 article, all of the work documented party activity from the 1950s and early 1960s, a period that pre-dated much of the perceived decline in local and other party organizations. As we have noted elsewhere (Frendreis and Gitelson 1993), with popular and scholarly accounts advancing the thesis of party decline, the stage was set for the contemporary period of research into the structure and activity of local parties.

The 1980s marked an important new generation of research on local party organizations beginning with the Party Transformation Study (PTS), the most systematic and broad-based research study generated in this century to examine state and local party structures (Cotter, Gibson, Bibby, and Huckshorn 1984; Gibson, Cotter, Bibby, and Huckshorn 1985). The PTS focused on the measurement and analysis of party organizations' roles and functions. In effect, Cotter and his colleagues asked the classic question of whether parties matter. They argued that local party organizations, in reacting to a changing political environment, maintain a fairly high level of programmatic activity and that their conclusions "[di]d not support the thesis of party decline" that was common in other accounts (1984:57).

Three significant conclusions about local party organizations stemmed from this work. First, despite the evolving and changing roles and functions of party organizations over the past three decades, local party organizations continued to be an integral and essential actor in the political process. This finding directly disputed the decline of party thesis. The second conclusion directly challenged Eldersveld's theory of "stratarchy," asserting that the party organizations at the national, state, and local levels were far more integrated than Eldersveld's model suggests. This view was also supported by the later work of Gibson, Frendreis, and Vertz (1989).[3] A third conclusion was that the strength of party organizations was independent of the strength of the party-in-the-electorate and the party-in-government.

Frendreis, Gibson, and Vertz, drawing on a subsequent survey of the PTS county organizations, found further evidence that local county party organizations were involved in electorally pertinent activities, "including candidate recruitment, joint planning with candidate organizations, and various independent campaign activities" (1990:225). These authors surmised that county party organizations are dynamic and autonomous political institutions and that party organizations do have an impact on electoral politics.

Some of the conclusions of this work have not gone unchallenged. In a 1986 study examining local party organizations in twenty-five New Jersey communities in Middlesex County, Lawson, Pomper, and Moakley (1986) took issue with Cotter and his colleagues regarding the prevalence of party organizational stratarchies and the legitimacy of Eldersveld's (1964) party decision-making model. A separate analysis of the New Jersey setting by Pomper (1990) also questioned the electoral relevance of local party activity. The work of Lawson and her colleagues, however, does seem to confirm the findings of the other studies that local party leaders "seek and get electoral linkage with the political process" and that those leaders are "active and they direct their activism into electoral campaigns" (Lawson et al. 1986:367).

Overall, then, the literature is mixed in its view of local party organizations. Although possessing a storied machine past, it is evident that the role of local parties has diminished over time. However, the most recent studies which have focused on local party organizational attributes describe organizations which are vital—and, in fact, are becoming stronger, not weaker. This paradox of organizations which are becoming structurally more developed, but functionally less effective, demands further investigation.

While many scholars are dubious that the parties are electorally irrelevant, there is relatively little empirical evidence that directly addresses the electoral role of local parties in the age of candidate-centered campaigning. Like studies of local party leaders, surveys of candidates reveal a modest role for local parties. Two candidate-based studies focusing on congressional races contribute to our understanding of the role of party organizations in the electoral process. Paul Herrnson's research (1986; 1988; 1993) makes it clear that party organizations, while not inconsequential, have less impact on the campaign process than a candidate's own organization, PACs, and campaign consultants. This general conclusion is important although it masks significant variation regarding specific campaign functions. While party organizations play a less important role in activities fundraising, at the same time they play a relatively significant role in volunteer recruitment and get-out-the-vote efforts (Herrnson 1986). A later study by Kazee and Thornberry (1990), focusing on the recruitment of congressional candidates, replicated the Herrnson findings, noting a moderate role for party organizations in this phase of the electoral process. Studies of party leaders suggest, however, that the overall role of local parties is greater for more local races at the county or state legislative district level (see Frendreis et al. 1990; Pomper 1990).

We have argued elsewhere that there are three reasons why studies of local parties should focus on lower level offices.[4] First, local party leaders themselves believe their organizations are most pertinent and effective with regard to lower-level offices. Second, lower-level offices, including state legislative and county offices, are accountable for public policy that is substantively important and collectively represents billions of dollars in annual revenues and expenditures. Third, what transpires at the local level is relevant for electoral and partisan politics at higher levels. For example, the underdevelopment of the Republican party in many parts of the South, may be more a function of party activity and partisan politics at the local level than it is of national and state-wide politics (Frendreis et al. 1990:231-232).

Local Party Organizations and the 1992 Election

This chapter focuses on the structural attributes and electoral roles of local party organizations. While our core analysis centers on a survey conducted of county party chairs in eight states in the 1992 elections, we also briefly report, from that same survey, on analysis appearing elsewhere (Frendreis, Gitelson, Fleming, and Layzell 1993) addressing the perspective of those people actually contesting elections—state legislative candidates—and their perceptions of the role of party organizations in the campaign process.

In 1992, we surveyed all Democratic and Republican county party leaders and all Democratic and Republican general election candidates for the upper and lower state legislative houses in eight states: Arizona, Colorado, Florida, Illinois, Missouri, South Carolina, Washington, and Wisconsin. These eight states were selected in order to provide representative coverage with respect to regions and the degree of party strength and competitiveness within each state (based on data reported in Cotter et al. 1984).

Two separate survey instruments were developed, one for chairs and one for candidates, but, where possible, the two sets of subjects were asked identical questions. In order to maintain comparability with previous research, our questions for candidates were modeled on those previously asked of congressional candidates (see Herrnson 1988), while our party chair survey was modeled on the PTS surveys (Gibson et al. 1989 and Cotter et al. 1984).[5] A total of 1,657 candidates for state legislative office and 1,016 county party leaders were surveyed. With valid responses from 986 state legislative candidates and 659 chairs, the response rates are 60 percent and 65 percent, respectively.

Our findings are organized in order to focus on three specific questions regarding the electoral roles of local parties:

1. What are the structural attributes and resources of contemporary local party organizations?
2. In what electoral activities do local parties actually engage?
3. What roles do local party leaders see their organizations playing in the 1992 elections?

In addition to these three questions, we will briefly address two issues regarding the electoral roles of local parties as perceived by state legislative candidates:

1. What roles do candidates see party organizations playing in the 1992 elections?
2. To what extent are the assessments of the parties' roles congruent between candidates and party leaders?

The Structural Strength of Local Party Organizations

In 1992, local party organizations continue to display the structural attributes noted in previous research. As a baseline for comparison, we have included in Table 8.1 comparable percentages reported in Gibson et al. (1985) for the 1979-80 PTS nationwide survey.[6] It is clear that in terms of these indicators of structural strength, local parties have not weakened over the last decade and, if anything, they have become slightly stronger. This finding is significant, since there is some indication that the structural strength of local parties has greater electoral consequences than their activity level in a given election cycle (Frendreis et al. 1990). Our findings here of continued structural strength parallel those reported by Gibson et al. (1989) for major county organizations for the 1980-84 period. Most differences over time are slight; the largest increases are seen when the party chair devotes more time to party business during nonelection periods and when the county organization has a telephone listing. There are few significant differences between the parties; the largest include a tendency for Democrats to hold more county committee meetings and for Republicans to have formal budgeting procedures.

This pattern of steady or slightly increasing structural strength should not mask the fact that these organizations remain essentially volunteer operations. Parties report the greatest level of development in areas requiring little or no expenditures—having officers, holding meetings, and having by-laws. In areas requiring the accumulation and outlay of cash—paid staff, formal budgeting, and maintenance of a year-round office—most local party organizations remain relatively underdeveloped. But, this lack of development does not represent a weakened state from a previous level of high structural strength.

Table 8.1 Structural Attributes of Local Party Organizations, 1980 and 1992.

	Percent Republicans 1980	Percent Democrats 1980	Percent Republicans 1992	Percent Democrat 1992
Has complete set of officers	81	90	92	94
Has at least 90% of chair positions filled	49	63	n/a	n/a
Chair works at least 6 hrs. per week (election period)	78	77	82	79
County committee meets at least bimonthly (election period)	57	59	57	75
Has constitution, rules, or bylaws	68	68	77	71
Has formal annual budget	31	20	34	23
Chair works at least 6 hrs. per week (nonelection period)	26	24	40	34
County committee meets at least bimonthly (nonelection period)	49	53	58	56
Has some paid, full-time staff	4	3	4	2
Has some paid, part-time staff	6	5	8	4
Chair receives salary	1	2	1	1
Has year-round office	14	12	21	12
Has telephone listing	16	11	27	21
Has campaign headquarters	60	55	59	57
Maximum N	1,872	1,984	330	352

Source: 1980 data reported in Gibson et al. 1985; 1992 survey by authors.

Taken as a whole, our findings support the early conclusions of the PTS regarding the structural strength of local party organizations in the United States.

The Local Party Chairs' View: The Electoral Role of Local Parties

Our survey of county party chairs found that local party organizations were active in various spheres of electoral politics during 1992.[7] The range of electoral operations covered everything from involvement in candidate recruitment to direct participation in campaign activities and responsibility for differing phases of individual candidates' campaigns. The prevailing opinion of county chairs was that their organizations were reasonably effective and productive as electoral actors.

Table 8.2 summarizes the percentages of Democratic and Republican chairs reporting that their party organization engaged in a variety of direct campaign activities during the 1992 election. An examination of the table reveals two patterns. First, as with structural strength, between the 1980 baseline year and 1992 there is no pattern of decline in campaign activity. In fact, the 1992 party organizations are a bit more active than the 1980 organizations. While there are declines of at least 5 percentage points in the organizations' reported activity in a few areas, such as voter registration and the buying of radio/TV time by Republican organizations, there are also increases of this magnitude in other activities for both the Democratic and Republican party organizations, including distribution of posters and lawn signs, distribution of campaign literature, arranging fundraising events, and organizing campaign events. This finding that party organizations are at least as active in 1992 as they were in 1980 also replicates the longitudinal findings of Gibson et al. (1989) for the shorter 1980-84 period.

A second pattern in Table 8.2 is that neither the Republican nor Democratic party has a distinct advantage with regard to direct campaign activities. Overall, the average Republican organization engaged in 9.0 of the 17 activities measured, while the average Democratic organization engaged in 9.4 activities. However, these differences, as well as the pairwise comparison between parties, are not statistically significant. But there were some Republican-Democratic differences that are statistically significant: Republican organizations are more likely to contribute money to candidates, while Democratic organizations are more apt to conduct registration drives, buy radio/TV time, coordinate PAC activity, and conduct get-out-the-vote efforts.

In addition to our findings regarding these direct campaign activities, party chairs also reported their organizations as actively involved in the campaigns of individual candidates. As the data in Table 8.2 indicate, over a quarter of each party related that their organization made formal or informal preprimary endorsements of candidates. An even larger percentage were involved in the broader process of candidate recruitment, with well over three-quarters of the chairs in each party reporting involvement in the recruitment of county and state legislative candidates. In all cases the percentages are higher for Republican organizations. The Republican-Democratic differences are statistically significant for all organizations for county and state legislative offices, but pairwise only for county offices. About two-thirds of the chairs report involvement in the recruitment of congressional candidates. The recruitment data reconfirm earlier results indicating that local chairs discern their role to be greater for lower-level partisan races than for higher-level races such as for Congress. Overall, these data represent an increase over the 1980 baseline and, in fact, exceed the comparable 1984 figures for major local party organizations reported by Gibson et al. (1989:Table 1).

Table 8.2 Campaign Activity Levels of Local Party Organizations, 1980 and 1992

	Percent Republicans 1980	Percent Democrats 1980	Percent Republicans 1992	Percent Democrat 1992
Direct Campaign Activity				
Distributes campaign literature	79	79	88	90
Arranges fundraising events	68	71	74	76
Organizes campaign events	65	68	77	81
Contributes money to candidates	70	62	75	67
Organizes telephone campaigns	65	61	58	62
Buys newspaper ads for party and candidates	62	62	60	65
Distributes posters or lawn signs	62	59	90	89
Coordinates county-level campaigns	56	57	57	59
Prepares press releases for party and candidates	55	55	62	65
Sends mailings to voters	59	47	58	51
Conducts registration drives	45	56	39	50
Organizes door-to-door canvassing	48	49	52	55
Buys radio/tv time for party and candidates	33	33	24	31
Utilizes public opinion surveys	16	11	15	15
Purchases bill board space	13	10	9	7
Coordinates PAC activity	n/a	n/a	4	10
Conducts get-out-the-vote effort	n/a	n/a	60	70
Candidate Recruitment				
"Very" or "somewhat" involved in candidate recruitment:				
For city and local offices	45	44	48	42
For county offices	71	69	94	87
For state legislative offices	75	74	86	81
For congressional offices	64	62	69	64
Makes formal or informal preprimary endorsements	28	32	31	27
Maximum N	1,872	1,984	330	352

Source: 1980 data reported in Gibson et al. 1985; 1992 survey by authors.

The party chairs were also asked to assess the importance of their own county organization in various aspects of candidates' campaigns. Our findings, presented in Table 8.3, generated three conclusions. First, county chairs overwhelmingly see their organizations as predominately local actors. With only a few minor exceptions, for each of the five campaign areas examined, there is a monotonic decline in chairs' evaluations of their organization's importance as the scope of the race increases. An analogous pattern holds for their assessment of their organizations' overall effect on electoral outcomes: chairs feel that the local party organizations are more effective for local offices and less effective for higher offices. Second, there is extraordinary similarity of viewpoint between Republican and Democratic chairs.[8] This similarity of perspective across party lines suggests that the parties have not cultivated different strategies at local levels. Third, while the chairs feel their organizations are of moderate importance to candidates' campaigns, they see their organizations as most important in such nuts-and-bolts areas as recruiting campaign volunteers, organizing campaign events, and get-out-the-vote efforts—each of which is a grass-roots activity emphasizing ties to local voters.

The Candidates' View: The Electoral Role of Local Parties

Thus far we have reported on the structural attributes and the electoral role of local party organizations as seen by county party chairs. But how do candidates see the involvement of county parties? Our survey of state legislative candidates reveals a very similar view of county parties, with a few expected differences. (These data are more fully presented in Frendreis et al. 1993.)

First, as with research on congressional races (Herrnson 1988), we found that family and friends were the most important factor in influencing a potential state legislative candidate's decision to run for office. However, local party organizations were the second most important factor affecting their recruitment. Second, our data show that state legislative candidates regard local party organizations as being of greatest benefit with regard to grass-roots activities like voter registration, organizing campaign events, recruiting volunteers, and get-out-the-vote efforts. Third, local party organizations are regarded as less important in campaign management and the development of campaign strategy. Apparently it is in this area that candidate-centered campaigning has taken over most fully.

Overall, the evaluations by state legislative candidates in 1992 suggest that candidate-centered campaigning is developing as much at this level as it is at higher levels of electoral politics. Candidates do not rely exclusively on local party organizations to facilitate and promote their races for office. At the same time, however, there is agreement between candidates and party chairs as to which aspects of a campaign local party organizations have the most and

Table 8.3 Chairs' Evaluations of the Importance of Their County Organization in Various Aspects of Candidates' Campaigns*

	Republicans	Democrats
Campaign Management and Strategy		
county candidates	3.21	3.05
state legislative candidates	2.67	2.62
congressional candidates	2.15	2.17
gubernatorial candidates	1.93	1.97
presidential candidate	1.68	1.84
Fundraising		
county candidates	3.21	3.11
state legislative candidates	2.81	2.74
congressional candidates	2.37	2.43
gubernatorial candidates	2.39	2.37
presidential candidate	1.96	2.08
Recruiting Volunteers		
county candidates	3.73	3.61
state legislative candidates	3.59	3.51
congressional candidates	3.33	3.23
gubernatorial candidates	3.34	3.25
the presidential candidate	3.16	3.20
Organizing Campaign Events		
county candidates	3.59	3.56
state legislative candidates	3.27	3.32
congressional candidates	2.94	2.98
gubernatorial candidates	2.78	2.73
presidential candidate	2.36	2.46
Get-Out-The-Vote		
county candidates	3.32	3.44
state legislative candidates	3.23	3.39
congressional candidates	3.13	3.36
gubernatorial candidates	3.15	3.31
presidential candidate	3.10	3.29
Maximum N	330	352

*Table entries are mean scores, measured on the following scale: 1=not important; 2=slightly important; 3=moderately important; 4=very important; 5=extremely important.
Source: Survey by authors.

least to offer. While there are substantial gaps between the absolute ratings the chairs and candidates give to the county party organizations, there is basic agreement on the relative importance of parties to the different aspects of campaigning. Local organizations are perceived by party chairs and state legislative candidates as most important in reaching out to the grass-roots—recruiting volunteers and getting voters to the polls—while least important to the creation and maintenance of the campaign infrastructure—fundraising and campaign management.

Local Political Parties and the Democratic Process

Contemporary debate over the status of party organizations has spanned the past four decades, beginning with the report of the American Political Science Association Committee on Political Parties (1950) calling for a "responsible party" system. That debate has engendered considerable concern over the state of parties in the post-World War II era. Indeed, a decade ago, a team of prominent political party scholars observed that "[t]he last twenty years have not been kind to American political parties" (Gibson et al. 1985:139). In fact, few American political institutions have seen their collapse (Broder 1971; Sundquist 1982; Crotty 1984; Wattenberg 1990, 1991b), and alternately, their revitalization (Schlesinger 1985; Kayden and Mahe 1985; Pomper 1981; Price 1984; Gitelson, Conway, and Feigert 1984), reported so often in scholarly publications, textbooks, and the popular press. Unquestionably, the past four decades have been marked by a volatile and changing party system.

We have argued here that any definitive evaluation of the tangible roles of local party organizations is hampered by the limited amount of contemporary research on their status. Further research may reveal the propensity for the continuing evolution of American parties; for simplicity we identify three possibilities (Frendreis and Gitelson 1993). First, American parties may be emerging into "responsible parties" (American Political Science Association Committee on Political Parties 1950). Although our research and PTS found an increase in organizational strength among local party organizations coupled with signs of a growing vertical integration of national, state, and local organizations, there is little evidence of movement toward the responsible party model.

A second prospect is what might be called the "disintegrating" model in which parties continue to lose influence with candidates and voters. Some research suggests that this is the case, particularly research on the hold parties exercise over the long-term loyalties of voters (e.g., Wattenberg 1990). Further support for this thesis is found in the evolving move from party-run to candidate-centered campaigns for major offices including presidential, gubernatorial, and congressional races. However, without further research, it is premature to assume the wholesale extension of this phenomenon to more local races.

We have chosen to label a third possibility the "adaptive brokerage" model. In this view, local parties (as well as national and state parties) have adapted to changes in the electoral environment, developing new roles, particularly that of bringing together candidates, consultants, and contributors. The specific role of political parties varies according to the electoral context. Where a party has been historically weak, the local party organization—aided by state and national organizations—may play a broader role in recruitment and direct electioneering. In more competitive areas and for higher visibility races, where candidate self-selection is the norm, adaptive brokerage parties would deliver resources to candidates—money, volunteers, newly registered voters—while the candidates themselves would be expected to deliver the votes. This view of parties as adaptive organizations was the view of the PTS researchers and seems to reflect the intuitions (and hopes) of many other party scholars (e.g., Gitelson, Conway, and Feigert 1984).

Essentially, the key unanswered research question is whether local parties are closer to the disintegrating model or the adaptive brokerage model. Democratic theory is not impartial with regard to these two possibilities, however. While adaptive brokerage parties may be less than perfect vehicles for the organization of political debate and the development of public policy, the most likely alternatives—electorally irrelevant parties—are wholly inadequate to the requirements of American politics. The need to better understand the evolving form and functions of local and other parties is more than a scholarly imperative; it is a practical necessity.

Notes

1. Key 1956; Cotter and Hennessy 1964; Huckshorn 1976; Conway 1983; Schlesinger 1985; Epstein 1986; Bibby 1986; Herrnson 1990; Paddock 1990; and Bibby 1990.

2. Both this research and the work on political machines is reviewed more extensively in Frendreis and Gitelson (1993) and Frendreis et al. (1993).

3. This difference in findings may be due to the time differences in the two studies, but by the 1980s, while party structure in the United States was not, strictly speaking, hierarchical, it was increasingly organizationally integrated.

4. For a fuller examination of this thesis, see Frendreis and Gitelson (1993) and Frendreis et al. (1993).

5. Copies of the complete questionnaires are available from the authors.

6. We are employing the earlier PTS data as a baseline because both data sets are based on surveys of the universe of county organizations, whereas the 1984 survey of county organizations by Gibson et al. (1989) oversampled major party organizations. Comparisons over time in this and other tables must be tentative, since such comparisons are between the 8 states surveyed in 1992 versus all 50 states surveyed by the PTS researchers. We note, however, that the 8 states surveyed in 1992 were selected in such a way as to be a representative grouping of states with regard to local party strength.

7. The results reported in this section are developed more fully in Frendreis et al. (1993).

8. Only 1 of the 25 Republican-Democratic differences is statistically significant (get-out-the-vote activities for congressional candidates)—exactly what would be expected by chance.

9

Sources of Activism in the 1992 Perot Campaign

Randall W. Partin
Lori M. Weber
Ronald B. Rapoport
Walter J. Stone

In the spring of 1992, H. Ross Perot moved from being an interested citizen-billionaire being interviewed on "Larry King Live" to a potential presidential candidate virtually overnight. There is no doubt that Perot benefited from having deep pockets, but without a cadre of volunteer activists committed to overcoming the barriers to an independent campaign (Rosenstone, Behr, and Lazarus 1984), he could not have succeeded in getting his name on the ballot in all 50 states, let alone garner a substantial portion of the popular vote in the November general election. In many respects, the mobilization of thousands of grass-roots activists in the spring and early summer of 1992 was the most remarkable feature of Perot's campaign. What caused these people to become active on behalf of H. Ross Perot during the 1992 campaign, and what are some of the possible consequences of that activism?

Sources of Third Party Activism

Explanations of political participation have long emphasized individual beliefs, attitudes, and resources (e.g., Verba and Nie 1972; Beck and Jennings 1982; Verba, Schlozman, Brady, and Nie 1993), although there is an equally long tradition emphasizing the importance of party mobilization (e.g., Katz and Eldersveld 1961; Crotty 1971; Kramer 1971; Beck 1974b). In their recent analysis of mobilization and political participation, Rosenstone and Hanson (1993) suggest that any complete explanation of participation must combine individual characteristics and resources with an understanding of mobilization effects. However, in the case of an independent candidacy like Ross Perot's in 1992, which individual attitudes and characteristics are likely to be important? How are mobilization effects likely to be manifested in a nonpartisan campaign?

In this chapter we present a preliminary analysis of the sources of activism in the Perot movement by examining three broad classes of potential explanation:

1. *Individual demographic characteristics typically associated with political participation, such as income, education, and age.* These are usually treated as politically relevant resources enabling individuals to bear the costs associated with political involvement. Similarly, they may help account for participation because they place individuals in social contexts where they are more likely to be induced by others to participate (Huckfeldt and Sprague 1992).

2. *Attitudes toward the candidates and parties.* Whether from a social-psychological or from rational-choice perspective, an individual's attitudes and preferences are relevant not only to vote choice, but to how involved they become in the campaigns. Exactly how these attitudes work in the context of a third-party campaign is not especially clear. However, Rosenstone, Behr, and Lazarus (1984) offer perhaps the most comprehensive theory of third-party support. They and others argue that roughly four groups of variables help account for support of third-party (and independent) candidates: perceived failures of the major parties, negative attitudes toward the major-party nominees, generalized alienation from the political system, and attraction to the independent candidate (cf Mazmanian 1974; Canfield 1984; Smallwood 1983; Carlson 1981; Gillespie 1993). For our purposes here, we reduce these factors to a simple "push-pull" model of Perot support based on attitudes toward the candidates and parties: potential activists are "pushed" away from the major-party campaigns by their disaffection from the two political parties and/or their nominees; simultaneously, they are "pulled" toward the Perot presidential bid by their attraction to him, either because of ideological considerations or based on positive general evaluations of him.[1]

3. *Mobilization effects.* In previous work on activism in contemporary presidential nomination campaigns, we have found that political mobilization from these contests tends to "carry over" to the general election (Stone, Atkeson, and Rapoport 1992). We have also found that this political mobilization "spills over" to activism in lower-level campaigns and perhaps even into party activity such as office holding, as well as interest-group activity (Rapoport, Stone, Partin, and McCann 1992). We argue that the highly visible nature of the contemporary nomination process draws people into campaign activity on behalf of nomination contenders. Once mobilized, they become ripe for involvement in other partisan contests.

We take these previous findings to be broadly consistent with the sorts of mobilization effects Rosenstone and Hanson (1993:174) discuss in describing the results of party appeals to potential activists. They suggest that such mobilization can affect perceptions of the stakes people have in political outcomes, and thereby encourage more involvement than otherwise would have occurred. These sorts of effects are easy to imagine at work in a party campaign where a formal apparatus exists to draw people into campaigns and other partisan arenas. Our research on nomination campaigns, however, leads us to ask whether similar kinds of mobilization effects may have been present in the Perot movement, deriving from either the major parties or interest groups activities. Indeed, the attitudes, habits, and skills learned in one electoral arena may transfer quite readily to another. Thus, we expect to find mobilization from parties and interest groups into the Perot movement.[2]

Data Sources

Our principal analysis is of a national sample of individuals who called the Perot toll-free telephone number during the spring and early summer of 1992. This is a sample of "potential" Perot supporters because merely calling the Perot phone bank did not necessarily constitute active support for Perot's candidacy. At the time we sampled from the data base in August of 1992, it contained the names of about 450,000 people who had called throughout the spring and early summer. We mailed questionnaires to a sample of 1901 just after Labor Day, and received usable responses from 1334 for a response rate of 70 percent. As it happened, Perot reentered the campaign on October 1, when all but a handful of questionnaires had been returned. Immediately following the 1992 election, we mailed a follow-up questionnaire to all respondents to the first wave. We received 944 responses to the post-election wave, for a response rate of 71 percent among respondents to the first wave, and just under 50 percent of the original sample.

During the early fall wave of the survey, we asked respondents about their activity levels for Perot prior to his dropping out of the race and for the candidates for the major party presidential nominations. We also asked about 1988 campaign activity levels in national, state, and local races. In addition, we included questions on attitudes toward and perceptions of the candidates as well as respondent demography. In the postelection wave, we asked about general election campaign involvement for Perot, Bush, and Clinton, and other subpresidential races. We repeated a range of attitudinal and perceptual items. Finally, in both waves we asked questions about involvement in a variety of political and nonpolitical organizations.

For purposes of describing our Perot sample, we make comparisons with the electorate by way of the National Election Study's (NES) 1992 Survey. Unfortunately, because Perot dropped out of the campaign in July, the NES asked very few questions about Ross Perot. Therefore, only limited comparisons with the national electorate are possible. We also compare the Perot activists with samples of 1992 activists drawn after the election from Iowa Democratic and Republican caucus attenders and Democratic attenders in Virginia.[3] These comparisons will allow us to define the contours of our sample of potential Perot activists by placing them in a context. In addition, we can get a preliminary feel for the viability of the broad explanations of Perot involvement by making these comparisons.

Who Were the Perot Activists?

As demonstrated in Table 9.1, our sample of potential Perot activists is relatively well off, highly educated, and white. In these ways it is different from the electorate as a whole, much as we would expect when comparing a relatively active population with the general public. Whereas only a quarter of the electorate falls into the greater than $50,000 annual income bracket, a plurality of the Perot sample (47.5 percent) is placed there. Similarly, only 23.5 percent of the national electorate achieved an education level of college graduate or postgraduate work while just under half of the Perot sample reached this level of educational attainment. With respect to age, the Perot

Table 9.1 Demographic Characteristics of the National Electorate, Potential Perot Volunteers, and Major Party Caucus Attenders in 1992

	National Electorate	Perot Activists	Caucus Attenders Democratic	Caucus Attenders Republican
Income				
Less Than $30,000	50.3%	25.2%	26.4%	33.8%
$30,000–$50,000	25.0%	27.3%	30.9%	32.2%
Greater Than $50,000	24.5%	47.5%	42.6%	34.1%
Education				
High School Grad or Less	51.9%	15.9%	19.8%	22.9%
Some College	24.6%	34.5%	21.2%	29.8%
College Grad or Postgraduate	23.5%	49.6%	58.9%	47.3%
Age				
Under 30	19.6%	8.5%	6.6%	8.1%
30–50	43.4%	42.1%	42.6%	38.3%
50–60	12.1%	18.3%	18.1%	19.2%
Over 60	24.9%	31.3%	32.7%	34.3%
Female	53.4%	37.9%	50.1%	40.6%
Nonwhite	15.3%	4.4%	5.9%	1.3%
N	2487	1334	764	385

Source: 1992 National Election Study; survey by authors.

sample is slightly older than the national electorate. Finally, our sample of potential Perot activists is remarkably unrepresentative of the national electorate when it comes to sex and race—only 38 percent of our sample is female (compared with 53.4 percent of the national electorate) and 4.4 percent of our sample is nonwhite (compared with 15.3 percent of the national electorate).

The first two of these demographic characteristics (income and education) are comparable to activists in general, while the last shows considerably smaller minority representation than among our sample of Democratic caucus attenders, but close to the typical percentages among Republicans. In sum, although our sample of potential Perot activists appears to differ from the national electorate with respect to demographics such as income, education, sex, and race, it seems to be comparable to major-party activists in these respects.

Table 9.2 presents the partisan affiliation and ideological self-placement of the Perot sample alongside that of the national electorate and those of our samples of Republican and Democratic caucus attenders. Not surprisingly, Perot activists are predominantly independent in their partisan attachments, with over 20 percent claiming strict independence and an additional 40 percent describing themselves as independents "leaning" toward one of the two major parties. In comparison, about 12 percent of the public and under 2 percent of caucus attenders are strict independents. Notice, too, that the potential Perot activist is slightly more Republican than Democratic; 23 percent identify with the former and 17 percent with the latter. In the electorate as a whole, Democrats held a 36 percent–25 percent advantage. Ideologically, the Perot sample is just right of center, with a bare plurality at the moderate position. The electorate as a whole is a bit more centrist, but also leans to the conservative side. On ideology, the Perot sample is far more representative of the public than party activists. As is typical of committed partisans, the Democratic caucus attenders were predominantly liberal, while Republican attenders were mostly conservative.

Table 9.3 presents activity levels for both the Perot and caucus attender samples in partisan campaigns in 1988 and in 1992 (comparable activity items are not available in the NES sample), as well as the percentages of each sample holding party office, and the degree of interest-group involvement. Overall, callers to Perot's toll-free telephone number were not political neophytes. With respect to the 1992 election year, our sample of potential Perot activists was remarkably involved in politics. Over 70 percent of the sample was active in some way for Ross Perot during the preconvention phase of the campaign.[4] Furthermore, over one-quarter of the sample participated in Democratic nomination campaigns, and just under 15 percent were active in the Republican nomination race. These rates of activity are about the same as those observed among party activists: fully 84 percent of the Perot

Table 9.2 Political Identification of the National Electorate, Potential Perot Volunteers, and Major Party Caucus Attenders in 1992

	National Electorate	Perot Sample	Caucus Attenders Democratic	Caucus Attenders Republican
Partisanship				
Strong Democrat	18.1%	7.3%	64.0%	0.0%
Democrat, not so strong	17.6%	9.6%	18.6%	0.3%
Independent, leaning Dem	14.4%	19.7%	13.0%	0.0%
Strict Independent	11.7%	21.1%	1.8%	1.5%
Independent, leaning Rep	12.4%	19.7%	1.5%	12.0%
Republican, not so strong	14.2%	13.0%	1.1%	22.2%
Strong Republican	11.2%	9.7%	0.0%	64.0%
Ideology				
Extremely liberal	2.7%	2.1%	8.3%	0.0%
Liberal	11.5%	16.3%	39.7%	1.5%
Slightly liberal	13.4%	13.4%	22.9%	2.9%
Middle of the road	31.4%	23.0%	17.0%	8.8%
Slightly conservative	20.3%	22.8%	7.9%	17.1%
Conservative	17.2%	22.9%	4.0%	56.9%
Extremely conservative	3.5%	4.6%	0.2%	12.7%
N	2487	1334	647	344

Source: 1992 National Election Study; survey by authors.

sample was active in a preconvention campaign for Perot or in one of the parties (not shown in Table 9.3). In comparison, 86 percent of the Democrats and 77 percent of the Republicans were active in their respective party's nomination campaigns, with only scattered activity for Perot among party activists.

In the general election stage of the 1992 campaign, activism for the eventual standard-bearer fell across the three columns in Table 9.3. Just over 60 percent of the Perot sample was active for the Perot-Stockdale ticket in the fall, while larger proportions of caucus attenders remained active after the convention for their respective nominees. Sub-presidential races were partisan and it is not surprising that the Perot sample shows lower rates of involvement than the party activists.

Even looking at party office, these Perot advocates show a significant level of involvement. About one in six either have held or are currently holding party office for one of the major parties (about half as great as the percentage for the party caucus participants). Finally, although the Perot sample was less

Sources of Activism in the 1992 Perot Campaign

Table 9.3 Political Activities among Perot Activists and Major Party Caucus Attenders in 1992

	Perot Activists	Caucus Attenders Democratic	Republican
Activism in early 1992			
Democratic nomination	28.5%	86.4%	4.7%
Republican nomination	14.9%	0.5%	77.1%
H. Ross Perot campaign	72.9%	4.5%	7.8%
General Election Activism, 1992			
Bush/Quayle	12.3%	2.3%	72.9%
Clinton/Gore	21.6%	75.9%	4.2%
Perot/Stockdale	62.0%	5.9%	5.7%
Republican House Race	9.1%	1.4%	42.2%
Democratic House Race	10.4%	25.9%	3.6%
Republican State/Local	10.5%	1.4%	43.8%
Democratic State/Local	13.0%	35.5%	2.1%
General Election Activism, 1988			
Bush/Quayle	22.8%	3.2%	68.2%
Dukakis/Bentsen	14.5%	55.0%	2.1%
Republican House Race	10.5%	0.9%	32.8%
Democratic House Race	10.5%	25.5%	1.0%
Republican State/Local	13.8%	0.5%	47.4%
Democratic State/Local	13.8%	34.5%	2.1%
Party Office-holding			
Democratic Office	10.2%	29.2%	1.0%
Republican Office	7.8%	0.3%	31.4%
Either Party Office	16.1%	29.3%	32.2%
Overall Levels of Group Activity			
Active in no groups	31.0%	28.8%	25.5%
Active in one group	24.9%	31.0%	31.9%
Active in two or more groups	44.1%	40.1%	42.6%

Source: Surveys by authors.

active in 1988 than partisan caucus participants, such is not the case when we turn to group activity. The percentage of our Perot sample that purports to be active in at least two groups (44.1 percent) is higher than the corresponding percentages from our sample of Democratic and Republican caucus attenders. As Table 9.3 shows, the potential Perot supporters' overall level of past group activity is almost precisely the same as for the two sets of caucus participants, if not higher.

Even this cursory examination of the history of political involvement among Perot respondents suggests possible links between the traditional parties, interest groups, and the Perot movement. These links may be consistent with a mobilization hypothesis: those drawn to activity by parties and groups may, as Rosenstone and Hanson (1993) suggest, become socialized to campaign activity and sensitized to their stake in electoral outcomes. In 1992, Ross Perot may have been able to tap into partisan and interest group quarters for his volunteer supporters, although it is clear that he mobilized a large cohort of newcomers to campaign activity as well.

Explaining Activism for Perot

Our strategy of sampling from Perot callers to identify activist volunteers in the 1992 Perot movement was successful. A substantial majority of our respondents were involved for Perot in some way, many quite extensively. At the same time, however, about 30 percent of the sample was not involved in the preconvention stage of the campaign, and almost 40 percent opted not to do anything for Perot after he redeclared in October. Indeed, only about 54 percent of our Perot respondents voted for the Dallas businessman. We thus have substantial variation *within* our sample of potential Perot volunteers. This variation allows us to explain activism on behalf of Perot by comparing those who became active with those who did not.

In searching for the sources of activism on behalf of Perot, we begin by drawing upon the three explanations outlined above: individual demographic characteristics, attitudes toward the parties and candidates, and mobilization effects of prior political activity. Despite the importance assigned to demographic factors in the literature, none of the social characteristics discussed above had any appreciable effect on activism for Perot (data not shown). Differences across age cohorts are small and inconsistent, both in the preconvention and fall stages of the campaign. Similarly, there are no consistent differences across the measures of education and income—although there does seem to be a small effect of income on pre-convention activity on behalf of Perot, with those with higher incomes being slightly more active. Gender and race likewise showed no significant differences. These sorts of characteristics therefore do not help explain activism *within a population predisposed toward activity for Perot*. We know from Table 9.1 that income, education, and sex differences between the Perot sample and the general population exist, but these differences do not help explain activism within the population of callers.

In addition to these measures of politically relevant resources, the "push-"pull" model of support leads us to consider a range of attitudinal and perceptual variables. Respondents attracted to Perot, or who perceived him as close to their own ideological preferences, should be more likely to become active on his behalf—hence the "pull" towards Perot. Table 9.4 presents the percent performing one or more activities on behalf of Perot during the early and late phase of the campaign by perceived proximity to Perot and by overall evaluation of Perot. In contrast to the demographic variables, these "pull" factors appear to have an effect. There is, for example, a monotonic effect of ideological proximity on activity. Likewise, overall affect toward Perot has an impact: those who gave positive evaluations were much more likely to be active for Perot in both phases of the campaign than were those who were neutral or negative. Finally, the percent of the popular vote the respondent expected Perot to win—a measure of the "electability" of Perot—is positively related to the level of activism on Perot's behalf. The relationship is positive and monotonic for both early and late Perot activity. This "electability" effect shows that respondents in our sample were susceptible to a "wasted vote" argument. As the expected success of Perot varied, the amount of activism on his behalf differed as well.

The "push" side of the explanation received a great deal of attention in 1992, and Perot himself played to this topic by being critical of the two parties and their candidates. Table 9.5 presents the effects of several evaluative measures of the two parties, of Bush and Clinton, and measures of long-standing affiliation with the major parties. As expected, the more negatively

Table 9.4 Evaluations of Ross Perot by Perot Activists

	Percent Active for Ross Perot	Percent Active for Perot/Stockdale
Proximity to Perot		
0 (closest)	84.1%	74.4%
1	79.4%	69.2%
2	65.2%	62.3%
3 (furthest)	58.8%	41.8%
Evaluations of Ross Perot		
Positive	86.2%	75.2%
Neutral	58.1%	46.6%
Negative	46.8%	36.8%
Predicted Vote for Perot		
31–100%	86.6%	85.4%
21–30%	77.0%	72.1%
11–20%	72.6%	65.3%
0–10%	65.0%	48.4%

Source: Survey by authors.

respondents viewed either party, the more likely they were to become active on behalf of Perot. Nearly 75 percent of the respondents who viewed either party or either nominee negatively were active on behalf of Ross Perot in the preconvention period, while somewhat lower percentages of those who were positive toward the major-party candidates and parties were active for Perot. The absolute percentages drop with respect to fall activity, but the monotonic relationship between evaluations of the parties and candidates and activity for Perot remains.

However, there is reason to suspect these findings do not adequately capture the "push" element in Perot activism. Respondents who affiliated with either major party may have viewed their own party/nominee favorably, and the opposite party/nominee negatively. This pattern could contribute to the relationships in Table 9.5 without really capturing a generalized discontent toward *both* parties. To check this, we present activity levels for respondents who viewed either both parties or both candidates negatively. These results remove the partisan effect and demonstrate a true "push" element. About 80 percent of the respondents who either viewed both parties or both nominees negatively were active for Perot in the preconvention period, and between 75 and 79 percent of the same respondents were active in the fall. On both these party and candidate indicators, activity levels were higher than in any of the categories of evaluation of the candidates or parties individually. This is added evidence in favor of the "push" effects.

Table 9.5 also shows that stronger partisans were less likely to become involved for Perot than weak partisans and strict independents. This is consistent with findings in other recent independent races (Converse, Miller, Rusk, and Wolfe 1969; Abramson, Aldrich, and Rohde 1994) and with the push-pull model because independence is associated with disaffection from the parties. Notice, too, that the drop-off in activity between the preconvention and fall phases of Perot's campaign is greatest among strong partisans (about 16 percent) and smallest among strict independents (7 percent). Independents may have been more susceptible to the "push" away from the major parties, whereas partisans were more likely to return to their party's nominee in the fall. Finally, as presented in Table 9.6, Republican identifiers as a whole were more likely to become involved in the Perot movement than Democrats. This is due to the significantly more negative attitudes Republicans had toward Bush than Democrats had toward Clinton.

In Table 9.6 we test the notion that past political activity stimulated involvement for Perot. This relationship is likely to be a good deal more complex than carryover effects from nomination to general election campaigns in the same party (Stone, Atkeson, and Rapoport 1992). Even nomination activists who supported a losing candidate are involved in a partisan contest that presumably unites all nomination activists in a common purpose. In the case of past partisan activity (which we have already seen is substantial), Perot activists must transfer their loyalties away from a party cause to an independ-

Table 9.5 Evaluations of the Major Parties and their Presidential Nominees by Perot Activists

	Percent Active for Ross Perot	Percent Active for Perot/Stockdale
Evaluations of the Republican Party		
Positive	55.4%	48.4%
Neutral	69.1%	61.7%
Negative	74.5%	62.9%
Evaluations of George Bush		
Positive	59.1%	54.0%
Neutral	68.6%	63.1%
Negative	75.0%	62.8%
Evaluations of the Democratic Party		
Positive	64.0%	35.9%
Neutral	70.7%	53.1%
Negative	73.4%	72.1%
Evaluations of Bill Clinton		
Positive	61.5%	38.3%
Neutral	73.0%	62.9%
Negative	74.2%	69.6%
Evaluations of both parties		
Negative	79.7%	75.7%
Evaluations of both nominees		
Negative	81.2%	79.2%
Strength of Party Identification		
Strong partisan	57.3%	40.9%
Weak partisan	68.6%	60.7%
Leaning independent	73.0%	64.6%
Strict independent	82.1%	75.1%
Partisanship		
Democrat	65.9%	49.4%
Republican	70.5%	66.2%

Source: Survey by authors.

ent candidate. This is clearly a less straightforward effect. As a result, it is not surprising that our results are inconsistent. While early activism for Perot increased as the level of presidential activity in 1988 increased, there is no relationship for later Perot activity in the fall stage of the campaign. This may reflect the difficulty of transferring to an independent candidate among those with past commitment to a partisan campaign. On the other hand, there is a clear and consistent effect of group activities on both early and late Perot support. Increases in past group activity (measured here as the number of groups a respondent was active in during the past year) appear to lead to increases in activism on behalf of Perot, both in the pre- and post-major party convention stages of the campaign.

In sum then, we find little support for the individual resources explanations for Perot activism. In contrast, the attitudinal explanations were supported by strong potential effects of an attraction or "pull" towards the Perot campaign and a similar "push" away from the major parties and their respective nominees. Finally, with regard to the mobilization explanations, we find weak evidence in support of a partisan mobilization effect, with those active in past partisan campaigns becoming active on behalf of Perot in the early stages of the campaign and no comparable effects on activism for Perot's general election bid. However, we find some suggestive support for mobilization from group activism, with those most active in groups also being more active on behalf of Ross Perot's presidential bid.

Table 9.6 Past Political and Group Activity by Perot Activists

	Percent Active for Ross Perot	Percent Active for Perot/Stockdale
General Election Activity, 1988		
0	68.0%	60.9%
1	68.8%	60.5%
2	74.6%	4.8%
Past Group Activities		
0	65.9%	51.5%
1	70.6%	63.0%
2	75.6%	69.6%
3	80.3%	68.9%

Source: Surveys by authors.

Multivariate Analysis

In order to capture adequately the impact of these possible explanations for activism on behalf of Ross Perot, we must estimate a multivariate model. By doing so, we will be able to control for some of the combined effect or spuriousness of these explanations. For example, the effect of past partisan activity on early Perot activity may be attenuated by strength of partisanship (already shown to affect Perot activism)—those with the strongest ties are less likely to support Perot by their actions. Not coincidentally, they are also those most active in past partisan campaigns (who are also less likely to become active for Perot). This analysis employs the same variables as above, including demographic characteristics, the "push-pull" attitudinal factors, partisan identification, expectation of Perot's vote, and levels of past participation.[5]

We present three parallel models predicting activism on behalf of Perot in both the early and late stages of the campaign. The first model predicts the degree of involvement in the early stage of the campaign. The second model predicts the degree of involvement in the general election stage of the campaign. Finally, we reestimate this second model including the possible mobilizing effects from the earlier stage of the campaign. The results of these analyses are presented in Table 9.7. Not surprisingly, given the absence of bivariate effects, the demographic variables have little impact on Perot activism, with sex falling just short of statistical significance in both models of general election activism.

The indices of negative ratings of the candidates and parties also do not quite reach statistical significance in explaining preconvention activity for Perot, but both are significant in the first general election equation (not controlling for mobilization earlier in the campaign). However, when controlling for mobilization in the early stage of the campaign, only the candidate index reaches the level of statistical significance, while the party index falls short. Strength of party identification has a reasonably strong (and highly significant) effect on preconvention involvement and general election involvement (from the first model), but just misses statistical significance in the fall once we controlled for preconvention mobilization.

Both evaluation and proximity to Perot (measuring a "pull" towards his campaign) affect participation in the spring and early summer, and in the general election stage. Once we control for the possible mobilization effects of preconvention Perot activism, both of these "pull" factors drop out of the model. This suggests that the effect of these variables on Perot activism in the fall was heavily mediated by activity in the spring-summer. That is, these attitudes generated activity for Perot in the preconvention period, but did not have an independent effect on involvement in the fall once spring activity is accounted for. Including preconvention activity in the fall equation fully taps

Table 9.7 Pre- and Post-Convention Activism for Perot: OLS Regression Analysis

	Pre-convention Activity	General Election Activity	General Election Activity
Demography			
Gender	0.089	0.208	0.156
Age	0.039	0.041	-0.013
Education	0.000	0.021	-0.041
"Push" Factors			
Negative ratings of candidates	0.081	0.105*	0.082*
Negative ratings of parties	0.060	0.104*	0.054
Strength of partisanship	0.159*	0.207*	0.081
"Pull" Factors			
Evaluation of Perot	0.431*	0.368*	0.120
Proximity of Perot	0.126*	0.096*	0.041
Participation Effects			
1988 campaign activity	0.113*	0.085	-0.019
Past group activity	0.090*	0.103*	0.039
Preconvention Perot activity	—	—	0.677*
Partisanship	0.120*	0.017*	0.055
Expected Perot vote	—	—	0.007*
Adjusted R^2	0.120	0.210	0.559
N	636	593	593

*Significant at the .05 level or better; figures are unstandardized regression coefficients.

any predisposition toward active support for Perot. Indeed, the same pattern is present for the participation variables. Both 1988 campaign activism and group involvement measures affect preconvention participation for Perot, past group activism affects general election activism for Perot (with no comparable effect of general election activism from 1988), and neither has an independent effect on general election activity once previous participation for Perot is taken into account.

Finally, there remains a tendency for Republicans to be more active for Perot than Democrats in the preconvention Perot campaign, even taking into account the other variables in the analysis. In addition, we can see that potential Perot activists were influenced by their perceptions of how well he would do in the fall campaign. Independent of the various affective measures, the more popular votes they thought he would receive, the more involved in his fall campaign they became. Candidate viability apparently affected potential activists' willingness to become involved in Perot's campaign.

Conclusion

Our research suggests mixed conclusions about the sources of active participation in the 1992 Perot movement. In the analysis of the Perot sample itself, we find very little effect of the usual demographic predictors of political participation. This does not mean the personal resources and other characteristics of Perot activists played no part in enabling their participation. We saw that the full Perot sample differed from the general population in quite predictable ways in income, education, and other measures. Since the population from which our Perot sample was drawn was self selected, these factors apparently had a greater impact on calling in to the Perot number in the first place than they did in differentiating among levels of activism among those who called.

We do find significant effects of our attitudinal measures and preliminary support for both the "push" and the "pull" sides of our model. The more attracted activists were to Perot, the more active they were, and the more repulsed they were by the major parties and their nominees, the more engaged in the Perot campaign they were. Perot attacked "politics as usual" and our evidence shows that he was successful in attracting a constituency of the discontented.

From the perspective of understanding the long-term consequences of the Perot movement for major party change, the participation effects we uncovered are perhaps most suggestive. We found support for the idea that past interest group and major-party involvement stimulated participation for Perot. This suggests that Perot activated volunteers who might have been available to the major parties had he not been on the scene. Of course, he also attracted substantial numbers of newcomers as well. Presidential campaigns are highly visible, permeable affairs that attract large numbers of activists who then remain involved and can change the face national politics. The Perot movement, while formally "nonpartisan" and antiparty, may ultimately have its greatest impact by affecting party politics in the years to come.

This may be the enduring legacy of the 1992 presidential election. Perot tapped massive discontent with politics as usual in the electorate. His supporters were energized in part because he was not part of the parties. At the same time, past involvement in the parties contributed to their willingness to volunteer in his campaign. Ties between the Perot and major-party campaigns suggest that the Perot movement in 1992 may stimulate party change by reorganizing party loyalties and perceptions and by drawing newcomers into the electoral process who may eventually move toward the parties. Perot's ability to hold the loyalties of his followers in 1992 will affect his political influence in the short term; the immense success his campaign had in identifying and mobilizing a constituency is likely to affect national politics in ways neither he nor anyone else can anticipate.

Notes

1. Elsewhere we have taken up the effects of more generalized alienation from the political system (Atkeson, McCann, Rapoport and Stone 1994). We have also considered the importance of "strategic" factors in explaining activism in a three-way race although that too deserves a more complete analysis than we can include here. The authors wish to acknowledge the Inter-University Consortium for Political and Social Research for access to the 1992 National Election Study.

2. Although we do not examine it here, we also expect to find mobilization from the Perot movement back into campaign activity for the major parties, particularly in the longer run.

3. We certainly do not argue that our caucus states somehow represent the entire nation, but we have found that cross-state variations within party samples are fairly small, especially on most of the indicators of interest in this paper (Abramowitz, McGlennon and Rapoport, 1983; Stone, Abramowitz, Rapoport 1989).

4. We asked the Perot sample about the following activities: collecting signatures for a ballot petition, attending meetings or rallies, trying to convince friends to vote for Perot, telephoning or door-to-door canvassing, organizing meetings or coffees, and holding a position in the campaign. Caucus attenders were asked a similar list, excluding collecting signatures. For purposes of Table 9.3, we count as active respondents those who have engaged in any of the activities.

5. The variable we employ is respondents' estimate of the popular vote Perot would receive in the fall election. We asked the question in our September-wave survey, when Perot was not a candidate. The variable, therefore, should be considered an imperfect estimate of respondents' perceptions of Perot's chances once he redeclared his candidacy in October. Interestingly, the aggregate mean estimates by the sample of each candidate's popular vote in November were almost exactly correct: Perot 18 percent, Bush 39 percent, and Clinton 49 percent.

PART THREE

Party Activities: A Closer Look

10

Women's Political Leadership and the State of the Parties

Barbara C. Burrell

What does the state of the parties have to do with women's political leadership in the United States? The women's movement has been one of the major social and political phenomena of the past quarter century. If the major parties were not to be marginalized, they would have to respond and adapt to feminism. But women have been vastly under-represented as activists, leaders, nominees, and elected officials within the Democratic and Republican parties. Even in 1992, women made up only 12 percent of all Democratic and Republican primary candidates for the U.S. House of Representatives and only 13.2 percent of all nonincumbent candidates.

Nevertheless, the parties have been affected by the revolution in women's roles in a number of ways. The difference in the voting behavior and attitudes of men and women in the 1980s, the so-called "gender gap," stimulated a party response. The Republicans were especially driven to action, as they appeared to be on the wrong side of these issues. Second, the increasing presence of women as party leaders is an element in the transformation of the parties. As I have stated elsewhere, women "may be leaders of organizations with little life or influence in the electoral process, or they may be catalysts in the revival of the parties" (Burrell 1993). Third, women's campaigns for public office have received much attention, culminating in the 1992 "Year of the American Woman in Politics."

All of these features of women's political participation—electoral, organizational, and candidacies—are related in their effect on the state of the parties. The gender gap has stimulated party efforts to recruit and promote women candidates and advance women in their organizations. The increased influence of women within the organizations has effected attitudes and party behavior toward women candidates. And partly as a result, increasing numbers of women have been major party nominees for national and statewide office.

This chapter outlines the development of these relationships in the contemporary party system. Major issues to be explored include the increased influence of women within the party organizations and the effect this change has had on the role of the parties in recruiting and supporting women candidates. Beyond description of these changes, there are theoretical questions concerning the importance of the state of the parties for those interested in women's political leadership. I conclude that strengthened political parties, particularly their organizational capacity, would be a positive force in women's pursuit of political leadership in the United States.

Women and Party Organizations

As suffrage appeared imminent, Carrie Chapman Catt, an earlier leader of the women's suffrage movement, urged women to target their political energies on the parties. "The only way to get things done is to get them done on the inside of a political party. . . . You will see the real thing in the center with the door locked tight. You will have a long hard fight before you get inside. . .but you must move right up to the center" (Chafe 1972:34). Although women achieved some sense of parity within the ranks of party activists early on, they did indeed have a long battle to gain influence.

Although contemporary feminists have often scorned the parties and party politics and have seen party organizations as something to be overcome, their activities suggest an acknowledgment of the importance of parties in the electoral process. The initial focus of the National Women's Political Caucus (NWPC) on gaining equality for women in the delegate selection process of the Democratic and Republican presidential nominations illustrates the significance of the parties to contemporary women's rights activists from their early years of organizing[1] (Shafer 1983; Baer and Bositis 1988). Since then the NWPC has established Democratic and Republican task forces to push for greater influence for women, to increase the number of women candidates each party nominates, and to promote women's issues within those organizations. In May 1976, for example, the two task forces held a joint press conference attacking the failure of both parties to achieve even the same number of women delegates they had in 1972 (Feit 1979). The Appointments and Elections Section of the 1976 Houston Women's Rights Convention adopted a plank which, among other things, called on the parties to "encourage and recruit women to run for office and adopt written plans to assure equal representation of women in all party activities, from the precinct to the national level, with special emphasis on equal representation on the delegations to all party conventions" (Bird 1977).

The parties thus have been targets of efforts by women activists during much of the contemporary era (Freeman 1988, 1989, 1993; Costain and Costain 1987). Within the organizations, staffers, professionals, strategists, managers, and even chairs and directors are more and more likely to be women (cf. Burrell 1994 for a more extended discussion of this "backstage revolution"). In 1988, Susan Estrich became the first woman to manage a presidential campaign when she took over the Dukakis race. Mary Matalin perhaps received the ultimate political insider compliment when in the 1992 presidential election she was referred to by the media as a "strategist" for the Bush campaign. Photos accompanying a *U.S. News and World Report* news story about the campaigns further illustrate the inroads women have made. The Bush campaign was represented by a picture of Mary Matalin in action and the Clinton camp was captured by a photo of Betsy Wright at her desk— and the story was not about women in politics (Baer 1992).

The issue of the presence and influence of women in party organizations has achieved such prominence that the presidential candidates were quizzed about it in the third debate of the 1992 election. Susan Rook asked the candidates, "I acknowledge that all of you have women and ethnic minorities working for you and working with you, but when we look at the circle of the key people closest to you—your inner circle of advisors—we see white men only. Why, and when will that change?" President Bush, in response, cited Margaret Tutwiler as a key person and then listed his cabinet appointees and his appointment record in general. Mr. Perot emphasized his history of hiring women in his business and the presence of his wife and "four beautiful daughters." Governor Clinton responded that he disagreed "that there are no women and minorities in important positions in my campaign. There are many." He went on to talk about his appointment record in Arkansas.

In 1993, women were chairs of eight Democratic and seven Republican state party organizations. They were also executive directors of 25 Democratic and eight Republican state parties. Two former female state party chairs serve in the 103rd Congress.[2] In its June/July 1993 issue, *Campaigns & Elections* highlighted "74 Women Who Are Changing American Politics." Twenty-nine of those women either currently or formerly held positions in party organizations.[3] Even though equality has yet to be achieved, a sea change has occurred within the parties regarding the role of women from a quarter of a century ago.

What accounts for this change? It is a confluence of factors. Women filled a vacuum as the parties became less central to the political lives of men. For example, Romney and Harrison describe the hiring of a group of women by the Republican National Committee in 1975: "there were about a dozen women who came in within six months or so of each other. There was no money and not much structure, and women were hired for jobs they might never have been offered if things had been more organized" (1987:182). Thus, party decline provided opportunities for women. And as the parties became more professional, different skills became more valuable. With college educations increasingly common among women, they are more likely to have these important skills—media expertise, computer skills, writing ability and especially public relations techniques. Feminists, too, played a role in promoting women within the parties. One prominent example has been Mary

Louise Smith, who became the first female chair of the Republican National Committee in 1974. She had been a founder of the National Women's Political Caucus-Iowa in 1973, and has continued to fight for women's rights within the party.

The Parties and Women Candidates

Both conventional wisdom and empirical data suggest party support for female candidates prior to 1980 was limited primarily to hopeless races. With the transformation of party leadership, party organizations are less of a barrier to women candidates. In addition, the structure of the electoral process also has changed leaving the parties with less control over nominations.

Past Efforts

Initial party efforts to increase the pool of women candidates and to assist their nominees consisted primarily of conferences, workshops, and a few targeted fundraising efforts. As early as 1974, the Democratic Party sponsored a "Campaign Conference for Democratic Women." Twelve hundred women attended and passed resolutions urging the party to do more to encourage women candidates. The conference occurred primarily because women in the party demanded it (Freeman 1987). Similar conferences did not happen within the Republican Party until nearly a decade later to offset the perceived negative effects of the gender gap in the 1980 election. Sessions geared toward the particular problems of female candidates became part of both parties' regional and national candidate training workshops during the 1980s.

Perhaps the most significant party effort prior to 1992 aimed at women candidates was Senator Richard Lugar's plan, in his capacity as chair of the Republican Senatorial Campaign Committee, to provide special funds for female Republican senatorial candidates in the 1984 election. He issued a press statement declaring: "a concerted drive by the Republican Party to stamp itself as the party of the woman elected official would serve our nation as well as it served our own political interests . . . The full political participation of women is a moral imperative for our society, and intelligent political goal for the Republican Party." Thus, he pledged to

> commit the RSCC to the maximum legal funding and support for any Republican woman who is nominated next year, regardless of how Democratic the state or apparently formidable the Democratic candidate. I am prepared to consider direct assistance to women candidates even prior to their nomination, a sharp departure from our usual policy (Lugar 1983).

The pledge to aid women in *primaries* was particularly significant. The parties traditionally do not get involved in primary elections because of the danger that the party-supported candidate might lose.

In 1988, for the first time, the national party platforms included statements endorsing "full and equal access of women and minorities to elective office and party endorsement" (Democrats) and "strong support for the efforts of women in seeking an equal role in government and [commitment] to the vigorous recruitment, training and campaign support for women candidates at all levels" (Republicans). These planks were symbolic statements and they were not substantive mandates to implement specific action. Their significance lies in the recognition of the problems women candidates face, and in the ability of influential party women to make that recognition explicit and public. However, no reference was made in either party's platform to women candidates in 1992. Indeed, conferences and workshops have become passé by the 1990s because women candidates have become more integrated into the parties.

The 1992 Election

The 1992 elections has been referred to as **the** "Year of the American Woman in Politics" after other years touted as such proved unworthy of the title. But Senator Bob Dole complained that it was the year of **Democratic** women in politics and that the media had been unfair to Republicans (Dole 1992). Yet, what made it a year of such prominence for women candidates was not a media bias against Republicans or for Democrats. It was the number of Democratic female nominees and the way in which they had obtained their party's nomination that attracted media attention. The Democratic women achieved media attention early on because they defeated establishment candidates, not because they were part of the establishment. They were viewed as outsiders and that is what made it a story for the press. In the past, Republicans had nominated women for national office, but they had not received the same type of publicity in part because they were "establishment" candidates. Had Republican Jane Doe defeated Senator Robert Dole in the primary, female Republican candidates would have received much more media exposure. In addition, significantly fewer Republican women sought their party's nomination in 1992. In the primaries, 121 female nonincumbent Democrats and 70 nonincumbent Republicans ran. Fifty-seven female Democrats competed in open seat primaries compared with 25 Republicans. Seventy Democrats and 36 Republicans won party nominations (including incumbents).

Democratic women became political stars by capturing the imagination of the country through their upset victories in party primaries. It began with Carol Moseley Braun's win over Senator Alan Dixon in Illinois and was enhanced by Lynn Yeakel's defeat of the Democratic lieutenant governor in Pennsylvania. The momentum continued when both Barbara Boxer and Dianne Feinstein won their senate primaries in California. Never before had two women simultaneously won their party's nomination for U.S. Senate from the same state.[4] Some feminists complained that had Feinstein been a man she would not have had primary opposition, that the party would have discouraged any opponents. But party organizations were basically irrelevant to the nomination of these women. Once women achieved so much success, however, and grabbed media attention, the party capitalized on it. This was especially well illustrated at the 1992 Democratic National Convention.

The Women's Caucus of the Democratic National Committee consists of women members of the DNC, accounting for approximately one-half of the national committee women in 1992. The Caucus played a prominent role in the convention with its daily "theme" meeting hosted by DNC Vice Chair Lynn Cutler. The first day focused on "Issues Moving Women in '92." The second day highlighted women candidates, an event cosponsored by the Women's Campaign Fund, EMILY's List, and the National Women's Political Caucus. On the third day abortion was discussed, and the final day featured "A Call to Arms." These daily sessions came to be seen as "the place to be"; among other things, both Bill and Hillary Clinton appeared at them. In addition, the caucus produced a booklet to help all candidates deal with gender issues, and each day included campaign training sessions for women candidates.

Thanks to Harriett Woods, president of the National Women's Political Caucus, the Democrats featured their women senatorial candidates on the opening night of their convention, dubbed "Ladies Night." Those who had already won nominations for the Senate were given the chance to speak on prime time to a national audience. This event won much applause for the party. Building on the splash women candidates had made in the primaries, the Democratic Senatorial Campaign Committee initiated the "Women's Council" in May of that year. This council was touted as the "only official party organization dedicated to recruiting and supporting women candidates" in its fact sheet. However, it was created too late to be active in recruiting efforts and did not get involved in primaries. It did raise $1.5 million which it allocated to ten Democratic women Senate nominees. In 1993, the Women's Campaign Council concentrated on expanding its female donor base and encouraging persons in that base to become more visible and involved in the party.

A much different situation existed for the Republicans in 1992. Although the Republican Party has historically received some praise for promoting women within the organization and as candidates (Freeman 1989), it has been criticized for holding seeming "antiwoman" public policy stands. Beginning in 1976, the Republican Party started to back away from its traditional support for the Equal Rights Amendment and began to take anti-abortion stances in its platform. In 1980, the process was completed and has remained ever since. Thus, moderate women (and men) in the party have found themselves in battle with the party leadership. Energy devoted to overturning these planks has taken away from efforts to encourage and support women candidates. The primary activity of the Republican Task Force of the National Women's Political Caucus in 1992, for example, was an attempt to modify the Republican platform's anti-abortion plank.

Indeed, it is widely felt that many potentially good female Republican candidates have not run because of the party's opposition to abortion rights and the difficulty of winning primaries against the right-wing of the party. Those who have run and won have expressed dismay at the party for not championing them more (Schwartz 1992). This was especially notable at the 1992 Republican National Convention when GOP women candidates were not showcased as their counterparts had been at the Democratic Convention. Instead they chose to spotlight women in the administration and, of course, in a controversial speech, Vice President Dan Quayle's wife Marilyn delivered a keynote address stressing women's traditional roles. Barbara Bush also gave a prime-time talk focusing on her family. The problem for the Republicans was how to advance a more public role for women while at the same time advocating a conservative political philosophy.

This is not to say that the Republican Party has become entirely antifeminist. At their 1992 convention, former Representative and Secretary of Labor Lynn Martin (who is pro-choice) nominated George Bush, while Kay Bailey Hutchinson was elected to the senate from Texas and Christine Todd Whitman as governor in New Jersey in 1993. Also, groups within the party are working on behalf of women candidates, including the WISH List, which held training sessions for female candidates in 1993, RENEW (Republican Network to Elect Women), and the National Federation of Republican Women. Jeanie Austen, Vice Chair of the Republican National Committee is bringing this group together. Of no little consequence, a majority of GOP female candidates for high office in 1992 were pro-choice.[5]

Women's Political Leadership and Renewed Party Organizations

The women's movement of the second half of the twentieth century has profoundly altered American political and social life. Women's rights activists have adopted insider strategies to affect change in the party system. Making the parties more "women-friendly" has been one of those strategies. In response, the parties have acted to increase the presence of women in leadership positions. But American parties have been in a weak position to substantially affect the number of women in elective office. One weakness has been the single-member district structure of the electoral process:

Generally the party list/proportional representation (PL/PR) system results in higher women's parliamentary representation than does the single member district system. . . . The single member district electoral system is a major cause of women's low representation in the U.S. House of Representatives and in the state legislatures (Rule and Norris 1992:44).

Another weakness is the inability of American parties to control nominations. As part of the Progressive Movement at the turn of the century, and later the opening-up of the system in the early 1970s, primary elections have become the means by which candidates are chosen to run under the party's label. Unlike other countries where the parties operate as private organizations, selecting their nominees and presenting them to the voters, American party nominees are chosen by voters. Thus, from a party organization perspective, the recruitment of different types of candidates is restricted.

This "fact of life" presents two possibilities. On the one hand, the entrepreneurial system allows individuals and groups historically shut out the opportunity to run. To be sure, much of the openness of the nomination system is a direct credit to the women's movement in the 1960s and 1970s. Candidates such as Lynn Yeakel, Carol Moseley Braun, and Dianne Feinstein need not seek the blessing of party organization officials—historically men—to launch their campaigns. Women might be hesitant to return to the smoke-filled rooms now that a bit of fresh air has been let in.

But on the other hand, the current system allows individuals to flood campaigns with personal funds and beat someone who may have labored within the party and developed responsible positions. Or it allows an extremely committed group, not necessarily representative of the majority of party adherents, to overwhelm the party structure in a primary election. Even if the parties encourage women to seek the nomination in winnable seats, there is no guarantee that they will get the nomination. Party organizations rarely get involved in primary elections, although they can, and do in some areas, operate under a system of preprimary endorsements. But these endorsements can be a negative asset; outsiders often use them to suggest the process is undemocratic. Thus, the idea that the parties can make greater efforts to run more women candidates rings hollow. In a sense, the success of early feminist activities—the opening up of the system—may now serve as golden handcuffs.

What role is left for the parties to increase the number of women in party affairs and elected office? We have seen that the organizational capacity of the party has increased over the last decade. Party units now represent the largest single source of contributions to congressional elections. As suggested in other chapters in this volume (chapters 11 and 12), there is considerable variance as to which candidates are slated for assistance—the foremost criteria being the closeness of the race. Yet, if the parties wish to develop a competitive edge in the long run, and if they take the gender gap seriously, they should broaden their targeting criteria to heighten the importance of female candidates. Moreover, if Paul Herrnson (1986, 1988) is correct that party organizations have become "brokerage" units, they can narrow the historic distance between large, nonparty contributors (PACs and fat cats) and women candidates. It would also be to the advantage of the parties to encourage *local* party organizations to support women candidates. They might draw up lists of potential candidates, aid their election efforts, and ultimately use these groups as "farm clubs" for higher level runs. After all, most of the successful women in congressional and senatorial elections in 1992 had considerable experience in governing and running for local office. Ultimately, the success of women in party politics will be judged by the number of female candidates the parties help get elected.

In recent times, women have become more prominent and skillful within the parties—both as insiders and as candidates. If parties continue to advance the cause of women it is likely they will remain viable instrument in the electoral process. If parties are primarily concerned with winning elections, this new direction simply makes good sense.

Notes

1. Anne and Douglas Costain have argued that the women's movement did not focus on the parties as a means to political power until the 1980s. They may have underestimated the extent to which transforming the parties was a tactic undertaken by elements of the women's rights community earlier (1987).

2. Nancy Pelosi, (D-Ca.) and Jennifer Dunn (R-Wa.)

3. Many of the others had strong ties to one of the major parties including such individuals as Hillary Clinton and Tipper Gore.

4. Of course it is an unusual set of circumstances when two senate seats in one state are open at the same time.

5. In 1993, 50 percent of the female Republican members of the U.S. House of Representatives voted to repeal the Hyde Amendment which prohibits federal financing of abortions, compared with only 4 percent of male Republicans.

11

Party Strategy and Political Reality: The Distribution of Congressional Campaign Committee Resources

Diana Dwyre

For the last two decades, the congressional campaign committees (CCCs) have provided the bulk of major party support to candidates for the United States House of Representatives. Yet, we know little about how these party units have spent their money over time. Previous studies have examined only one election cycle at a time and have only looked at CCCs' disbursements together with those from other national party committees (Herrnson 1989, 1992; Jacobson 1980; 1985–86; 1993). This gap has not gone unnoticed. Barbara Sinclair suggests that "Comprehensive studies of the growth in size, function, and technological sophistication of the [congressional campaign] committees and of their changing patters of giving are still lacking . . . Certainly the committees deserve more attention . . ." (1990:128). Biersack and Wilcox point out that "no effort at longitudinal analysis has been attempted [to gauge] the critical role of party resources in effecting a rational and efficient allocation of financial support" (1990:225).

This chapter examines ten years of CCC allocations to House candidates during the five election cycles in the 1980s. Federal Election Commission (FEC) campaign finance data are used,[1] as well as interviews with congressional campaign committee directors and staff. Findings suggest a seat maximization strategy generally guides resource distribution, but that there is some slippage, much of which can be explained by party status, availability of resources, and regulatory restrictions.

The Congressional Campaign Committees and Party Goals

The congressional campaign committees, also known as "the hill committees," are *the* party force in contemporary congressional elections (see chapter 6).[2] In 1988, the two hill committees—the Democratic Congressional Campaign Committee (DCCC) and the National Republican Congressional Committee (NRCC)—accounted for some 91 percent of party spending in House and Senate races (Sorauf and Wilson 1990:190). Although the House CCCs do not contribute to every congressional campaign, they assist most House candidates in some way. For example, in 1988 the Democratic Congressional Campaign Committee made cash contributions and/or coordinated expenditures[3] to 83 percent of the party's general election candidates, and the National Republican Congressional Committee gave to 84 percent of their House candidates.

For nonincumbents in close races—candidates for which party assistance can make the most difference—the proportion of funds from the party can be considerable, possibly turning an otherwise hopeless bid into a strong challenge. Herrnson reports that in 1988 "party money accounted for almost 14 percent of the general election funds spent by, or on behalf of, Republican non-incumbent candidates for the House" (1992:61). Party support is also thought to be more valuable than other money: it is often given as "seed money" early in a campaign and in-kind services are sometimes worth more than their reported value.[4] The role of the congressional campaign committees is thus significant beyond the actual contributions made to House candidates.

But do the national parties' CCCs distribute their resources in a rational manner? Have spending patters changed over time? In order to answer these questions it is necessary to first understand party goals. American political parties are wholly motivated neither by ideological or policy goals nor by electoral success. Rather, a division of labor among party units exists whereby different segments of the party are *primarily* responsible for each of these goals.

As the in-government structure, a party's caucus (or conference, as the Republicans call it) is primarily responsible for policy development. Yet it is also concerned with electoral success in order to affect the policy process. As an electoral organization, a congressional campaign committee is responsible for electing members to government. This is not to suggest the hill committees are incapable of promoting the party's policy objectives, simply that they will do so only if it does not interfere with the goal of winning elections. It is not surprising that scholars have found little evidence that these organizations follow a loyalty maximizing strategy when distributing resources (see, for example, Porter 1993; Wilhite and Theilmann 1989).

A more subtle method of party influence may, however, be at work. Kayden and Mahe (1985:187) maintain that the issue-oriented assistance the parties provide candidates (party-line issue papers, advice, research, and so forth) contributes to a higher level of cohesion among partisans in Congress. Jacobson has also noted that "some credit for Republican unity clearly belongs to the national party's electoral work. Party committees had of course assisted many of the new [1980] Republican members with campaign money and services and so established some degree of obligation" (1985:166; see also Leyden and Borrelli 1990). Indeed, party cohesion in the House increased during the 1980s, along with the activities of the congressional campaign committees. But it is these more subtle influences rather than any concerted attempt by the committees to induce party loyalty that may have contributed to the increase in party unity.

Winning may not be everything, but it is the overriding concern of the congressional campaign committees in allocating resources. As past DCCC chair Beryl Anthony noted: "There is ultimately one way to judge the success of the DCCC: does it win races?" (The Washington Post 1989)

An Efficient Distribution of Party Resources

An efficient distribution of resources requires that a CCC distribute its funds to candidates in accordance with their likelihood of getting elected. Overall, the return on investments will *generally* be greatest for open seat candidates, followed by challengers and then incumbents. Candidates of any type in close races clearly offer a greater potential return for the party than sure winners or sure losers.

Open seat candidates represent the best chance for a party to *gain* a House seat. As former NRCC Director Tom Cole explained, "Clearly an open seat situation is a seat you're going to look harder at. . . you may actually do more in an open seat than a Republican seat now held by a Democrat, because he's got the advantage of incumbency."[5] Indeed, both parties invest heavily in most open seat races—particularly the NRCC in an effort to win more seats and move closer to majority status.

Challenger races pose a variety of possibilities. A challenger in a close race might receive a large marginal gain from an added dollar spent while a challenger with little chance of defeating a strong incumbent might gain substantially with the first dollars spent, because of increased name recognition, but quickly reach a point of diminishing returns. Other challengers might be able to achieve their highest level of gain once into the campaign if political circumstances change in their favor and they have the resources to take advantage of them (Jacobson 1985–1986; 1993:132–135).

Incumbents are generally less needful, for they enjoy a tremendous fundraising advantage over challengers as well as the perks of office such as franked mail and travel allowances.[6] First term incumbents, however, are more vulnerable to a strong challenge than more senior members. Jacobson suggests that in 1982 "Democrats were especially likely to challenge Republicans first elected in 1980 and thus thought to have comparatively precarious holds on their districts" (1985–86:615). In 1986, 34 percent of all newly elected House members (16 of the 48) won with over 60 percent of the general election vote, while 86 percent of all other incumbents won by that margin.[7] Freshman incumbents are simply less safe than other incumbents, and the CCCs should give more to these members.

There are, however, less direct ways that a hill committee might pursue its goal of winning elections. Both the NRCC and the DCCC contribute to incumbents who eventually win by large margins, a strategy that has been characterized as a waste of party money (Jacobson 1993:118). They justify these allocations as a means to insure that seemingly safe incumbents avoid serious challenges in the first place. They are investments that help the party *retain* House seats. The Democratic organization may be more inclined to support seemingly safe incumbents in order to protect its majority status, particularly in years when incumbents are thought to be vulnerable. Genie Norris, DCCC Executive Director, explains:

> The main focus is to have as many Democrats in Congress as there are, and the first place you start is making sure the people that are there stay there . . . The electorate is very volatile . . . nobody's entirely safe . . . So, we don't look at somebody who won big the last time and say we don't commit any attention to them, because every race is different and every year is different.[8]

The Republicans protect their incumbents by giving each an in-kind donation—"the equivalent of $5000 in a two year cycle that can be used for services, communications programs, satellite feeds, studio time, and things of that nature." It is used to "help the person avoid a race in the first place."[9] Party decision-makers themselves do not think that spending on incumbents, even on some who appear electorally safe, is an inefficient use of party resources.

Often, "four-year plans" are implemented. That is, both CCCs invest in challengers with little chance of winning, believing that support in the current election will provide increased name recognition and enhance the candidate's viability the next time around. What looks to be an inefficient use of party money in one election may actually serve the party's seat maximization goal in the next. Given the dearth of experienced Republican challengers, especially in the South (Jacobson 1990:63-65), the Republican organization may be particularly inclined to use this strategy.

Other concerns that might deter a party from funding only candidates in close races include attempts to elect more women and minorities. While both CCCs report that they do not consider gender or race in the distribution of resources, both have made efforts to *recruit* women and minority candidates— an activity that requires some expenditure of party funds. Such efforts, while seemingly less efficient, may well attract voters in the long-run.

Constraints on the Efficient Distribution of Party Resources

While seat maximization—in its various forms—guides congressional committee activity, there are several constraints. Some of these pressures are less difficult to overcome, but all potentially limit a party's resource distribution efficiency.

Federal Election Campaign Act

A significant constraint on the distribution of party resources is the Federal Election Campaign Act (FECA). Political parties can give House candidates $10,000 in cash and in-kind contributions; $5,000 for the primary and $5,000 for the general election. They are also allowed to make coordinated expenditures on behalf of candidates. These limits are not only higher than those for direct contributions, they are adjusted for inflation, so that the limit for House campaigns (originally $10,000) had reached $27,620 by 1992. On top of that, a state party, which often does not have the funds to take advantage of coordinated spending on behalf of federal candidates, may pass its limit on to the national party committees through an "agency agreement," effectively doubling the congressional campaign committee's spending limit.[10] In 1992, a CCC could potentially contribute $65,240 to a House candidate: $10,000 in contributions plus $55,240 in coordinated expenditures (the CCC's limit plus a state party's limit passed on with an agency agreement).

Although these exemptions in FEC regulations allow parties to have higher spending limits than PACs and individuals, they often pose a serious obstacle to allocating party funds in a fully efficient manner: "Once the limits are reached, party committees can do no more for a candidate, even if the election is close and more money might make a difference. Hence the law restricts a party's ability to pursue its collective electoral goal of winning the largest possible share of seats" (Jacobson 1985-86:611). The Republicans are affected more by the spending limits due to their relative wealth. This may be why the Democrats, by 1990, had nearly caught up to the Republicans in the *amount* they spent on cash contributions and coordinated expenditures despite fewer overall resources.[11]

Information

The hill committees need accurate information in order to determine which races to fund. They rely on a variety of sources that do not always prove to be accurate. Each CCC generally determines whether or not it is important to defend incumbents or to be more offensive, to place special emphasis on open seats, or to groom candidates for future elections. But a miscalculation of these factors could lead to a misallocation of party funds. They must also remain flexible in order to take advantage of changing conditions late in the campaign season. Neither party took advantage of a strong anti-incumbent sentiment that reached a high point late in the 1990 campaign because possible challengers had made their final decisions to run long before the fall and the hill committees had determined their spending priorities much earlier (Jacobson 1993). Indeed, both CCCs have, in the past, finalized their lists of targeted races by April.

The campaign committees conduct surveys and focus groups, encourage candidates to do their own polls, and closely watch local newspapers in order to track the progress of candidates. Both committees maintain in-house polling experts and are able to provide this service at cut-rate prices, or they contract it out in bulk orders. The Republicans, because of their greater resources, are able to do more tracking surveys than the Democrats and may have a statistical edge in directing campaign funds where most needed. The CCCs also use field staff who report on the situation in districts, the quality of candidates and their challengers, their financial capabilities, the local political climate, and so forth. Field staff personnel are seasoned political operatives with extensive experience. Clearly, information from any of these sources is potentially inaccurate and may therefore limit a party committee's ability to use its resources most efficiently.

Incumbent Pressures

Because the hill committees are creatures of the legislative parties and are controlled by members of the party caucuses, there may be significant pressures to use resources simply for reelection. Giving resources to incumbents who generally do not need additional campaign funds leaves less money for challengers and open seat candidates. Yet, as discussed earlier, both parties' CCCs allocate funds to some incumbents who end up winning by large margins in order to help avoid a serious challenge in the first place. It is difficult to determine if an incumbent is vulnerable to a challenge and even harder to determine if party resources helped avoid such a challenge.

When asked whether incumbents influence funding decisions, former DCCC Executive Director Les Francis said, "Sure, . . . we'll have to do some of that . . . if it's an incumbent who has helped us raise a lot of money, or it's particularly critical to the leadership . . . you do it."[12] In their study of 1980 and 1982 congressional campaign committee allocations, Wilhite and Theilmann found that those incumbents who served on the NRCC received larger contributions than those Republican candidates who did not (1989:16, 18). Such allocations may serve other party goals, but they do little to help the party maximize seats.

Candidate Quality

Sometimes there are not enough high quality candidates for a party to support. The lack of quality candidates to challenge the Democratic majority in the House has indeed been a serious limitation on the Republican party's ability to pursue sound resource distribution strategies. It does not matter how much money the Republicans have; without good candidates and in the context of FECA limitations, they will not present a serious challenge to the Democrats' control of the house.

A Longitudinal View of Resource Distribution

Have the CCCs allocated their resources in a manner consistent with the goal of winning as many House seats as possible? Have their spending patterns changed over time? Figure 11.1 shows the average total CCC allocation (contributions plus coordinated expenditures) by competitiveness of races and candidate status for House elections from 1980 to 1988. The figures are adjusted for inflation in 1984 dollars. Competitive candidates are those who received between 40 and 60 percent of the general election vote. Of course, the actual general election vote does not represent the information available to the CCCs when they made their allocation decisions. Polling data and other information the parties use is not public information and it is closely guarded by the parties, candidates, and polling consultants even after the election.[13] As these figures indicate, the hill committees have done a fairly good job of ascertaining the closeness of races.

The most obvious party difference is the disparity in wealth between the two party committees. The NRCC was able to give much larger average contributions to its candidates than was the DCCC, and the greater resources controlled by the NRCC enabled it to distribute those resources more efficiently than its Democratic counterpart (Sorauf 1988:140). Although each party committee started out the 1980s barely distinguishing between different types of competitive candidates, the NRCC quickly moved to giving more to close nonincumbents and decreasing its allocations to marginal incumbents. This is again consistent with the Republicans' need to gain seats. The Democrats gave more to incumbents in close races than to other marginal candidates until 1984, when they began to distribute resources more strategically under Tony Coelho's leadership.

The figure also clearly shows that both the DCCC and the NRCC increasingly gave larger average contributions to competitive candidates than to noncompetitive candidates. The growing gap over time between average contributions to competitive candidates and those to noncompetitive candidates suggests that both committees have become more focused on the

Figure 11.1 Average CCC Allocations by Competitiveness of Race and Candidate Status, 1980-1988

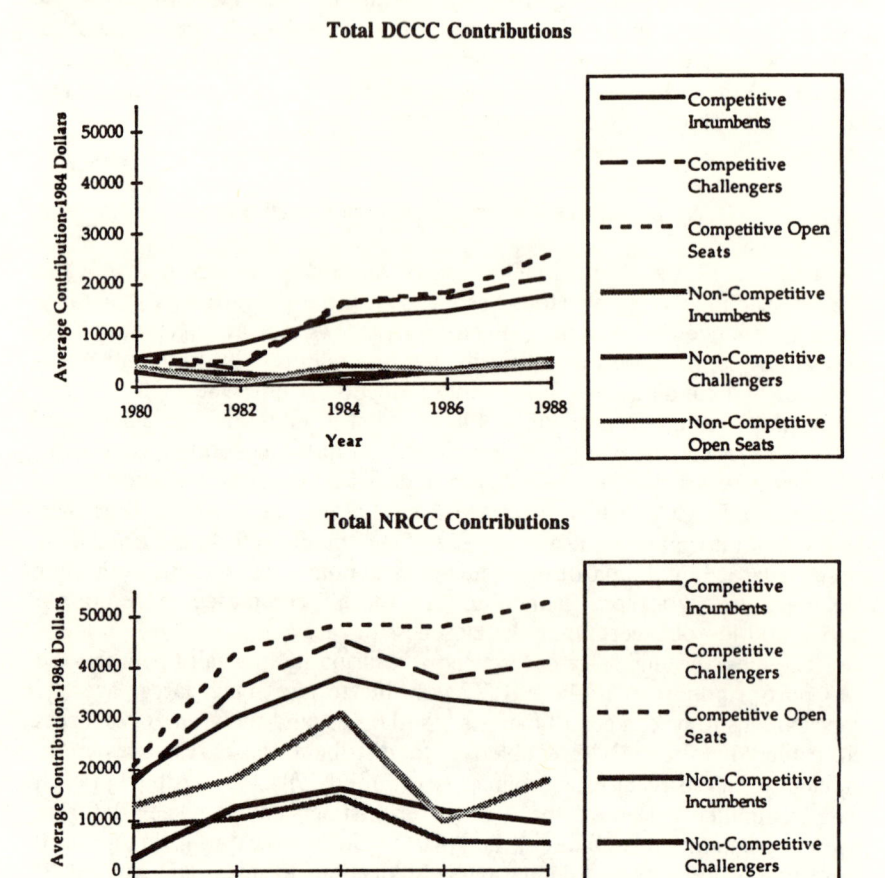

Total DCCC Contributions

Total NRCC Contributions

Note: All figures adjusted for inflation in 1984 dollars. "Total Contributions" includes both direct contributions and coordinated expenditures made by the party committees. A competitive candidate is one who received between 40 and 60 percent of the general election vote.
Source: Federal Election Commission.

seat maximization goal. This trend is more pronounced for the DCCC, anexpected development since the Democrats needed the most improvement in this area. Indeed, this improvement in their efficiency is most evident after 1982, precisely when newly-elected DCCC chairman Tony Coelho broke with the past tradition of supporting every Democratic candidate regardless of need and "decided to ignore those Democrats with 'safe' seats and concentrate resources on close races" (Easterbrook 1986:32; Jackson 1988:231, 289-91).

Other trends and patterns become clear with a longitudinal view. The NRCC after 1980 and the DCCC after 1982 gave smaller average contributions to competitive incumbents than to other competitive candidates, indicating each party's improved ability to deny its safe incumbents funds for the benefit of the more needy competitive challengers and open seat candidates. This kind of strategy—concentrating resources on close races, and denying contributions to incumbents who can more easily raise campaign funds from PACs and individuals—helps parties win *more* seats. Thus, as expected, a pattern of giving to challengers is more pronounced for the Republicans, because they must *gain* seats to achieve majority status in the House.

There are a few other party differences. The Democratic committee increased its allocations to competitive challengers each year after 1982, perhaps because the DCCC had more money to allocate. However, there was a decline in average NRCC allocations to competitive challengers after 1984, not only because the Republicans were unable to find high quality challengers, but because their net receipts decreased substantially after 1984—going from a high point of $59,270,741 in 1984, to $37,639,975 in 1986, and dropping to $28,377,978 in 1988 constant dollars (Federal Election Commission 1980-1988).

A Closer Look: The Distribution of CCC Resources in 1986

In order to assess the efficiency of allocations, I have developed a hypothetical distribution of resources for the 1986 election given FECA contribution limits and each party's level of resources.[14] This hypothetical distribution of party resources accounts for the number of candidates running in each category and thus offers a good test for the actual distribution of party resources. Tables 11.1 and 11.2 show this hypothetical distribution against the actual distribution.[15] The tables list the types of candidates in the descending order of funding priority. The hypothetical distribution in the next column follows this order and takes into account the FECA and resource constraints faced by the parties. The data is also disaggregated to separate first-term incumbents from more senior incumbents.

It was a midterm election year in 1986, when the party controlling the White House (the Republicans in this case) traditionally loses seats, and in fact, the Democrats won back control of the Senate. Much of the country was deep in recession, particularly farming and textile states. The stage was set for the Democrats to make substantial gains in the House. An efficient strategy called for DCCC investment in competitive challengers and open seat candidates, since incumbents had little to worry about in an off-year election with a sluggish economy easily blamed on the Republican administration.

However, Table 11.1 shows that the DCCC did not follow this strategy. For example, they gave higher average contributions to the two competitive freshman incumbents running in 1986 than to Democratic challengers and open seat candidates in close races, a strategy that may have contributed to the party's unimpressive showing (a gain of only five seats). In their study of the 1986 congressional elections, Jacobson and Kernell found that national issues proved helpful to challengers with enough resources to take advantage of them (1990:84-85). The DCCC seems to have missed some opportunities.

Perhaps the Democrats' comfortable majority in the House motivated the party to hold on to recent gains rather than to make new ones. Indeed, after the election, DCCC Chair Tony Coelho said that since the Democrats had lost only 14 seats in Reagan's 1984 landslide election the party did not have to make up for much lost ground: "We can't win back seats we didn't lose" (Watson 1986:2842). It appears that the Democrats were satisfied with the size of their majority. Note, for example, the DCCC's relatively higher average contributions to noncompetitive first-termers than to other noncompetitive candidates, reflecting the party's emphasis on seat protection.

Incumbent pressures may have contributed significantly to their lack of efficiency in the distribution of its campaign resources, but the DCCC's almost blind emphasis on seat protection (particularly newly won seats) can explain much of the inefficiency. The DCCC got half of the equation right: it gave more to competitive than noncompetitive candidates, but it followed the party's general inclination to protect incumbents just when the opportunity to win *more* seats should have motivated the committee to direct resources elsewhere. In at least one case the DCCC's support of a challenger paid off. Mississippi's Mike Espy received the largest DCCC allocation in 1986 ($52,641 in contributions and coordinated expenditures), and he became the first black House member from Mississippi since Republican John Lynch left the House in 1883.

As Tables 11.1 and 11.2 show, the Democrats also suffered from a lack of resources in 1986. The NRCC gave in excess of two and one-half times more to its competitive challengers than the Democrats allocated to challengers in close races. Competitive Republican incumbents received almost twice as much from their organization. The NRCC's generous support of its competitive candidates no doubt helped the party keep its losses to a minimum, as did the less-than-strategic allocation practices of the DCCC.

Although NRCC receipts fell in 1986 and the committee had less money to contribute to candidates, it was able to provide generous sums to competitive Republican candidates: the NRCC exceeded the regular maximum limit of $31,810 for virtually all of its competitive candidates and therefore must have made agency agreements with state parties for them.[16] The fact that the NRCC found it necessary to increase its spending limits through agency agreements with state parties illustrates the constraint that the FECA contribution limits impose on the CCC's ability to efficiently distribute its resources.

Conclusion

The results of this analysis indicate that both parties' CCCs are highly motivated by winning. Both improved the efficiency of their distribution decisions over time, a finding about which previous studies of single election years could only speculate. The most important factor in the distribution of party resources for both party committees, but especially for the NRCC, was found to be competitiveness. Both the NRCC and the DCCC gave larger average allocations to competitive than to noncompetitive candidates. However, each committee faced different constraints. The DCCC was and still is limited by its lack of resources. As a result, its allocations were not only small, but the overall distribution was not especially efficient. Furthermore, the DCCC's lack of resources to spend on gauging the competitiveness of races, conducting opposition research, and supporting field staff personnel meant decisions were less grounded in accurate information and allocations more apt to be poorly targeted.

The NRCC's relative wealth actually deterred the committee from distributing its resources as efficiently as possible: FECA contribution limits forced the Republican Committee to direct funds away from the most competitive candidates once limits were reached. The FECA contribution limits compelled the NRCC to make special arrangements with state parties (i.e., agency agreements) in order to spend more on the most competitive candidates. The limits also forced the Republicans to allocate generous sums to candidates who either did not need the funds (i.e., safe incumbents) or had no chance of winning.

Each party's status in the House also affected the way it distributed resources. For instance, the Democrats place great emphasis on seat protection in order to *maintain* their majority status. They tend to automatically direct funds to incumbents, particularly to the more vulnerable freshmen. Previous studies have characterized such allocations as inefficient, but such a strategy is not always so. For example, when the political tide is flowing against a party it is quite rational for it to protect its incumbents.

Table 11.1 Hypothetical and Actual Distribution of DCCC Resources to US House Candidates, 1986

	% of Total Candidates Running (n)	An Efficient Distribution of Party Resources (Hypothetical) $	% of Total	Mean Allocation (Hypothetical) $	Actual Distribution of Party Resources $	% of Total	Mean Allocation (n) $
Competitive Open Seat Cand.	6.1 (26)	827,060a	39.7	31,810	484,679	23.3	19,387 (25)
Competitive Challengers	8.9 (38)	763,440b	36.7	20,091b	695,528	33.4	18,303 (38)
Competitive Freshman Incum.	0.5 (2)	47,715c	2.3	23,857c	63,496	3.0	31,748 (2)
Competitive Other Incum.	5.9 (25)	397,625d	19.1	15,905	259,877	12.5	13,678 (19)
Noncompetitive Open Seat Candidates	4.2 (18)	6,218e	0.3	345	71,160	3.4	5,930 (12)
Noncompetitive Challengers	25.6 (109)	23,590	1.1	216	195,067	9.4	2,672 (73)
Noncompetitive Freshman Incum.	2.3 (10)	1,803	0.1	180	29,429	1.4	4,204 (7)
Noncompetitive Other Incum.	46.5 (198)	15,569	0.7	79	283,784	13.6	2,604 (109)
TOTAL	100.0 (426)	2,083,020			2,083,020		

Note: Competitive candidates are those who received 40 to 60 percent of the general election vote. Party allocations include contributions to candidates and coordinated expenditures on behalf of candidates (i.e., 441a(d) expenditures).

a. The hypothetical model gives competitive open seat candidates the *regular* maximum total contribution (contributions plus coordinated expenditures) without increased coordinated spending from agency agreements with state parties, because the Democrats did not have the resources to spend at such levels.

b. This figure based on giving the 20 closest challengers (those receiving 45 to 55 percent of the general election vote) three-quarters of the *regular* maximum total contribution. The remaining 18 competitive challengers receive one-half the regular maximum total contribution.

c. Competitive freshman are given three-quarters of the regular maximum total contribution.

d. Other competitive incumbents are given one-half the regular maximum total contribution.

e. What is left after funding the competitive candidates is distributed among the noncompetitive challengers, with noncompetitive open seat candidates receiving the next largest allocations, and noncompetitive incumbents the smallest allocations.

Source: Federal Election Commission.

Table 11.2 Hypothetical and Actual Distribution of NRCC Resources to US House Candidates, 1986

	% of Total Candidates Running (n)	An Efficient Distribution of Party Resources (Hypothetical) $	% of Total	Mean Allocation (Hypothetical)	Actual Distribution of Party Resources $	% of Total	Actual Mean Allocation (n)
Competitive Open Seat Cand.	7.0 (27)	$ 1,447,740a	25.7	$ 53,620	$ 1,502,783	26.6	$ 51,820 (29)
Competitive Challengers	5.7 (22)	1,179,640a	20.9	53,620	857,808	15.2	40,848 (21)
Competitive Freshman Incum.	4.2 (16)	857,920a	15.2	53,620	667,969	11.8	41,748 (16)
Competitive Other Incum.	5.7 (22)	1,179,640a	20.9	53,620	892,121	15.8	33,042 (27)
Noncompetitive Open Seat Candidates	4.2 (16)	87,941b	1.6	5,496	215,160	3.8	19,560 (11)
Noncompetitive Challengers	41.6 (160)	644,902	11.4	4,031	817,051	14.5	13,618 (73)
Noncompetitive Freshman Incum.	3.9 (15)	48,856	0.9	3,257	104,137	1.9	8,678 (12)
Noncompetitive Other Incum.	27.5 (106)	195,425	3.4	1,844	585,035	10.4	5,572 (105)
TOTAL	100.0 (385)	5,642,064			5,642,064		

Note: Competitive candidates are those who received 40 to 60 percent of the general election vote. Party allocations include contributions to candidates and coordinated expenditures on behalf of candidates (i.e., 441a(d) expenditures).
a. Because of the Republicans' financial strength and the FECA contribution limits, the NRCC negotiated many agency agreements with state parties and doubled its coordinated spending on quite a few candidates. Therefore, the hypothetical model gives all competitive candidates (open seat, challenger, and incumbents) this higher maximum allocation ($53,620).
b. What is left after fully funding the competitive candidates is distributed among the noncompetitive candidates, with noncompetitive open seat candidates receiving the largest allocations, noncompetitive challengers the next largest, and noncompetitive incumbents the smallest allocations.
Source: Federal Election Commission.

Furthermore, both parties allocate funds to many incumbents who end up winning by large margins, for such allocations are made early in the campaign and are designed to help the incumbent avoid a serious challenge in the first place.

The Democrats, however, may follow this protection strategy to a fault—even when conditions dictate otherwise and create opportunities to pick up more seats. In 1982 and in 1986, when recessions under a Republican administration insured the safety of Democratic incumbents, the DCCC still directed large sums to incumbents.

The Republican committee's activity also confirms that a party's numerical status in the House can greatly influence its campaign committee's resource distribution decisions. As the minority party, the Republicans are highly motivated to gain seats. The longitudinal analysis (Figure 11.1) shows that the NRCC did indeed direct the bulk of its resources to non-incumbent candidates after 1982. Yet the Republican committee also supported incumbents by giving each a $5,000 in kind contribution. Perhaps if the NRCC were not financially secure, not restricted by the FECA limits, and the spread between them and the Democrats not so large, it might use these resources on nonincumbents.

A reform proposal that enjoys support among scholars and others suggests that increasing or removing party contribution limits would not only curb the influence of PACs, but also help make congressional elections more competitive. Parties are thought to allocate campaign resources more rationally (i.e., to challengers) than other contributors (Alexander 1992:172; Sabato 1989:51). Nevertheless, this analysis shows that not only do both parties quite rationally protect their incumbents, but they also focus more intensely on open seat candidates than on challengers. There is little reason to believe the hill committees will stop supporting incumbents or directing large sums to open seat races if contribution limits are raised or removed.

Notes

1. Campaign finance data were made available in part by the Inter-university Consortium for Political and Social Research. The data for *Campaign Expenditures in the United States: Reports on Financial Activity* were originally collected by the Federal Election Commission. Neither the collector of the original data noThis data set is hereafter referred to as "FEC, *Reports on Financial Activity.*"

2. The same was found to be true for similar campaign committees on the state level in New York, where the legislative campaign committees have come to play a larger role than the state parties in state legislative elections (see Dwyre and Stonecash 1992).

3. Coordinated expenditures (or 441a(d) expenditures) are party expenditures made in coordination with candidates but spent by the party on behalf of candidates.

4. For example, if the party CCC conducts a poll for a candidate, the reported value of that poll diminishes as time passes. Therefore, the CCCs often put off delivering the results of the poll to a candidate until it has depreciated so that the party committee can contribute more to that candidate before reaching the contribution limit.

5. Personal interview with Tom Cole, former NRCC Executive Director, November 13, 1991.

6. In 1992, House incumbents spent on average almost seven times more than their challengers (Federal Election Commission 1992). In 1990, 80 percent of all political action committee (PAC) money went to incumbents, only 6 percent to challengers, and 14 percent to open seat candidates (Ornstein, Mann and Malbin 1992:91-92). Incumbents also attract the greatest share of contributions from private individuals, taking in 49 percent of all of the money contributed by individuals to House candidates in 1992 (Federal Eelection Commission March 4, 1993a).

7. Election figures compiled by author from *Congressional Quarterly Weekly Report*, November 8, 1986:2864-2871 and November 12, 1988:3301-3307; and Ornstein, Mann and Malbin 1992:61.

8. Personal interview, October 27, 1993.

9. Personal interview with former NRCC Executive Director Tom Cole, November 11, 1991; see also "Rules of the National Republican Congressional Committee," 2.

10. This larger amount is also the coordinated expenditure limit for states with only one House member.

11. In 1990, the Democrats spent $4,208,964 on contributions to and coordinated expenditures on behalf of House candidates and the Republicans spent $5,028,550 (Ornstein, Mann and Malbin 1992:95).

12. Personal interview, November 8, 1991.

13. Green, Robins and Krasno have discussed this problem and have noted that the available sources, such as Congressional Quarterly's preelection forecasts (which they call a "journalistic finger-in-the wind") and media polls, provide neither accurate vote expectations nor the same kind of information available to candidates and parties from the polls they commission: " . . . there are no easy substitutes for polling information that is both accurate and *known* to be used by incumbents [and parties]. Such data are not easy to come by . . ." (Green, Robins and Krasno, 1991:11-13; see also Green and Krasno 1990:371)

14. 1986 FEC limits for party allocations to congressional candidates: the contribution limit was $10,000 ($5,000 for the primary and $5,000 for the general election); and the *regular* coordinated expenditure limit was $21,810, while the coordinated expenditure limit when an agency agreement was made with a state party or in a state with only one House member was $43,620. The total *regular* maximum contribution limit was therefore $31,810, and the maximum limit with an agency agreement or for a state with one representative was $53,620.

15. The hypothetical distribution of party resources presented in the tables is clearly not the only efficient distribution that is possible. Indeed, efficiency is characterized according to a very strict standard, whereby the parties are expected to allocate funds almost exclusively to marginal candidates. The hypothetical model for each party might therefore appear top heavy, because nearly all of each party's resources are allocated to competitive candidates in recognition of the primary goal of maximizing seats. However, since "competitiveness" is operationalized generously—a competitive candidate is one who receives between 40 and 60 percent of the general election vote—the model avoids the danger of a party targeting too narrowly, a mistake that would cause the party to miss opportunities to win seats (Jacobson 1993).

16. A full 97 percent of Republican competitive open seat candidates, 76 percent of the party's close challengers, 81 percent of its competitive freshmen incumbents, and 63 percent of the marginal nonfreshman incumbents received allocations over the regular maximum limit. Remember that an agency agreement allows a state party to pass on its contribution limit to the national party, thus potentially doubling the national committee's contribution limit for a congressional candidate.

12

Party Resource Allocation: The Timing of Contributions and Coordinated Expenditures

Janet M. Box-Steffensmeier

The institutionalization of the national parties and their increasing role in congressional politics have been the major impetuses behind studies of party resource allocation. Party money is important to candidates for a number of reasons. First, national party contributions serve as a cue for political action committees (PACs) and individuals to make contributions, so party money is essentially multiplied. Second, parties are the largest single source of money for most candidates. Finally, the value of party contributions has been posited as being worth more than the reported value because party contributions are often "in-kind benefits," and because of the timing of contributions (Herrnson 1992; Biersack, Herrnson, and Wilcox 1993). The primary questions of past research on party allocation strategy have been: Who gets party resources and how much? Additional insight into party strategy may be obtained by asking: When do candidates get party resources?

The need for longitudinal research on party allocation strategies has been pointed out by Biersack and Wilcox (1990) as well as Sinclair (1990). Dwyre (chapter 11) provides a well-crafted longitudinal analysis across elections from 1980 to 1988. This chapter differs by focusing on party allocation strategy *within* an election cycle. Longitudinal research of this sort is important for understanding the dynamics of campaigns.

This chapter is organized as follows. First, the literature on party resource allocation is discussed and it is shown that existing theory and empirical research can be used to predict which candidate characteristics affect when resources are received. Second, the question of timing is added to the existing literature. Third, contrasts and comparisons among the timing of contributions from parties, PACs, and individuals are drawn. Finally, an event history analysis is undertaken to assess the factors that influence the timing of party resource allocation strategies in congressional campaigns.

Party Resource Allocation in Congressional Races

Past research about the parties' role in campaign finance has concluded that candidates in competitive elections have been the recipients of party resources (Sorauf 1988; Herrnson 1990). Jacobson and Kernell (1983) argue that seat maximization is the parties' primary goal. Jacobson (1985–86) extends this by showing that organizational differences between the parties are important to understanding the distribution of party resources in 1982. Herrnson (1989) builds upon Jacobson's insight regarding the importance of the national parties' organizational characteristics and concludes 1) Republicans place the greatest emphasis on competitiveness, campaign quality, geographic location, and candidate status when distributing coordinated expenditures; and 2) Democrats place the greatest emphasis on candidate status (1989:317–18).

There is an ongoing debate over whether parties also consider party loyalty when distributing campaign resources. Wilhite and Theilmann (1989) and Leyden and Borrelli (1990) argue that party resources are not only distributed to maximize seats, but that past party loyalty is also a factor. Herrnson strongly disagrees: "They [the national parties] are not concerned with the formulation of public policy, nor do they take members' policy positions into consideration when distributing campaign money or services. National party activities are aimed at the attainment or expansion of electoral majorities, not the building of policy majorities" (1992:68).

In addition, Dwyre (1992) does not find support for the loyalty thesis and points out that the Wilhite and Theilmann (1989) and Leyden and Borrelli (1990) empirical studies have limited explanatory value because only winning incumbents are examined. The current evidence leans in favor of the seat maximization theory.

This theory holds that the competitiveness of the election is the primary variable used to explain party resource allocation decisions. Competitiveness is typically measured as the general election outcome, which appears to be a reasonable approximation. The current evidence also shows that incumbency status is important to understanding party resource allocation strategies (Herrnson 1989). Dwyre (1992) uses aggregate data and interviews to draw her conclusions. Using disaggregated data, I have shown elsewhere that war chests deter challenger entry, which indicates that incumbency status should be an important consideration in party allocation strategy, especially regarding timing (Box-Steffensmeier 1993). Based upon these findings, early party contribution to incumbents is consistent with the seat maximization argument; by giving to incumbents early, parties may help incumbents avoid competitive races. This argument is consistent with anecdotal and journalistic evidence as well.

Whether the incumbent is a member of the Democratic Congressional Campaign Committee (DCCC) or the National Republican Congressional

Committee (NRCC) has also been shown to be an important explanatory variable (Jacobson 1985-86; Wilhite and Theilmann 1989). The hypothesis is that sitting on these committees assures the member of receiving party resources. This hypothesis contradicts seat maximization theory since, in most cases, incumbents are well-funded.

In addition, whether or not the congressional race is in the South was shown to be important by Herrnson (1989), Squire (1989), and Box-Steffensmeier (1993). Southern races are still more likely to be uncontested or have low quality challengers because of one party dominance and "traditionalistic" political culture (Elazar 1984). Herrnson's (1989) results suggest, however, that targeting Southern races may be a strategy that varies from year to year.

Finally, the literature agrees that the quality of the challengers is also a factor in party allocation strategy (Herrnson 1989 and Dwyre 1992). High quality challengers should receive early party money and candidates facing high quality challengers from the opposing party should not.

Incorporating the Element of Time

Campaigns are obviously dynamic phenomena. However, the majority of models in the literature are static and use temporally aggregated data.[1] The importance of the timing of money is often mentioned in the campaigns and elections literature. Cheney (1980) suggests that early money is particularly valuable and adds, "a creative political scientist probably could analyze the timing of contributions and perhaps prove or disprove my theory" (1980:252). Biersack and Wilcox (1990) point out that if early money is critical to a candidate's success, then who gives early contributions and to whom is of particular interest since these contributors are likely to be more influential. They argue in more general terms that an explicit examination of the link between when contributors give and the candidate attributes that influence them is a top priority since it will ". . . enhance our ability to anticipate shifts in allocation strategies and to understand their causes and impact" (1990:237). Ample anecdotal and journalistic accounts also support the supposition that candidates, campaign strategists, and contributors pay attention to timing and that the effect of money varies over the course of the campaign (Beaudry and Schaeffer 1986).

Based on the dynamic conceptualization of campaigns and recognition that there are distinct stages within them (Box-Steffensmeier and Lin 1992), it is expected that the timing of financial transactions is critical to both the contributor and recipient. In order to sustain this expectation, the distribution of money within an election cycle should not be equal over time. Of more interest here, there should be discernable differences among the timing strategies of different contributors. After all, individual donors, PACS and parties are likely to have different motivations when making contributions to a campaign. The literature suggests that individuals and PACs would be most likely to contribute to incumbents very early and very late in the campaign to minimize risk. On the other hand, parties are more likely to give to challengers and in the middle of campaigns. This pattern reflects the unwillingness of parties not only to take sides in primaries, but also to become involved in riskier campaigns.[2]

What follows is a test of these expectations using temporally disaggregated contributions from individuals, PACs, and parties for contested House elections in which an incumbent ran for reelection in 1986.[3] After a brief description of the timing of contributions by source, event history analysis (a proportional hazard model)[4] is used to analyze the timing of party contributions and coordinated expenditures in terms of the variables discussed above: competitiveness of the race, incumbency status, challenger quality, membership on the NRCC and DCCC, and geographic location of the district.[5]

Who Receives Party Resources and When?

Table 12.1 presents the temporally disaggregated contributions from individuals, PACs, and parties for contested House elections in which an incumbent ran for reelection in 1986.[6] As a group, individuals contribute more money than PACs and both contribute more than parties. There are two periods, the first and last, in which PAC contributions to incumbents exceed individual contributions; the discrepancy is even larger when comparing median contributions. The first and last stages are exactly when previous research has shown that expenditures will have the greatest impact on electoral outcomes (Box-Steffensmeier and Lin 1992). This implies that candidates will value these contributions more and, subsequently, contributors who provide money during these stages are gaining more per dollar than those giving in other stages.

On the other hand, parties give the bulk of their money in periods five and six. Period five begins when the majority of primaries are over. This is consistent with the goal of parties to remain neutral during primaries. In addition, Box-Steffensmeier and Lin (1992) show that money has a big effect during these periods. So party contributions appear to be consistent with seat maximization theory. The money given very early in the election cycle is also shown to have a large effect. More risk is involved in giving money early since it is more difficult to predict accurately who will win. However, early incumbent contributions is an important strategy that may insulate an incumbent from facing a challenger (Box-Steffensmeier 1993) and serve as a cue to other contributors.

Table 12.1 Congressional Contributions by Source, Incumbency Status, and Timing 1986

Individuals

Period	Incumbents % of the Mean	Total	Challengers % of the Mean	Total	% of the Mean	Total
1	$19,033	8	$18,238	11	$795	1
2	34,767	15	31,766	19	3,001	5
3	25,619	11	20,310	12	5,308	9
4	45,357	20	32,020	19	13,336	23
5	56,646	25	36,962	22	19,684	34
6	15,167	7	9,830	6	5,337	9
7	32,019	14	21,809	13	10,211	18
1-7	228,608		170,935		57,672	

PACs

1	$18,610	10	$18,471	11	$138	1
2	24,928	13	24,641	15	286	1
3	15,173	8	14,459	9	713	3
4	37,315	21	33,246	20	4,068	19
5	44,272	24	36,796	22	7,476	36
6	15,563	8	12,513	7	3,049	15
7	31,566	17	26,333	16	5,233	25
1-7	187,427		166,462		20,964	0

Parties

1	$193	7	$120	12	$0	0
2	40	2	25	3	0	0
3	35	1	21	2	1	0
4	0	0	0	0	0	0
5	1204	46	464	47	285	45
6	1127	43	352	36	349	55
7	0	0	0	0	0	0
1-7	2600		982		635	

N = 246 candidates
Source: Federal Election Commission.

Candidates' status helps to further clarify the timing of contribution by individuals, PACs, and parties. Of course, all contributors are expected to give more to incumbents than to challengers because of the high incumbent reelection rate. But if any kind of contributor behaves differently, it is expected to be the parties because party contributions come from one, or at most a few, organizations whose motive is often reduced to maximizing seats strictly by party label (Jacobson 1985-86; Herrnson 1989). These expectations are borne out: parties more evenly divide their resources between incumbents and challengers. Overall, individuals and PACs individuals give contributions to challengers later than to incumbents. Specifically, challengers begin to receive contributions when the primaries begin, which is after the first three periods. Parties show a much more modest version of the same pattern, giving more than one-half of their funds to challengers in period 6.

Thus, in contrast to individuals and PACs, parties give more to challengers and later in the campaign. But which kinds of candidates receive the most support from parties? Tables 12.2 through 1254 test a proportional hazard model first for Republican and Democratic contributions and then for Republican and Democratic coordinated expenditures. These data are from the 1992 election cycle.[7] In interpreting these tables, a negative β indicates earlier receipts of contributions, while a positive signs denotes later ones.

Table 12.2 looks at the patterns of Republican party contributions. First, the type of candidate most likely to receive early party contributions is not a member of the NRCC. This is consistent with the seat maximization hypothesis discussed earlier and contradicts the idea that NRCC members seek self-oriented goals rather than party goals. Since incumbents were "running scared" in 1992, these results are especially strong. Second, candidates in competitive elections are more likely to receive early Republican contributions. This result is also central to the seat maximization theory.

Third, all of the variables designed to pick up the effects of incumbency are significant, indicating that incumbency status is an important determinant of who receives early party contributions. The final incumbency variable reveals that in races with two incumbents (due to the 1990 redistricting) candidates are likely to receive early party contributions. These patterns are also consistent with seat maximization.

Fourth, the candidate-quality variables indicate that high quality Republican challengers receive early party contributions. Republicans running against high quality Democratic challengers do not. Finally, geography apparently did not play a role in the Republicans' contribution strategy. Republicans did not target Southern Democrats in their allocation strategy despite Republican candidates getting stronger in the South and Democratic candidates' fears of being targeted.

Table 12.3 provides the analogous results for Democratic contributions. The type of candidate most likely to receive early Democratic contributions is not a member of the DCCC, faces a low quality Republican challenger (one that the party may see as more realistic to defeat), and is in a competitive race and a Southern district. Democrats were protecting potentially vulnerable Democratic incumbents by targeting Southern races. In contrast to the Republicans' timing contribution strategy, incumbency and the quality of the Democratic challenger was not as important to Democrats. These patterns are also consistent with the seat-maximization strategy.

Party Resource Allocation

Table 12.2 Cox Proportional Hazard Model for 1992 Republican Contributions over the Election Cycle

Variable	Coefficient	Std. Error	t-ratio
NRCC	-0.5792	0.0448	-12.916*
Competitiveness	-0.0140	0.0023	-6.111*
Uncontested	-0.2165	0.0921	-2.350*
Double Incumbent	0.5653	0.0731	7.736*
Open Race	-0.4943	0.0843	-5.865*
Quality1	-0.1239	0.0461	-2.689*
Quality2	0.2773	0.0482	5.759*
South	-0.0724	0.0414	-1.747

Quality1: quality of Democratic challenger
Quality2: quality of Republican challenger
* Signicant at .05 level or better
Chi-Squared (8) = 433.76
Significance Level = 0.00
N = 3310 contributions

Table 12.3 Cox Proportional Hazard Model for 1992 Democratic Contributions over the Election Cycle

Variable	Coefficient	Std. Error	t-ratio
DCCC	-0.2159	0.0839	-2.573*
Competitiveness	-0.0207	0.0038	-5.402*
Uncontested	0.0833	0.2016	0.413
Double Incumbent	0.5121	0.09425	5.433*
Open Race	.0412	0.2228	0.185
Quality1	0.0294	0.0910	0.323
Quality2	-0.2532	0.0857	-2.955*
South	0.2350	0.07478	3.142*

Quality1: quality of Democratic challenger
Quality2: quality of Republican challenger
* Signicant at .05 level or better
Chi-Squared (8) = 98.10
Significance Level = 0.00
N = 1020 contributions

Table 12.4 reports the results of a similar analysis for Republican coordinated expenditures. The signs of the explanatory variables are exactly the same as the results for Republican contributions. However, only NRCC membership, competitiveness, and uncontested races achieve significance. This suggests that Republicans economized more when making coordinated expenditures. Coordinated expenditures may be the route to emphasizing the races in which the party is particularly interested. Thus, the larger and more sophisticated coordinated expenditures are more narrowly targeted, as the seat-maximization would suggest.

Table 12.5 contains the results for Democratic coordinated expenditures. The signs are the same as those for Democratic contributions, except for two of the incumbency status variables. However, none of the incumbency status variables are significant. Only the DCCC variable is significant for Democratic coordinated expenditures. This suggests that Democratic coordinated expenditures were targeted to safer incumbents. This is the one finding that does not fully support the seat-maximization hypotheses.

Conclusion

The contribution strategies of party organizations are primarily driven by a desire to win elections. Like other sources of funds, congressional parties support candidates with the best chance of winning both in aggregate and within campaigns themselves. However, unlike other sources of money, parties give more to challengers and during the middle portion of the campaign. Thus, these committees do not participate in primaries and their funds are usually allocated before the last push in the campaign. Overall, the evidence supports the conclusions that the congressional parties are most concerned with maximizing the number of seats (Jacobson and Kernell 1983). In this sense, the congressional parties fund candidates that are best able to win rather than candidates that are best for the policy agenda of the party. Such a lack of ideological or policy focus is consistent with other studies of party strategy.

These findings suggest routes for future research. First, timing is an important aspect of contributions and needs to be investigated further. Party money may well serve as a cue for other contributions, and thus enhance the influence of party donations. And second, the use of split population models may help distinguish between the effect of the occurrence of a contribution and its timing.

Table 12.4 Cox Proportional Hazard Model for 1992 Republican Coordinated Expenditures over the Election Cycle

Variable	Coefficient	Std. Error	t-ratio
NRCC	-0.4224	0.1169	-3.614*
Competitiveness	-0.0319	0.0040	-8.004*
Uncontested	-0.7486	0.2623	-2.854*
Double Incumbent	0.0714	0.0708	1.008
Open Race	-0.0082	0.1979	-0.041
Quality1	-0.1377	0.0828	-1.662
Quality2	0.1066	0.0716	1.488
South	-0.0948	0.0651	-1.457

Quality1: quality of Democratic challenger
Quality2: quality of Republican challenger
* Signicant at .05 level or better
Chi-Squared (8) = 16.08
Significance Level = 0.04
N = 2830 Coordinated Expenditures

Table 12.5 Cox Proportional Hazard Model for 1992 Democratic Coordinated Expenditures over the Election Cycle

Variable	Coefficient	Std. Error	t-ratio
DCCC	-0.1625	0.0487	-3.333*
Competitiveness	-0.0006	0.0023	-0.243
Uncontested	-0.1567	0.1543	-1.016
Double Incumbent	0.0035	0.0572	0.060
Open Race	-0.0590	0.1047	-0.563
Quality1	0.0072	0.0510	0.141
Quality2	-0.0360	0.0526	-0.685
South	0.0340	0.0442	0.769

Quality1: quality of Democratic challenger
Quality2: quality of Republican challenger
* Signicant at .05 level or better
Chi-Squared (8) = 16.08
Significance Level = 0.04
N = 2830 Coordinated Expenditures

Notes

1. See Alexander 1992; Jacobson 1980; Green and Krasno 1988; Goldenberg and Traugott 1984.

2. See Jacobson and Kernell 1983; Cotter, Gibson, Bibby, and Huckshorn 1984; Eismeier and Pollock 1986; Wilcox 1989.

3. The data used here consist of all party contributions and coordinated expenditures for House campaigns made during the 1985-86 election cycle available from the Federal Elections Commission. The monetary data are recorded by the week of the transaction in seven periods as follows: 1. January 1, 1985, to June 30, 1985; 2. July 1, 1985, to December 31, 1985; 3. January 1, 1986, to March 31, 1986; 4. April 1, 1986, to June 30, 1986; 5. July 1, 1986, to September 30, 1986; 6. October 1, 1986, to October 15, 1986; and 7. October 16, 1986, to November 24, 1986.

4. Event history analysis is a regression-like procedure for longitudinal data. Event history analysis focuses on analyzing the length of time until an event occurs. Here the event is a party contribution or coordinated expenditure. Cox's proportional hazards model allows one to estimate the effects of individual characteristics on survival times without having to assume a particular form for the distribution function (or the density or hazard). Explanatory variables can be added to this model, so it is used to determine which variables have significant effects on length of time until a candidate receives a party contribution or expenditure. The model is based on the hazard rate at time t, $h(t,x) = h(t,0)e^{\beta'x}$ where $h(t,0)$ is the baseline hazard rate at time t for covariate vector 0, x are the covariates, and β is estimated.

5. The independent variables in the model were operationalized as follows: *Competitiveness* is the final 1992 vote outcome. *Incumbency* takes into account the status of the candidates with regard to incumbency; three dummy variables are used: *Uncontested* equals 1 if the race is uncontested; *Double incumbent* equals 1 if there are two incumbents running due to redistricting; *Open race* equals 1 if it is an open race. The base category is a race between an incumbent and challenger. *Quality* captures the quality of the challengers; *Quality1* indicates whether or not the Democratic challenger has held previous political office; *Quality2* is coded similarly for Republican challengers. Congressional Campaign Committees *(NRCC/DCCC)* is a dummy variable equal to one if the candidate is a member of the NRCC or the DCCC depending upon whether Republican or Democratic resource allocation strategy is being examined. *South* is a dummy variable indicating whether or not the congressional district is in a Southern state.

6. The within-subject-by-between-subject repeated measures ANOVA was done on a pairwise basis for all three sources and confirms that each source follows a different contribution timing strategy.

7. The data used here consist of all party contributions and coordinated expenditures for House campaigns made during the 1991-92 election cycle available from the Federal Elections Commission (see note 3).

13

Explaining Party Leadership Activity among House Freshmen: The Classes of 1980-1988

Stephen A. Borrelli
Kevin M. Leyden

Party leadership in the House of Representatives is now more visible, active, and powerful than at any time since the "Czarist Speakership" at the turn of the century (Rohde 1991; Sinclair 1992; Davidson 1992). Party leaders play a central role on most major issues that confront the House; leaders' participation now extends far beyond the building coalitions on the floor to all stages of the legislative process (Sinclair 1992). And while House members' campaigns are still primarily "candidate-centered," congressional party leaders and party committees are now playing an historically unprecedented role in recruiting, advising, and funding candidates (Herrnson 1988; Sorauf 1988). More than at any time in recent memory, the question of who gets recruited to party leadership positions is of interest to scholars and political practitioners alike.

In this chapter, we examine recruitment of *freshman* House members to positions within party leadership organizations during the 1980s. We believe that these early entrances onto the leadership ladder deserve more attention than they have received. As the House parties have extended the leadership hierarchy to include even the most junior members, some members are able to get on a "leadership track" from the day they begin service. While we know that contests for the more senior leadership positions are influenced by the intricate internal politics of the House parties, previous research does not indicate whether access to lower-level leadership positions is equally complex.

We suspect that there are predictable, systematic forces—mainly having to do with members' qualifications and experiences prior to their House service—that tend to "select in" some freshmen and "select out" others for participation in formal leadership groups. Specifically, we hypothesize that freshmen with state legislative experience, experience as party leaders in the state legislature, experience in statewide elective office, and/or experience as leaders of state party organizations, as well as freshmen who relied heavily on party support to win election to the House, are more likely than their colleagues to attain congressional party leadership positions during their first terms in office. The evidence from the 1980s largely supports these expectations, at least for the Democratic freshmen. To the extent that early accession to leadership positions gives members an advantage in future contests, this suggests that a likely "leadership class" of freshman Democrats can be systematically identified within each incoming freshman class.

The Recruitment of Freshmen to Party Leadership

Most of the existing recruitment studies focus on contests for the very top party leadership positions: Speaker, majority/minority leader, and/or majority/minority whip. In identifying the factors associated with successful movement to the leadership, most authors have concentrated on attributes of the candidates' *congressional* careers: how often they voted with the party in the past, the services they have performed for other members, the previous committee and leadership positions they have held within the House, and the style of the campaign they have waged for their desired position (see Polsby 1963; Peabody 1976; Brown and Peabody 1987; Canon 1989). As Loomis (1984) has reminded us, however, recent developments in the size and structure of the party leadership should lead us to expand the focus of our study of leadership recruitment. Loomis argues that the Watergate and post-Watergate freshman classes have sought to participate in leadership activities at an earlier stage in their careers than was the case a generation ago. And House party leaders have responded to these demands by greatly expanding the number of leadership positions available to junior members; the Democrats expanded their whip system from 20 slots in 1961 to 104 slots in 1991, and both parties have developed extensive systems of permanent and temporary leadership task forces to deal with specific issues (Little and Patterson 1993). Leaders were not just being generous by offering junior members these additional rungs on the leadership ladder. The expansion of the Democratic leadership, for example, is part of a deliberate "strategy of inclusion" that provides clear benefits to the senior leaders: in addition to more "eyes" and "ears" on Capitol Hill, the strategy gives senior leaders the opportunity to get to know junior members, to socialize them to party norms, and to groom some of them for future leadership roles (Sinclair 1981; Garand and Clayton 1986).

Understanding House leadership today, therefore, requires looking at a larger number of members and looking at them earlier in their House careers. Assuming freshman entry into the leadership follows any kind of systematic patterns, those patterns must be determined largely by the *precongressional* experiences and qualifications of freshman members.[1]

In the following sections, we propose that freshmen possessing certain kinds of objective qualifications and experiences are generally more likely to *want* positions in the leadership structure and more likely to be *approved* for such positions by those who appoint or elect leaders. We do not deny that there are many routes a freshman can take to the leadership, and that each case involves a somewhat unique combination of self-selection and selection by others. Even so, we suspect that freshmen's prior legislative or party experience will affect their motivations to seek leadership positions *and* others' motivations to allow them to get leadership positions strongly and consistently enough to allow us to predict freshman leadership attainment with a fairly simple empirical model. Underlying all of the hypotheses below is the theory that freshmen with precongressional experience working in or with political parties are more likely to join the House leadership than those lacking in such experience.

Background and Experience

State Legislative Experience. *Freshmen with extensive experience serving in a state legislature are more likely to attain Congressional leadership positions than are those with little or no state legislative experience.*

State legislative experience has been cited as the most frequent, if not the best, kind of preparation for successful House careers (Canon 1990); we expect that it will be an especially good predictor of successful attainment of leadership status during the first term. First, we think that longtime members of state legislatures should be more motivated to seek leadership positions than their colleagues lacking in such service. In addition, the typical state legislator is probably more thoroughly socialized in the norms of supporting the party than would be a public official or private citizen who has not served in such a partisan setting. Just as important is the possibility that current leaders and caucus members may think of experienced legislators as better qualified for such positions. Finally, experienced state legislators may be more skilled at lobbying and campaigning their colleagues in order to achieve leadership positions. Berkman (1993) finds that state legislators, particularly those from states with professionalized legislatures, have "institutional and policy mastery" that equips them to rise to prestigious committee positions faster than their colleagues. We see no reason why early attainment of party leadership posts should not follow the same pattern. In the analysis below, we measure state legislative experience simply as the total number of years a member served in either chamber of a state legislature prior to his or her arrival in Congress; members with no experience are coded "0."[2]

Prior Leadership Service. *Freshmen who have served as party leaders in the state legislature are more likely to attain House leadership positions than their colleagues without such experience.*

Even if state legislators as a group were not especially interested in joining the leadership, and/or more attractive as leadership candidates, we might still expect that those former state legislators with the most directly transferable background in legislative party leadership—those who had been elected to major party leadership positions while in the state legislative chamber—would be more willing and/or able than other freshmen to continue such service in the House. We coded members as state legislative leaders if their biographical data indicated service as a state legislative majority or minority leader, president of a legislative chamber, assistant majority or minority leader, and/or chair of a legislative party caucus. The leadership variable is coded as a simple dichotomy, with "1" indicating a stint of service as a leader.

Service with Party Organizations. Freshmen who have served as top-ranking officials in a national, state, county, or city political party committee are more likely to attain House leadership positions than their colleagues without such experience.

In examining the possible effects of previous party organizational service, we move beyond direct legislative experience to suggest that a general prior commitment to and affiliation with party organizations influences a member's willingness and/or opportunity to serve as a party leader in the House (see Price 1992). Those with a record of service to party organizations have demonstrated party loyalty (which might make them an attractive leadership candidate to others, and more likely to volunteer for often thankless and time-consuming party duties). Moreover, state party officials are used to thinking of parties as teams, negotiating with different factions within the party, and putting party success above pure policy concerns, all of which might be useful skills for a legislative leader. There is also a strong possibility that a typical former party official has had more previous opportunities to meet and work with other House members (at least those from his or her home state) whose support might be helpful in attaining a House leadership post. In the analysis below, we treat party organization leadership as another dichotomy; a code of "1" if he or she has any prior service as an executive officer (chair, president, secretary, and/or treasurer) in any national, state, or local party organization, and 0 otherwise.

Statewide Elected Office. Freshmen who have won statewide elective office prior to their House service are more likely to attain House leadership positions than their colleagues without such experience.

A number of considerations lead us to this expectation. A successful run for statewide office requires impressive political skills and connections (and, in many states, substantial party connections), as well as fundraising ability. One would think these talents would be respected by colleagues and current leaders as evidence of House leadership potential. While it is true that states vary greatly in the extent to which parties and partisanship matter in state elections, we can say (as we did in the case of former state legislators) that most elected governors, judges, and statewide executive officials run on a party ticket and have some experience with the kind of intraparty and interparty negotiation required of House party leaders. And, as in the case of prior legislative service, a former state official—particularly someone who has had the privileges and perks of executive office—might be less satisfied with routine congressional responsibilities and more apt to seek positions of greater authority. This variable is also coded as a dichotomy, with "1" indicating some service in statewide elective office, and "0" indicating no evidence of such service in a member's biography.

Political and Electoral Characteristics

So far we have discussed qualifications and background characteristics that might mark a freshman as a potential House party leader before he or she begins, or even considers, a House campaign. As Richard Fenno (1978) and others have recently emphasized, however, we should also consider the possible effect of the campaign experience itself on members' activities and opportunities once in office. Fenno points out that members continue to employ the styles, strategies, and issues developed during the campaign in their legislative work. In this vein, we suspect that attitudes toward political parties developed during the campaign might influence members' willingness and/or ability to participate in House party leadership activities after the election. We hypothesize that members' initial campaign experience might affect movement to the leadership in three specific ways.

Levels of Party Involvement in the Campaign. *Freshmen whose campaigns exhibited relatively heavy involvement on the part of party campaign organizations are more likely to attain party leadership positions than are their colleagues whose campaigns showed less party committee involvement.*

The proportion of a candidate's campaign expenses funded by party coordinated expenditures might conceivably affect both a member's motivation to seek party leadership positions and others' willingness to award him or her such a position. A member who benefited relatively heavily from party support might feel some obligation to "return the favor" by devoting hours to party service.[3] Alternatively, members might not be motivated so much by gratitude as by a simple awareness—based on their personal experience of receiving significant party assistance—that the leadership controls tangible resources that members value highly and a simple desire to attain positions through which they can help decide who gets these resources. Turning to the "demand side," we propose that leaders and colleagues might regard a heavy party investment in a freshman's campaign as a sign that the freshman won the confidence and trust of the party leaders in charge of doling out the funds and was able to work successfully with them in a winning campaign. Such considerations might lead colleagues to decide that a freshman has leadership potential.

We should note that party funding of congressional campaigns can be in the form of direct contributions to a candidate's campaign as well as coordinated expenditures. We use only measures of coordinated party expenditures, for two reasons. First, the legal ceilings on such funds are much higher than those for direct contributions. Second, the expenditure of coordinated funds involves much closer cooperation between party officials and the candidate's campaign personnel than do direct contributions to the candidate's campaign. It is this campaign cooperation that we believe would best predict a member's continued affiliation with the party leadership once elected. This variable is operationalized as the percentage of total campaign receipts received in the form of "coordinated expenditures" made by party campaign committees on the candidate's behalf.[4]

Margin of Victory. *Freshmen who ran in especially close elections are less likely to attain party leadership positions than are their colleagues with larger electoral margins.*

Our initial expectation was that the freshmen, their senior colleagues, and current party leaders might all share the belief that marginal members should forego party responsibilities and concentrate on constituency service in the interests of protecting their seat. In other words, both the opportunities for marginal members to obtain leadership slots and their motivations to do so would be reduced. However, we cannot dismiss the possibility of an effect working in the other direction; perhaps in some situations freshmen and/or their more senior colleagues feel that the additional power and prestige of an early party leadership position might actually help a marginal freshman get reelected. We measure "closeness" as the difference between the freshman's percentage of the vote and that of his or her nearest competitor.

Ideological Considerations. *Democratic freshmen from districts where Presidents Reagan or Bush ran relatively strongly are less likely to attain party leadership positions than are their colleagues from weak Reagan/Bush districts; Republican freshmen from strong Reagan/Bush districts should be more likely than their colleagues to attain party leadership positions.*

In general, we expect that Republicans running in strong Reagan or Bush districts would be most likely to find satisfaction and electoral benefit in party service, and that Democrats from strong Reagan or Bush districts would be most uncomfortable helping to implement the largely liberal Democratic leadership agenda. Similarly, we would expect that those who select future leaders might be wary of ideologically conflicted members and most trusting of members whose personal and district ideologies are most consistent with the party "norms." Students of Congress have traditionally assumed that members tend to choose ideological "middlemen" as their leaders (Sinclair 1990:124–25).

There are reasons, however, to expect that members from ideologically atypical districts might not be disadvantaged, or could even be advantaged, in their bids for leadership posts. There have been recent efforts, particularly within the Democratic party, to make the party leadership more responsive to the full range of party opinion, including appointing conservative Southern Democrats to whip and task force positions (Rohde 1991:185).[5]

Structural Factors

We realize that attainment of leadership position is more than just a matter of member ambition and approval among one's colleagues. There are structural constraints on the number of opportunities available to a would-be freshman leader. The most severe constraints are those imposed by both parties' campaign and committee assignment committees: in order to ensure broad geographic representation on these bodies, slots are formally reserved for members from particular states. Although the exact method of reservation varies, as a general hypothesis we can safely say:

State and Regional Delegations. The larger the number of House colleagues of the same party in a given freshman's state delegation, the less likely that freshman is to attain a leadership position.

Even on leadership committees where there is no formal allocation of seats to states or a looser allocation according to regions (as in the whip systems), there may be informal norms preventing members from the larger states from gaining too many positions. In addition, both parties may have a particular interest in making sure that the South is represented on leadership committees, given the recent complaints about underrepresentation by Southern Democrats (see Rohde 1991) and the Republicans' interest in winning and holding seats in this increasingly competitive region. Accordingly, Southern freshmen are also more likely to attain leadership positions—in both parties—than are non-Southern freshmen. We thus include a variable indicating the total number of state copartisans during the member's freshman term (including the freshman in question), as well as a dummy variable for "South" (defined as the old Confederacy).

Cohort Effects. Finally, we also need to control for time-specific structural factors that may make it inherently more difficult for freshmen elected at certain times to join the leadership during their first term. Our purpose is to formulate a general model of freshman leadership attainment, and apply it to a data set including freshmen classes from five different Congresses (the 97th through 101st, i.e., the classes elected between 1980 and 1988). Throughout this period, the top party leadership made decisions to expand or contract the size of leadership groups and to create or eliminate spots reserved for freshmen members. Moreover, the size of freshman classes varied greatly from year to year; a larger freshman class might mean more competition for leadership spots (although it might also mean more vacancies on leadership committees due to retirement or defeat). Because all these factors vary from Congress to Congress, we attempt to capture them through the inclusion of four dummy variables representing membership in different freshmen classes (1982, 1984, 1986, and 1988, with 1980 being the excluded category).[6]

Research Design

Two data sets are employed in the analysis, one consisting of all Democrats newly elected to the House during the period November 1980–December 1989, and the other consisting of all Republicans newly elected to the House during the same period.[7] Separate analysis of the two parties' freshmen is necessary because of the different organizational structure of the two parties and because of possible differences in access to leadership positions due to the longtime majority status of the Democratic party.

Our dependent variables represent the successful achievement of various leadership positions by an individual member during his or her first House term (for members elected in 1980, the period under examination would be 1981–1982; for members elected in 1982, it would be 1983–84, etc.) Hibbing (1991) and others who have studied movements into leadership positions have tended to consider the entirety of the congressional career and are especially interested in the length of time it takes "the typical member" to begin a career in the leadership (see also Polsby 1968; Canon 1989). Here we focus on the earliest possible movement to the leadership, that occurring in the first term. In so doing, we are introducing an automatic control for seniority; if we compare freshmen members' progress in the first term only, we are forced to pay attention to variables other than length of service that distinguish those involved in party governance from those less involved.

Which leadership positions should we consider in constructing our dependent variables? In other words, how broadly should we define "party leadership?" For the purposes of this paper we focus on what could be called the "middle management" level of the party leadership, and we choose to look at those committees most closely associated with the *party* organizations. While some of the standing committees do have leadership status, recruitment to these committees has been much more extensively studied (Shepsle 1978; Smith and Deering 1984), and there is likely to be some controversy as to exactly which committees "deserve" this status. For the Democrats, we analyze entry into the whip system (whether or not a member becomes a deputy whip, assistant whip, at-large whip, zone whip, or a caucus representative within the whip system), the Steering and Policy Committee (which makes all nominations to Democratic committee slots, coordinates committee activity, and formulates Democratic policy positions), and the Democratic National Congressional Campaign Committee (which provides campaign assistance to Democratic House candidates). For the Republicans, we look at freshmen attainment of positions within the whip system (which include deputy whips, regional whips, assistant regional whips, class whips, and the "strategy" whips employed in 1989–90), the Republican Policy Committee (which formulates party positions on pending issues), the Republican Research Committee (which studies and evaluates policy alternatives), the Republican Committee on Committees (which makes Republican committee assignments), and the National Republican Congressional Campaign Committee (which assists House Republican campaigns).[8] The primary source for all data on committee membership is the *Congressional Quarterly Almanac* for the year corresponding to the beginning of each new Congress.[9]

Findings and Discussion: The Democrats

The first, and most general, version of our "leadership attainment" variable for freshmen Democrats is an index encompassing first-term membership in three different leadership organizations. A member receives one point for service in each of the following: the DCCC, the Steering and Policy Committee, and the whip organization. The maximum value, then, is "3" and the minimum value "0." Table 13.1 presents the results of an OLS regression of this index on the various predictors described above.

Table 13.1 indicates that precongressional experience matters. Variables measuring the number of years a member served as a state legislator, whether a member served as a state legislative leader, and whether a member held a statewide elective office are all significantly and positively correlated with our dependent variable. In addition, we find the number of Democratic members in a state delegation also to be significant in the hypothesized direction; increased competition from fellow members of the state delegation tends to inhibit leadership service. There is also a significant positive relationship between district vote for Republican presidents and successful freshmen leadership attainment. This relationship is somewhat surprising, in that it suggests Democrats from relatively strong Republican districts are more likely to successfully join the leadership team. Whether this is a result of an attempt by leaders, caucus members, and/or would-be leaders to moderate the Democratic party's ideological profile, or an attempt by the party to "spotlight" members from traditionally Republican territory, remains a topic for future research.

The model presented in Table 13.1 accounts for a third of the variance in the leadership attainment index. Given the wide variety of selection methods used to fill these committees and the traditional view of leadership recruitment as an idiosyncratic and highly personalized process, our general model does a respectable job of distinguishing leaders from nonleaders with a small set of general variables. We realize, however, that each arm of the party leadership emphasizes different functions (vote counting and mobilization for the whips, committee assignments for the Steering and Policy Committee, and electoral support for the DCCC). It is very possible that not all of the variables do equally well in predicting freshman membership on each of the committees. Combining three leadership positions into one index might obscure important committee-specific patterns. For this reason we decided to estimate logit models predicting first-term membership (scored "0" for nonmembership, "1" for membership) on each individual leadership committee. Unfortunately, problems with lack of variation in some of the variables and multicollinearity prevent us from being able to estimate a fully specified model predicting Steering and Policy Committee membership.

We are able to estimate meaningful models predicting DCCC membership and assignment to the Democratic whip organization. The DCCC model is presented in Table 13.2. State or local party organization leadership, years of state legislative experience, and statewide elective office experience are all significant predictors of freshman DCCC membership. These are exactly the kinds of experiences—those related to campaigning, fundraising, and other aspects of electoral politics—we would think to be most directly relevant to the purposes of the DCCC; the selection process for the DCCC clearly favors those who are already familiar with the type of work the DCCC does. By way of contrast, experience as a state legislative leader does not correlate with DCCC service. Prior state legislative leadership is apparently not considered an important qualification for DCCC service. As expected, given the empha-

Table 13.1 Leadership Attainment Among Democratic Freshmen, Classes of 1980–1988 (OLS)

Indep. Variable	Coefficient	Std. Error	t-Ratio
Years as State Legislator	.015	.008	1.83*
State Legislative Leader	.316	.124	2.55**
Party Organization Leader	.140	.111	1.30
Held Statewide Office	.701	.172	4.07***
% Campaign $ in Coord. Exp.	-.000	.012	-.01
District % for Repub. Pres.	.009	.004	2.09**
Margin	.002	.248	-1.38
Dem. Reps. in State	.012	.005	-2.19**
South	.090	.085	-1.06
Class of 1980	.010	.110	.90
Class of 1984	.131	.172	.76
Class of 1986	.174	.133	1.30
Class of 1988	.160	.139	1.15
Constant	-.343	.248	-1.38

Dependent Variable = Total number of positions held during freshmen term on the following committees: Democratic Congressional Campaign Committee, Democratic Steering and Policy Committee, and The Whip Organization.
R^2 = .31
n = 143
* $p < .10$; ** $p < .05$; *** $p < .01$ (two-tailed)
Source: See text.

sis on geographic representation in the DCCC, having a large number of copartisans from the same state appears to be a significant disadvantage for would-be first term members.

Perhaps the most intriguing, but not unanticipated, result concerns the effect of heavy party financing during the previous campaign on a member's appointment to the DCCC; the larger the percentage of a member's total receipts derived from coordinated spending by the party, the higher the probability a member will join the DCCC during his or her first term. As we mentioned, a number of different causal processes could bring about this result. One possibility is that members heavily aided by party contributions become more aware than their colleagues of the personal and institutional value of having viable party campaign committees and thus more motivated to seek campaign committee positions. Another is that members who received a great deal of coordinated aid might be most familiar to current

Table 13.2 Freshman Term Membership on the Democratic Congressional Campaign Committee, Classes of 1980–1988 (Logit Model)

Indep. Variable	Coefficient	Std. Error	t-Ratio
Years as State Legislator	.090	.048	1.87*
State Legislative Leader	-.092	.525	-.18
Party Organization Leader	1.007	.437	2.31**
Held Statewide Office	1.444	.573	2.52**
% Campaign $ in Coord. Exp.	.141	.048	2.13**
District % for Repub. Pres.	.020	.027	.75
Margin	.005	.010	.48
Dem. Reps. in State	-.162	.066	-2.44**
South	.240	.400	.60
Class of 1982	.584	.728	.80
Class of 1984	.070	.925	.08
Class of 1986	-.602	.847	-.71
Class of 1988	-.173	.832	-.21
Constant	-2.670	1.925	-1.39

Dependent Variable = "1" if member joined DCCC during his or her first term, "0" otherwise.
Dhrymes Pseudo-R^2 = .41
n = 143
* $p < .10$; ** $p < .05$; *** $p < .01$
Source: See text.

DCCC members and to the current party leadership, who are involved in targeting members for aid (Herrnson 1989). The important point is that party financial support, which did not appear to be related to leadership attainment, generally speaking (see Table 13.1), is very much related to membership on the committee that handles this support.

Table 13.3 shows the results of a model of whip organization membership. Again, the variables relating to prior political experience show an intuitive pattern. Past experience in the most analogous position to that of House whip—state legislative leader—is a strong predictor of whip service, and so are years of legislative experience and prior service in statewide elective office. This time, it is party *organizational* leadership that appears less relevant, as the data indicate that organization leadership is statistically unrelated to freshman whip service. Since party organizational leaders are concerned almost exclusively with electoral politics, and state legislative leaders are more heavily involved in coalition-building and policy making within the legislature, it is not hard to see why legislative leadership might be considered a relevant qualification for a whip position while party organizational leadership would be less so.

Two additional findings in the whip model deserve mention. First, district-level presidential election results, which did not affect recruitment to the DCCC, do appear to have an impact on recruitment to whip positions; members from relatively strong Reagan or Bush districts were more likely to join the whip organization. As mentioned earlier, further research is necessary to determine whether this is a product of "revolt from below," "inclusion from the top," or a combination of such forces. Finally, members who were most reliant on coordinated funding were significantly less likely to serve as whips.[10]

Findings and Discussion: Republicans

As with the Democrats, we begin by estimating an OLS model predicting an index of overall party involvement among freshmen (Table 13.4). The Republican index has a possible range of 0-5, counting membership in five leadership organizations: the NRCC, the Republican Committee on Committees, the Republican Policy Committee, the Republican Research Committee, and the whip office.

Table 13.4 suggest that first-term membership in the Republican leadership is largely driven by structural factors, and is not as dependent on members' political experience as was the case for the Democrats. Republicans from states with few or no other Republicans found it much easier to gain early admission to the leadership circle, and members elected in 1986 were significantly less likely than those elected in the baseline year of

Table 13.3 Freshman Term Membership in the Democratic Whip Organization, Classes of 1980-1988 (Logit Model)

Indep. Variable	Coefficient	Std. Error	t-Ratio
Years as State Legislator	.071	.034	2.06**
State Legislative Leader	1.010	.415	2.44**
Party Organization Leader	-.466	.522	-.89
Held Statewide Office	1.033	.586	1.76*
% Campaign $ in Coord. Exp.	-.165	.090	-1.84*
District % for Rep. Pres.	.040	.024	1.68*
Margin	-.016	.013	-1.23
Dem. Reps. in State	-.011	.022	-.50
South	-.512	.392	-1.31
Class of 1982	.210	.504	.42
Class of 1984	.418	.819	.51
Class of 1986	1.206	.626	1.92*
Class of 1988	1.240	.608	2.04**
Constant	-3.634	1.487	-2.44

Dependent Variable = "1" if member became a whip during his or her first term, "0" otherwise (see text for definition of whips).
Dhrymes Pseudo-R^2 = .34
n = 143
* $p < .10$; ** $p < .05$; *** $p < .01$
Source: See text.

1980 to do so.[11] None of the political background variables emerges as significant or even nearly so, and the overall fit of the model is clearly inferior to that of the Democratic analogue presented in Table 13.1.

Our ability to perform analysis of membership on each individual committee is again subject to limitations imposed by the structure of our data. We can estimate a fully specified logit regression model of NRCC recruitment (Table 13.5) which modestly replicates some of the findings of the corresponding Democratic model. (Note that in the interests of conserving space, the coefficients presented in Table 13.5 represent only those variables that were close to statistical significance in their respective models.) Prior service as a state or local party organization leader and service in statewide elective office are both weakly correlated with NRCC membership, the former at a .20 level of significance and the latter at a .10 level. Less intuitive relationships of roughly the same level of significance emerge for the margin variable and the years of legislative service variable. It is not at all clear why prior legislative service would inhibit NRCC membership; perhaps the slight tendency for marginal members to be more successful at winning NRCC spots suggests a perception—by would-be NRCC members or those who select them—that such service might help them in future electoral contests.

Models predicting Committee on Committees membership and Policy Committee membership can be estimated only if the statewide elective office variable is not entered (Table 13.5).[12] The Committee on Committees results are dominated by the committee's requirement of broad geographic representation; members from states with large Republican delegations are significantly disadvantaged in attaining membership. In addition, members of the 1984 and 1986 classes are significantly less likely than those elected in 1980 to join the Committee on Committees as freshmen. The only substantive effect that is even close to statistical significance is that for district Republican presidential vote. If we take this variable to represent the conservativeness of the district, and that in turn to indicate the potential conservativeness of its representative, this pattern is consistent with what we know about the standing committee assignment process. To the extent that the Republican Conference and leadership wants to ensure that the Republican members of important committees represent "typical" party views, they would be well advised to appoint conservative members to the Committee on Committees.

Selection to the Republican Policy Committee is virtually unpredictable with the data at our disposal. Aside from slight tendencies for some classes to gain admission more frequently than others, there seem to be no systematic patterns relating member characteristics to Committee membership. Finally, obtaining meaningful results for models of Research Committee and whip system membership requires the elimination of several potentially important variables, and we are reluctant to draw conclusions from deliberately underspecified models.

Conclusions

When political scientists and journalists have written about leadership contests, they have usually chosen to discuss the "heavy weight" contests between experienced legislators for the positions at the highest rungs of the leadership ladder. The explanations for who wins and loses these contests typically focus on internal congressional politics: who follows the norms, who votes with the party, who makes the best media spokesperson, who can call in the most debts from other members, and so forth. In the postreform House, however, contests for leadership positions involve many more members, at much earlier stages in their careers, than was the case a generation ago. In fact, Canon (1989) argues that as a legislative party becomes more institutionalized in its leadership hierarchy (which has clearly happened to the House Democrats), leadership contests at the top become routine or nonexistent, and the real scramble for power occurs lower in the party ranks.

It would seem difficult to predict leadership attainment among members with little or no seniority; it is tempting to conclude that early leadership success is due to intangible factors such as luck, charisma, and attitude. In this paper, however, we have shown that freshman entry onto the leadership ladder shows systematic patterns. The success of individual members at gaining leadership positions can be predicted on the basis of structural constraints, and, especially for the Democrats, objectively measured member characteristics. The process of early recruitment to leadership does not favor all equally, nor does it arbitrarily discriminate in favor of a mysterious select few. Particularly for Democrats, the process favors those with predictably relevant qualifications. To varying degrees, depending on the number and type of leadership committees in question, prior state legislative service, state legislative leadership, prior service in statewide elective office, prior service on a state or local party committee, and/or relatively high reliance on party coordinated party funds in the most recent campaign can be shown to steer Democrats toward early leadership posts.

We hope to have raised a number of topics for future research throughout. First and foremost among them would be explaining why Republican moves to the leadership are less dependent on prior political experience. Two explanations come to mind. Perhaps the House Republican leadership ladder is simply more fluid and less structured than that of the majority Democratic party. This claim has already been made with respect to the top levels of Republican leadership (Canon 1989); it may true of the lower levels as well. This fluidity, in turn, might be caused by the semipermanent minority status of House Republicans. For a congressional party that has been frustrated in both its policy and political ambitions for most of the last fifty years, it may make little sense to develop a highly structured leadership selection process. Republicans might be willing to experiment with inexperienced or unorthodox leaders (such as a Newt Gingrich) in a continuing effort to find something that works (Bader and Jones 1993:294–295).

A second possible explanation for the lack of a clear Republican pattern involves the differences in career paths between Republicans and Democrats (Fiorina 1994). It may be the case that Republican politicians tend to value previous elective office experience less when selecting leaders, either because relatively fewer incumbent Republicans have elective office experience themselves, or because of an ideological distrust of "career politicians" (Jacobson 1990; Maisel 1992). Republicans have been consistently less likely than Democrats to offer politically experienced House challengers and open seat candidates in recent years. Out of necessity or choice, Republican candidates are less likely than Democrats to have followed traditional paths to high political office. Our results raise the possibility that the Republican tendency to undervalue professional politicians may continue even within the House chamber.

We should also note that our measure of state copartisans, which in most cases predicts leadership committee membership for both parties, is no less interesting because we label it a "structural" variable. Our results suggest members from small states and/or states which are typically hostile to their party are given an important head start in the quest for leadership positions. The extent to which members are able and willing to exploit this advantage later in their congressional careers is worth further investigation.

In this chapter, we have discussed our hypotheses and findings primarily in the context of the literature on Congress, because, appropriately enough, that is where most of the work on party leadership recruitment has originated. We conclude, however, by expressing our hope that we have in some small way advanced the study of political parties more generally. Parties are often advertised as performing a crucial linkage function in American democracy. In a political system splintered into various branches and levels in an extremely large and diverse society, political parties are supposed to be a cohesive force that can bridge the gaps inherent in our constitutional structure. Our results suggest one way in which this linkage can and does occur. Democratic freshmen who have been active in party affairs in their state legislatures are more likely to continue in such a role at the national level. Moreover, Democratic freshmen who have served as officers in state party organizations, and/or who have been helped by party organizations in their campaigns, are more likely to serve on the DCCC once in Congress. Despite the growing alienation from the parties at the mass level, party linkages at the elite level—between party-as-organization and party-in-government, and between state and Federal parties—persist, and merit continued attention from academics, journalists, and political practitioners.

Notes

1. While we deal here with the correlates of attainment of leadership positions by freshman members in their first terms, we also maintain that precongressional experience variables might also help to explain movements to the leadership by more senior members with considerable congressional experience under their belts. Fenno (1978) has argued that precongressional office and campaign experience has a lingering effect on legislators' attitudes and behavior, and Barber (1992) has long maintained that a politician's first independent political experiences have a profound and lasting influence.

2. All biographical data on freshmen come from various editions of *The Almanac of American Politics*, *The Congressional Staff Directory*, and *Politics in America*. In all cases, at least two of these sources were checked; in most cases, all three were consulted.

3. Following the same logic, we have elsewhere explored the possibility that party contributions to members' campaigns might influence their propensities to vote with the party on roll call votes (Leyden and Borrelli 1990).

4. See Herrnson (1989), Sorauf (1988), and Leyden and Borrelli (1990) for further discussion of the quantitative and qualitative differences between coordinated and direct party funding. Our sources for financial data were various (final) editions of FEC Reports on Financial Activity, U.S. Senate and House Campaigns.

5. Our sources for electoral data were various editions of Congressional Quarterly's *Politics in America* and Congressional Quarterly's *Almanac*. The presidential vote variable is simply the raw percentage of district votes for the Republican presidential candidate if the most recent presidential election was 1984 or 1988; if the most recent election was the three-way race of 1980, we used the Republican percentage of the two-party district vote.

6. Members elected in special elections are included in our data; they are lumped in with the freshmen elected during the previous general election, so that members elected between December 1980 and November 1982 are considered members of the class of 1980, etc.

7. Four freshmen Republicans in our data set had previously held and lost U.S. House seats before their "new" election to the House. We consider them freshmen because their prior interrupted service, under House rules, is not supposed to give them any seniority over their freshmen colleagues.

8. The Democratic Study Group (which conducts research and disseminates information) was not coded as being part of the Democratic leadership in this analysis. The DSG originated as an insurgent group within the party and remains officially independent of the leadership. The DSG is unique for other reasons; a DSG staffer (personal interview, 1993) told us that the nominal membership of the Democratic Study Group has reached the point where the Study Group is almost identical to the Democratic Caucus. This said, there are reasons why the DSG "should" be considered as a viable part of the leadership (see Little and Patterson 1993). In an earlier draft of this chapter we included an additional table that included the DSG as a part of our Democratic leadership index. With a few exceptions, the results were generally similar but weaker than those presented in Table 13.1.

9. Most of the party committees retained the same basic size and structure throughout the period under examination, but there are some major exceptions. The Republicans gradually expanded their whip organization from 23 members in 1983–1984 to 29 in 1987–1988, then reduced it to 18 members in 1989–1990. The reported membership of the Republican Committee on Committees was cut in half between the 1987–1988 and 1989–1990. Both the size and structure of the Research Committee were altered during the period of our study; the committee had about twenty members until 1985–1986, when *Congressional Quarterly* reported no membership, and then reemerged in 1987–1988 with a reported membership of all Republican members! In order to preserve some kind of equivalence across time for our analysis, we considered chairmanship of a Research Committee task force as the criterion for Research Committee membership in 1987–1988, and membership in the executive committee of the Research Committee as a threshold for membership in 1989–1990.

10. At first we thought this might reflect a tendency for whip positions and DCCC positions (which are related to coordinated funding) to be mutually exclusive; on closer examination, this appears not to be the case.

11. The near-significant negative effect of the 1984 coefficient is somewhat artificial: as we stated earlier, we could not locate a list of Research Committee membership for 1985–1986, and so the maximum possible index score for the 1984 freshmen is "4," not "5."

12. The problem is limited variance; only four Republican freshmen throughout this entire period are reported as having experience in statewide elective office.

14

State Legislative Campaign Committees: New Partners or New Competitors?

Daniel M. Shea

Those who lament party atrophy have found refuge in a host of recent organizational studies. A new generation of scholars have resurrected the structural approach to studying parties and, if not directly challenged the demise perspective, certainly complicated the debate. The party may not be "over" just yet. Indeed, evidence of growth and adaptation seems straightforward; party organizations have more and are doing more. At nearly every level budgets are larger, staffing is up, and party clients (candidates) are receiving greater assistance. One might even go so far as to speculate this surge is a by-product of decline in other areas—principally mass partisanship.

An important component of the resurgent view has been the rapid development of legislative campaign committees (LCCs).[1] At the national level these units, often referred to as the "hill committees," blossomed during the early 1980s and are now seen as integral parts of the national party organizations (Herrnson 1986, 1988; Jacobson 1992; Adamany 1984). Prior to the late 1970s, few state legislative caucuses had established centralized campaign units—notable exceptions being in Wisconsin, California, and New York. During the past decade, however, they flourished and today are found in 40 states.

In addition to financial help, state-level LCCs furnish extensive high-tech campaign services: polling, computer data-base facilities, direct mail services and electronic media production. Many state-level LCCs provide incumbent, challenge, and open seat candidates with assistance which far outweighs that of traditional party units and political action committees (Jewell and Olson 1988). In several states they have become the dominant player in state legislative elections (Shea forthcoming; Dwyre and Stonecash 1993; Gierzynski 1992; Giles and Pritchard 1985; Johnson 1987; Redfield and Van Der Slik 1992; Loftus 1985; Jewell 1986).

Perhaps eager to find party renewal, most students of parties welcome state LCCs as evidence of party "adjustment" or "adaptation." John Bibby, a leading scholar in the field, notes: "State legislative campaign committees, composed of incumbent legislators, operate in both the upper and lower chambers of most state legislatures. These committees have become the principle party-support institutions for legislative campaigns in many states" (1990:31). Anthony Gierzynski, in one of only two full length work on state-level LCCs to date, suggests they have: "developed, or are developing into what are indisputably party organizations . . . Adaptation [to the modern political environment] has spread to the state level" (1992:116-119).

Nevertheless, the theoretical synthesis of LCCs with an overarching "party" may conceal profound changes in state legislative politics, modes of campaigning, and party dynamics. For one thing, it is not clear that LCCs are linked with traditional geographic party organizations. Although Diana Dwyre and Jeffrey Stonecash (1993) suggest the only way to accurately gauge the strength of party committees in New York, for example, is to include LCCs within the assessment, Malcolm Jewell and David Olson note that "in practice [LCCs in New York] are about as autonomous as possible" (1988:222). Recent works on several states seem no less contradictory (Gierzynski 1992; Shea forthcoming).

Where do LCCs fit in today's political environment and how are they different from other party organizations? Are they simply appendages of existing party structures, or are they more akin to PACs and campaign consulting firms? What variables might lead LCCs to resemble and to work alongside traditional parties more so than others? Before we rush to congratulate the adaptability of parties it seems reasonable first to assess whether these new units are linked with traditional geographic party organizations. Certainly, if they are not, a host of questions regarding their activities, goals and impact on existing structures are raised.

This research seeks to shed light on the linkage question. Specifically, it examines the extent to which state-level LCCs are tied, both formally and programmatically, to traditional state party committees. It also seeks to discern what variables play a role in this new dynamic.

Overall, the results suggest that formal bonds and programmatic interdependence are sporadic. In some states LCCs are clearly partners with the state party committee while in others they are only distant cousins. Legislative professionalization emerges as the most noteworthy control; states with professional legislatures are considerably more likely to hold fully autonomous LCCs than are those with part-time bodies.

Searching for Linkages

As noted above, one of the foremost issues raised by the development of state-level legislative campaign committees is the extent to which they are coupled with traditional party committees (Dwyre and Stonecash 1993; Shea Forthcoming; Gierzynski 1992). It should be noted that this issue sets aside any comparison of activities and goals. Although LCCs may reside and conduct projects independent of state party committees, what they do and what they seek to accomplish may be similar. This would suggest they are no less "party-like." The aim here is to take the first step by looking at formal and informal interactions.

Formal Ties

For some scholars, such as Duverger (1954), the prescribed articulation between party subunits is a critical ingredient of that organization. With regard to LCCs and state party organizations such linkages refer to party bylaws or state statutes. Simply put, are LCCs formally connected with party organizations—as appendages, branches, or service agents?

There are several reasons to suggest formal ties would be common. For one, "party" committees have been granted, in both state and federal law, advantages over nonparty organizations. Twenty-two states now have programs of tax-assisted funding for state parties (Alexander 1992:141-142), and all party committees receive the lowest possible postage rates. As party appendages these advantages would also apply to LCCs. Second, those who control LCCs may wish for them to be seen as benign, party organizations. At the very least there is an air of secrecy, particularly in states with professional legislatures. The use of state employees as operatives is common but, perhaps, improper.[2] Third, our political system is dominated by a pervasive sense of localism. The idea of nonparty organizations created to infuse campaigns with external resources may run counter to this norm. In sum, we would expect most LCCs to be legally linked to the state party committee.

Project Interdependence

Formal linkages may tell only part of the story. A functional interdependence may exist where the two organizations come to rely upon one another for assistance. Because winning elections might certainly be a shared goal,[3] we would expect a high level of cooperation and interaction. One must be cautious, however, when assessing this dimension. Speaking of party subunit interaction, Cotter et al. point out:

> Interdependence . . . implies joint activity toward common goals, or it implies a process of reciprocity in which the party organizations at different levels assist each other in achieving their goals. When one level of the organization consistently exploits another for its own purposes, such an asymmetrical relationship cannot be considered interdependent (1984:72).

Additionally, cooperation along a very narrow range of activities does not imply organizational interdependence.

In order to be even more precise, we can divide interdependence into three clusters: 1. institutional support activities, 2. candidate-directed services, and 3. material interdependence.

Institutional support activities are those projects aimed at sustaining an organization. For both LCCs and traditional party organization fundraising, recruiting candidates, and services to subunits are examples. On the whole, *few* institutional support linkages are expected. The ability for LCCs to win state legislative elections is a function of available resources. Conceivably, certain broad-based goals of traditional party organizations, such as full slating and support for the entire ticket, *may* not coincide with—or even run counter to—LCC objectives. It seems reasonable, then, to expect each unit to focus on its own support activities. What is more, Cotter et al. found very low levels of institutional support interdependence between county and state committees (1984:73), and we would be hardpressed to suggest how relation would be different.

Candidate-directed activities refer to the services provided candidates, such as financial support, media assistance, survey research, direct mail, telephone canvassing, and so on. By pooling resources and expertise both the LCCs and the state party organization might benefit from greater economies of scale.

We can further break down candidate-directed activities into *strategic considerations* and *tangible services*. The former relates to behind-the-scene judgments which determine the direction of a campaign and the appropriate mix of activities, and the later to specific activities—that is, the implementation of strategic decisions.

Interdependence is expected to be greater for tangible services than for strategic considerations. These new units may frequently call upon party committees to assist with labor-intensive projects. Cooperation on strategic decisions, however, will be scant. Most LCCs are highly technical, staffed by professionals, and it is doubtful they would call upon party activists (generally "amateurs") for strategic advice.

Material interdependence means the sharing of facilities, equipment, and personnel. Again, economies of scale would suggest the two units interact along this dimension. Yet, one advantage of a physical dualism would be unambiguous control of resources. Another important consideration relates to fundraising. A pronounced distinction between traditional party organizations and LCCs is the ability for donors to funnel gifts directly to legislative leaders through the latter. By doing so, contributors might feel as though they are getting a bigger bang for the buck—greater access to the influential. The appearance of being merged with the state committee (by sharing a headquarters, and so forth) may reduce this advantage. In the long run LCCs might be better off remaining physically apart from the state committee.

Data and Methodology

State legislative campaign committee studies to date have focused on either campaign finance data or interviews with LCC officials. This study, while also utilizing finance data, sought the views of state *party* leaders. In December of 1992, surveys were mailed to the leaders of each Democratic and Republican state party committee in all 50 states. In total, 49 of the 100 organizations returned the survey; 36 of these respondents have LCCs in their state. There are 30 Republican and 19 Democratic organizations included in the sample; 23 of the Republicans and 13 of the Democrats are from LCC states.[4] The geographic distribution of the sample appears random. It is also evenly divided between party chairs and executive officers, with a majority of the latter being Republican. The survey is supplemented with aggregate data, including demographics, LCC disclosure information, state committee data, the degree of interparty competition, and numerous other state-level measures.

Findings

The Formal Relationship

Respondents were asked to note the legal/formal relationship between their organization and the LCCs within their state. Table 14.1 notes the results, controlled by party. Expectations are only modestly supported; 56 percent suggested there were no formal linkages.[5] A slightly larger share of Republican organizations are nonaligned, but the difference between the parties appears minimal. The most frequent comment concerning the type of legal arrangement between the units was that the LCCs are "auxiliary" organizations or "branch" committees.

Beyond a fixed, legal arrangement, respondents were asked how the state party leaders thought LCCs in their state "fit into the overall party structure." Sixty-six percent said they were *not* part of the party organization. Surprisingly, several of the respondents (30 percent) who noted a legal relationship, also said the LCCs were *not* part of the state party organization.

Regarding another query,[6] only *one* respondent suggested that their organization controlled the activities of the LCCs. This was most surprising because the sample is, after all, composed of party leaders. Apparently, LCCs are generally perceived as autonomous regardless of explicit legal ties. This finding holds true for both parties. It was also telling that just 12 percent of the respondents noted a "legislative caucus" was responsible for LCC activities. Rather, 45 percent said legislative leaders and another 26 percent said a "small group of legislators"[7] ran the show.

Table 14.1 Formal Linkages Between LCCs and State Party Committees Controlled by Party of Respondent

	Legal Relationship	No Legal Relationship	Total
Republicans	38%	62%	66%
	(8)	(13)	(21)
Democrats	55%	45%	34%
	(6)	(5)	(11)
	44%	56%	100%
	(14)	(18)	N=33

The Question Read: "Do you know if there is any *formal* or legal relationship between these organizations and the party state committee? If so, what is this relationship?"
Source: Survey by author.

We might speculate the formal dualism would be most acute in states where LCCs are fully developed and have bountiful resources; only well-funded organizations will have the luxury of being autonomous. Although the small sample makes generalizations difficult, a cross-tabulation between legal linkages and LCC resources[8] revealed 75 percent of the well funded LCCs are autonomous units, as compared to 50 percent in the middle-range group and 66 percent in the low category.

One additional control was the extent of state laws supportive of parties.[9] A relationship does appear to exist: states with laws sympathetic to parties are twice as likely to find LCCs formally linked than are states without such laws. This would seem to support the conjecture that utilitarian considerations at least in part guide the formal LCC-state committee relationship.

Programmatic Linkages

Although the exact import of legal ties may be hard to discern, nonformal linkages, or programmatic interdependence, may say a good deal about this new relationship. How often and on what types of activities do state party committees interact with LCCs? While there may be no legal tie, by working together and sharing facilities/equipment they may be part of the same "team." The opposite may also be true.

Institutional Support Activities

Activities designed to sustain the organization, such as raising money, often require a good deal of time and effort. Table 14.2 notes the results of

Table 14.3 Financial Interdependence between LCCs and State Party Committee

	Frequency	Percent
Does State Party Give to LCCs?		
Yes	11	33%
Yes, but very little	3	9
No	14	49
		N=30
Do LCCs Give to State Party?		
Yes	8	24%
Yes, but very little	8	24
No	13	39
		N=29

The Questions Read: What is the financial relationship between the state committee and these organizations? That is, does the state committee contribute money to these organizations? Do these organizations contribute funds to the state party committee?
Source: Survey by author.

two questions regarding a financial interdependence between the state party committees and the LCCS. The first is whether the state committee contributes funds to the LCCs, and the second asks whether the LCCs help fund state party activities.

Again, the sample appears to be divided. Approximately 40 percent of the state committees give financial help to the LCCs and roughly one-half suggested LCCs help fund state party activities. A cross-tabulation between these questions suggests, generally speaking, financial interdependence either flows in both directions or not at all. Only two of the respondents that answered "no" to the first question answered "yes" to the second. Surprisingly, legal ties do not emerge as a noteworthy control, suggesting legal articulation has little bearing on institutional support activities.

With regard to fundraising *projects*, findings are similar. Only 24 percent noted their state committee worked regularly with LCCs to raise money (for either organization). A second query asked the chairs to use a ten-point scale to rank the level of coordination between the state committee and the LCCs on fundraising projects (1 being "very distant" and 10 being "very close"). The mean response was a 4.9. Forty-three percent noted a value of "3" or less.[10] There appeared to be a similar degree of cooperation on other institutional support activities. The mean level of cooperation on get-out-the-vote drives, using that same ten-point scale, was 6.5. For voter registration drives it was 5.1, and for recruiting candidates the average value was 6.5.[11]

Three bivariate ordinary least square (OLS) regressions were used, where LCC resources (measured in dollars) are introduced as the independent variable. The dependent variables are the ten-point scales measuring cooperation on fundraising, GOTV drives and candidate recruitment (each considered institutional support activities). A negative relationship was expected; that is, the more resources held by the LCCs, the lower the level of cooperation with the state party committee. Again, autonomy may be a luxury of the affluent. Results are found in Table 14.4

Only one of the coefficients (Recruit Candidates) is in the expected direction. Better funded LCCs appear to be somewhat more likely to cooperate with state committees on voter mobilization programs and fundraising activities but the regression coefficients are modest. A similar analysis, not reported here, was conducted for level of party competition.[12] Overall, increased party competition seems to lower institutional support linkages. Each of the regression coefficients are in the negative direction but are again modest; the r-squares are each less than four percent. While this finding is certainly tentative, neither does it support the notion that growing competition leads to the unification of candidate nuclei, as suggested by Schlesinger (1984, 1985, 1991).

Another control was whether the respondent's organization held a majority or minority position in the state. We might expect units out of power to interact with one another more frequently than those in the majority.[13] Findings suggest this is not the case; majority units are just as likely to work together as were minority ones. And LCCs in states with a mixed party status are *less* likely to interact with the party than are LCCs in states with a clear majority/minority division.

Table 14.4 Bivariate OLS Regression with LCC Resources ($) as Independent Variable and Ten-Point Cooperation Scales as Dependent Variables

Dependent Variables:	Slope	S.E.	R-Square	N*
Voter Mobilization	.0010	.001	.38	10
Fundraising	.0006	.001	.17	30
Recruit Candidates	-.0004	.001	.01	27

* The N fluctuates due to the varying number of respondents that suggested the LCCs in their state engage in each activity.
Source: Survey by author.

Candidate Directed Activities

A second area of interdependence may be candidate-directed activities. Here it was conjectured that interdependence would be greater for tangible activities than for strategic considerations. Respondents were asked to use a ten-point scale to assess their organization's input in LCC resource allocation decisions. A significant portion indicated they had very little say; 44 percent answered with "4" or less. Although the mean response was 5.0, the mode answer was "1" (seven respondents).

Introducing the respondent's party as a control produced an interesting finding. Democrats were less likely to interact along this dimension than were Republicans. Also, responses were normally distributed for the Republicans, but for Democrats significantly skewed toward the low end of the scale. In fact, 66 percent of the Democrats noted a score of "4" or less, and only eight percent marked "8" or higher.

A second set of queries referred to a list of tangible services. Expectations that interdependence would be greater here are supported. As Table 14.5 notes, the mean for each of the items is higher than for the strategic cooperation average (5.0). Candidate seminars and direct mail stand out as cooperative efforts. In addition to having the largest standard deviation, the survey research question produced a bimodal response frequency. It appears as though either the two units work together extensively on polling, or not at all.

Table 14.5 Cooperation between LCCs and State Committees on Tangible Candidate-Directed Activities

Activity	Mean Response	S.D.
Campaign Seminars	7.1	3.4
Direct Mail Assistance	6.8	3.0
Media Assistance	5.9	3.4
Survey Research	5.8	3.9
Contributing $ to Candidates	5.5	3.1

S.D. = Standard Deviation
N = > 22 for each item.

The cooperation scale query read: "Please use the ten-point scale to describe the degree of cooperation between the state committee and the legislative campaign committee for each project. In other words, do you work together on the activity?"
Source: Survey by author.

Austin Ranney's frequently used party competition scale was introduced as an independent variable (see note 12) in an OLS regression. Each of the candidate-directed cooperation scales were again used as the dependent variables. Results are found in Table 14.6. Coefficients again suggest interparty competition does not significantly increase LCCs/state party linkages.

Material Interdependence

Two questions were used to assess this dimension; whether the two units shared the same physical space, and whether certain staff worked for both organizations. Only 24 percent (8) of the respondents reported that the state committee and the LCCs were located in the same building. Slightly more respondents noted joint staff (31 percent), but on the whole material interdependence seems to be the exception rather than the rule. Neither LCC strength, legal ties, or level of interparty competition had any significant impact on this finding.

Table 14.6 Bivariate OLS Regressions between Level of Party Competition and Candidate-Directed Interdependence Scales*

Activity (Dep Variable)	Slope	S.E.	R-Square
Strategic Cooperation	.04	.05	.03
Tangible Benefits			
Contributions $ to Candidates	.08	.06	.06
Survey Research	.06	.12	.02
Media Assistance	.03	.08	.01
Direct Mail	.02	.09	.01
Candidate Seminars	-.02	.08	.01

N= > 22 for each item.

*The independent variable is inter-party competition and dependent variables are cooperation scales. The former is based on the aggregate outcome of a set of state-wide elections. It was extracted from Bibby, et. al. (1990). For more information on the cooperation scales, see Table 14.6.
Source: Survey by author.

Linkages and Legislative Professionalization

Simply put, findings thus far suggest some LCCs are tied to state committees while others not. None of the controls examined have provided much explanatory power. Party status and legal linkages do little to explain levels of interdependence. Nor does the extent of either state committee or LCC resources. Degree of party competition was perhaps most revealing; the null findings seem to contradict scholarly conjecture and perhaps conventional wisdom that uncertainty would lead to the merging of campaign organizations. One important dimension yet to be examined is legislative professionalization.

The professionalization, or "congressionalization", of state legislatures has been one of the most dramatic changes in state politics over the last few decades (Rosenthal 1990; Patterson 1990; Squier 1988). In the past, the archetypical state legislature consisted of amateur members, few resources and staff, and little ancillary support. The length of legislative session was short, and the average state legislator held his/her seat for two or three terms. Members conducted policy research and constituent services personally. They generally held other jobs; legislative salaries—if there were any—were meager.

The growth of state government during the 1960s and 1970s and the New Federalism movement of the 1980s, enhanced the professionalization of many state legislatures. Changes can be grouped into three areas: the style and organization of legislative life; the locus of power; and the instruments of power. The principal change in legislative style has been the growing perception that legislative service is a career, rather than a temporary interlude. Longer sessions, higher salaries, increased tenure, and a growing number of legislators who view their jobs as professions are each clear evidence of this transformation. With regard to locus of power, throughout much of this century state legislatures were overshadowed by the executive and/or urban party bosses. At roughly the same time many of the urban machines declined, resources and staff within the legislature expanded. Power slowly shifted from these external forces to legislative leaders. Finally, the instruments of power available to legislative leaders have changed. The creation of in-house research units and legislative commissions has allowed these bodies to reduce their dependency on administrative agencies.

It is conjectured that each of these dynamics may play a role in keeping LCCs away from the traditional party organization. As rank-and-file members see their posts as professions, they will be inclined to keep their campaign organization (the LCC) narrowly focused and under their direct control. Along with growing policy and budgetary autonomy, LCCs might be viewed by legislative leaders as simply a new external resource. What is more, these units grant legislative leaders autonomy from traditional party organizations—generally under the governor's control—to reward or punish caucus members, secure their own leadership posts, and/or augment the caucus. A measure of legislative professionalization is therefore introduced as a control. The distance between LCCs and state party committees, for both legal and interdependent dimensions, is believed to be greatest in states with professional legislatures.

There are several ways we might measure legislative professionalization.[14] A parsimonious index has been developed by Kurtz (1992). He uses a three-point scale based on member pay, length of session, and staffing levels. States with part time bodies are scored "1", with hybrid bodies "2", and with highly professional legislatures "3."

At the outset it is worthwhile to note *every* state in the professional category has legislative campaign committees, roughly 60 percent of states with hybrid bodies and only 50 percent of the states with part-time legislatures have these units.

For both legal ties and notions of "overall fit," levels of legislative professionalization appeared to play an important role. Seventy percent of the respondents from states with full-time legislatures noted *no* formal relationship, compared with 28 percent in hybrid states and 36 percent in part-time states.

Results regarding programmatic linkages point to one of the most striking findings in the data set. The relationship between legislative professionalization and project interdependence—both institutional support and candidate-directed—is consistently negative. In other words, the more professional a state's legislature, the less likely the LCCs within that state will interact with the state party committee. Table 14.7 lists the correlations between the interaction scales noted above and the legislative professionalization scale. The top set of variables refer to institutional support activities and the bottom to candidate-directed services. Although a few of the coefficients are modest, *every* one is in a negative direction and several are quite strong.

Legislative professionalization was also telling with regard to material interdependence. Only 14 percent of the respondents from professional states said their organization shared either office space or personnel with the LCCs. Over 50 percent from part-time states suggested this type of cooperation occurred.

Discussion

This research sought to answer two questions; are state-level legislative campaign committees linked with traditional state party committees; and what are the forces that influence this relationship. With regard to the former, a mixed bag was found. Roughly one half of the respondents suggested there were legal or formal ties between the units. Concerning project interdependence, linkages were also found to be modest. This was particu-

Table 14.7 Correlation between Measures of Project Interdependence and Legislative Professionalization

Activity	Correlation	N*
Fundraising	-.86	30
Recruiting Candidates	-.81	27
Voter Registration	-.58	8
Voter Mobilization Programs	-.28	10
Candidate Seminars	-.94	24
Media Assistance	-.86	23
Survey Research	-.63	16
Direct Mail	-.19	19
Strategic Cooperation	-.06	34
Contributing $ to Candidates	-.01	29

* The N fluctuates due to the varying number of respondents that suggested the LCCs in their state engage in each activity.
Legislative professionalization is based three criteria: legislative pay, length of session, and staffing levels. For a complete break-down, see Kurtz (1992).
Source: Survey by author.

larly true with regard to institutional support activities. Although there seems to be a level of cooperation on tangible candidate activities, joint strategic decision making was sparse. However, in each of these areas the degree to which the respondent's state legislature was professionalized proved to be an important control. Levels of project interdependence, in particular, were much lower in states with full-time legislatures than in ones with part-time bodies.

Several components might help explain the import of legislative professionalization. As state legislative service becomes fulltime, well paying, and prestigious, members begin to view these posts as professions. Ehrenhalt's argument (1992) that contemporary legislators represent a different breed, primarily because they see their service as a career rather than a temporary stopping ground, may be a key part of the dynamic between LCCs and traditional parties. The more the job is worth keeping, the more channelled the objectives and activities of the LCCs—and consequently their distance from traditional party organizations.

A second, related possibility is that professionalization places an added emphasis on majority party control. This is certainly true in states such as New York, California, and Illinois where the power and perks accompanying majority status are profound, including complete control over the flow of legislation. Majority control may too spill into campaign resources. Rather than being a tool of membership or an appendage of the state party, perhaps LCCs in professionalized states are instruments of caucus leadership. As such, their foremost goal may be to secure and maintaining a majority. Gierzynski's (1992) finding that LCCs appear more willing to fund close races rather then safe reelection campaigns seems to buttress this argument.

Finally, with the expansion of legislative duties and resources comes the growth of professional staff.[15] Instead of being granted their jobs as patronage or working on a part-time basis, as in the past, modern legislative staff are hired for their skills. They are paid very well and often hold their jobs at the discretion of caucus leadership. They are not the product of party politics but of universities and graduate schools. Many of these professionals are involved (at least on a part-time basis) with LCC activities. In brief, not only are their paychecks directly tied to the success of the caucus, but they have few material or ideological links with the traditional party. Interactions with that organization will thus be calculated from purely an instrumental vantage.

What does this imply about the future of state parties? It is hard to say how powerful, autonomous legislative campaign units will impact traditional party structures. Much of this question relates to the activities and goals of these new units—issues not addressed here. At the very least, this research calls into question elements of the party adjustment/growth perspective. It seems tenuous, at best, to lump LCC and state party resources together when assessing "party" viability—as is often done (Gierzynski and Breaux 1992; Dwyre and Stonecash 1993). In states with professional legislatures, the very states where LCC resources are the greatest, the two units are often structurally and programmatically distinct. With the trend toward full-time state legislatures, it is certainly possible that linkages found in some states will become strained in the near future.

We might also speculate as to whether the two will compete for resources. Contributors might find LCCs more attractive than traditional party units. And why not, as these seem to be extensions of caucus leadership, those that control the flow of legislation. If one is interested in influencing policy or gaining favor with decision makers, it may be more effective to send money to LCC officials than to party leaders. And, as the power of these new units increases they become even more attractive to contributors. Although campaign money may not be zero-sum, growth in one sphere certainly does not imply growth in the other. In this light, LCCs may be even more damaging than candidate-centered campaigns or PACs.

State-level LCCs have only recently caught the eye of scholars. The first impulse was to congratulate parties for their adaptability. Parties have been important organizations, linking average citizens with their government. They have helped coalesce an exceedingly complex system and give voters a choice, both in candidates and in policies. They encourage participation, mediate conflict, and empower the economically disadvantaged. Any indication of party resurgence may be, for some, hard to resist.

Nevertheless, as sovereign, office and level-specific campaign machines, the impact of LCCs on traditional parties—and for that matter popular governance—may be serious. They may be fueling what Burnham calls the "accelerated decomposition of nominally partisan coalitions across office specific and level specific lines" (1989:20). As the power and influence of these organizations grows, the powers and activities performed by traditional party organizations may well decline. Rather than being evidence of party renewal, state LCCS may be yet another agent in the radical recomposition of the American political system (Burnham 1989). This may *not* be the "party" we had in mind.

Notes

1. These units are referred to by some scholars as "legislative caucus campaign committees."

2. Legislative campaign committee operatives in New York were recently accused of conducting their activities while on the state payroll. In the fall of 1987 Manfred Ohrenstein, Minority Leader of the New York State Senate, was indicted on 564 counts of conspiracy, grand larceny, and related charges. He had, the prosecution argued, used state employees solely for the purpose of running campaigns. One of the counts claimed operatives were paid up to $10,000 per month in state monies. Ohrenstein argued the indictment violated the line between legislative and executive affairs and that no law had been passed limiting such practices. Although this claim carried little weight in the lower courts, it was supported by the New York State Court of Appeals in the fall of 1990.

3. While the range of LCC concerns may be debated, and is, (Gierzynski 1992; Shea 1993), few would argue winning elections is not their top priority. The same would hold true for traditional geographic party organizations.

4. Because this distribution is clearly not optimal, a close eye will be kept on party as a control.

5. Throughout the survey respondents were asked to provide both perceptual and some factual information. This question, as well as several others to follow, deals with the latter. There are certainly other ways of collecting this information—including a review of all 100 state party by-laws. The slight advantages of such a method are, however, far outweighed by the costs.

6. This was an open-ended question which read: "Who controls their activities?"

7. I am tempted to conclude these "small groups" are indeed composed of legislative leaders, but we can not be sure.

8. The latter was created by combining Gierzynski's (1992) data with Jewell and Olson's (1986) figures. Combined, 20 (of 34) LCC states have aggregate figures—twelve of which are included in our sample.

9. This measure was compiled from an Advisory Commission on Intergovernmental Affairs Report (1984).

10. Again, party differences were minimal. Legal connections between the units also had little impact. In fact, of the state committees with legal links to the LCCs, more worked independently to raise money than together.

11. These questions were only asked to those respondents who believed the LCCs in their state engaged in these activities. Obviously, if an LCC does not conduct get-out-the-vote drives, for example, linkage questions along this dimension are moot. In a way, then, our measure is a rather soft test of interdependence.

12. Party competition is measured using Austin Ranney's scale, recalculated for 1988 (Bibby 1990). Here the aggregate outcomes of several state-wide elections are used; the more evenly divided the totals (between the two major parties), the higher the interparty competition ranking.

13. One limit to this control is the difficulty in defining "minority" or "majority" party status. Three components should be considered: the party's position in the House; the party's status in the Senate; and the party of the governor. Consequently, I divided the sample into three groups: respondents whose party controls all three components (majority); respondents whose party controls none of the components (minority), and respondents from mixed party states (mixed). From these calculations, of the 100 state party committees, 16 are majority units, 16 are minority units, and 68 are mixed. In the sample, four are majority, seven are minority, and twenty-five are mixed.

14. John Grumm (1970), for example, suggests there are at least four dimensions: compensation of legislators, length of session, expenditures for legislative service and operations, and "legislative service scores." While his index is certainly comprehensive, it is not used here because it is rather dated.

15. I realize the inverse may have occurred. That is, the growth of staff has lead to increase legislative activity. At the very least, there may be a reciprocal relationship.

PART FOUR

Party Policy, Culture, and Values

15

A Tale of Two Parties: National Committee Policy Initiatives Since 1992

Laura Berkowitz
Steve Lilienthal

There is consensus that American politics is in trouble, and many of the complaints focus on the failures of the system. Dissatisfaction with the economy, frustration with foreign policy, and disgust with government gridlock all contribute to this disenchantment. The American electorate, characterized by declining efficacy and increased levels of alienation and apathy, regard political parties as having lost touch. Not only is the intensity of partisanship declining, but the percentage of the electorate who view themselves as "independent" is now over 40 percent. There is a growing perception that the current party system is incapable of responding to the challenges of the 1990s.

The parties themselves are aware of these difficulties, and are recognizing that people want to be appraised of the specific policy directions. Bill Brock, a former Republican national chair, expressed the problem cogently: "Voters don't have the foggiest idea of what we stand for in terms of governance" (Cook 1993). Parties are mindful of the chord struck by Ross Perot's charge that they are not responsive to citizens' concerns. The electorate not only wants to know what the parties stand for, but also want to be included in creating those policies.

Both the Democratic and Republican National Committees (DNC and RNC) have instituted new programs to facilitate party policy making and involve their own grassroots membership. These initiatives include meetings, publications, surveys, new organizations, television programs, and media events aimed at furthering dialogue about issues and party philosophy. The potential of these innovations to make the national committees into significant forces for formulating and articulating policy proposals is the focus of this essay.

Information used for this analysis was developed from personal and telephone interviews.[1] Findings suggest a genuine commitment to enlarge the scope of party activities. There appears to be enthusiasm for the idea that involvement in "the business of ideas" is not only needed to reinvigorate the national parties, but also may be necessary for their survival. This represents a significant change in the focus of the national committees; it is widely believed that preoccupation with electoral activities seems no longer sufficient to meet the challenges of the last decade of the twentieth century.

Past Attempts At Party Policy Making

Policy considerations have always been a secondary concern for the national committees. Their involvement in issues is related to their electoral role and their function as a communication forum for state and national party leaders. The DNC and RNC have traditionally exerted some limited influence in candidate selection and recruitment. Also, their national convention responsibilities include constructing a party platform, which necessitates policy considerations. In-party national committees have worked to promote the president's program, while out-parties have employed a defensive strategy, often responding to presidential initiatives by simply criticizing his or her proposals.

There are several factors which restrict the policy-making role of the national committees. Their historic lack of a strong policy orientation, competition with others to speak for the parties, little political influence over party office holders, and the coalition nature of the parties all serve as constraining influences (Hames 1994). In the past there have been proposals for the national organizations to become more involved in policy development. Perhaps the most noted was the 1950 report of the American Political Science Association Committee on Political Parties, *Toward a More Responsible Two-Party System*. The report warned there is a "chance that the electorate will turn its back upon the two parties unless they become more participatory and issue-oriented. Those who suggest that election should deal with personalities but not with programs suggest at the same time that party membership mean nothing at all" (1950:28). The report urged "formulations of programs linking state and local issues to questions of national and international concern [that would] help overcome unduly narrow views of party" (1950:67). The programs were supposed to "bubble up" from the grassroots level. Having the parties place more emphasis "upon policy and the interrelationship of problems at the various levels of government [would make] association with a party . . . interesting and attractive to many who hold aloof today" (1950:67).

There have also been previous attempts by both parties to become more policy oriented. In 1956 the Democrats formed the Democratic Advisory Council (DAC) to serve as a policy-making body between conventions

(Roberts 1994). Nine years later the Republicans created the Republican Coordinating Committee (RCC) in response to the devastating Goldwater defeat (Bibby 1994). Both initiatives, although short-lived, did succeed in mobilizing party elites to produce consensus. Policy position papers were generated by both groups. The RCC was more successful at articulating coherent policy positions, but some planks of the DAC platforms were used by the congressional candidates and the Kennedy presidential campaign. However, both organizations labored under handicaps that limited their effectiveness. Both were nonparticipatory, elite-based organizations. The policy positions agreed upon at their meetings did not necessarily translate into broad party-wide consensus. A similar problem bedeviled policy groups established with the national committees, such as under RNC Chair Bill Brock (Klinkner 1994) and DNC Chair Charles Manatt (Menefee-Libey 1994).

One of the few attempts at broader based, participatory policy formation was the Democrat's abortive midpresidential conventions of 1974 and 1978. These meetings did not produce a strong consensus, and were eventually disbanded. However, they are noteworthy in that they foreshadowed both parties' current efforts to include a wider range of participants in developing policy stands.

The potential for national committees to advance policy direction is much greater today than at any previous period. The parties recognize that there is a danger they may be viewed as mere vote-getting organizations at the very time the public hungers for meaningful choices and a belief that their choices will make a difference. The way campaigns are conducted has also contributed to the growing alienation of the electorate from the parties. Media driven, candidate-centered campaigns serve to minimize the voters' role, and the increased reliance on computerized voting lists, mass mailing, and phone banks combine to depersonalize the connection between the party organization and its members. Substantive policy alternatives have been reduced to subliminal imagery and pictorial allusion (Lowi 1992a). However, technology is now being utilized to bridge the gap with the electorate. Innovations such as satellite and cable television are heralded as ways to again involve partisans who found their role devalued by the rise of mass media and computer technology. The parties hope that these techniques can provide activists with an opportunity to help shape the party's message. They also expect these new technologies and their expanded policy orientation will attract new constituents. While both parties seem eager to embrace this new technology, differences in how each committee has chosen to apply technological innovations will also be reviewed. The eventual success of these recent outreach attempts is yet unclear, as is their influence on the long-term prospects of both major parties.

Republicans: Leading the Pack Again

Policy Making

The Republican Party has made the strongest early commitment to better communicate coherent principles and policies to voters. RNC Chair, Haley Barbour, recently noted: "the National Committee must take the lead in emphasizing the principles that unite . . . [We] need a strong party per se, and must resist allowing the party to become subservient to any candidate, officeholder, or faction" (1993b:1). Tenets of private enterprise, market economics, free trade, reduced government regulation, peace through strength, public and personal security, opposition to drugs and crime, and a belief in traditional family values are the policy stands being pushed by the party.

Republicans have established the National Policy Forum (NPF), which holds town meetings across the country and allows politicians and the public, not all of whom are Republicans, to discuss issues. Officially, the NPF operates independently of the RNC, although both organizations share the same chair, Haley Barbour, and the former is widely perceived as an arm of the latter. According to Mary Crawford, Communication Director of the NPF, one rationale for legally disassociating the NPF from the RNC is to include Independents and even disaffected Democrats in its actualities. In response to questions regarding the partisan nature of the meetings, Crawford stressed their participatory nature and likened the sixty NPF forums to "think tanks in reverse." In these meetings held across the country, local elected representatives and a panel of experts give short presentations on a particular policy issue to stimulate discussion. They then actively seek input from the audience; two-way communication is encouraged. She stresses how important it is that people feel included and recognize that their concerns are important in determining the policy of the party.

The RNC is also directly involved in other modes of two-way communication. Over 800,000 party officials, elected officials, donors, and activists were recently polled by mail for their input on issues ranging from the budget to social policies. Almost 140,000 questionnaires were returned, a response rate which reflects the respondents' intense interest in expressing their views. Responses repeatedly expressed frustration that the GOP had not solicited or advocated the views of its grassroots membership.

The Republicans are also relying on more traditional means of communicating with voters. The NPF has reissued the journal *Commonsense*, which the Republican National Committee had published in the late 1970s and early 1980s. Two issues have been published by the spring of 1994 and plans are to continue publishing indefinitely. According to editor Judith Van Rest, articles deal with domestic and foreign policy topics and are geared toward fostering the discussion of ideas. It may not influence Republican policy making directly, but is intended to present a forum for the consideration of issues. Circulation is approximately 20,000, and recipients include mayors, governors, members of Congress, heads of university political science departments, and think tanks. While the RNC has no prior editorial approval on its contents and it operates under a separate copyright from the previous journal, Barbour reads all submissions.

New Technologies

Just as the Republicans proved more adept at harnessing the power of television advertising in the 1950s and computer technology and direct mail and survey research in the 1960s and 1970s, they are once again leading the Democrats in the use of cable and satellite television to communicate with their membership. If the widespread use of television advertising and computers replaced the old-style political gathering and citizen participation in politics, the GOP's use of cable and satellite television are helping to bring them back.

The RNC leaders realize that they have only scratched the surface of the new technology. Barbour suggests: "We're just starting to use technology in the way a lot of businesses and industries have been using it" (Seib 1994). They utilize satellite technology for its new *Rising Tide* television program. This weekly one hour news program, cohosted by Barbour and RNC Deputy Communications Director Leigh Ann Metzger, is broadcast by satellite to 4,000 local GOP organizations. *Rising Tide* accepts calls from viewers, and is structured along the lines of a news magazine. An RNC advertisement promises "Whether it's welfare reform in Wisconsin, reaching out to minorities in urban America, or a tough stand on crime in Virginia, *Rising Tide* keeps you plugged into Republican messages and ideas at the local level."[2] RNC communications director Chuck Greener notes that its weekly airing enables the program to present up-to-the-minute news about important legislative and political events of consequence to Republican activists. For example, a show in mid-February featured a discussion with New York City mayor Rudy Guiliani on crime and the failure of the parole system. Segments also included discussions with Governor George Allen (R-VA) and GOP media consultant Greg Stevens on how the crime issue was used to win the governorship in 1992. College Republicans, Young Republicans, and local Republican Women's groups often plan their meetings around the broadcasts of *Rising Tide*.

State parties have also started to work in conjunction with the RNC to make use of the new satellite technology. Washington state's Republican Party used the RNC's television facilities to link up party activists attending precinct caucuses with Senate Minority Leader Bob Dole (R-KS), Sen. Slade

Gorton (R-WA), and Rep. Jennifer Dunn (R-WA). Both cable and satellites were used to carry "The 1994 Republican Community Forum," during which those in attendance submitted issues questionnaires.

Another attempt to initiate dialogue between office holders and party activists is Lamar Alexander's Republican Exchange Satellite Network (RESN), which sponsors *Republican Neighborhood Meetings*. RESN spokesperson Kevin Phillips estimates that the April 1994 broadcast was received by 2,500 neighborhood groups. Originally, they were carried by satellite but have now been picked up by over one hundred cable companies with a potential audience of over 31 million. An "Electronic Blackboard" collects viewer's toll-free calls on a host of issues. Innovative segments help keep viewers watching; *The Tennessee Journal* publisher M. Lee Smith has dubbed Alexander "The new Mr. Rogers in the GOP neighborhood" (M.L. Smith 1993:A-9).

Democrats: Following Clinton's Lead

Policy Making

While Democrats are also concerned about encouraging dialogue on issues, they are concentrating primarily on developing new means of communicating the priorities of the President to the party's grassroots. The DNC is combining its traditional role of building and financing the party's national political apparatus with generating support for Clinton's programs (Barnes 1993). According to Craig Smith, former DNC Political Director, the role of party used to be solely focused on elections, yet both message development and lobbying are needed today to actively promote the president's legislative agenda (Tisinger 1993). The DNC and the White House work in tandem on common goals and coordinated strategy. The National Committee is concentrating on generating grassroots support, while the White House has focused its efforts primarily on Congress.

The energized atmosphere at the DNC is attributable to the first opportunity in twelve years for the Democrats to initiate policy and control the policy agenda. Anita Perez-Ferguson, Education Director for the DNC, remarked in a recent interview that there is a significant difference in reacting to a Republican president's initiatives and following the lead of one's own president. Health care reform and economic programs are high on the President's agenda and therefore the DNC's agenda. The National Health Care Campaign, launched by the DNC in the fall of 1993, typifies this approach: the deployment of resources to mobilize the governing party around an issue-oriented agenda.

The DNC has organized telephone banks, blanketed editorial page editors with letters and op-ed pieces, and sponsored activities designed to attract the attention of the press (Tisinger 1993). Arranging for trained and fully briefed surrogate speakers to address local groups on health care is another new service of the national committee. They are augmenting grassroots mobilization efforts with an advertising blitz, including extensive radio and TV advertisements supporting the president's economic plan. DNC Chair David Wilhelm estimates that these efforts cost between $1.5 million and $1.7 million, and they resulted in over 1.5 million telephone calls to Congress supporting the President's economic plan (Barnes 1993b). They are also spending approximately $2 million on polling to help White House policy makers determine which issues are of paramount concern to voters (Lambro 1994).

Wilhelm has heralded the creation of an "activist network" that also seeks to establish a "full scale dialogue between people and their government, and people and their party."[3] He emphasized that a "citizens' lobby," formed to fight the special interests in Washington on issues of concern to working families, will be designed to reach Americans who feel disenfranchised by politics as usual.

A recently expanded staff permits the DNC to broaden the scope of its outreach programs. Prior to 1992, the main focus of the National Committee was regional communication and the election of more Democrats; efforts were organized around geographic and regional lines. These regional undertakings have been expanded to include a network of constituency groups whose sole focus was to build communication around common issues. Alice Travis, Assistant Executive Director of the DNC, sees the Constituency Division and the Division of Government Affairs, both of which were founded in 1992, as significant innovations. The Division of Government Affairs has expanded the means by which Democratic office holders on both the local and state level are given relevant information on policy, elections, and all aspects of the party activity. The Constituency Division is an outreach to specific groups of Democrats who share mutual interests. The Youth Division, Asian-American group, women's group, and individuals concerned with disability issues are examples of initiatives geared toward activating specific elements of the party. Instead of party elites determining policy for the party's various constituencies, it is hoped that these groups will contribute input to insure their particular concerns are addressed.

New Technologies

The Health Care Outreach's innovations are examples of how the Democrats are also embracing technologies of the 1990s. According to Deputy Press Secretary Adam Sohn, the DNC has conducted two video teleconferences with health care spokesperson Hillary Rodham Clinton. Using hookups with five different media sites, approximately 500 community activists were afforded opportunities to direct questions to the first lady. Sohn sees video teleconferences as an important new mechanism for direct two-way party communication.

During the 1992 campaign the DNC assisted the Wisconsin Democratic Party with two statewide issue forums with party activists via satellite. Undecided voters and those leaning toward supporting the Democratic ticket were also invited by phone and mail solicitation to watch the meetings. Regional sites included a sports bar and a college campus. Senator Bill Bradley (D-NJ), Governor David Walters (D-OK) and then DNC Chair Ron Brown participated in the forums, which also featured local candidates. Guests answered phoned-in questions from the regional audiences.

Former state party executive director Jonathan Sender estimates well over 1,000 people attended both meetings. The impact of the meetings resonated well beyond the halls: television stations would pick up the broadcasts and use excerpts in their newscasts. The *Wisconsin State Journal* credited the "video town hall meetings with providing a chance for people who otherwise never think or talk about politics to do so. That's what an election year should be all about" (1992:11-A).

The DNC has also made use of satellite technology in more conventional terms, such as press conferences. One interesting event was conducted in mid-April 1994 when Americans were filing their tax returns. To demonstrate how limited the impact on raising middle-class taxes the tax program would be, Chairman Wilhelm appeared at a large baseball stadium with only 1.2 percent of the seats filled—the exact number Democrats claimed would pay more under the Clinton tax increase. The event was beamed to television news stations across the country.

Another important communication innovation of the DNC is the "morning briefs," communications which are sent to approximately 2,000 individuals, including state party chairs, big city mayors, Democratic state officials, and grassroots activists by fax at least three times a week. They have been tremendously successful at communicating current party positions and topics of interest. As one might expect, much attention has been given to health care issues. Recipients are encouraged to further disseminate the morning briefings. For example, the New York State Democratic Committee regularly distributes copies to its local party committees. In all, it is estimated that the morning briefs have a circulation of over 10,000.

Since 1993 the DNC has routinely conducted "satellite media tours" with cabinet secretaries to discuss issues of importance. Its constituency outreach also utilizes this technology to facilitate communication with local groups. However, the Democrats have not approximated the RNC's programming on a regular basis. Catherine Moore, Press Secretary for the DNC, has voiced skepticism about the effectiveness of such programs. "What is the value of reaching people who you are already reaching? I wonder if the Republicans are reaching the people that are already with them" (Lambrecht 1994:4A).

Constraints on the Shift to Issues

While there is much enthusiasm about both parties' recent policy orientation and new mechanisms to communicate about issues, there are reasons for skepticism about the long term impact of these initiatives. The national committees have little longstanding commitment to policy making. They are by nature very responsive to the state and local committees, which have picked their own officers, nominated their own candidates, developed their own policy stands, and raised and disbursed their own funds without regard for the national committees (Beck and Sorauf 1992). They have become a significant force in American politics by building internal cohesion, as well as attaining financial and organizational resources. In fact, their "nuts and bolts" efforts have been directed toward providing services and funds to individual candidates and campaigns, not in the development of policy.

While the national committees have achieved some measure of autonomy, primarily through their fundraising success, they have no scheme for creating policy. The president and other office holders have always been the source of policy and dictated the agenda for the party in power. Kenneth Hill, Vice President of the National Policy Forum, explains: "The whole process of policy development over the last twelve years (when GOP presidents held the White House) was an assistant secretary sitting in a Washington office telling everybody what the policy was." The out-party has historically relied on congressional leaders to articulate its concerns.

Thus, there is no guarantee that these longstanding tendencies will change with this new-found enthusiasm for policy pronouncements and discussion. For example, the DNC's role in mobilizing grassroots support for the Clinton health care campaign has been drastically reduced in the last year. Control has shifted to Senator Jay Rockefeller's health care reform project, and the DNC now primarily serves as a purchasing agent for television advertisements (Kosova 1994).

There is also a danger that the DNC is likely to become less a vehicle to promote an issue agenda within the party and to the public and more a public relations shop for Clinton's 1996 reelection campaign. Many other Democrats fear their own campaign needs will be shortchanged by the DNC. Instead, its resources will be expended lobbing for the President's programs: "That is important to us, but we also need a first-rate political operation up and running. We've got to turn our attention to reelecting Democrats" (Barnes 1993b:2834). Congressional leaders are careful to guard their own party leadership roles; party unity does not extend to automatically accepting DNC pronouncements with which they disagree. For example, Wilhelm recently attacked the president's congressional Whitewater critics at a DNC meeting in Cleveland. His words were repudiated the following day by Speaker of the

House Thomas Foley. Foley suggested, on national television, that personal attacks on members of Congress make for bad politics (Grove 1994).

There is also a certain amount of skepticism about how long the RNC chair will remain an important party spokesperson. Many anticipate a change when the presidential primary season is in full swing with the front runner encroaching on that position, and the eventual nominee usurping it. The influence wielded by the nominee and national chair in drafting the RNC 1996 platform is also a matter of speculation.

Another fundamental problem with the national committees taking the lead in policy initiatives stems from the nature of the parties. Each are comprised of broad-based coalitions. Authoritative policy statements have often fragmented these coalitions. The extreme positions of the left wing of the Democratic Party in the 1970s caused long-term damage. According to DNC Political Director Don Switzer, "There will always be disagreements on policy in our party. But our party learned its lessons in 1980 when we tore ourselves apart . . . This is our president. We're not about to get into a suicide war and tear ourselves apart for 1996" (Lambro 1994). Much the same thing threatens the Republicans on social issues. RNC Chair Barbour warns that the Republican party must "be especially diligent in showing that we are a diverse, inclusive, and tolerant party: that we understand that in a party large enough to elect a president everyone will not always agree on everything" (1993b). Morton Blackwell, a member of the RNC from Virginia, expressed concern that the NPF's plan to air different policy positions might backfire and foster disagreements. It could encourage publicity about disputes within the party and portray "the image of a Republican Party badly divided and fighting itself on these issues" (Berke 1993). Thus, both parties are well aware of the potential booby traps in fermenting debate.

Conclusion

In order for the National Committees to aggressively advance policy initiatives, they must walk a fine line. The DNC and RNC must avoid stepping on the toes of congressional leaders, state and local organizations, constituencies within the party, and candidates who look to them for support. If they completely avoid controversy and decisiveness, their efforts may be reduced to meaningless platitudes and broad generalities. These may not offend anyone, but neither will they give anyone a clear sense of direction.

There are many indications that the national committees are sincere in their commitment to move toward a more "responsible" role than merely dispensing cash and technological services. American politicians are experts at running campaigns that emphasize their own merits rather than party programs. Perhaps the new initiatives will enhance the role of the National Committees in attracting better, more qualified candidates. Individuals committed to the party's philosophical direction might be motivated to run for office due to the appeal of a coherent policy stand by the national committees.

The success of Perot in 1992 was a clear signal that the major parties should begin to develop programs which link them and the citizenry on issues and around broad philosophical principles. Ongoing participatory policy forums will not only improve communication, but also may result in a more thoughtful, coherent party platform which directly addresses the voters' concerns. Perhaps the unrealized goals of the RCC and DAC will be achieved, and issue position documents will be produced on a regular basis. These policy stances would not be dictated from the top but would arise bottom up, the result of a grassroots consensus. Technologies developed in this decade may facilitate this dialogue. While it is premature to evaluate the success of these endeavors, recent policy initiatives may well affect the role and the future prospects of both national parties.

Notes

1. Information for this article was obtained through several personal interviews: Mary Crawford, March 1994; Kenneth Hill, summer, 1993; Anita Perez-Ferguson, March 1994; Kevin Phillips, April 1994; Adam Sohn, May, 1994; Alice Travis, May 1994; Judith Van Rest, April 1994.

2. RNC advertisement (March-April 1994).

3. Remarks of David Wilhelm before the DNC Executive Committee Meeting, Albuquerque, NM, June 26, 1993.

16

The Democratic Leadership Council: Institutionalizing a Party Faction

Jon F. Hale

Bill Clinton captured the Democratic party nomination and won the presidency as "a different kind of Democrat." He touted a new governing philosophy based on opportunity, responsibility, and community; this theme was designed to appeal to the mainstream voters who had been increasingly deserting the party in past presidential elections. This message, however, did not come out of thin air; it was developed by the Democratic Leadership Council (DLC), a policy-oriented organization unconnected with the Democratic National Committee. This chapter examines the development and institutionalization of the DLC, founded in 1985 by a political entrepreneur and a group of moderate Democrats.[1] The DLC helped pull Democratic elected officials back into national party affairs, established a niche for itself as a developer of ideas and policy within the party, and served as a springboard for the Clinton candidacy. Moreover, the institutionalization of the DLC assures that it will continue to play a significant role in Democratic party politics and presidential nominations.[2]

The Birth of the DLC

Many specific factors may lead to the development of alternative party structures. These preconditions result in the belief that the existing party is not meeting the needs of its members. This appears to be the case with the DLC. Perceptions of a liberal bias within the national Democratic Party arose from reforms in the delegate selection process. The McGovern/Fraser Reform Commission and numerous subsequent ones limited the control of formal party leaders over the presidential nomination process and forced representatives of the "official" party to compete for delegate positions on an equal footing. The result was a sharp decline in the participation of elected officials and an overall increase in the influence of liberal activists.[3] This trend was reinforced by the growing number of new style politicians who put together personal political "enterprises" largely independent of party organizations (Loomis 1988; Ehrenhalt 1991). Among Democrats, these politicians tended to distance themselves from presidential politics, seeing no advantage in tying themselves to a national party perceived by many as too liberal. While this distancing strategy was an important self-preservation tool, it helped assure the dominance of liberal activists in presidential politics.

The first organization to emerge because of this perceived institutional bias was the Committee on Party Effectiveness (CPE) formed by a group of House Democrats. When a party loses the White House, as the Democrats did in 1980, the task of idea and policy development is generally ceded to the congressional party. From 1981 to 1984 the CPE attempted, in the words of its former leader Rep. Gillis Long (LA), "to reassess our Party's direction and redefine our message" (National House Democratic Caucus 1984). The CPE produced policy documents that were applauded politely as a first attempt by Democrats to find their voice in the 1980s (Price 1984:284). A 1982 document included a well-received paper on long-term economic policy, written by Long and Reps. Richard Gephardt (MO) and Tim Wirth (CO). It was seen as an attempt to reorient Democrats away from their emphasis on redistribution toward goals of restoring growth and opportunity (CPE 1982). A more detailed document was submitted to the Platform Committee at the 1984 convention, but the group's contribution was overwhelmed by the sheer size of the 45,000-word final platform.

Nonetheless, CPE was the forerunner of the DC. This House-based organization articulated several of the major themes later fleshed out by the DC: economic growth and opportunity, reciprocal responsibility, community, and assertive American leadership in global affairs. It was run by Long's top assistant, Al From, who would later found the DC, and Will Marshall, who would become From's top assistant at the DC. What is more, 27 of the 41 CPE members would later become DC members.[4]

The Early DC, 1985-1988

The 1984 election accelerated the demand for the formation of an alternative party organization. Democratic nominee Walter Mondale had built his nomination around the party's liberal wing and as a result was strongly supported *within* the party, but had little appeal among the general electorate. As Pomper notes, "Mondale personified the problem of the Democratic party generally, the need to define a more general vision from the clash of competing factions" (1985:16). In fact, Mondale mixed relatively moderate economic positions with liberal stances on social and defense/foreign policy issues, but his call for a tax increase to reduce the deficit was portrayed by Republicans as an attempt to make the white middle class pay more taxes for government programs that benefitted an array of special interests—especially blacks—in the Democratic Party (Edsall 1991:205).

Not only was the party message perceived as too liberal in 1984, it was viewed as having a profound negative effect on the entire Democratic ticket. During the 1984 campaign Republicans tied themselves closely to the popular Reagan-Bush ticket, while labeling Democratic opponents as "Mondale liberals." In his state-by-state survey of campaigns in the deep South, for example, Lamis (1990) found the use of this tactic in virtually every Senate and competitive House race. Particularly disturbing to Democrats were the losses of two moderate Senate candidates, Sen. Walter "Dee" Huddleston (KY) and Gov. James B. Hunt (NC). These defeats served as "a sober warning to southern Democrats of the national party's negative impact" (Cohen 1986:270). As then-Senator Lawton Chiles (FL) stated "Most of us had been running away from the Democratic Party for years. But we were beginning to see that you couldn't enjoy the luxury of that anymore. Maybe some of us would survive, but there wasn't going to be a Democratic Party behind us in our state" (Barnes 1986:19). Thus, the 1984 election created a "market" for membership in the DC among Democratic elected officials who believed the party's national message was too liberal and who worried about the impact of the national party identity on their own political careers.

This market was tapped through the political entrepreneurship of Al From. Formerly Executive Director of the House Caucus under Gillis Long, From was well respected on Capitol Hill. His tenure at the caucus ended when Long's term expired in 1984 and his association with Long ended in January 1985 when the Louisiana congressman died. The formation of the DC was announced in February 1985. As one founding member later remarked, "Al From was looking for a job. He had an idea, and he made it work."

From's idea was to influence the movement of the national party away from its post-1968 liberalism, making it more competitive at the presidential level and less of a burden for Democratic candidates at the state and local level. He believed the party needed a more moderate message in order to re-enlist Democratic elected officials into national party affairs. He conceived the DC as a supplementary policy-oriented organization, with a membership consisting of elected officials only.

The initial DC leadership cadre consisted of elected officials who stood to gain from the achievement of the organization's political goals, and those who had worked closely with From in the House Caucus. Governor Chuck Robb (VA), Senator Sam Nunn (GA), and Representative Richard Gephardt (MO) were the primary DC spokesmen at the news conference announcing the group's formation. Governor Bruce Babbitt (AR), Senator Lawton Chiles (FL), and Representative James Jones (OK) were also heavily involved in the DC's initial activities. The DC was initially perceived as a stalking horse for southern, moderate presidential candidates in 1988, Robb and Nunn in particular, and this association helped get the DC off the ground. These prominent officials linked the group to financial contributors and publicized its goals through a series of appearances and media events. In brief, their association with the DC "helped with prestige and money, and helped make the organization seem vital and attractive," according to Bruce Reed, the DC Policy Director.

To recruit members, the DC offered a mix of selective benefits to supplement the collective benefits associated with the organization's political goals. Generally, these selective benefits helped elected officials attain their primary goal of reelection, policy making, representation, and influence (Fenno 1973 and Loomis 1982). Membership was a little more costly than contacting the DLC and asking to be put on the list. Nominal dues were requested, but not required; DLC membership was akin to membership in many congressional caucuses.

Interviews in 1991 revealed that some DLC members regarded their involvement as a central component of their political world, while others saw it as largely peripheral to other activities. Nonetheless, every member interviewed indicated that the DLC provided some form of selective benefit. Table 16.1 provides a rough outline of the benefits members believed they receive from the organization and the career goals served by each.

The DLC's membership grew rapidly, more than doubling from 1985 to 1986, then again from 1986 to 1988, as noted in Table 16.2. Membership growth was especially robust in the House; several members suggested that the benefits of DLC membership helped them establish an identity in Washington. Others believed House members were eager to sign on simply because of their propensity to join informal caucuses and because of the personal influence of Gephardt.

Table 16.1 Benefits Associated with DLC Membership

Type of Benefit	Career Goals Served
1. Advertisement in constituency as nonliberal Democrat	reelection, influence
2. Information exchange	policy making
3. Participation in policy development activities	policy making, influence
4. Organizational vehicle for pursuing centrist policy interests in Washington	influence, policy
5. Alternative leadership structure	influence
6. Association with like-minded colleagues	policy making, influence
7. Doing something to help the party	influence

Table 16.2 DLC Membership, 1985-1988

Office	Year			
	1985	1986	1987	1988
Senators	14	19	24	27
Representatives	17	79	99	106
Governors	10	12	14	16
State & Local	N/A	N/A	N/A	46
TOTAL	41	110	137	195

Relationship to Party

The founding of the DLC sparked controversy within the Democratic Party. To many, it was seen as a statement of no-confidence aimed at the new DNC chair, Paul Kirk, and his ability to reinvigorate the party after the 1984 landslide defeat. Kirk supporters feared the new organization would attract the party's up-and-coming centrist leadership and undercut Kirk's efforts to moderate the party from within (Gailey 1985). From, however, denied the DLC had anything against Kirk himself: "It is important to have an autonomous group constantly pushing for change. To be effective, we need to be without the institutional restraints Kirk has" (Cohen 1986). Yet, in an effort to head off the formation of the DLC, Kirk appointed his own policy council, the Democratic Policy Commission, just days before the DLC announced its founding (Gailey 1985).

Once the DLC was in operation both Kirk and the DLC played down their differences. To recruit and retain members, the DLC needed to be perceived as an elite group of elected officials, uniquely qualified to formulate party positions—not as a threat to the DNC. For his part, Kirk needed to be perceived as having the support of centrist elements of the party if his efforts to reduce the influence of liberal activists were to succeed. By March 1986, Kirk could speak of his "positive, constructive relationship" with the DLC (Stengel 1986), and by 1988, Jesse Jackson was complaining that Kirk was "getting too cozy with the DLC" (Elving 1988).

The 1988 Campaign

Few saw the DLC's horizons extending beyond 1988, when it was assumed the Democrats would have a good chance to retake the White House. If the DLC were to change the image of the party, the proof would come during the 1988 nomination process. Although four DLC members sought the nomination, their performances disappointed the DLC and seemed to confirm perceptions that a moderate candidate could not win the Democratic nomination. Of the DLC member-candidates, only Gore ran openly as a moderate. Assessing the first four years, From noted: "We were fine until the presidential nominating process got going in earnest, but then that process defines the party."

The initial success, then, of the DLC was rather limited. The group's message centered on creating the impression that there was life at the party's center, but there was little in the way of an agenda. The DLC's efforts, along with those of DNC chair Paul Kirk, helped chart a more moderate course for the party by 1988, but there was no new centrist message or agenda for Democratic candidates to run on. Nevertheless, the DLC had become a viable organization by 1988, with nearly 200 members and growing financial clout.

Institutionalization of the DLC

The defeat of Michael Dukakis in the 1988 election prompted intraparty debate over the causes of his defeat. While party liberals generally blamed the messenger, and his poorly executed campaign, the DLC blamed the message, seeing Dukakis's defeat as symptomatic of a party with no alternative to the liberalism caricatured so effectively by the Bush campaign (Hale 1993). Al From noted: "Dukakis erased the (liberal) graffiti on the wall but put nothing on it, and Bush painted it for him. Dukakis never articulated an alternative vision for the country, allowing Bush to use wedge issues against him. At that point we decided to increase the intellectual effort within the DLC." Henceforth, the push would be for the DLC to become less of a benign forum for elected Democrats to discuss issues and political imagemaker for moderates, and more of an ideas-based movement focused on shaping a specific, mainstream alternative message for the party.

Expansion of Activities, 1989–1992

To accomplish this mission, the DLC became a more complex organization after 1988. It undertook four major initiatives: (1) an expanded fundraising effort, including a project termed the "DLC network," used to target under-40 contributors; (2) an effort to extend membership to state and local officials and to create state DLC chapters; (3) development of a think tank, the Progressive Policy Institute (PPI); and (4) creation of a bimonthly publication, *The New Democrat*, designed to spread the DLC message to all Democratic elected officials and grass-roots supporters. The DLC staff also expanded to fifteen, with various functional specializations, and there were three PPI staff, plus three resident scholars. The think tank, magazine, and the organization of state DLC chapters required substantial amounts of money. The annual budget in the DLC's early years was around $500,000. Much of this was raised in large contributions from executives, lawyers, lobbyists, and other Democratic financial patrons supportive of the DLC's goals. Early stalwarts like Nunn, Robb, and Gephardt also attracted financial support to the organization. The annual budget of the post-1988 DLC pushed the $2 million mark, with corporate sponsorships bringing in substantial amounts. Of 100 DLC "Sustaining Members" in 1991–92, 57 were corporations and another dozen were professional or trade associations. The energy, health care, insurance, pharmaceutical, retail, and tobacco industries were all represented.

With its new focus on recruiting members from state and local officials, the DLC expanded its membership substantially. As Table 16.3 notes, membership growth among senators, representatives, and governors slowed, indicating that the DLC had probably maximized its recruitment from those offices. After 1988, about half of sitting Democrats in Congress and Democratic governors were DLC members.

Perhaps recognizing that the DLC could fulfill a policy development function, and that no other intraparty entity was doing it, Ron Brown, who replaced Kirk as DNC chair in 1989, treated the DLC as a firmly established supplementary party organization and never challenged the DLC's claims to represent "the ideas wing" of the party. Early in his tenure, Brown appeared at the DLC's 1989 annual meeting to demonstrate, following Kirk's lead, his commitment to moderation in the party (Edsall and Schwartz 1989). When the DLC's 1990 annual meeting was inadvertently scheduled at the same time as a DNC meeting, Brown shuttled back and forth to attend both and emphasized common ground rather than disagreements. In 1991, Brown attended the DLC's Cleveland convention and praised its efforts to develop ideas for the party. He did warn, however, that the party "cannot tolerate code word debates, push-off political maneuvering, or litmus tests by any part of our party."[5] But the chairman's comments had little appreciable affect on the DLC's efforts to distinguish its ideas from those of party liberals.

The "New Democrat" Message

The intellectual task of developing the centrist message fell to the PPI. An analysis of PPI publications between 1989 and 1992 suggests three phases of development: 1. the establishment of the political rationale for a new Democratic message; 2. the articulation of the core values of a new message; and 3. the development of an agenda and specific policy positions.[6]

The effort to establish a political rationale began in earnest immediately following the 1988 election when PPI published "The Politics of Evasion" (Galston and Kamarck 1989). Taking aim at those who suggested there was little wrong with the Democrats' message, the political scientists who put the

Table 16.3 DLC Membership, 1989-1992

Office*	1989	1990	1991	1992
Senators	29	29	32	32
Representatives	106	115	138	142
Governors	15	21	25	28
State & Local	59	222	381	502
TOTAL	209	387	476	704

* Includes former office-holders

report together argued that the "liberal fundamentalism" with which the Democratic Party had become associated was beyond salvation in national elections. Making use of polling data, they argued that the public saw both Mondale and Dukakis as too liberal. And making use of registration and voting data, they argued that the Democratic ticket would have fared no better in 1988 had more extensive mobilization efforts been undertaken. Taking exception with those who saw in 1988 the outlines of a new liberal electoral vote coalition emerging, the PPI authors contended that no Democrat could win the White House by writing off the South. Finally, the authors warned that the Democratic majorities below the presidential level were imperiled by the possibility of secular, "trickle-down" realignment.

This critique of "liberal fundamentalism" was touted by the DLC throughout 1989 and was a focus of that year's annual conference in Philadelphia. For 1990, the emphasis turned to establishing a set of core values that would serve as the foundation of the "New Democrat" message. This appears to have been a relatively straightforward task. Themes of opportunity, responsibility, and community—unveiled ceremoniously at the 1990 New Orleans conference—had been on the minds of From and PPI President Will Marshall since the CPE days in the early 1980s.

Yet the DLC faced a problem in clarifying its message: how to differentiate itself from both the left and right sides of the political spectrum without appearing to be simply posturing in the middle. This seemed the tendency of the early DLC and is often typical of centrist groups (see Pridham 1988). The DLC centrists tried to extricate themselves from this dilemma by constructing an approach that questioned the relevance of the conventional liberal-conservative spectrum. Similar to the claims advanced by Reich (1987) and Dionne (1991), the DLC argued that liberal fundamentalism and Reagan-Bush conservatism were presenting "false choices." They proclaimed their message as a "progressive, third way" to address the problems of the 1990s.

With election-year politics looming, the DLC and PPI fleshed out its agenda and policy positions in 1991, adopting the "New Choice Resolutions" in Cleveland. Its policy positions reinforced the "New Democrats'" faith in a "reinvented," activist government and clarified their differences with Republicans. To a far greater extent than Republicans, the "New Democrats" were willing to use government to promote economic growth and assure equal opportunity. To this end, they supported increased public investment, and a restoration of progressivity to the tax code. Indeed, these "New Democrats" differed with Republicans on a plethora of issues, including environmental protection, health care, family leave, the guaranteed working wage, abortion, handgun control, and national service.

The DLC and Bill Clinton

The development of new ideas is primarily an interelection process, but the acceptance of new ideas ultimately depends on the party's candidates. Rather than creating a message and agenda out of whole cloth, candidates are "both consumers and interpreters of policy ideas generated within the party" (Price 1984:291). Presidential candidates and, ultimately administrations, need intellectual fuel to campaign and to govern (Hargrove and Nelson 1983). Just as Kennedy was able to draw on the ideas developed by the Democratic Advisory Council and Reagan was able to draw on the ideas percolating in the conservative intellectual establishment in the late 1970s, the DLC sought to do the same for the next Democratic nominee and administration.

Clinton as DLC Chair, 1990–91

With this in mind, From set out to recruit a chair for the DLC in 1991 who would be considered a plausible 1992 candidate. At the very least, the chair needed to be someone who could command the attention of other potential candidates. Bill Clinton quickly emerged as best-suited for the task. From (1993) later stated, "What I had seen of him in 1987 and 1988 indicated to me that of all the politicians I've ever dealt with in Democratic party politics, this guy understood the importance of values in politics. And I believe the problem the Democrats have is that they think in programmatic terms while the people think in values terms." Added Will Marshall: "We thought Bill Clinton had the intellectual capacity to synthesize our new ideas with the old verities of the party into a new governing philosophy. He was the obvious choice for the DLC; there wasn't anyone else who had those talents."
The DLC's 1991 annual meeting in Cleveland showcased Clinton along with its "New Choice" agenda. Not considered in the top echelon of potential Democratic contenders prior to the Cleveland meeting, the Arkansas Governor's stock rose considerably thereafter (Balz 1991). Throughout 1990

and 1991, Clinton and From traveled, at DLC expense, to more than two dozen states to set up state DLC chapters. Among other things, this allowed Clinton to try on the message and to establish extensive state-level contacts.

The 1992 Presidential Campaign

The DLC connection paid off handsomely for Bill Clinton in 1992. His position helped him raise all-important early money, develop state-level campaign organizations, and collect endorsements from contacts made through the DLC. In Georgia, where Clinton needed a victory to slow Paul Tsongas's post-New Hampshire momentum, he was boosted by the endorsements and support of Nunn, Gov. Zell Miller, and Rep. John Lewis, the former civil rights activist (Balz and Dewer 1992). All three were fellow DLC members. Clinton was also helped by DLC members in Congress. One week after his New Hampshire defeat, 37 of Clinton's first 52 superdelegate endorsements came from DLC members. At that time, Harkin, Kerrey, and Tsongas had 12 endorsements each, one-third of which consisted of DLC members (*Congressional Quarterly Weekly Report* 1992). Most of the high-profile African-Americans who endorsed Clinton prior to Super Tuesday were DLC members as well.[7]

Perhaps even more important, Clinton picked up the DLC message and ran with it. When announcing his entry into the campaign in October 1991, Clinton spoke of the need to reinvent government, broaden opportunity, require greater responsibility on the part of citizens, and restore a sense of community. Eschewing ideological labels, Clinton took a page straight out of the 1991 New Choice Resolutions: "The change I seek and the change that we must all seek, isn't liberal or conservative. It's different and it's both" (in Toner 1991d).

Because Clinton entered the campaign after most other prominent moderates had announced decisions not to run, both he and those at the DLC assumed he would be the only moderate in a field of liberals. They also assumed the nomination campaign would be the final battleground for the intra-party struggle between the "New Democrats" and the liberals, whose strongest potential candidate was New York Governor Mario Cuomo. Clinton would define himself as a "New Democrat" and even if he lost the nomination to Cuomo, he would be well-positioned for 1996 if Cuomo lost the general election (Goldman and Matthews 1992b). Ultimately, however, the only traditional liberal in the race, Iowa Senator Tom Harkin, received little support and Clinton found himself to the left of his chief competitor, Tsongas, on the foremost issue of the campaign—the economy. Clinton's message was blurred further because of the time spent explaining character issues. As a result, even though he stayed well within the parameters of the DLC message, Clinton had trouble establishing himself as "a different kind of Democrat."

A renewed effort to appeal to the middle began with the selection of Al Gore, a fellow DLC member, as Clinton's running mate, and continued with the adoption of the Democratic Party platform. The Democratic National Convention was well-choreographed to convey the "New Democrat" message and was entitled "A New Covenant with the American People," echoing the main themes of the DLC.

The text of the platform was structured around notions of opportunity, responsibility, and community. A comparison of the platform with the DLC's New Choice Program reveals striking similarities. Of 51 subheadings in the Democratic Platform, 37 were in agreement with agenda items in the DLC's New Choice Draft and the other 14 items were in rough accordance with the DLC document. Nothing in the Democratic Platform was in disagreement.

Clinton won the general election because of widespread concern over the state of the economy. Yet, his emphasis on middle-of-the-road issues before and after the convention may well have made it easier for many voters to support the Democratic nominee. The argument could be made that Clinton's election simply shows that any Democrat could have defeated George Bush in 1992, given the state of the economy. Others would suggest, however, that Clinton's "New Democrat" credentials put him in the position to compete with Bush on a level playing field for the mantle of economic leadership. Before the election, models used to forecast the outcome on the basis of economic indicators predicted Bush would win (Pennar 1992). In other words, economic conditions were poor, but not so poor that Bush was a sure loser. The "New Democrat" identity made it possible for Clinton to preempt the Republican tactic of using cultural issues as a wedge to separate white, middle-class voters away from the Democrats—a tactic that would have been used against a liberal candidate to divert attention from the economy.

The Clinton Administration

Clinton's election largely fulfilled the mission of the DLC and raised the question of what the group's purpose would be during the Clinton presidency. Going out of business is not in the nature of organized groups, and, given the institutionalization of the DLC, disbandment was probably out of the question. A postelection fundraiser brought in $3.3 million, a testament to the DLC's reputation as having helped elect a president (Grove 1992).

Al From played a prominent role in the transition period as Clinton's advisor for domestic affairs. Ultimately, a number of DLC members and staffers received administration appointments, as Table 16.4 shows.

Despite these successes, the overall number of "New Democrats" appointed was relatively small. As Rep. David Price (NC), an active DLC member noted, "there was some sense that we have not had a full cadre of

Table 16.4 DLC Alumni in Clinton Administration

Office	Name	DLC Position
President	Bill Clinton	Chair
Vice President	Al Gore	Member
Secretary of Treasury	Lloyd Bentsen	Member
Secretary of Defense	Les Aspin	Member
Secretary of the Interior	Bruce Babbitt	Member
Secretary of Agriculture	Mike Espy	Member
Secretary of Labor	Robert Reich	Board of Advisors
Secretary of Housing	Henry Cisneros	Member
Secretary of Education	Richard Riley	Member
Director of OMB	Leon Panetta	Member
Deputy Assistant for Domestic Policy	Bruce Reed	DLC Policy Director
Assistant for Domestic Policy	Bill Galston	PPI Fellow
Counselor, National Security Council	Jeremy Rosner	PPI Vice President
Domestic Policy Advisor (V-P Gore)	Elaine Kamarck	PPI Senior Fellow
Assistant Secretary of Labor	Doug Ross	PPI Fellow
White House Political Affairs staff	Linda Moore	DLC Field Director

people to recommend for Administration positions" (Barnes 1993:1408). From's perception was that many of the key policy-making positions in the Administration went to party liberals:

> Of the dozen of so people who were the backbone of the DLC, most of them are in the government, but that's not many compared to all the people the interest groups have who are geared toward protecting all the old programs and approaches of the party. So we need to build a much bigger infrastructure if we want to change this party in a governing sense.

This personnel problem has helped crystallize the DLC's purpose during the Clinton Administration. In the short-term, it meant that the DLC would have to monitor the administration closely for deviations from the "New Democrat" agenda. In the long-term, it meant the DLC would have to devise ways to develop an infrastructure of political actors and activists committed to the "New Democrat" agenda.

The relationship between the new president and the DLC thus got off to a rocky beginning. Taking a page from the right-wing Heritage Foundation, which published *Mandate for Leadership* in 1981 (Heatherly 1981), the PPI published *Mandate for Change* (Marshal and Schram 1993) in early 1993. This was a 340-page primer on the "New Democrat" agenda with a brief introduction by President-elect Clinton. Three months into the administration From and Marshall (1993a) wrote that the new president seemed to be "oscillating between the old and new politics." The DLC-PPI leaders urged Clinton to get to work on the "New Democrat" initiatives, to attack entrenched interests and programs more boldly, and to justify his actions more resolutely in terms of the core values he articulated during the campaign.

In May of 1993, the DLC strongly opposed the nomination of Lani Guinier to a Justice Department post (Barnes 1993a), and in July, with much fanfare, released the results of a poll of Perot supporters conducted by White House pollster Stanley Greenberg. They argued that Clinton's best bet to woo Perot voters in 1996 would be to govern as a "New Democrat" (From and Marshall 1993b).

In the second half of 1993 Clinton pursued a "reinventing government" initiative, pushed NAFTA through Congress, and began touting "New Democrat" ideas on crime and welfare reform. Nevertheless, by the end of the year trouble was brewing between Clinton and some prominent DLC officials over budget cuts and health care reform. The administration opposed an effort led by Rep. Tim Penny (MN), a DLC stalwart for several years, for a second round of deeper spending cuts. More significant was a health care bill that rapidly gained bipartisan support in Congress, sponsored by DLC chair Sen. John Breaux (LA) and DLC member Rep. Jim Cooper (TN). By not mandating universal coverage, the Cooper-Breaux bill struck at the heart of Clinton's own health care reform proposal (Balz 1993). By early 1994, the DLC itself had not repudiated the call for universal coverage contained in *Mandate for Change*, but many of its members in Congress were supporting the Cooper-Breaux alternative.

The cost of success for the DLC appears to be the group's inability to control the on-going definition of what it means to be a "New Democrat." Speaking to the DLC conference in December of 1993, Clinton proclaimed that he was proud to have campaigned and to govern as a "New Democrat." As long as he embraces the "New Democrat" label, the president's words and actions will define precisely what it means.

New Directions in Party Organization

What does the experience of the DLC portend for the future of American party organizations? It suggests a model for intraparty groups to organize and change the party's policy direction. It also illustrates the weakness of the official parties in policy development. Supplemental party organizations tend to emerge to fulfill functions that the official party is neglecting (Lawson and Merkl 1989; Loomis 1982). The national party organizations have never been well equipped to fulfill the function of ideas development largely because of the heterogeneity of the parties themselves. Policy development groups sanctioned by either the national party organization or the congressional party face pressures to represent the party as a whole. When such groups attempt to define party policy, the result is often a watered-down statement that practically everyone can agree on, but that is equally easy to ignore. This has been the fate of most policy councils. The major exception is the Democratic Advisory Council (DAC), set up after the 1956 election by DNC chair Paul Butler (Roberts 1994). The DAC was successful precisely because Butler ignored pressure to defer ideas development to the congressional party or to balance the group and filled it instead with party liberals, who proceeded to define the message and agenda of the party for the 1960s (Arden 1988, Peters 1990).

What the experience of both the DAC and the DLC suggest is that parties cannot forge new directions without a fight. Most of Butler's successors at the DNC have been brokers between party factions and thus unwilling to risk their limited political capital on policy development. Independence from the official party gave the DLC the ability to develop its message and give it a sharper definition than is generally possible within party organizations. Once the message was developed, Clinton carried the flag and won.

The DLC, as a supplementary policy-oriented organization, provides a model for factions who wish to hone their message in preparation for intraparty warfare. The DLC's success helped spawn the 1991 formation of a liberal Democratic group called the Coalition for Democratic Values and, in the aftermath of the 1992 election, at least one moderate Republican group, patterned after the DLC (Zaldivar 1992). Even the new leaders of the Israeli party Likud, reeling from its 1993 election defeat, have consulted with DLC officials on how to develop a new party message.

The DLC also illustrates a method for getting elected officials involved in party policy debates. In the candidate-centered era, elected officials must view involvement in party affairs as furthering their primary career goals, be they reelection, policy making, or institutional influence. The DLC was structured around that basic premise. It enhanced members' reelection goals by providing a "moderate" party organization with which they could identify, while continuing to distance themselves from the liberal wing of the party. It enhanced members' policy-making goals by providing ideas, policy information, and forums for discussion. The DLC enhanced members' influence generally by serving as an alternative leadership structure to enhance personal influence and leadership skills. The success of the DLC is tied to this incentive structure. Without it, the DLC would not have drawn the membership or leadership necessary to carry the "New Democrat" message into the electoral arena. As parties move toward becoming what Pomper (1992:114–115) has called "leadership coalitions," which are "centered on and largely directed by the principal public office-holders elected under the party label" rather than by ideologically motivated activist groups, organizations such as the DLC, may be increasingly central to the development of party messages.

Notes

1. Research for this chapter was supported by grants from the Dirksen Center, the Carl Albert Center, and the University of Oklahoma Research Council. The Social Science Research Institute at Northern Illinois University provided facilities for writing and research. Thanks to all of these entities for their generous support.

2. The information in this chapter is based on interviews with principal figures in the DLC (elected officials, DLC leaders, and various staffers), attendance at various DLC and Democratic party meetings between 1991 and 1993, documents provided by the DLC, and periodical accounts. Of the nearly four dozen interviews conducted for this research, twenty-five were conducted with Members of Congress and eight with congressional aides, most on the condition that they would not be identified. Interviewees outside of Congress who agreed to interviews on the record are identified in the text.

3. The withdrawal of Democratic senators and representatives was particularly acute after 1968. In that year 61 percent of senators and 32 percent of representatives attended the convention. In the three subsequent conventions, the percentage of senators attending averaged 20 percent and the percentage of representatives attending averaged 13 percent (Shafer 1988: 138).

4. Figures are based on lists of CPE members in *Renewing America's Promise* (National-House Democratic Caucus 1984; also see Committee on Party Effectiveness 1982) and of DLC members in the DLC 1991 National Convention program (DC 1991a). In addition, at least a dozen patrons who helped finance the publication of *Renewing America's Promise* subsequently became DLC contributors.

5. Ron Brown address before the Democratic Leadership Council, 1991.

6. The following discussion of the DLC message and agenda is based on DLC (1988; 1990; 1991b; 1992).

7. These included Reps. Lewis, Mike Espy (MS), William Jefferson (LA) and Floyd Flake (NY) and Mayors Maynard Jackson (Atlanta) and Kurt Schmoke (Baltimore). See "Democratic Endorsements" (1992).

17

Proclaiming Party Identity: A View from the Platforms

Terri Susan Fine

Symbols are a key component of political persuasion and one that is particularly important for political parties. After all, mobilizing political support lies at the heart of party activity, and failure to be persuasive can have devastating consequences. Symbols are valuable in reaching out to the mass public because they dramatically communicate the party's identity, foster antagonism toward the rival party, and illustrate the party's value to its constituencies. In light of declining partisanship and rising split-ticket voting, symbols are a powerful means of demonstrating how one party can better serve voters' values and interests. Indeed, symbols may give an uninformed and disinterested electorate cues with policy relevance.

Party platforms provide an excellent opportunity for the use of symbols to frame the party's identity, discredit the opposition, and appeal to key constituencies. They are the only written documents adopted by representatives of the party faithful, and as such express the party's core beliefs. In addition, they reveal the party's perception of itself, its expectations of the voting public, and its understanding of the competitive situation.

The following analysis is an exploratory look at the role of symbols in party platforms. It begins by outlining the use of symbolism in the persuasion process, including a discussion of the various kinds of symbols and how they might be utilized by parties. Then the discussion turns to the use of symbols in the 1992 Republican and Democratic platforms and what they tell us about each party's perception of its own identity, prospects for public support, and understanding of the competition they faced.

Political Persuasion and Party Platforms

Political persuasion is a conscious communication process where the sender of the information is attempting to achieve cognitive and/or behavioral change on the part of the receiver (Barner-Barry and Rosenwein 1985). A requisite element of the persuasion process is shared meanings, images, myths, and symbols (Nimmo and Coombs 1980; Edelman 1971). Two factors must exist in order for persuasion to occur. First, there must be a receiver of the communication. Persuasion will not ensue without an audience that is receptive to the message. Facilitating the process requires a common language or vocabulary. This vocabulary need not hold the same meaning to both the sender and receiver, but the sender must incorporate language into the message that will likely elicit predictable responses from the receiver.

The three key elements of persuasive communication are arguments, evidence, and goals. Once the sender has outlined the proposed course of action, arguments favoring it must be communicated. These arguments require factual evidence for support and statements of the goals to be achieved (Barner-Barry and Rosenwein 1985:159). Political symbols are an important currency for this process because they are meaningful to both sides of the interaction. Symbols are political objects that have been endowed with meaning, value, or significance, and can thus serve as a rallying point for mobilizing support (Elder and Cobb 1983:17). They allow political leaders to summarize, classify, or efficiently communicate their agenda. Symbols can thus suggest arguments, serve as evidence, and illustrate goals in the process of persuading voters to support a particular agenda.

By using symbols, leaders try to establish their own identity by drawing on common myths (identity symbols), thus implicitly making arguments on their behalf; distinguish themselves from their opponents by linking them to undesirable things (oppositional symbols), therefore providing evidence for their arguments; and by summoning up heroes and villains from the past (condensational symbols) that point to their goals.

Myths are important to political persuasion because they hold meaning among significant numbers of people (Barner-Barry and Rosenwein 1985:199; Edelman 1971). Political leaders who cue myths by means of symbols in their written and oral communication are using a common language:

> Because myths are frequently couched in terms of or revolve around specific symbols, they not only give substantive content to one's political world view but also tend to define how that content is to be linked to specific political symbols. In this sense, myths represent prepackaged symbolic orientations that are simply internalized (Elder and Cobb 1983:54).

Party myths allow the public to develop a psychic connection to government and politics, and thus serve as shorthand for arguments in favor of the party. They help voters cope with ever-changing policy environments and political leadership by tying these actions and individuals to a particular set of values under a common party banner. Drawing on these myths is a potent means of establishing and reestablishing the party's identity. Oppositional symbols illustrate what is wrong with the rival party by linking it to poor values, bad behavior, and unpopular activities. Such symbols are often couched in terms of the presenting party's own myths, thus offering tangible evidence of the negative consequences of supporting its rivals. Making distinctions with oppositional symbols bolsters the argument in favor of one party by providing evidence of the failing of the other.

Condensational symbols summarize and condense experiences, feelings, and beliefs, and hold complex, emotional meaning beyond a clear definition of the object being used as a symbol (Firth 1973; Edelman 1964; Sapir 1934). Political leaders often take on heroic or villainous meaning, and their names become associated with key concerns and aspirations. Thus, condensational symbols bring to mind commonly accepted goals of the parties, either directly by citing heroes or indirectly by reference to villains from the opposition.

Party platforms provide a strong vehicle for political persuasion: as written guidelines for campaigning and governance, they are designed to proclaim the party's program to potential supporters and motivate public support to achieve its goals. Consistent with the requisite elements of the persuasion process, platforms include arguments, evidence, and goals. Symbols are a potent means to communicate these matters. After all, political socialization includes attachment to political objects (policies, public figures, events) that are then associated with party labels (Hess and Torney 1967:96).

The following analysis focuses on the use of symbols in the 1992 Democratic and Republican Platforms. The first section will analyze the framing of party identity by means of symbols linked to common myths, followed by a discussion of the oppositional symbols employed, and finally, a look at the condensational symbols. The implications of these symbols for the party's expectations regarding the public and its understanding of the competitive situation in 1992 will be addressed as well.

Who Are We? Shaping Party Identities with Symbols

The 1992 party platforms reveal stark differences between the identities of the Republican and Democratic Parties. The Republicans enjoyed the advantage of incumbency, but were hampered by a weak president. The Democrats carried two burdens: challenger status and reputation. Both parties spoke to these matters. In addition, each party's symbolism revealed their expectations of voters and their understanding of the competitive situation.

Early on, each party put forth its basic myths within the context of a new approach.[1] The Democrats offered a "new covenant" based on expanding opportunity while promoting greater individual responsibility and restoring community. By comparison, the Republicans offered a "new paradigm" or a "new consensus" founded on individual choice/empowerment and decentralized authority. Symbolic meaning was attached to these phrases in terms of the prevailing myths of each party: aiding the "common man" for the Democrats, enhancing "individual freedom" for the Republicans (see Table 17.1).

The term "new," in and of itself, is symbolic because it suggests a directional change. One might expect that the challenging party would be unique in putting forth a symbol indicating that the old ways will cease. Yet both parties promised change founded on existing principles. Both organizations believed the public wanted an alternative, and each used their platform to suggest their responsiveness to this demand for change. Although each party benefited from controlling at least one branch of government, the demand for change warranted seeking control of the other branch.

In framing their identities, each party took into account public expectations and the competitive situation it confronted. The Republicans used incumbency to argue that they had achieved a great deal, but that even more was possible in the future. Indeed, much of what was "new" about their agenda was, in fact, "old," if perhaps unrealized. On the other hand, the Democrats directly confronted their reputation and electoral misfortunes: "We welcome the close scrutiny of the American people, including Americans who may have thought the Democratic Party had forgotten its way, as well as all who know us as the champion for those who have been denied a chance"

Interestingly, the language chosen for outlining party myths suggests similar beliefs: each party argued that the best government could do was nurture the individual spirit and provide the necessary support system.

Table 17.1 Identity Symbols in the 1992 Democratic and Republican Parties

Democrats

Symbol: "New Covenant"
Meaning: Expanding opportunity for all citizens (broad based, non-inflationary economic growth and the opportunity that flows from it) while expecting individual responsibility (ethics practiced, values instilled, pride in work, and religious faith followed) in the context of restored community (strengthen families and neighborhoods, public schools, religious institutions, charitable organizations, civic groups and other voluntary associations).

Republicans

Symbol: "New Paradigm" or "New Consensus"
Meaning: Individual Choice/Empowerment (prosperity and process through individual opportunity and freedom) in the context of decentralized governmental authority ("Government has a legitimate role to play in our national life, but government must never dominate that life." "Bureaucracy is the enemy of initiative and self-reliance").

However, it is the meaning attached to these symbols that differentiates the two parties. Approaching government performance in this fashion seemed appropriate in light of the fiscal and economic woes of the country. The Democrats sought a government that would responsibly help people help themselves, while the Republicans argued that reducing government would unleash individual initiative.

Tattle Tales: Telling on the Enemy

Both parties utilized oppositional symbols that were couched in terms of their own party myths, and each spoke of the evils of its enemy (Table 17.2). The Republicans attempted to discredit the Democrats by tagging them as "liberal" and linking them to "bureaucracy" and "trickle-down government," (a play on the Democrats' accusation that Republicans believed in "trickle-down economics"). The Democrats, by contrast, avoided ideological language in framing their identity, even when they were distinguishing themselves from the Republicans. They chose instead to focus on the inactivity of the Republican administration with such symbols as "do-nothing government" and "gridlock."

Table 17.2 Oppositional Symbols in the 1992 Democratic and Republican Platforms

Democrats

Symbol: "Do-nothing government"
Meaning: Republicans believe "government has no role"; irresponsibility, neglect.

Symbol: "Gridlock"
Meaning: Republicans engage in "politics of diversion and evasion"; "everyone in Washington blaming one another for inaction"

Republicans

Symbol: "Bureaucracy"
Meaning: Democrats advocate bureaucracy, which is the enemy of initiative and self-reliance; big government is danger to liberty and prosperity.

Symbol: "Trickle-down government"
Meaning: Democrats believe in over-taxation, hyper-regulation, mega-government

The oppositional symbols included in these platforms outline the differences between each party's electoral and historical circumstances. The Republicans were advantaged by negative public sentiment toward previous Democratic presidents and candidates as well as their prior success attaching negative meaning to liberalism. The Republican Party used oppositional symbols more often than the Democrats, a tactic that reflected their successful negative campaign strategy in 1988. They were determined to remind voters of the unpopularity of recent Democratic presidents and presidential nominees.

In seeking to foster a new image of their party, the Democrats put forth their vision to draw distinctions between their historical reputation and the opposing camp's suggestions. Negative perceptions of Presidents Carter and Johnson, as well as previous Democratic presidential candidates, compelled the Democrats to confront their reputation. In so doing, they sought to persuade the public that they had rehabilitated by developing a new approach that was the better alternative to the Republicans. This persuasion strategy coupled self-deprecating remarks with anti-Republican discourse.

> The Revolution of 1992 is about a radical change in the way government operates—not the Republican proposition that government has no role nor the old notion that there's a program for every problem, but a shift to a more efficient, flexible and results-oriented government.... We believe in activist government, but it must work in a different, more responsive way.
>
> We reject both the do-nothing government of the last 12 years and the big government theory that says we can hamstring business and tax and spend our way to prosperity. Instead, we offer a third way.

Condensational Symbols: Personalizing the Parties

Condensational symbols provide easily recognized names and images that facilitate party linkage with current and past political issues. Condensational symbols provide the parties with easy shorthand for political persuasion. While both parties incorporated condensational symbols in their platforms, positive ones greatly outnumbered negative ones. As with oppositional symbols, the Republicans were helped by recent Democratic woes. The Democrats were blessed by a weak opponent and a difficult economy. Both parties described the first president bearing their moniker in a positive light, and the latest president from the rival party was portrayed negatively (Table 17.3).

The Democrats emphasized Thomas Jefferson and his commitment to "activist, responsive and decentralized government," and then moved forward to the twentieth century to FDR and Harry Truman. Although the latter were both "old" Democrats, they were founders of the present-day Democratic coalition and predated the more recent party woes. The Republicans showed a similar pattern, beginning with Abraham Lincoln, who is celebrated for his

Proclaiming Party Identity

commitment to individual freedom and initiative, and then moving forward to Theodore Roosevelt, identified with social responsibility, and Ronald Reagan, noted for strong foreign policy. All told, these presidents encapsulate the key goals of each party.

The absence of certain condensational symbols in the Democratic platform is also noteworthy. A recurring theme throughout the Clinton campaign was his reverence for, and homage to, John F. Kennedy. Clinton's efforts to associate himself with this strong condensational symbol were especially pronounced at the Democratic National Convention. During the

---

Table 17.3 Condensational Symbols in the 1992 Democratic and Republicans Platforms.

Democrats

Symbol: Thomas Jefferson
Meaning: Spirit of revolution; believed in activist, responsive, decentralized government.

Symbol: Franklin Delano Roosevelt
Meaning: "Faith in America demands that we recognize the new terms of the old social contract. In the strength of great hope we must all shoulder our common load."

Symbol: Harry S Truman
Meaning: Redefined "global security with bold approaches to tough challenges."

Symbol: George Bush
Meaning: "America's leadership is indifferent at home and uncertain in the world."

Republicans

Symbol: Abraham Lincoln
Meaning: "The legitimate object of government is to do for a community of people whatever they need to have done, but cannot do at all, or cannot so well do, for themselves in their separate and individual capacities."

Symbol: Theodore Roosevelt
Meaning: Believed that corporations have responsibilities to society, conscience alone should prevent outrages.

Symbol: Ronald Reagan
Meaning: Foreign policy legacy because he swept away communism and America won the Cold War.

Symbol: Jimmy Carter
Meaning: "Are we safer and stronger today, in 1992, than we were in 1980, when Jimmy Carter was the Democrat president?"

balloting on the third night of the convention, he walked to the podium amid great fanfare right after the Ohio delegation had cast the necessary votes for his nomination. He thanked the delegates like another Democrat had done about thirty years earlier. The following evening, a short film included a segment where Clinton, as a young man, met President Kennedy. Clinton's voice-over text described how that experience motivated him to pursue a public service career. Yet the platform made no mention of Kennedy. Kennedy's image as an "old Democrat" may have prompted the exclusion of his name because it would be inconsistent with the "New Covenant" model that was being projected.

The Democrats also avoided two obvious negative condensational symbols: Richard Nixon and Ronald Reagan. Nixon's reemergence as an elder statesman with foreign policy expertise may have hindered a successful negative association with government corruption. More likely was the perception that Nixon had not hurt either the Reagan or Bush campaigns. In addition, Reagan's lingering popularity meant that the Democrats would not successfully portray him negatively. Instead, "Republican Administration over the last 12 years" or a variation thereof, was selected as a symbol.

Conclusion

Platforms provide the parties with the opportunity to tell the public who they are and what they stand for; the use of symbols is an integral part of this presentation. More importantly, symbols assist with all three elements of the process of persuasion, argument, evidence, and goals. The 1992 platforms refer to party myths to frame identity, the employment of oppositional symbols to illustrate the failings of the opposition, and the deployment of condensational symbols to articulate key goals. The competitive environment further facilitates this process because a known enemy can be identified and information about the opposition can be easily integrated in the persuasive message. Thus, a party's electoral situation strongly influences the way it uses symbols. In 1992, both parties promised a new direction, understood in terms of their dominant myths, their expectations of the electorate, and their understanding of their competitive situation.

This brief analysis of symbols in party platforms suggests an avenue for future research. The use of symbols in other forums such as speeches, campaign literature, and advertising campaigns may be quite revealing. And connecting such symbols back to their sources and forward to their effect on both elites and the electorate could tell us a great deal about how parties understand the persuasive process, as well as how persuasion takes place. It may be, for instance, that there is more substantive and policy content in party messages than is commonly realized. While symbols are hardly substitutes for detailed and differentiated party programs—and informed debate about them—they may give an uninformed and uninterested electorate cues on which to make judgements. Hence the careful analysis of the role of symbols in party proclamations may reveal more depth to party identity than is commonly supposed.

Notes

1. All references to the 1992 party platforms are taken from *Congressional Quarterly Weekly Report* Volume 50, Number 29 (Democratic Platform) and Number 34 (Republican Platform).

18

Party Culture and Party Behavior

Philip Klinkner

The notion of party culture is familiar to even the most casual observers of party organizations. At a superficial level, many political scientists have commented upon the striking differences one sees in the appearance and operation of the Republican and Democratic Party headquarters. At a deeper level is the recognition that Republicans and Democrats are often fundamentally different in their behavior and outlook, independent from differences in ideology. As William Crotty notes: "Despite their deceptively similar governing forums, national and local party structures, and even—to the unpracticed eye—apparent unity on such matters as general policy, the two national parties are distinctively separate entities, each with its own traditions, social roots, and organizational and personal values" (1983:205–206).

Yet, party culture is only rarely discussed as a relevant device for studying and understanding party organizations. For proponents of rational choice theory, notions of distinct party cultures run directly counter to their view that parties are best viewed as symmetrical organizations, indistinguishable from one another in their single-minded pursuit for office. The distinctive cultural traits of the parties are either ignored or written off as irrelevant to their larger purposes. More traditional analysts of party organizations are more likely to recognize differences in the culture of the two parties, but only rarely do they attribute any significance to these differences.

This lack of attention to party culture is regrettable. Party culture, as I hope to show, provides a useful tool for analyzing and explaining the behavior of party organizations. For example, much of the Democratic Party's focus on procedural matters stems, in large part, from a party culture that stresses inclusion and participation, while the Republican Party's emphasis on organizational and managerial activities arises from a party culture that values the techniques and technology of business enterprises.

In analyzing party cultures and the roles that they play in the behavior of party organizations, I will first attempt to show how other fields have defined and used the concept of culture to explain the behavior of organizations. Second, I will describe the cultural attributes of the Democratic and

Republican Parties. Finally, I will review the ways in which party culture may influence the behavior of party organizations.

Theories of Organizational Culture

While political scientists might be unwilling to rely upon cultural concepts to explain the behavior of party organizations, such is not the case in other disciplines that study organizations. In fact, analyses of "organizational culture" have long played an important role in sociology, administrative and management sciences, and organizational theory. Today, organizational culture is a widespread and important device for understanding the behavior of business organizations and public bureaucracies (Shafritz and Ott 1986). In fact, thinking about organizational culture has begun to go from the theoretical to the practical, as more and more firms seeks to "reengineer" their cultures to meet changing competitive environments (Hammer and Champy 1993).

Within these disciplines, the concept of organizational culture encompasses the following:

> [I]t is the culture that exists in an organization, something akin to societal culture. It is comprised of many intangible things such as values, beliefs, assumptions, perceptions, behavioral norms, artifacts, and patterns of behavior. It is the unseen and unobservable force that is always behind the organizational activities that *can* be seen and observed . . . organizational culture is a social energy that moves people to act. "Culture is to the organization what personality is to the individual—a hidden, yet unifying theme that provides meaning, direction, and mobilization" (Ott 1989:1).

The most specific and common definition of organizational culture is offered by Edgar Schein. According to him, organizational culture consists of:

> A pattern of basic assumptions—invented, discovered, or developed by a given group as it learns to cope with its problems of external adaptation and internal integration—that has worked well enough to be considered valid and, therefore, to be taught to new members as the correct way to perceive, think, and feel in relation to those problems (1985:12).

Organizational culture rests upon certain basic assumptions held by the members of an organization which condition their behavior. Over time, these assumptions become imbedded in the minds of those within an organization, becoming the types of routines and procedures which define "the way we do things here." Thus, in organizations with strong cultures, these assumptions become powerful enough to influence or control the behavior of the organization. For example, with business firms, the culture of an organization may prevent it from making the changes necessary to adapt to an altered environment (Ott 1989:3–5 and Schein 1985).

An organization's culture represents the composite of several factors: the societal culture in which the organization resides, the nature of the organization's business and its business environment, the social and professional background of the organization's members, the impact of important leaders, particularly those who help found the organization, and the historical memory of important or crisis events, among others. Since these factors will differ from organization to organization, no two organizations will display the same culture. Moreover, the culture of an organization may be strong or weak, depending upon the degree to which these factors reinforce one another and the perceived accuracy and success of the assumptions underlying the culture.

Once developed, an organization's culture tends to remain strong and resistant to change. This endurance results from several factors. First, organizations tend to recruit and hire individuals who already possess the assumptions and attributes found in its culture. According to Schein, an "organization is likely to look for new members who already have the 'right' set of assumptions, beliefs, and values" (1990:115). Such a process is natural, since those who hold these views will be more likely to seek positions in such organizations, and the organizations will more readily select persons who seem most likely to "fit" their organization. Second, organizations socialize new members into the basic assumptions and norms of their culture. This acculturation takes many forms, from formal instruction in the organization's standard procedures and routines to the more informal "learning the ropes" which all new members absorb over time. Third, organizations tend to marginalize or remove members who deviate too strongly from the basic precepts of its culture (Ott 1989:87-97).

While often strong and stable, organizational cultures are not static; they can and do evolve over time. Several factors may trigger such an evolution. One is a changing external environment. When an organization confronts new problems and situations, it may find that the old behaviors, procedures, and routines dictated by its culture no longer work. Such stresses, if strong and persistent enough, will usually lead to change in the organization's culture. Strong and dynamic leaders may also play a role in changing an organization's culture, particularly when they are able to exercise decisive and effective leadership in a period of stress or crisis.[1] Finally, an organization's culture will evolve to reflect changes in the larger society in which it resides.

Republican and Democratic Party Cultures

Using the definition and descriptions of organizational culture gleaned from other disciplines, how might one characterize the cultures of Republican and Democratic Party organizations? An analysis of the Republican and Democratic National Committees (RNC and DNC) indicates that each possesses a distinctive culture. With the RNC, there is a focus on the technical and managerial aspects of party activities, "nuts and bolts" and "business values." The Democrats, however, have a culture that focuses on party procedures, making it a much more democratic party. They are continually concerned about inclusion and representation within the party and they tend to see the party as both the arena and arbiter for such questions.[2]

The Republicans: The Culture of Business

One important element in the development of an organization's culture is the social background of its members. In this respect, the Republicans are the party of business. The relationship between Republicans and the business world has traditionally been understood in ideological terms, but that relationship encompasses more than just supporting the political agenda of the business community. Much more so than Democrats, Republicans tend to come from business backgrounds, they associate with business people, they admire and emulate the efficiency of business organizations, and, as a result, their culture shows a marked similarity with that of the business world (Kayden and Mahe 1985:69).

One aspect of the business-like culture of the Republicans is their reliance on business technology and methods in their approach to party activities. Over the last 30 years, the Republicans have been much more likely to use techniques first developed and perfected by the private sector—direct-mail solicitation, computerized data bases, professional consultants, marketing research, and television advertising. Democrats, on the other hand, tend to lack familiarity with such techniques. Where Republicans often seek to copy technological and managerial innovations from the private sector, Democrats have usually viewed such methods as extraneous to the more expressive purposes of political activity.

The business orientation of the GOP has been evident since at least the 1950s, when Hugh Bone observed that the Republicans were explicit in their desire to run the RNC "like a corporation," and he quotes Stewart Alsop's description of the RNC as looking like the "home of a large and successful business concern." In contrast, he found the Democrats to be much more informal and disorganized (Bone 1958:44–45). A few years later, Cotter and Hennessy made a similar observation, stating that while each of the Democratic national committees does "what it damn well pleases," the "Republicans approach the problem of national party financing with business-like matter-of-factness" (Cotter and Hennessy 1964:176–178).

Though made thirty years ago, these observations still provide an accurate description of current differences between the parties. In a more recent analysis of national party activity in congressional races, Paul Herrnson states that Democratic Party staff members "work in a highly politicized environ-

Party Culture and Party Behavior   279

ment which lacks the business-like ethos of its Republican counterpart" (1989:317-18). According to John Bibby:

> The observer of DNC and RNC meetings is immediately struck by the fact that the differences between the two committees go well beyond their respective sizes Differences in style of operation and party constituencies are apparent. Republican National Committee meetings are extremely well organized and professionally staffed. There is an air of formality and relative order about the conduct of the meetings. DNC meetings are less well organized, informal, and have a rather ad hoc character. Orderliness prevails in RNC sessions, while confusion is common at DNC meetings (1992:85-86).

My own observations of the national party operations and staff reinforce this view. On several visits to both party headquarters, I quickly noted the modern and efficient operation of the Republicans, in contrast with the informal and less organized Democrats. A trip to the RNC is like visiting an investment bank, while going to DNC was akin to stopping by the offices of junior faculty members at a small college.[3]

One important clue to understanding the culture of an organization is the language that its members use to describe their activities and goals (Ott 1989:22-31). Not surprisingly, Republicans speak of politics in much the same terms as business people speak of an industry or a market. One of the best example of how Republicans use business terms to describe politics comes from a 1962 speech by Dwight Eisenhower. According to him:

> We [the Republican Party] have a good bill of fare, or you might say, stock of goods on the shelf, but the trouble is that we think that because they are good in the cans and packages, we can let them get dusty on the shelves . . .
> The Democrats have less value in their goods, but they paint up the can, tidy up the store, and then they have a better, more appealing idea to put before a prospective customer.
> Now, I think we ought to read this very objectively and see wherein we are weak and wherein we are strong, and if we are happy with the package . . . I think we should find out whether this [the Republican program] is saleable and we ought to use salesmanship in getting it before the public (Kesaris, Reel 2, Frames 354-55).

In interviews with the leadership of the RNC, business and managerial language was frequently used, while such terms where almost never heard from Democrats. The Republicans constantly relied on phrases like, "make the sale," "marketing" a candidate or an idea, the "corporate wheel" of the party, and "distribution system," among others. Indicative of this reliance on business terms is the campaign manifesto used by Haley Barbour in his successful 1992 bid for RNC Chair, which describes the RNC as a "Board of Directors" with the chair as the "CEO" and "manager" who must "ensure productivity, accountability and quality control" by relying on "good business practice" (Barbour 1993).

The most commonly used term among Republicans is former RNC chairman Ray Bliss's favorite expression, "nuts and bolts." Nearly every RNC member or RNC staff person that I have ever spoken to describes the efforts and purpose of the RNC in these terms. Additionally, in 1993, each of the contenders for the RNC chairship sought to use the "nuts and bolts" label to characterize their proposed efforts. Certainly Ray Bliss's success and high regard within the party help to account for the common and continued use of this term, but it also seems likely that accurately reflects the technical and business-oriented nature of the Republican Party.

In addition to their role as the "party of business," the high degree of homogeneity within the Republican Party is another likely reason for its "nuts and bolts" culture. According to Jo Freeman, the social homogeneity of the Republican Party helps to create a sense of trust "The Republican Party sees itself as an organic whole whose parts are interdependent. Republican activists are expected to be good soldiers who respect leadership and whose only important political commitment is to the Republican Party" (1986:339).

In turn, this centralization and hierarchy creates an environment hospitable to the "nuts and bolts" activities used by the Republicans. In her words, a party "which is hierarchical, unitary and in which power flows downward" will be better "able to use more of its resources for attaining its goals and direct them more efficiently" (Frantzich 1989:90, 345).

The Republicans' experience as a minority party also seems to have helped shape their party culture, contributing to their affinity for "nuts and bolts" activities. Perhaps following another example from the private sector, the Republicans have emulated Avis Rental Cars by acting according to the claim, "We're number two, so we try harder." According to Cotter and Hennessy, the behavior of the RNC might be explained as "the frugality of the minority party aware that organization may compensate for numbers" (1964:183). Since their banishment to minority party status in the 1930s, the Republicans have often operated on the assumption that while they might be outnumbered by the Democrats, their emphasis on organization would serve as an equalizer. As one study of party organizations states:

> The Republicans, in the first years of the New Deal, preached organization for the out party as the key to mitigating the adverse consequences of Democratic hegemony. In subsequent decades they practiced organization as a key to reversing electoral adversity. In short, the national party organizational elites in the 1920s and 1930s perceived a relationship between long-term electoral trends and organizational strength (Cotter, Gibson, Bibby, and Huckshorn 1984:164).

As with cultures in other types of organizations, the role of leadership, particularly Ray Bliss and Bill Brock, has also influenced the culture of the RNC. Each came from predominantly Democratic areas where superior organization was the Republican party's only hope and each first succeeded by building political organizations capable of competing with the numerically larger Democrats. Bliss first began in politics in Akron, Ohio, where the Democratic Party, bolstered by the political organization of the rubber workers' union, dominated local elections. He eventually moved on to the larger stage of Ohio state politics, but here, once again, the Democrats had an edge in voter registration. Bill Brock began his political career in the solidly Democratic South, becoming the first Republican elected to Congress from his district in Tennessee since the 1920s.

While serving as RNC chairman, both Bliss and Brock emphasized the importance of party organization that they had gained from their previous experiences. And in both cases the strategy was perceived as successful since the Republican Party won the White House during their tenure. As a result, they are held in high esteem by their colleagues and successors, who often refer to them in tones best described as reverential. Their methods are still used although they have long since departed from the RNC.

As much as Bliss and Brock might have influenced the culture of the Republican Party, it is also reasonable to see these two leaders as products of that same party culture. As mentioned above, organizations tend to recruit persons who share its cultural values. One can see evidence of this process at work in the selection of Bliss and Brock as RNC chairs. Both men had reputations as nonideological leaders who would emphasize organization and activities over factional maneuvering, characteristics that fit well with the existing Republican culture (Klinkner 1992:chs. 4, 7).

The Democrats: The Culture of Democracy

While Republicans have a cultural affinity toward business, the primary cultural referents for Democrats are interest and constituency groups. Many of these Democratic groups—women, minorities, gays, labor, and others—have traditionally perceived themselves as powerless and locked out of America's important social and political circles. According to Jo Freeman, Democrats "do not think of themselves as the center of society. The party's components think of themselves as outsiders pounding on the door seeking programs that will facilitate entry into the mainstream. Thus the party is very responsive to any groups, including such social pariahs as gays and lesbians, that claim to be left out" (1986:338). These groups view the Democratic Party as an arena and a vehicle to achieve the representation and power denied to them by other groups and institutions. Freeman adds that representing these groups "does not mean the articulation of a single coherent program for the betterment of the nation but the inclusion of all relevant groups and viewpoints. Their concept of representation is delegatory, in which accurate reflection of the parts is necessary to the welfare of the whole" (1986:337). This view is supported by the observations of a recent DNC official, who states that the Democratic Party allows these groups to "express their heart and soul." Moreover, in her view, the Democratic Party is the only instrument for this expression, since the Republican Party is "not big enough to give them any power" (Klinkner 1992:332).

Attempting to achieve an "accurate reflection of the parts" led the Democrats to stress procedural reforms during the 1970s and 1980s. These reforms were intended to provide each of the party's constituent elements representation in party circles. Even those Democrats who criticized the particulars of the party's reform efforts did not challenge the idea that the party should strive to be as open and inclusive as possible. Instead, they tended to argue over the extent of reform necessary or that by opening the party to such groups as blacks, women, and young people, the reforms had inadvertently excluded other groups, such as organized labor, or blue-collar whites (Klinkner 1992:chs. 5,6). In short, nearly every element in the Democratic Party is devoted to making it a democratic party.

The Democrats' cultural biases can also be seen in their language. Where Republicans speak of "markets" and "nuts and bolts," the Democrats rely on terms like "voice," "representation," "inclusion," "participation," "empowerment," "fairness," and "democracy." Such terms are rarely used by Republicans.

While Democrats revel in their concern for internal party democracy and the consequent focus on procedural reforms, Republicans approach such matters with a distinctly different attitude. The party has not engaged in significant procedural reform since 1912, and when current Republicans are asked why they did not undertake procedural reforms similar to those of the Democrats, their responses fall into one of two categories. One answer is the along the lines of, "Why would we want to do something like that?" The second is not so much an answer as an uncomprehending stare, much as one might get if you had asked them why the Republican Party had not called for a confiscatory tax system, a command economy, or unilateral disarmament.

The quest for inclusiveness that spurred much of the Democrats' procedural efforts is not absent in Republican Party. Many, if not most, Republicans want to make their party more inclusive, particularly of women and minorities, but they are willing to do so only as long as these new entrants act as Republicans rather than as organized groups. According to an organizer of the Republican Women's Task Force at the 1976 convention, the Republican Party is not "an interest group party. And consequently the Republican Women's Task Force is viewed with skepticism. Party regulars have a hard time adjusting to the presence of an organized interest" (Pressman 1978:682). Not surprisingly, constituency groups within the Republican Party seem unwilling to challenge this attitude and, therefore, usually do not attempt to voice strenuously their demands within party circles.

In comparison, the Democratic Party seems much more attractive to new groups since the Democrats do not require group loyalties to be replaced by party loyalties. The culture of the Democratic Party is such that interest and constituency groups are allowed, even encouraged to organize and pressure the party. Furthermore, the Democrats often offer new groups, by virtue of their legitimacy as a group, direct representation and power in the party decision-making process. Though the DNC under Paul Kirk began to temper its formal support for constituency groups, their role still remains very strong (Klinkner 1994).

The different approaches of the parties to organized interest groups is best summed up by John Bibby, who states:

> The major subunits of RNC gatherings are meetings of state chairmen and regional associations. There are also informal meetings of various ideological and candidate factions. The DNC has all of these types of subunits and factions, but in addition has active caucuses for blacks, Hispanics, and women which have played a major role in DNC meetings. . . . There is no comparable specialized representational structure—formal or informal—within the RNC. This no doubt reflects the important role which organized interest groups have traditionally played within the Democratic coalition. By contrast, the Republicans, with their more homogeneous constituency and middle class orientation, have had a less extensive and explicit relationship with organized groups (1992:86).

Just as the homogeneity of the Republican Party bolsters its organizational tendencies and reduces the role of interest groups within the party, the heterogeneity of the Democrats reinforces their affinity for procedural matters. Party procedure provides the Democrats with the "consultation, representation, and participation" required of a heterogeneous party and is an expression of cultural makeup of the Democratic Party (Freeman 1986:351). On the other hand, the more homogeneous party Republicans need less of this and, consequently, are less disposed to tinker with procedures.

The Democrats' heterogeneity also limits their ability to carry out organizational reforms as easily as the Republicans. Without the bonds of trust established by a homogeneous membership, it becomes very difficult to institute the centralization and hierarchy necessary for a business-like organization. Organizational decisions are scrutinized not only for their effectiveness, but also for the impact that they will have on the party's constituencies, which often makes those decisions more difficult to implement.

This difference between the parties emerges in discussions with members and staffs of the national committees. As for the Republicans, one gets the impression that the chair is given great latitude to make and implement decisions for the party. These decisions do not necessarily have unanimous agreement, but most seem willing to defer to the judgment of the party leadership. With Democrats, however, one constantly hears of how decisions, even those regarding relatively minor matters, must be cleared with important constituency groups. For example, after Paul Kirk became chair in 1985, the DNC took great efforts to ensure that minority-owned businesses received an adequate proportion of DNC business. One DNC staffer commented, anonymously, "Working at the DNC is a Noah's Ark kind of thing. You have to make sure to have two of everybody before you do anything" (Klinkner 1994).

Since the 1930s, the Democrats have viewed themselves as the majority party, a perception that has also aided their predilection for procedure.[4] As the majority party, the Democrats believe they will naturally win every election so long as they are united and procedure provides the means by which the party can achieve unity, or so the thinking goes with many Democrats. The history of Democratic Party reforms provides evidence of such reasoning. They have continually attempted to devise a procedure for nominating presidential candidates that satisfies the desires of all party constituencies and thus keeps them unified for the general election. After 1968 the party reformed itself to bring back the McCarthy supporters who had defected or stayed at home. After 1972 they took steps to give greater say to the state and local party officials and union leaders who had abandoned McGovern. After 1980 the Democrats created the superdelegates to give more representation to elected officials. After 1984 the DNC supported "Super Tuesday" to give conservative whites more influence over the nomination. The Democrats have seemed to operate under the assumption that if only they could construct an ideal nomination system that properly represents each of the party's constituencies, then the perfect nominee would emerge, leading a unified party to victory. To some extent the party's 1992 nominee, Bill Clinton, succeeded in this effort, though it is uncertain how much the Democrat's nominating system influenced his nomination and election (Klinkner 1994).

A final reinforcement to the procedural impulse in the Democratic Party is the impact of the 1968 election. How an organization deals with critical incidents, such as a challenge to authority, has a strong influence on its culture. According to Edgar Schein:

> One can see in [organizations] how norms and beliefs arise around the way members respond to critical incidents. Something emotionally charged or anxiety producing may happen, such as an attack by a member on the leader. Because everyone witnesses it and because tension is high when the attack occurs, the immediate next set of behaviors tends to create a norm (1990:115).

The events of 1968, culminating in the riots outside of the Democratic convention in Chicago, were "emotionally charged and anxiety producing" for the Democrats, and their response to those events had an important impact on its culture. In 1968 liberal insurgents challenged the traditional leadership of the Democratic Party. The party leadership responded to that challenge by beginning a series of procedural reforms that would open up the party to insurgent groups. This helped to create a cultural norm in which it was legitimate for party constituencies to demand procedural changes and for the party leadership to provide such changes as a method of unifying the party.

Party Culture and Party Behavior

How might the cultures of the Democratic and Republican Party organizations influence their behavior? Elsewhere (Klinkner 1992; 1994), I have argued that party culture is the chief factor in determining the response of out-party national committees to presidential election losses. Between 1960 and 1992, the Republican National Committee relied on organizational rebuilding efforts (defined as improvements in financial operations, media usage, candidate recruitment, polling, issue development, data analysis, and fundraising) to respond to each of its losses in the preceding presidential election. The best known examples of this were the party-building activities of Bliss and Brock. In the same period, the Democrats were nearly as consistent in their reliance on procedural reforms (defined as changes in their rules and procedures for internal governance and the selection of presidential candidates and convention delegates) to respond to their losses (see Table 18.1).

Though the Democrats during the 1980s did make an effort to include organizational improvements, even these partial exceptions do not contradict the type of behavior posited by theories of organizational culture. The Democrats' efforts to incorporate nonprocedural responses came during a period of stress and crisis (a string of poor performances in presidential elections) which is usually associated with change in an organization's culture, and the continued presence of procedural reforms shows the endurance and evolutionary nature of cultural norms.

Table 18.1 Out-Parties Responses 1960–1992

Period	Losing Party	Response
1960–1964	Republicans	Organizational
1964–1968	Republicans	Organizational
1968–1972	Democrats	Procedural
1972–1976	Democrats	Procedural
1976–1980	Republicans	Organizational
1980–1984	Democrats	Procedural/Organizational
1984–1988	Democrats	Procedural/Organizational
1988–1992	Democrats	Procedural/Organizational
1992–1996	Republicans	Organizational

The way in which the parties went about selecting these responses also shows the importance of culture in understanding party organizations. Unlike rational choice theories of party behavior, the parties not only failed to select responses used by the other party, but also rarely even considered doing so. Instead of engaging in a "rational" search for the most efficient means of responding to their defeat, objectively assessing the causes of their loss and considering all possible responses on their merits, the parties tended to assess their defeats in ways that led them to rely on the measures that they had employed in the past and that fit with their culture. For example, the RNC consistently viewed their losses as the result of poor grass-roots party organization and an excessive focus on internal party divisions, thus causing them to rely on the type of nonideological, "nuts and bolts" rebuilding that fit so well with their party culture. On the other hand, the Democrats tended to view their losses as the result of failing to give the proper amount of voice and representation to each of the party's various constituencies, which not surprisingly led them to the types of procedural reforms characteristic of their culture. In short, rather than selecting the most appropriate response for the cause of their defeat, it seems that the parties usually selected the cause of defeat most appropriate for their party culture (Klinkner 1994).

It is unlikely that the influence of party culture on the behavior of party organizations begins and ends with how the national committees respond to defeat. Another way party culture might influence the party behavior is in the creation and maintenance of competitive advantages. Research on business firms suggests that culture might be a reason why some firms develop sustained competitive advantages, and the same might be true for parties (Barney 1986). From 1968 to 1988, the Republican Party had a sustained competitive advantage in presidential elections, which might be accounted for in part by the ability of its party organization to develop a unified message and run a technologically sophisticated campaign, two activities that seem directly influenced by a party culture which emphasizes hierarchy, unity, and intensive use of technology. During this same period, the Democrats have had a sustained competitive advantage in congressional races. A party culture which emphasizes decentralization and diversity might help to account for their ability to develop the vast coalition of groups interest—black and white, North and South, urban and rural, liberal and conservative—that allows them to consistently win the majority of seats in Congress.[5]

Party culture might also disadvantage a party organization. As mentioned previously, organizational cultures change very slowly, thus a firm or a party, blinded by a culture that no longer fits current realities, might find itself at a distinct disadvantage. One might argue that the Democrats' excessive concern with questions of voice and representation, and the consequent emphasis on procedural reforms, handicapped it during the 1970s and 1980s when it should have, like the RNC at that time, been improving its fundraising and ability to provided services to campaigns and state and local parties.

The same might be true of the Republicans in the aftermath of their defeat in 1992. The "back to the future" contest for Chair of the RNC in January 1993 saw each of the contenders trying to lead the party in the 1990s by wrapping themselves in the memory of Bliss and Brock and emphasizing the techniques used in the 1960s and 1970s. The eventual winner, Haley Barbour was very explicit in his desire to "be a nuts and bolts organizational leader like Ray Bliss or Bill Brock" (Barbour 1993a).[7] As they entered their fourth decade of "nuts and bolts" organizational efforts, no one in the Republican Party seemed willing to consider whether the point of diminishing returns for these activities had already been reached.

From the preceding analysis of the national committees it seems clear that party culture can have a significant influence upon the behavior of party organizations. While culture is not determinative, it does provide an important and often significant element in the behavior of party organizations, an element that is often lacking in other types of analysis. Most importantly, an emphasis on party culture can help remind us that party organizations are not symmetrical organizations possessed by the single-minded purpose of winning the next election. Instead, the organizations of the two parties are distinct entities, displaying characteristics unique to their membership and historical experience. By taking party culture into account, perhaps future research can provide richer and more realistic explanations of party behavior.

Notes

1. This point is echoed by Herrnson and Menefee-Libey's discussion (1990) of entrepreneurial party leaders, though organizational culture theorists would argue that an organization's culture has a powerful constraining effect on such leaders.

2. The following descriptions of party cultures draws heavily from my analysis of out-party national committees from 1956 to the present. (See Klinkner 1992 and Klinkner 1994).

3. While I am a junior faculty member at a small college, I imply no value judgment with this observation since my wife works for an investment bank. Not surprisingly, she is a Republican and I am a Democrat.

4. The Democrats' perception that they are the natural majority party seems, at first glance, to contradict their belief that they are the party of the nation's out-groups. Yet most Democrats would attribute their "out" status not to their lack of numbers, but to their lack of political representation, economic power, and social respect.

5. See Ehrenhalt (1991) for a related argument.

6. One might attribute the Republicans' desire to return to "nuts and bolts" of the 1960s and 1970s to the recent trend in popular culture to resurrect artifacts of fashion and music from these decades, but unlike platform shoes and disco, the "nuts and bolts" trend never went out of style with the Republicans.

19

Responsible Political Parties and the Decentering of American Metropolitan Areas

Michael Margolis
David Resnick

The highest achievements of man are language and wind-swift thought, and city-dwelling habits.—Sophocles, *Antigone,* circa 441 B.C.

The lights are much brighter there,
You can forget all your troubles, forget all your cares
So go downtown . . . Tony Hatch, "Downtown," 1965.

I came here from Oregon in April, 1982. I have been downtown about six times in 11 years. I live in Springdale. I have ready access to Forest Fair Mall, Tri-County Mall, Northgate Mall, various supermarkets etc. There are numerous movie houses in the area, a library, post office, parks, pools, etc. If I never see downtown Cincinnati again, I will have lost nothing. (Letter to the Editor, *Cincinnati Enquirer* August 17, 1993)

Much of the recent literature on American political parties at the local level has focused upon their "revitalization" and "transformation." Researchers have suggested that local parties have increased their organizational efficiency and professionalism (Cotter et. al. 1984:ch. 1; Schlesinger 1991:chs. 1,7). As such, researchers have measured the extent to which parties register new voters, recruit candidates for local office, consult with and coordinate the efforts of local candidates' campaign organizations, raise money, distribute literature, and otherwise publicize candidates' qualifications, campaign activities, and policy positions. Contrary to popular and scholarly perceptions of decline, several important studies have produced evidence of revitalized party activity at the local level (cf. Frendreis and Gitelson 1993). In addition, even though local parties continue to act independently, the Democratic and Republican party organizations have become more integrated across levels of government. As the national and state party organizations have acquired professional staff and permanent headquarters, they have increased their capacity to provide research and polling services, technical assistance, training for candidates and campaign managers, and cash transfers in support of local electoral campaigns, especially for Congress and the state legislatures (Cotter et al. 1984:ch. 4; Cutler 1993; Gibson and Scarrow 1993; Herrnson 1993; Pitney 1993; Sturrock et al. 1994).

How local political parties interact with office holders and community organizations in addressing the problems of governing metropolitan areas, however, has received less attention. The lack of attention stems in part from the financial and logistical difficulties of collecting data on the thousands of local party organizations that operate under diverse state laws. Study is further complicated by the formal nonpartisanship of about half the municipalities, not to mention the governing bodies of many special districts (Margolis 1993:33; Herson and Boland 1990:chs. 7, 12).

Furthermore, there is a disjunction between the governmental units for which local parties run candidates and the scope of the problems which affect metropolitan areas. The borders of these problems do not correspond to electoral or jurisdictional boundaries of cities, townships, counties, or in some cases, even states (Dahl 1967; Rusk 1993). This disjunction creates problems for political analysis. Just as the boundaries within a metropolitan area tend to narrow the perspectives that public officials, party leaders, community activists, and the mass media bring to metropolitan problems, so they tend to limit the purview that political scientists bring to the problems they choose to study. Political institutions often place constraints over how political actors perceive problems and solutions. When political scientists focus on political actors too closely, they are liable to accept the actors' own understanding of the real and the possible. This leads them to underestimate the influence that institutions have on the actors' day-to-day political behavior (cf. March and Olsen 1984:743-47).[1]

This chapter looks into how local political parties operate in metropolitan areas (MA).[2] Our concerns go beyond the parties' ability to recruit and run candidates for local elective office. In particular, we ask how, if at all, local party leaders have altered their strategies and behaviors to adjust to the relative (and sometimes absolute) shrinkage of the population and resources of central cities (and counties) even as population and resources of MAs have grown. The party organization may hold a virtual monopoly on partisan elective offices by maintaining the loyalty and support of the party-in-the-electorate; but it is another matter for that party to work with candidates and elected officials toward solutions to the problems of declining central cities surrounded by burgeoning suburban municipalities, villages, and townships. The latter role calls for party organizations to link the party-in-government to the party-in-the-electorate (cf. Price 1984:ch. 4).

We find that local party organizations have been reluctant to recognize the new urban circumstances, however, and slow to adjust their operations to accommodate them. More broadly, we conclude that local parties are not alone: other political, civic, and market institutions have also been reluctant to address metropolitan problems. This gives rise to calls for public authorities to surrender their resources and power to nonpartisan quasi-governmental entities designed to take on these issues. A proposal to create an independent management corporation to run downtown Cincinnati like a suburban shopping mall is a good example.

In the next section we review the nature of the changes in the central cities and how these have affected urban lifestyles. We then discuss the role that theorists have argued "responsible parties" should play in democratic politics. This is followed by an examination of how well local parties fulfill this role: in this section we present data on local parties in Hamilton County, the central county of the Cincinnati Consolidated Metropolitan Statistical Area (CMSA). Finally, we present our tentative conclusions and suggestions for further research.

The Decentered American City

Once upon a time, before the authors of this chapter became political scientists, the downtowns of America's great cities held a special wonder. They boasted ornate first-run movie houses, great legitimate theaters, concert halls, museums, churches, cathedrals, libraries, the biggest and best hotels, skyscrapers, restaurants, night clubs, department stores, specialty retailers, even stadiums, coliseums, and arenas. Built mostly along rivers or natural harbors, they were centers of transportation and commerce, the areas at which the highways and railroads converged. As late as the 1950s, respectable folks still "dressed up" before "going downtown."

The cities themselves still had the flavor of self-contained economic units. Many of the factories, markets, and warehouses that served the cities lay within their boundaries. Most of the businesses were still locally owned, and even the larger corporate enterprises usually had their home offices near their factories. The cities also served as the principal local markets for the farms in the surrounding areas.

Since midcentury, metropolitan areas of the United States have undergone a process of "decentering." The typical decentered MA no longer consists of a central city hub surrounded by a wheel of suburbs connected by spokes of railways and highways. The new metropolitan area may even lack a dominant urban center, and its geographic borders are not at all obvious to the casual observer. It consists of interspersed residential, recreational, industrial, and commercial zones that not only sprawl across traditional governmental units like cities or counties, but often extend across state lines. These dispersed elements are connected by grids of highways and, served by scattered shopping malls.

As the metropolitan areas have grown, the central cities' populations have declined, not only relative to the total population of their MAs, but often in absolute numbers. As disproportionate numbers of middle and upper class urban dwellers have moved outside the central cities' limits, the relative (and in some cases absolute) affluence of the central cities has declined. As industries have moved their plants to cheaper tracts outside the cities' boundaries, the cities' tax bases have shrunk.

Meanwhile, crime in central cities has increased relative to population. The cities have also become burdened with problems of air and water pollution, public transportation, public education, and poor housing stock. Providing adequate street and bridge maintenance, public sanitation, trash collection, solid waste disposal, police, fire, emergency medical services, public parking, and traffic control present further problems.

The central cities now have disproportionately nonwhite and poor populations; most of the surrounding suburbs remain disproportionately white and affluent. A generation of suburbanites has no familiarity with the life of the old downtown. For most Americans under forty, the city center is at best a place to which they or some friends or acquaintances must commute to work. Fortunately, when they function properly, the superhighways (and in some cities, systems of rapid transit) can safely whisk suburbanites back and forth between their homes and downtown without requiring their paying much attention to the deteriorating city neighborhoods through which they pass.[3]

Far from being cultural wastelands, suburban communities have developed their own theater groups, night clubs, movie complexes, restaurants, and even symphony orchestras. The shopping centers, easily reached by automobile, provide clusters of services, including community meeting rooms. And in contrast to downtown, parking is usually free.

Kenwood Towne Centre is an example from the Cincinnati area. The "Towne Centre" is a shopping mall composed of specialty shops, restaurants, three department store "anchors," and a movie complex, but it serves as a reference point, art gallery, social center, and tourist attraction. Realtors advertise developments as located in Kenwood; people refer to themselves as living in Kenwood; Montgomery and Kenwood Roads even have signs telling drivers they are entering Kenwood. The energy of the old city center—restaurants, office complexes, hospitals—radiates along the highway grids near Towne Centre.

But governmentally, Kenwood Towne Centre is the center of a town that does not exist. It has no mayor. Its "citizens" elect no representatives. An anonymous corporation controls what businesses are established in the Towne Centre, what types of public messages are tolerated, what art is displayed, how many seats are provided in common areas, even what the temperature will be. The corporation employs a private security force to maintain law and order. Nominally, the Towne Centre and all the surrounding households and businesses fall under the jurisdiction of four elected officials of Sycamore

Township—a three person board of trustees and a clerk. Notwithstanding their location in Sycamore Township, the Towne Centre and the surrounding complex draw people from various cities and townships throughout the Cincinnati area, including residents of the city of Cincinnati proper. More generally:

> Families create their own "cities" out of the destinations they can reach (usually by car) in a reasonable length of time. Indeed, distance in the new cities is generally measured in terms of time rather than blocks or miles....*The pattern formed by these destinations represents "the city" for that particular family or individual.* The more varied one's destinations, the richer and more diverse is one's personal "city." The new city is a city *a la carte* (Fishman 1992:19).

As the decentered American city stretches across local governmental (and sometimes state) jurisdictions, developing and implementing public policies that address its problems becomes more complex. Officials or governmental bodies elected at the county level or below are disinclined to take responsibility for area-wide problems, such as public transportation, environmental pollution, economic development, low-cost housing, or crime. Indeed, most, elected officials we interviewed (see below) emphasized their efforts to do the best job governing their particular bailiwick, not taking on metro-wide problems. Even though certain metropolitan problems affect their localities, officials suggested that their constituents hold them responsible only for those problems for which they have formal legal authority.[4]

Those who want the public authorities to attack these problems face a dilemma. Either they must call for state or federal government to impose policies that intervene in local affairs, or they must call for local authorities to surrender powers to special districts or quasi-public commissions usually not elected by the public and not scrutinized by their representatives. Responsible political party organizations, at least in theory, offer one potential solution to this dilemma.

Parties and Metropolitan Politics in a Democracy

Political scientists who favor a "responsible parties" model of governance have argued that of all the major organizations that participate in American politics, political parties are "critical to achieving democratic accountability and responsiveness, to relating citizens to their broader political community, and to developing a capacity for cooperation and for addressing hard problems within and between the organs of government" (Price 1984:116; American Political Science Association Committee on Political Parties 1950). Only the parties are expected by law to have one or more of their representatives—either elected or appointed—placed in every electoral precinct in the nation. Only the parties are so permeable that citizens can gain the rights and privileges of membership simply by declaring their desire to join. Only the parties have elected members who exercise public authority in nearly every locality and at all levels of government. Just as American political parties counteract the separation of executive, legislative, judicial, and state versus federal powers, so too they can overcome the separation of powers and jurisdictions within MAs.

In its strong form the responsible party model calls upon party organizations to recruit candidates, conduct election campaigns, and develop principles, platforms, or programs which their candidates pledge to support. Once elected, public officials have a duty to implement these programs to the extent practicable. They must communicate and consult with party leaders, and they must work with other elected officials, especially members of their own party, to develop the appropriate public policies to achieve these programs.

In its weak form, the responsible parties model calls for parties to register voters, raise funds, recruit candidates, and conduct electoral campaigns, but not for them to generate party programs and policies that their candidates are pledged to implement. Candidates need only declare their agreement with general party principles. Between elections parties facilitate communication between elected officials and interest groups and among officials at different levels of government. The success of public policy, however, depends upon the demands of various interests among the electorate and the ideas and abilities elected officials. As a rule, the party is indifferent to the content of the policies (cf. Frendreis and Gitelson 1993; Schlesinger 1991:ch. 6).

In theory, responsible parties are the ordinary citizens' best hope for exerting control over decision-making elites. Without responsible parties, theorists suggest, elections tend to degenerate into exercises in demagoguery. And once elected, most officials lack the connections to forge the coalitions necessary to carry out their campaign promises. The policy process tends to be dominated by well-organized, and often well-endowed, interest groups with their own particular agenda. Public policy leadership, if any, tends to fall to officials like presidents, governors, and mayors, who have privileged access to the mass media (cf. Bachrach 1967; Ginsberg 1986; Lowi 1979).

Democracy generally begins at the local level. Here citizens can organize parties or interest groups to press their demands and to elect representatives to satisfy them. The scale of government is small and politics is more understandable and less intimidating. Moreover, the cost of political participation is usually not exorbitant. Guided by parties or local interest groups, citizens can engage in a rich exchange of ideas, facilitated by new communication technologies (Abramson et al. 1988).

The responsible parties model, however, is not the only model for effective democratic politics at the local level. In response to the corruption of a few powerful turn-of-the-century party "machines," the reform movement developed a nonpartisan model. Local government should concern itself with "efficient business-like" delivery of services, not with matters of partisan politics. For municipalities this nonpartisan politics is often facilitated by a council-manager form of government. In this form of government, an "honest, representative" nonpartisan council determines basic policy "that would work for the general interest of the city," and the city manager determines the best way to implement that policy (Charter Research Institute 1991:5).[5] For townships in Ohio this ideal can be realized through a limited government headed by four elected officials: a single administrative clerk and a nonpartisan board of three trustees with no legislative powers beyond those delegated by the state.[6] "There is no Democratic way to pick up garbage. There is no Republican way to pave a street: only an honest and efficient way"—so went one of the original Charter rallying cries still pertinent today (Charter Committee 1988:7).

There is a limit to the ability of a council-manager government to carry on its policies in a business like manner. A city government, unlike a business, cannot follow its customers when they move to the suburbs. The nonpartisan model can work as long as the city maintains a "great, orderly, prosperous, middle-class backbone." Unfortunately for Cincinnati and other declining central cities:

> The great, orderly, prosperous, middle-class backbone of the city that made city manager government work is now the ... backbone of the suburbs. And those economically segregated suburban municipalities are now bigger than the city they surround ...
> City managers are just the ticket for places like [affluent suburbs] where the most intractable problems have to do with traffic lights and where the social issues have to do with prom dates. City government in Cincinnati has problems ... like crack cocaine, teenage pregnancy, racial isolation, suburban shopping malls, radio talk shows and institutionalized panhandling. Political problems.
> Fountain Square West [a prime block of downtown real estate earmarked for retail development] is not a management problem, it's a political problem. The city needs a political leader to jawbone, flatter, threaten, wheedle, and knock heads until the right store gets built. ... The city manager just can't (Pyle 1993:25-26).

Even among traditional opponents of powerful local party organizations, partisan politics may be coming back into vogue. As the central cities' resources have diminished, cities with strong mayors have been able to garner more federal and state dollars through grants than those with council-manager governments. They also have been able to lure more private investment back into the city center (Herson and Boland 1990:chs. 14-15; Cole 1974; *Cincinnati Enquirer* 1993).[7] There is a trend among central cities to change from council-manager to a strong mayoral forms of government. St. Petersburg, Florida, has abandoned its city manager. Toledo has just elected its first strong mayor. Dallas, Sacramento, and Dade County (Miami, Florida) are contemplating similar changes. Even Cincinnati's leadership have discussed revising the city charter to grant more power to the mayor (*Cincinnati Enquirer* 1993).

Nevertheless, no one contends that central cities can solve their major problems by reforming their charters. Regardless of their formal powers, strong mayors will still be leading central cities without the resources to solve their problems on their own. The leadership of villages, townships, smaller cities, and counties must become convinced that their communities have an important stake in the fate of the central cities. Otherwise, the cities are bound to decline further as high paying jobs and capital continue to flow toward the suburbs (Herson and Boland 1991:442-45).

Two other mechanisms have been proposed to bring city and suburbs together: nonpartisan quasi-governmental commissions that plan and implement public policies and special metropolitan authorities that provide or regulate particular services. Nonpartisan commissions, a time-honored tradition in Cincinnati, usually arise in MAs with council-manager cities. Metropolitan authorities usually arise when several neighboring communities in the MA have been individually burdened by problems of sewage, waste disposal, pollution, public education, transportation, or safety.

In recent years the federal government has begun to require that local communities conform to regional plans for clean air and water and public transportation. Metropolitan Planning Organizations, often regional Councils of Government composed of representatives from local governments, have been given greater control of the distribution of federal largess throughout the MAs (Rusk 1993:112; OKI 1993). As we shall see in the next section, both city and suburban public and party leaders see the greatest potential for fostering greater cooperation between central city and suburban governments in these regional councils.[8]

Responsible Parties in the Decentered Metropolitan Area

If local party organizations operated in accordance with the responsible parties model, we would expect parties to play a significant role in addressing the problems of the decentered MA. The model calls for parties to raise funds, recruit candidates, assist in their electoral campaigns, maintain communication with officials between elections, and impose some form of party discipline. In addition, if the strong form of the responsible parties model applied, we would expect that parties that develop platforms or policy positions to deal with local and metropolitan problems, that agreement with these party positions would be a precondition for party endorsement, and that elected officials would consult regularly with party leaders to implement them.

In most cases, metropolitan problems such as traffic flow, sewage, air pollution, water purification, and crime control impinge upon life in the municipalities, villages, and townships outside the central cities. Even if local party organizations did not address metropolitan problems, we would still expect to find that other organizations, public officeholders, or civic-minded individuals would. As we suggested above, however, most of these groups and individuals have no responsibility to the general public. Only elected officeholders are directly responsible to constituent publics, and only those commissions or intergovernmental bodies appointed by elected officials have clear responsibility to the public's representatives. Actions of civic-minded individuals, independent commissions, or other organizations—even those appointed by public administrators—are at least two steps removed from review by the electorate.

If success for local party organizations were winning office in the short term and fostering policies that preserved their electoral and organizational advantages in the long term, we could declare local party organizations healthy and flourishing. Paradoxically, we could make this judgment even if their actions were largely irrelevant to solving the pressing problems of the MAs in which they operated. Indeed, we believe this sort of reasoning accounts for the judgment of researchers who present evidence that local parties have increased their resources since the 1950s and conclude that "the level of party organizational activity is in general far higher today than it was in the past, and, as a result, the effectiveness of parties is most likely increasing rather significantly" (Gibson and Scarrow 1993:240).

Our concerns, however, extend beyond short- and long-term electoral effectiveness. We are interested in determining the extent to which local party organizations play a responsible role in dealing with metropolitan political problems. To this end we have reviewed the judgments of party scholars about the political activities of local party organizations; we have examined recent studies of how political and civic organizations and actors have addressed the problems of decentered MAs; and finally, we have conducted our own investigation of the role of local political party organizations in addressing the problems of the Cincinnati CMSA. To anticipate our findings: we uncovered few instances of party organizations playing what we have described as a responsible role in metropolitan governance. Our interviews with Hamilton County party leaders and public officials revealed not only the political parties' low level of involvement in addressing metropolitan problems, but a low interest—and among some officials, a low comprehension—regarding any responsible role party organizations could or should take in addressing these problems.

Even though party scholars have debated the proper policy roles that American political parties should play at various levels of government, limited resources have forced most researchers to focus on higher levels of government.[9] Most research, in fact, concerns the organization and behavior of national party committees. Relatively less is known about the policy efforts of most state party organizations. A general pattern of increased professionalism and electoral effectiveness of state party committees, however, has led researchers to suggest that state parties too are playing a stronger policy role than in the past. This is particularly true with regard to candidate recruitment where state parties are increasingly moving into the roles that satisfy what we have called the weak model of responsible party governance (Gibson and Scarrow 1993:244).

Political scientists have done much less research on the policy roles of local party organizations than they have on the roles of national and state organizations. We know that local parties can no longer provide sufficient material incentives, such as local jobs and patronage, to gain mass electoral support. However, we have little evidence that they have successfully substituted ideological or policy (purposive) incentives in their stead. What evidence there is suggests that personal loyalty to candidates provides a more common motivation for party workers than does loyalty to party policies (Keefe 1991:25–27; Margolis and Owen 1985). Moreover, despite increased party professionalism at the state and national levels and increased electoral activity at the local levels, candidate-centered rather than party-centered campaigns remain the norm at all levels of government (Crotty ed. 1986; Salmore and Salmore 1989:255–56).

Local party organizations do not seem to be directly involved in addressing metropolitan problems. The *Cincinnati Enquirer's* extensive report on "saving" the downtowns of seven midwest cities suggests that local political parties have made little, if any, impact on public policies aimed at revitalizing the city centers. Although the *Enquirer's* reporters conducted interviews with public officials, business and civic leaders, and ordinary citizens, they spoke to no one in his or her capacity as a party official. In fact, the political parties received only two significant mentions in some twenty-two full pages of newsprint.[10]

Nonetheless, it can be argued that researchers have failed to find local party organizations playing significant policy roles simply because they have not looked very hard. Most studies of local parties, after all, have focused on how well parties have performed electoral tasks. Other studies of urban politics have tended to focus on how officeholders, local elites, and interest groups—not political parties—have addressed the problems of central cities.

Our study makes a deliberate effort to look at the policy role of local political parties. Beginning in July 1993, we conducted interviews with party leaders and public officeholders in the Cincinnati CMSA. The interviews were designed specifically to assess both the roles parties currently play in developing policy for the CMSA and the roles that party leaders and public officials wanted them to play.[11]

On the surface, the Hamilton County Democratic and Republican party organizations look stronger than average. Each has a permanent headquarters staffed by full- or part-time professionals. Each has auxiliary clubs or affiliated organizations. Each endorses candidates for local office, raises and disburses campaign funds, does mailings, and makes phone calls on behalf of party candidates.[12] Moreover, the city of Cincinnati itself has a third party, the Charter Committee, that also maintains a permanent headquarters with a professional staff, endorses candidates for city council, and carries out other tasks similar to those performed by the Democratic and Republican party organizations.[13] Electorally, these parties are remarkably successful. Nearly every elected officeholder in the county is affiliated with one of them, even though election for Cincinnati City Council, township trustees, and some municipal councils are officially nonpartisan.

When we scratch beneath the surface, however, a less flattering organizational picture emerges. While each of the parties has a role in endorsing candidates, party officials readily admit that most candidates are in fact self-starters. There is little, if any, active candidate recruitment. The party endorsements go mainly to incumbents and to those self-starters who party officials judge to be most electable.[14] Even after endorsement candidates remain mostly on their own. The party endorsement confers a bona fides that helps candidates garner coverage in the local news media; it also facilitates access to lists of individuals who have contributed to the campaigns of previously endorsed candidates. The parties do little, however, to develop issues or strategies for the campaign; nor do they normally distribute substantial funds to support particular candidates.[15] By and large, candidates must develop their own personal organizations. In fact, officeholders report that many precinct executives—mostly Democrats—cannot even be relied upon to pass out party slate cards on election day.

The city of Cincinnati has lost approximately 138,000 people since 1970. Its 362,000 residents now comprise less than 40 percent of the county's population, and barely one quarter of those living in the CMSA. Nonetheless, the county parties do little tracking of where their voters have moved. Each of the county party subunits—township, village, and municipal party committees—essentially runs its own electoral operation. Both county parties concentrate the lion's share of their efforts on winning offices in the city of Cincinnati and county-wide. If anything, the parties still devote more attention to city than to county politics and elections.

Neither the party leaders nor the officeholders whom we interviewed indicated they had made significant adjustments to their electoral strategies or their policies to accommodate metropolitan problems. County party leaders lamented the flight of the middle class from the city to suburbs together with the attendant loss of revenues, stable neighborhoods, and potential for political and civic leadership. Nevertheless, they had nothing more to suggest concerning how the parties or government could cope with these problems beyond setting up (another) independent commission to study them.

Party leaders and public officials showed a remarkable tendency not only to focus almost exclusively on problems within their own particular bailiwick, but also on problems related to their own formal responsibilities. Democratic and Republican party leaders saw their organizations as primarily in a struggle to control the Cincinnati City Council, the County Board of Commissioners, and the independent County Offices. The Executive Director of the Charter Committee emphasized that Charter had to reinvigorate its city organization before it could concern itself with metropolitan problems. County officials claimed they did not have power to do much for the subunits of government, particularly the city of Cincinnati. Township and municipal officials outside the central city expressed concern about the problems of public safety, parking, and shopping downtown, but pointed out that they could not do much about them. Their constituents were more concerned with maintaining local roads and providing good local schools, police, and fire protection. Air and water pollution were problems, but they did not view them as their responsibility nor, as they saw it, did their constituents. Public transportation was a problem only if a local municipality lacked access to a line for those who needed to commute to the central city.[16]

Except for federally mandated contact through the Regional (Ohio-Kentucky-Indiana called "OKI") Council of Governments, interviewees reported little or no contact with their counterparts in other counties in the CMSA. Indeed, Roxanne Qualls, the Cincinnati Council representative to the OKI, indicated that most elected officials didn't even know who their counterparts were in counties across the state borders. Although the federal government now requires that OKI certify that all new local initiatives accord with regional plans for public transportation and pollution control, the idea of metropolitan government remains an anathema. Interviewees generally saw metropolitan government (or "unigov") as the intrusion of big government into local matters.[17]

The parties have no long-term strategies. When we asked party leaders what they would do differently if they had all the money and staff they could use, they answered that they would continue to do what they do now, only more effectively. They would hire more staff, conduct surveys of voters, spend more money to advertise candidates, improve party headquarters, and the like. None expressed any desire to win over electors by promoting any ideas or recruiting better candidates.

In sum, although the local parties remain electorally successful, neither their leaders nor their public officeholders envision them fulfilling the active policy role called for by the strong model of party responsibility. In fact, the party leaders generally are not interested in policy at all. Nor do the parties fully satisfy the criteria of the weak model of responsibility. They don't raise much money, they do little active recruitment of candidates, they rarely attempt to enforce party discipline, and even these rare attempts usually fail.

Conclusions

Political scientists are worried about the changes in the American political system that might make the political parties irrelevant. There has been a significant amount of research on local parties focused on the question of decline and possible revitalization, but most of that research has been centered on the political party as an electoral organization. There is relatively little research on other aspects of local party behavior which might erode the significance of party in American politics. Political scientists have argued that the electoral role is the key role of political parties. If they do not perform that role successfully, they are much less likely to perform other roles successfully, such as political socialization, facilitation of mass political participation, leadership recruitment, agenda setting, policy development, and the like.

Yet even if the electoral role of local political parties is a necessary condition for them to remain significant players in the nonelectoral aspects of American politics, it is not a sufficient one. Party organization and electoral influence may be on the road to recovery, and yet the role of parties may still be in a relative decline. Local parties in Cincinnati define their role very narrowly and show little interest in broadening their understanding of what they actually should do. Parties seem to be simply trying to survive and make a good showing in the next election.

Parties must have both the will and the opportunity to play other roles. It is not sufficient to assume that if they have a continuing place in the electoral arena they will automatically fulfill other functions that theorists have assigned them. At the local level we have a myriad of local jurisdictions. Political parties have the potential to unify our fragmented political system by uniting both citizens and officeholders across jurisdictions, thereby making local politics less parochial (cf. Beck and Sorauf 1993:16; Price 1984:116).

It has become a cliché to say that all politics is local. Whatever weight such a generalization carries at the national level, it certainly carries much more at the local level. The problems in a small town may actually be regional problems, but local politics is local. The problem of parochialism cuts across the question of whether or not we have responsible political parties. Even if local parties conformed to the responsible party model, providing party principles and programs, controlling the process of nomination and imposing party discipline upon elected officials, they would not necessarily have any impact on the problems of fragmentation and parochialism. In theory the party label, the party principles, and the organization as a whole are not constrained by the legal boundaries and powers which comprise local jurisdictions. The practice of local politics is full of self-imposed constraints.

Because political parties have been narrowly defined as electoral organizations, the logic of responsible parties has been turned inside out. Responsible parties are supposed to elect candidates in order to achieve public policy goals. Elections are the means; policies and programs are the ends. But for local parties in Hamilton County, electoral victory is the goal, and policies and programs are but one of the less important means of achieving this goal.

According to Beck and Sorauf the entire argument for responsible political parties "rests on replacing individual or group responsibility for governing with responsibility of the political party" (Becka and Sorauf 1993:452). Yet, for the most part, the local political parties in our study prefer to shun responsibility. They prefer leaving political responsibility to public officeholders and others. The party will render candidates assistance, often rather minimal, during electoral campaigns. But once they are elected, the officeholders become the visible standard-bearers of political responsibility. Between elections the party fades into the background.

Even this picture of individual political responsibility is too optimistic. Individual standard-bearers often prefer to hand the standard to someone else, anyone else, who seems capable of handling the tough issues. The tendency of local political parties to shun responsibility for governing is something they share with local officeholders. Elected officials try to maintain that whatever is wrong is not their problem, and even if it is their problem you can't really expect them to solve it. Is there too much crime in the central city? Neither the suburban nor the county politicians have jurisdiction; and how can the voters expect the city officials alone to control the out-of-state drug traffic coming up I-75? Is traffic snarled? Are the sewers backing up? Is much of the housing dilapidated? These are problems that require the resources of state or federal authorities, the efforts of civic association, or the investment of private corporations. Local politicians are constantly searching for nonpolitical solutions that relieve them of responsibility for making tough decisions. The seeming inability of local political parties to respond creatively to the changing urban environment is symptomatic of a general loss of faith in the ability of government to solve political problems.

Consider the following editorial from the August 18, 1993, *Cincinnati Enquirer*. It is written to back a new plan for the revitalization of downtown Cincinnati. The plan advocates targeting affluent downtown workers while still working on long-term plans to compete with suburban malls. What is interesting about the editorial is not the viability of the proposed solutions to Cincinnati's urban problems, but the assumptions it makes about the political process at the local level:

> At last, steps are being taken to form an independent group to do for downtown what management companies do for malls. It's an idea whose time came and went elsewhere. Leadership has been lackluster: city council bickers, staff is shell-shocked by turnover and firings and a posse of committees rides off in all directions to rescue downtown . . .

Key groups such as the Downtown Progress Committee have been weak. The city leans on the Cincinnati Business Committee like a crutch. The Chamber of Commerce has not been the catalyst it could be. And egos have eclipsed the sun in a struggle for obsessive control.

But now downtown business leaders at the Chamber of Commerce, the Cincinnati Business Committee and the Downtown Progress Committee, with acting City Manager Frank Dawson, are getting their act together.

The goal under discussion: raise up to $1.4 million to form an independent management corporation.

By comparison, suburban malls often spend more each year for marketing, management and security. Half of the $1.4 million goal may be sought from business, half from taxpayers. That sounds like a big hit on taxpayers . . . But without revival, the tax base will shrink with each closed business, as taxpayers are stuck with a swelling bill for city services.

An umbrella management corporation could finally tackle parking, security, promotions, development and a shopping list of other issues.

The preferred solution is the establishment of a nonprofit management company to implement suggestions in a plan commissioned by the city council, but actually developed by private consultants. The plan is a true nonpartisan plan, not a Democratic, Republican, or Charterite plan. Even more significant is that the editorial does not even conceptualize the problems as remotely partisan. The solutions to the city problems will not arise from the existing electoral political process. That is, the way out of the spiraling decline of the core city is not to back the candidates or platforms of one of the established political parties. The answer is not to throw the rascals out and elect new members to the city council.

Cincinnati is one of the few remaining core cities in CMSAs which still operates under the council-manager form of government, but the proposed solution also does not draw upon old-fashioned reform ideology. It does not blame partisanship for thwarting the political process. Nor does the proposed solution call for a more competent city manager. Increasing the powers of city government, reorganizing its bureaucracy, and eliminating political bottlenecks seemingly could not provide the city with the means to execute the new plan for reviving downtown Cincinnati.

The difficulty goes much deeper. Local government is incompetent to implement workable solutions. Yet the free market is not viewed as the alternative to incompetent government. The editorial assumes that if market forces are allowed to continue, the core city faces ongoing decline. More and more retail merchants will move to the suburbs or simply go out of business. Another sign that market forces alone cannot revive downtown is the suggestion that significant public tax money is necessary to implement this plan; the collective self-interest of downtown merchants is not sufficient.

A revitalized downtown will benefit both city taxpayers and business interests, yet the means for achieving collective renewal require a model that combines the virtues of both public and private management. The solution proposed by the *Enquirer* is to establish a quasi-governmental entity which would do what both the free market and municipal government are incapable of doing. The solution might be called "reform-reform" government or privatized government. Appropriately, the model for this entity is the suburban shopping mall. People often blame the decline of the old central city on suburban shopping malls. They say that malls create a substitute for main street and a sanitized middle class version of the old lively cityscape where, among other things, politics and political problems have vanished. Self-government has been replaced by faceless management corporations.

The solution to the decline of Cincinnati is to treat the center city like a shopping mall. The core city must be made more like the suburbs and treated as simply another shopping node. It must be adapted to the lifestyle and assumptions of suburban retail shoppers, to the citizens of the suburbs accustomed to their own way of interacting with city services. The city itself is struggling to adapt to this new reality, but the political party is nowhere in evidence. It is irrelevant and has nearly vanished. Privatized government does not even have to fight entrenched city political machines for reform. It simply has to build a consensus and have the political system turn over power and money.

Whether this model will in fact be embraced by the city of Cincinnati is difficult to predict. It has apparently proven itself in other old core cities which have employed some form of the new privatized method for economic renewal (*Cincinnati Enquirer* 1993). The political system seemingly cannot provide leadership and expertise. The business community by itself cannot organize a successful revitalization campaign. Only the new nonprofit semipublic management structures can do what in the past had been done either by local government, by the market, or by local government in partnership with business. What role does the local political party organization have in this major process of urban transformation? Seemingly, little or none.

Researchers have heralded the news that the reported terminal decline of local political parties has been greatly exaggerated. They claim to have found a revitalized and transformed party organization. Yet from the perspective of those who look for responsible parties to play a dynamic role in the process of governing, such optimism seems unwarranted. Local parties may not be declining as electoral organizations, but instead of confronting the new realities of decentered metropolitan areas, they are conducting business as usual.

We end on a rather pessimistic note. Though much of the data for our study come from the Cincinnati region and further research in other metropolitan areas will be necessary to confirm our findings, we still feel confident about our overall conclusions. The old central core city has undergone a profound transformation, but local political parties have not responded. Despite our hopes to the contrary, we find no evidence that they intend to respond in the future.[18]

Notes

1. For example, the *Cincinnati Enquirer* distributed three separate fall election guides in the Sunday paper of October 24, 1993. Readers received the guide for Hamilton County (Cincinnati and suburbs), the guide for Clermont, Butler, and Warren Counties (Southwestern Ohio), or the guide for Boone, Campbell, and Kenton Counties (Northern Kentucky). No special section covered Dearborn Counties, Indiana, Gallatin, Grant, and Pendleton Counties, Kentucky, or Brown County, Ohio. In short, the *Enquirer* prepared no comprehensive (or summary) guide for the metropolitan area for which it is the principal newspaper.

2. A Metropolitan Area (MA) consists of a central city with a minimum population of 50,000 or an urbanized area of 100,000 or more people (75,000 in New England) as defined by the Bureau of the Census. Geographically, an MA consists of one or more central counties, but it may also include adjacent counties with strong economic or social ties to the center. For statistical purposes an MA is designated either as a Metropolitan Statistical Area (MSA) or as a Primary Metropolitan Statistical Area (PMSA) of a larger Consolidated Metropolitan Statistical Area (CMSA). CMSAs consists of MAs over 1,000,000 people that have one or more large central cities. CMSAs may contain smaller PMSAs. The key requirements for determining the boundaries of an MA are that the outlying counties (or cities in New England) have specified social and economic relationships to the central counties as measured by levels of commuting, population density, urban population, and population growth (U.S. Department of Commerce, 1992). Ordinarily, no governmental unit to which citizens elect representatives corresponds to the boundaries of the MA.

3. Actually, more people commute from suburb to suburb than from suburb to central city. More offices are located in the suburbs than in central cities. Suburbs also have more retail sales than do central cities. (See Fishman 1992:12–17).

4. There is also some evidence that voters do not hold local government responsible for problems like layoffs and unemployment. (See Margolis, Burtt, and McLaughlin 1986:22)

5. The philosophy behind Cincinnati's Home Rule Charter remains as baldly "good government" as it was in 1924 when the voters adopted the Council-Manager form championed by the National Municipal League. ". . . council should hire a City Manager with a thorough knowledge of municipal services and proven skills as a professional administrator. This system was also inaugurated to depoliticize the city administration, and the Manager is responsible for running departments and programs without political bias. Council hammers out those political decisions that are part of the legislative process in a democracy, while the Manager is free to deal with the nuts and bolts of a large municipal administration" (Charter Research Institute 1991:5). See also Seasongood (1954).

6. See Dorsey (1993:59) for a paean to township governments of "limited power, decisions by peers, [and] administration by consensus."

7. Of the six midwest cities the *Enquirer* team compared with Cincinnati, the four with the most vibrant downtowns—Cleveland, Columbus, Indianapolis and Louisville,—have strong mayors, while the two with the most depressed centers—Dayton and Toledo—have city managers.

8. We skip a discussion of the pros and cons of metropolitan government simply because consolidated metropolitan government is not a viable possibility at this time. Only three major consolidations have occurred in metropolitan areas over 250,000 since 1907: Indianapolis,

Indiana (1969); Jacksonville, Florida (1967) and Nashville, Tennessee (1962) (Herson and Boland 1990:260 ff.).

9. Schlesinger (1991:ch. 1), for example, argues that policy concerns detract from the parties' main mission: electing candidates to office. Gibson et al. (1989) on the other hand, argue that ideology can help rather than hinder electoral success. On the difficulty of doing comparative studies of local party organizations, see Margolis (1993).

10. In both instances, the state party organization, rather than the local party, played a critical role. The first involved the Republican business leaders of Cleveland seeking Governor James Rhodes' blessing for his Lieutenant Governor, George Voinovich, to return to the city and run for mayor against the politically unpalatable (and increasingly unpopular) Democratic incumbent, Dennis Kucinich. The second involved Louisville Democrats petitioning the Democratically controlled state legislature to authorize a referendum to allow their mayor to serve three consecutive four-year terms instead of being limited to only one term. In each case, we have at best an instance of the state or local party organization acting in accordance with the precepts of the weak model of party responsibility to recruit or retain a strong candidate. A consolidated copy of the full series can be obtained from the *Enquirer*.

11. Interviews were conducted by the authors in person or by telephone using a directed list of questions, but not a formal interview protocol. They lasted between 30 and 120 minutes. See below (after the references) for a list of interviewees.

12. The Republican Party is far better organized: it has a bigger budget, larger staff, more active committees, and more active affiliated organizations.

13. The Charter Committee is technically not a party. Ohio law requires that organizations maintain a statewide presence in order to qualify as official parties. (See Sturrock et al. 1994).

14. This appears to be consistent with endorsement processes in other localities (See Maisel et al. 1990:150-52).

15. Neither of the major parties develops a platform or principles to which candidates are asked to adhere. Rarely do the parties repudiate one of their own, regardless of his or her performance. When the Republicans did refuse to endorse incumbent Guy Guckenberger for Council in 1989, he ran successfully as an independent Republican. (The party subsequently relented and appointed him to a vacancy on the County Board of Commissioners). The Democrats were happy to endorse Tyrone Yates in 1993 even though he was first appointed and then subsequently elected to Council as a Charterite. The Republicans have been similarly happy to accept Democratic turncoats, such as Kenneth Blackwell and James Cissell. The Charter Committee's principles preclude their imposing any more guidance on candidates than the general admonition to campaign and to govern "for the good of the whole city" as opposed to any particular neighborhood or special interest (see Miller 1993).

16. Even here the view of transportation is rather parochial. County Commission Chairman, Robert Dowlin, recently complained that even the OKI metropolitan transportation plan assumes everyone wants to travel downtown. "I don't see enough cross-town transportation. There are as many jobs in Blue Ash as there are in downtown Cincinnati." (Calhoun 1993).

17. Qualls' recent elevation from council member to mayor has signaled a new emphasis on regional concerns. Her "State of the City Address" (January 6, 1994) called for regional cooperation to solve the city's problems. Among other things, she proposed formation of a Cincinnati/Northern Kentucky port authority to tackle big ticket projects like financing a new stadium and expanding regional convention facilities. This regional focus is her own initiative. The local Democratic party has never taken any position on these issues, and Qualls has always run as an independent Democrat.

18. Interviews: **Tim Burke**, Chairman, Hamilton County Democratic Party, August 1993-present; face to face, August 19, 1993. **Loi Conway**, Executive Director of Charter

Committee; face to face, , August 3, 1993. **Robert Dorsey**, Chairman, Anderson Township Board of Trustees, Republican; face to face, August 19, 1993. **Robert Dowlin**, President, Hamilton County Board of Commissioners, Republican, Former Mayor, City of Sharonville; face to face, August 23, 1993. **Gregory Jarvis**, City Manager, Covington, Kentucky; face to face, October 7, 1993. **Thomas Luken**, Former Mayor of Cincinnati, former Member of Congress, Chairman, Hamilton County Democratic Party, 1991–93; successful candidate for City Council, 1993; face to face, August 25, 1993. Also short interview by telephone in July. **Zane Miller**, Former Ward Chairman, Cincinnati Democratic Committee, Campaign Manager for Southwestern Ohio, Eugene McCarthy for President, 1968, Professor of History and Co-Director, Center for Neighborhood and Community Studies, University of Cincinnati; face to face, August 12, 1993. **Roxanne Qualls**, Member, Cincinnati City Council, Democrat, Council Representative to OKI Regional Council of Governments, Elected mayor in November 1993; Telephone, August 27, 1993. **Brewster Rhoads**, Democratic party campaign consultant and manager, Member, Hamilton County Democratic Executive and Steering Committees; face to face, October 11, 1993. **Dusty Rhodes**, Hamilton County Auditor, Democrat; face to face, August 27, 1993. **Eugene Ruehlmann**, Chairman, Hamilton County Republican Committee, Former Mayor of Cincinnati; face to face, August 16, 1993. **Greg Vehr**, Executive Director, Hamilton County Republican Committee; face to face, August 16, 1993. **Brandon Wiers**, Former Mayor of City of Forest Park, Member, Commission on County Government Reform, Member of Forest Park Democratic Committee, Served on commission as representative of Charter Committee of Cincinnati, Forest Park has nonpartisan council-manager charter; face to face, August 17, 1993. **Tyrone Yates**, Member, Cincinnati City Council, Democrat, elected as Charterite for 1991–1993 term, Former Democratic Party Candidate for Congress, Adjunct Associate Professor of Political Science, University of Cincinnati; Short interviews: face to face and by telephone: July 1993.

PART FIVE

Reconceptualizing Parties: 1992 and Beyond

The Resurgence of Party Organization?
A Dissent from the New Orthodoxy

John J. Coleman

Forty years ago, the American Political Science Association's Committee on Political Parties (1950) precipitated a storm of controversy with a critique of American parties. While many political scientists were sympathetic to the committee's call for responsible parties, an equally sizable contingent agreed with Pendleton Herring's (1940) classic analysis: the United States had parties appropriate to its political culture and government structure, attempts to change these parties were probably futile, and any such changes would be dangerous for American democracy.

Twenty years ago, scholars began to diagnose the decline of American parties as central organizing structures in American politics.[1] Many writers pointed to decline stretching half a century or longer, while others argued that the decline was particularly severe in the postwar period. In effect these writers viewed even the parties criticized by the APSA party report to be preferable to the parties of the late 1960s.

Today, a new orthodoxy in party organization scholarship challenges the party decline analysis. With few exceptions, writers concentrating on party organizations argue that parties are more active and more significant than earlier literature implied. According to this view, the party decline school mistakenly assumed that problems in Congress and in the electorate indicated the decline of the party *system* and, by extension, party organizations. While these scholars concede that the strength of the party system cannot be inferred from the strength of party organizations, they also argue that such an assessment has to include party organizations (Gibson, Cotter, Bibby, Huckshorn 1983:194). The logical implication of this analysis is that the party system is stronger than the party decline model implies. The irony is rich: the "revivalists," who usually express sympathy with the Herring view of parties, argue that some of what the APSA committee demanded has come to pass and the American political order is better for it (see inventory in Baer and Bositis 1993:appendix). But they challenge the "declinists" who grudgingly accepted the Herring-approved political parties of the early postwar period.

Once we move beyond the notion of increased party activity, several shortcomings in the recent party revival literature become clear. Here I address several of these deficiencies. Because it is done so well in many of the sources I cite, I will not provide an extensive review of the findings in the literature. Moreover, despite a critical tone, this essay should not be construed as a wholesale indictment on an impressive body of research. Recent party organization research has filled a large gap in the study of parties, addressed with precision several anomalies in that larger literature, been innovative in measurement and research design, and proven remarkably cumulative. My objective is to point out research gaps and to encourage a more integrated analysis of the party system.

The New Orthodoxy

The past decade has seen a sea change among party scholars regarding the health of party organizations in the United States. Where fifteen years ago there was consensus that party organizations were weak, today the consensus argues that party organizations are revitalized, resurgent, and relevant. Scholars have conducted large-scale surveys of state and county party chairs and found that those organizations report performing more activities today than at any time since the second World War.[2] Campaign finance studies indicate that ever-larger sums pass through the hands of various party committees on the national, state, and county (local) levels and that these funds, with some party differences, are generally targeted toward competitive races.[3] These scholars are enthused about what they see happening with the party organizations and are convinced that "parties matter" (Gibson and Scarrow 1993).

Virtually all party scholars agree that there has been real change in party activity on the national, state, and county levels. But there are some peculiarities in the data. Cotter, Gibson, Bibby, and Huckshorn (1984:39, 54), for example, find that most of the increase in state and county party organizational strength occurred in the 1960s, which is not widely considered the heyday of party organizational resurgence. Indeed, Herrnson and Menefee-Libey (1990), *begin* their overview of party organizational change in the late 1960s, and many writers focus on changes in the late 1970s and early 1980s. A second disturbance in the claims about party organizations concerns the status of local parties. Most of the literature focuses on county party organizations, and here, like with the national and state parties, the consensus is that parties are doing more today than previously (cf. Lawson, Pomper, and Moakley 1986). Studies of cities, however, show a more mixed pattern, with the authors in Crotty (1986) generally encouraged by what they see while authors like Ware (1985) argue city party organizations have lost so many of their traditional functions, especially control of nominations, that they are but a shell of their former selves (Johnston 1979).

Despite these peculiarities in the data, the case that party organizations are performing more activities and raising more funds today is strong enough that one can not get very far arguing that it is not so. But armed with this data, the party organization literature has leapt too quickly to words like "resurgence" and "revitalization." Increased activity should only be the *start* of a conception of resurgent parties. That conception also needs to account for the party organizations' relations with other actors and institutions in the political universe. To make a business analogy, over the past few years there has been much speculation in the business press about the troubles afflicting the International Business Machines Corporation (IBM). Suppose that with new leadership, IBM was to begin restructuring and reallocating organizational responsibilities, changing prices, and introducing new product lines. It is difficult to imagine that we would hear much about IBM being resurgent and revitalized unless customers returned to IBM products and IBM's profitability improved, even if analysts admired IBM's efforts. Even praising the company's ability to hold its market share steady would be considered at best a backhanded compliment. We should ask the same questions of parties: are the customers returning and are the parties increasing their "market" share? One might argue that if market share is measured as the percentage of offices held by the two major parties or by candidates' use of party services, then indeed market share is high and perhaps growing. But if market share is measured in other ways—such as the percentage of voters given enough incentive to turn out to vote—a different picture might well emerge. However one measures the benchmarks, the point is that resurgence is indicated not by organizational restructuring alone but by the *effects* of restructuring.

Bringing the Voters Back In

One striking anomaly in the contemporary party system is that scholars argue party organizations are reviving while the public has become increasingly skeptical about the relevance of political parties to governing and the desirability of partisan activity (Fiorna 1980; Burnham 1982; Brady 1990; Milkis 1993). More citizens say that interest groups better represent them than do political parties, and the interest group advantage is particularly heavy among the young (Advisory Commission on Intergovernmental Relations 1986:52). Record numbers of voters split their tickets and record numbers of districts have split outcomes—that is, supporting a president of one party and a member of Congress from another. Voting patterns are increasingly inconsistent: it is harder to predict what will happen in one race by knowing the outcome in another and it is harder to predict voting patterns two years hence based on voting patterns today. Only half the electorate bothers to vote in presidential elections while about one-third votes in off-year congressional elections. Electoral turnout varies substantially across states and across offices; in the absence of a gubernatorial campaign, turnout is low. Local turnout is usually low as well. In 1992, nineteen percent of the voting public supported an independent candidate for president who had held no political office, was all but unknown seven months before the election, and did almost no campaigning in the traditional sense.

It is difficult to understand any of these developments through the lenses provided by party organization theory. Perhaps one could argue that decreasing party loyalty is a sign of party organizational strength: that is, the organizations have become so effective at campaigning that they uproot traditional voter loyalties (Cotter, Gibson, Bibby, and Huckshorn 1984:103). Perhaps organizational strength would explain the phenomenon of segmented or dual partisanship, but segmented partisanship is difficult to correlate with the data indicating that party organizations are also becoming more integrated—unless national-state-local integration is devoid of substantive policy content. But we know that this is certainly not true for the Republicans and their widely praised service-provision activities for candidates at all levels. These arguments reverse the causation in Schlesinger's (1991) much-cited formulation that decreases in voter loyalty led to increased party organizational efforts (it is not clear in Schlesinger what led to the decreased loyalties). In short, no compelling case has been made within the organizational framework to explain increasingly variable voting patterns across offices and years.

Thus, widespread lack of trust in parties and the increasing tendency for voters to view parties as unnecessary and perhaps unhelpful appendages to the political system pose a large puzzle for the new orthodoxy (Wattenberg 1990). Now, this is not to argue that antipartisan attitudes are unique to the present period because they have to one extent or another been a common part of American political culture (Epstein 1986). But the level of disgust and bitterness with "politics as usual" is exceptionally high—and political parties are surely part of "politics as usual." Though today many political scientists do indeed scoff at the public's discontent, suggesting that the public is either spoiled, ignorant, manipulated by demagogues, or all three,[4] the negative public mood is reflected in turnout, voting behavior, and attitudes toward parties. Though party organizations have increased their activity levels, voters are unimpressed. Ross Perot may not be easy to explain in any context, but within the celebration of party resurgence and revitalization in the party organization literature he becomes an enormous enigma. If the dominance of offices and votes by the two major parties is a measure of party strength, then it is hard to understand why one-fifth of the electorate abandoned the parties' presidential candidates *after* a sustained period of party "resurgence."[5]

One might argue that this discontent is a result of particularly effective campaign tactics spearheaded by party strategists. From this reading, discontent is actually a result of party organizational strength. Certainly many postmortem analyses of the 1988 Bush campaign reached such a conclusion. But for the party organizations, such a resolution is hardly satisfactory because it suggests one of two things: 1. party organizations help candidates whip up discontent about real issues to win office, but along with party-in-government they are unable to do anything to restore public confidence once in office—i.e., the problems are real but the parties are unable to effect any change; or 2. party organizations help whip up discontent about nonexistent or irrelevant problems. The first alternative suggests a collapse of accountability in the political system, at least accountability oriented around political parties; the second suggests that party organizations willingly debase public discourse to win office, which raises disturbing normative issues (see below).

The striking contrast between the literature on party organizations and observations on partisanship in the electorate results from the dominance of supply-side analysis in this literature, namely, examining what parties are doing (or say they are doing). From such analysis it is easy to conclude that parties are resurgent—parties must be stronger if they are doing more rather than less.[6] But what this literature has ignored is the demand-side represented by the electorate. While studies of late nineteenth and early twentieth century party organizations place a great deal of emphasis on the interaction between party officials and the citizenry (McGeer 1986; Bridges 1986; Shefter 1976, 1986; cf. Brown and Halaby 1987), studies of recent party organization stress what the party is supplying and de-emphasize how the public is responding. The emerging "truncated" or service-provider model of the party teaches us about changes in modern campaigning, but not about the broader place of party in American politics. How much must public discontent with the parties grow before organizational studies recognize the implications of those negative signs for party "revitalization" or "resurgence"? Is it more important that targeted party activity might raise turnout two or three percentage points in a given election *or* that turnout has dropped steadily over time and is lower now than when the party organizations were "weak"? Only an unduly narrow view of party organization can suggest our primary interest is whether candidates think party assistance is helpful.

A handful of studies do look closely at the link between party organization (or party competition, which is not necessarily the same thing) and public response. These studies stress primarily the parties' direct and indirect influence on turnout; they usually find that party activities indeed have some impact.[7] But if public response to turnout efforts is a valid part of party organization scholarship, why not public views or behavior toward party? One argument might be party organizations see voter turnout as one of their functions, but public attitudes toward parties are not in their purview. This argument misses the point. Intended or not, party behavior through governing is a public act and may produce public discontent. Parties ignoring this discontent because "it's not our problem" have a history of being deformed through reforms. Public opinion matters.

What about linkage at the other end? Although my focus is on the linkage between party organizations and voters, studies of the connection between party organizations and party-in-government have been similarly limited. Two strong supporters of contemporary party organizations acknowledge that "much less is known about how party organizations affect public policy" (Gibson and Scarrow 1993:245) than about how they affect elections. They note that while there is some possibility that these organizations can affect policy direction, on the whole it is "highly doubtful that [they] have much of an ideological effect" (1993:245) once public officials take office. But, they point out, there is some possibility for affecting party policy at the margin through the recruitment and nomination process (Gibson, Frendreis, and Vertz 1989). One small group of recent studies does attempt to discern whether party organization activity has any influence on elected officials' policy decisions; the influence is at best slight (Cotter et. al 1984; Leyden and Borrelli 1990; Dwyre 1992, 1993). As Lawson, Pomper, and Moakley (1986:368, 369) point out, our knowledge about the parties' performance as linkages between citizens and the state "remain[s] fragmentary and inconclusive."

Methodological obstacles have surely been one hindrance to examining the linkage between party organizations and party-in-government. Cotter, Gibson, Bibby, and Huckshorn's warning in their discussion of party organization relationships with elected officeholders that "these interpretations must be treated as only suggestive because of the small number of cases, the lack of control variables, and uncertainty about the appropriateness of generalizing from the high and low strength ranges that are actually party-specific" (1984:118) gives a good sense of the difficulties. Similar complexities face the analyst examining whether party organizations influence election results.

Linkage at both ends—citizen to party organization and organization to elected officeholder—is strained. But because I believe the problems with voters deserve special attention, I have placed extra emphasis on the former. If parties' "raison d'être is to create a substantive connection between rulers and ruled" (Lawson 1980:3),[8] then we have a problem if voters pay little attention to party efforts or their antipathy to party grows. It is misleading to cast stepped-up party activity as yet another indication of party "resurgence."

Before drawing such conclusions, we need to look beyond party intentions to their results, and these results must encompass the behavior and perceptions of the public as well as candidates.

Accentuate the Positive, Ignore the Normative

Part of the reason that party organization scholars have been eager to move the discipline away from the notion of party decline is that these scholars tend to believe deeply in the positive contributions parties make to the American political system. Even though many and probably most disagree passionately with E. E. Schattschneider's vision of the ideal political party for the United States, they typically endorse Schattschneider's frequently-noted contention that "modern democracy is unthinkable save in terms of the parties" (1942:1). When party organization students contend that "parties matter," they are making both an empirical and normative statement.[9]

Despite this normative endorsement of parties, the organization literature has been surprisingly quiet about key features of American politics during the era of resurgent party organizations. Beyond the problem of the electorate's response to party organizational changes are questions concerning practices in American politics that are directly related to the parties' service-provider activities. The results of these activities have not always been pretty. Yet the party organization literature has said little about their normative implications.

Our interest in the health of political parties should not be divorced from our interest in the health of politics or the political system. For example, the new orthodoxy is generally very positive about the efforts of the parties to raise and distribute more campaign funds and their efforts to coexist peacefully with interest groups and political action committees. Yet other studies raise troubling questions about the parties' increasing reliance on raising huge sums of money from special interests (Edsall 1984; Ferguson and Rogers 1986). The implicit stance of organization theorists is that the parties' *ability* to raise this money is more significant than the *effects* of this reliance on massive fundraising. Are party organizations part of the problem with money in politics or part of the solution? Are they making a bad situation—the intersection of money and politics—worse? Indeed, the intersection of money and politics is a significant aspect of the public discontent mentioned above. It is one thing to note that a party committee is holding a "breakfast" for important contributors; it is quite another to ignore that these activities may resonate very poorly within the public at large and may, in the long run, be harmful for the credibility and legitimacy of political parties. The party organizations' tremendous "success" at funneling "soft money" into campaigns raises similar problems. While some studies make the plausible argument that parties make the situation less distasteful than it might be by serving as an intermediary of funds for candidates—and as the largest single provider for most candidates (Herrnson 1988, 1990)—these important normative questions are discussed infrequently.

Another normative issue concerns voter turnout. As I mentioned above, several studies indicate that party mobilization efforts can have a positive impact on voter turnout. But studies of organization tend to ignore the flip side—parties can and do effectively demobilize as well (Shefter 1984; Piven and Cloward 1989). This is certainly not news, as the trajectory of Southern politics after the turn of the century makes clear. Rosenstone and Hansen (1993:162–77, 215) attribute the bulk of the decline in turnout since the early 1960s to decreasing efforts to mobilize voters by various organizations, including most prominently the political parties. One explanation is that the parties have chosen to de-emphasize labor-intensive mobilization in the new capital-and-technology-intensive electoral system (Frantzich 1989). While officials and workers in party organizations may not have the luxury to contemplate the participatory implications of this kind of shift, it is incumbent upon party organization scholars to do so. Organizational adaptation that is rational in the short term may not prove to be so in the long term.

The point here is simple: we either believe that declining turnout is bad for the political system or we do not. If we do, we need to be clear about the parties' contribution to something we consider corrosive to democracy. Without denying the need for technological adaptation and sophistication, we can question whether the extent of the move *away* from labor-intensive mobilization is as inevitable as it is normally portrayed. It may be the case that county chairs see their efforts as most significant in "grass-roots activity emphasizing ties to local people" such as organizing campaign events and get-out-the-vote drives (Frendreis, Gitelson, Flemming, and Layzell 1993:10), but the dismal state of turnout (especially in local races) has to lead one to question how effective or extensive these activities are. What do we want from parties? A party organization and party system that I would label resurgent or revitalized would not be one that witnesses sustained declining participation or one with participation levels as low as at present.

A third normative issue concerns the quality of modern campaigns. As party organizations claim increasing involvement in recruiting candidates, assisting the strategy and conduct of campaigns, and acting as intermediaries between the candidates and the private market of campaign services (Maisel, Fowler, Jones, and Stone 1990; Kazee and Thornberry 1990; Frendreis, Gibson, and Vertz 1990), they should be judged on the quality of these campaigns. I do not want to overstate this point. The organization literature is, it seems to me, very careful to avoid projecting party organizations as the lead institutions in contemporary campaigns but rather as the supporting cast for candidate organizations (which some students might, of course, reasonably note as a sign of party decline). Again, while party organizations do not have the luxury of stepping back to analyze the quality of campaigns, political scientists, even those enthused about the changes in party organizations, should. There are plausible arguments on each side of this issue—some argue that modern campaigns are informative (Popkin 1991) while others assert that campaigns have become shrill, uninformative, divisive, and unrelated to the real tasks of governance that follow the election (Blumenthal 1990; Dionne 1991; Bennett 1992). Are the resurgent party organizations helping corrode the discourse of American campaigns? If campaigning is increasingly divorced from governing, we should question the contributions of institutions intimately involved in campaigns and campaign strategy.

The point of these examples is that such normative issues should not be ignored by the proponents of party organizational resurgence. The literature lacks a critical appraisal of the content of the activities the parties perform. By way of contrast, analyses of interest groups often manage to merge support of interest group involvement in the political process with critical assessments of the impact of interest groups on the political system. This omission is important, for as Lawson, Pomper, and Moakley (1986:369) note, "the parties, including their hard-working activists, may be willing to endure public contempt so long as they win elections, but how long will the public tolerate such parties?"

Successful at What?

One message found throughout the party organization literature is that party organizations play an important role in American politics. Surprisingly, however, the exact nature of the success achieved by these organizations is often left vague. And measures of success that appear obvious are overlooked. This problem is related to the more general tendency to focus on activities and pay less attention to effects.

Most studies on party organization are particularly impressed with the efforts of the Republican Party to restructure its organizational apparatus, upgrade its service capacities, and improve the product it offers candidates and potential candidates. What is surprising, however, is the lack of hard data in the literature showing that the Republican efforts have made much difference in the electoral landscape. Republican organizational efforts have probably boosted the party's fortunes in the South, though certainly the internal collapse of the Democrats was also a factor. But more generally one can ask: where is the evidence that Republicans have received much of a return on the massive amounts of money they have spent on campaigning over the past decade or so? Perhaps the Republican capture of the Senate in 1980 was due in large part to Republican organizational efforts, with the cooperation of sympathetic groups like the National Conservative Political Action Committee. Some scholars argue plausibly that Republican losses might have been much more severe in the deep recession of 1982 (e.g., Jacobson 1985-86) if not for the efforts of the Republican campaign committees but the data is not hard.[10] Other possibilities—general approval of the Reagan governmental-reduction agenda, skepticism about Democratic competence given recent experience, lack of a Democratic program, a change in political culture that increased the level of unemployment necessary to create political outrage—are also plausible. For all the apparent Republican advantages in party organization, both at the national and state level, one might have expected some larger payoff.

Beyond the question of recent Republican "success," evidence is mixed regarding the effect of party organizations on election outcomes. Gibson and Scarrow (1993:242-43) note that evidence suggests party organizations made a difference in election outcomes in specific cases. Cotter et al. (1984), on the other hand, found that over time a party's relative electoral success (measured by the Ranney index) bore little relationship to the strength of its state party organizations. A mild to moderate relationship was, however, uncovered for nonsouth gubernatorial elections. Both studies properly note the methodological difficulties inherent in teasing out the effect of party organizations on election results.

Success is also related to what writers believe the important role of the parties to be. As mentioned above, the service-provider and party-as-broker views have clearly gained ground in recent years, but it is not generally acknowledged that we should consider the set of tasks confronting parties—or that they choose to confront—when we estimate whether party organizations are resurgent and revitalized. In other words, what are we expecting parties to do? The more limited our expectations, the more likely we see success and resurgence. Ware perhaps puts this point most clearly when he observes that

> A strong party organization is one which at the very least, can determine who will be the party's candidates, can decide (broadly) the issues on which electoral campaigns will be fought by its candidates, contributes the 'lion's share' of resources to the candidates' elections campaigns, and has influence over appointments made by elected public officials (1988:x).

For scholars the question must be whether the "successes" garnered by the truncated party are as significant as the "successes" of past parties as depicted by Ware.

An increasing party role in campaign finance is seen by many as a key success of modern party organizations. But while it is true that the parties raise more money than previously and that they use that money more carefully, it is also the case that legislative campaign committees have become dominant in the funding of legislative races. Rather than increasing the influence of party or working to pull parts of the party together, Sorauf and Wilson (1990) argue that the dominance of the legislative campaign committees reflects an effort by legislators to remain autonomous from the wider party (see chapter 14). Therefore the increasing role for the parties in this aspect of campaign finance may increase the likelihood of party members winning but it does not, as Sorauf and Wilson suggest, increase the integration of the party.

Another irony regarding success is that as party organizations became more efficient in campaign finance and campaign assistance, fewer members of the parties in Congress needed the services as incumbency reelection rates and margins increased. When one half of the challenger party's adherents abandon party identification to support their incumbent member of Congress (Abramson, Aldrich, and Rohde 1994), the incumbent's party organization is being asked to play a truly relevant role in fewer contests. This is useful, because it allows parties to concentrate their resources, but it does suggest how much of the electoral universe is largely beyond the influence of party organizations.

As noted above, organization scholars are careful to avoid attributing too much influence or strength to party organizations. In campaigns, for example, the party is clearly seen as a supporting institution to the candidate. Yet the line between success and failure is perilously close. To take the most recent data as an example, Frendreis et al. (chapter 8) report that state legislative candidates rate county party organizations as slightly effective only in recruiting campaign volunteers and getting-out-the-vote. On organizing campaign events, fundraising, and campaign management and development of strategy, the county parties rate somewhere between "not important" to "slightly important." Even discounting for candidate hubris, this is of rather minimal importance. It is difficult to imagine that someone attracted to the party decline idea would find this evidence particularly challenging. The literature needs to provide a better sense of why *this level* of influence matters. Party organization students clearly want to believe that parties are an important and necessary part of modern campaigns and elections, even if idealistic, responsible parties are implausible: "While adaptive brokerage parties may be less than perfect vehicles for the organization of political debate and the development of public policy, the alternative—electorally irrelevant parties—are wholly inadequate to the requirements of American politics" (Frendreis et al. 1993:14). But scholars need to spell out *why* these parties would be wholly inadequate. Indeed, Bledsoe and Welch suggest that this electoral role may be the *least* significant one parties perform and not one they need perform alone: "Though these other agents [interest groups, political action committees, consultants, etc.] can replace the party organization as an election vehicle, they contribute nothing to the process of governing: the coalition building, political accountability, and policy coherence that may be offered by a healthy party system" (1987:265).

Fighting the Last Battle

One reason for the shortcomings in the party organization literature, I believe, is an ongoing interest in challenging the thesis of party decline. The argument between these schools is remarkably reminiscent of the responsible parties vs. functional (or indigenous) parties dispute that swept the field forty years ago. But like that dispute, today's debate has become unproductive.

First, there has been a tendency in the organization literature to overstate the central thrust of the decline argument. While some decline analysts projected an extremely dim view of party prospects, most writers on decline were making the simple point that the contemporary parties were in several respects less central to the political process than they were previously. It is correct to note that they usually overlooked party organizations. But it seems to me unhelpful to caricature the party decline approach with terms like "demise," "prophets," "strident," "impressionistic," "exaggerate," "swamped," or "decimated," or to suggest that party decline theorists yearned only for the "golden age" of party modeled on a "few" urban political machines or "disciplined, socialist" parties as found in Europe (all in Patterson 1989).[11]

For many decline writers it was difficult to imagine the trends changing dramatically. As we know, however, the trends did partially change: parties in the Congress and party organizations both showed new signs of life in the 1980s. But when most of the decline arguments were being written, it was indeed difficult to see signs of renewal. This was especially true because of the lack of any overarching theory of party that integrated the developments at each geographic level of party and for each of the three major party components. Yet rather than exaggerate or falsely assume party decline, the decline theorists did not typically make arguments that were incompatible with "the facts" as presented in the party organization literature. Herrnson (1988), for example, accepts that the party organizations from World War II to the mid-1970s were clearly inferior to and of lesser significance than the party organizations before the war. For a decline writer to *assume* weak party organizations was not advisable, but apparently not incorrect. Herrnson argues that the party organizations adapted and took on new roles after the mid-1970s and that the party organizations now fit their environment well (Herrnson 1988:30). But he does acknowledge that they may not be needed to the same degree they were in the environment of the late nineteenth century—i.e., the "constituent" nature of and demands on parties had shrunk (Lowi 1975 and also chapter 4).

With its interest in demonstrating that at least part of the party system was not declining, a second problem is that the party organization literature has placed too little emphasis on integrating party theory. As I stated above, this relative neglect has meant turning a blind eye to the response of the public to the improvements in party organizational strength. Cotter et al.

(1984:167), for example, who *are* interested in integrating party organizations into the bigger party picture, devote but one paragraph to the relations between party organizations and the public, and that one paragraph seems to dismiss the reality or significance of negative public perceptions.[12] I would suggest that the failure to deal with normative questions also stems from this desire to demonstrate that not all of the party system has declined. While this approach was perhaps warranted at the outset, it has now become counterproductive.

Third, there is a real risk of walking into the same analytical trap that ensnared writers on party decline: if you build your theory on only one part of the data trend you find it very difficult to explain how that trend might stop. The variables examined by party decline analyses pointed in the direction of future decline; by limiting the dependent variable to periods of decline, declinists overlooked independent variables that might alter the trend. Today, the party organization literature faces the same problem. To build more theory into these studies, revivalists need to consider seriously what could disrupt the projected trajectory of ever more involved, ever more relevant party organizations.

Finally, this concern with fighting the last battle leads to the use of a "counteracting" party model (see Cotter and Bibby 1980:26–27, for an early example; see Frendreis, Gibson, and Vertz 1990 for a recent treatment). This model suggests that even if there is some sign of decline elsewhere in the party system, say among voters, the revival in party organization "counteracts" that decline. Unfortunately, it is not clear what is entailed in counteracting other parts of the political system. What would be different if this counteraction did not occur? How do we know? How does this "counteraction" affect what happens in those areas that might indeed be in decline; i.e., what does this mean for the "counteracted"? How are party organizations different because they play a counteracting rather than parallel role with other party elements? A stronger version of the counteracting model argues that party organizational resurgence *depended* on party decline among voters (Schlesinger 1991). But while this idea may be consistent with recent American politics, a look back to the late nineteenth century suggests that this is not a general principle of party development. A more modest version asserts that strong party organizations have counteracted party decline elsewhere in the system, "thus making the party system more resilient to antiparty and dealigning influences" (Bibby et al. 1983:26). But how do we know if these organizations have indeed made the system more resilient—what is the null expectation? Looking at the recent developments in public opinion and behavior makes one wonder just how effective these counteractive party organizations have been in resisting these influences.

Searching for Integration: "The State of the Parties"

I have suggested in this chapter some reasons to question the new orthodoxy that party organizations are "resurgent" or "revitalized." In conclusion I want to focus less on the organizations per se and more on the political science analysis of these organizations.

Party scholars need to take seriously the goal of integrating party theory and probing the relationships between different parts of the party system. Herrnson reports that

> Some analysts have questioned the propriety of using evidence about the party-in-the-electorate and the party-in-government to support the hypothesis that political parties in general, and especially party organizations, are in decline. Blurring the distinctions between the three dimensions of the political party may lead to a misunderstanding of the nature of party development and result in faulty conclusions about the condition of party organizations (1988:5).

I am not arguing that the distinctions be blurred, only that we understand better how these aspects of party fit together. Indeed, many party organization studies touch on these connections. I am not arguing that we aim for faulty conclusions, only that we recognize that because the party system fits together it is misleading to ignore the other components when studying any one of the three. If there is finally something called "party" that exists beyond these individual components, it is at least partially defined as the centrality of party organizations, party-in-government, and party-in-the-electorate to the way in which the business of democracy gets done: selecting candidates and running campaigns, deciding how to vote, designing and implementing public policy, and so on. If voters were exceptionally loyal to parties and thought they mattered greatly, but parties in Congress were hardly cohesive and party organizations did next to nothing, I would be uncomfortable talking about parties being healthy. Similarly, it is unwise to overlook party-in-government but especially public opinion and political behavior when assessing the health of the party system even if it has active organizations. When party organizations begin to pull the electorate along as they perform their activities, my enthusiasm about the revitalization of American party organizations and the party system will increase.

Though there are good reasons to begin integrating party theory, less clear is how one goes about this (Epstein 1986; Schlesinger 1991). Elsewhere I make the argument that party decline—*and* party improvement—can be understood only if parties are analyzed within their structural and policy settings (Coleman 1993, 1994). For the postwar period, this means tying party decline to the construction of a "fiscal state" in the 1930s and 1940s that oriented party competition around macroeconomic management issues on which the parties in Congress tended to converge at crucial moments (e.g., recessions). At the same time, this state structurally limited party responsibility for the economy. Voters, sensibly, paid decreasing attention to parties, and either exited the electorate or focused on individual candidates. When this macroeconomic system began to crumble in the stagflation of the 1970s, the collapse of the Keynesian consensus created an opening for improvement in the status of political parties.[13] Increased party cohesiveness in Congress and new attempts to enhance the capacities of party organizations reflected this improvement. But enough of the fiscal state remained intact that these changes did not filter down to the electorate. Because elites and voters can restructure the state, especially at crisis points, the decline of party need not be inevitable or irreversible. From this approach, "the state of the parties" is a phrase rich in meaning.

There are three important points here. First, this kind of approach suggests that party organizational resurgence occurred when it did for some concrete reasons. Herrnson and Menefee-Libey's (1990) outline of the development of party organization since 1968 is a necessary but not sufficient explanation of what happened because it overlooks the success of the parties' fundraising efforts from the donors' perspective. To understand the changes in party organization over the past twenty-five years, we need to know why donors were particularly willing to give in the late 1970s. With the collapse of the postwar macroeconomic governing consensus and dramatic changes emerging in the global economy, it is not surprising that concerned elites and members of the middle class would find Republican appeals to be particularly attractive. That is, Republican organizational improvement depended crucially on the availability of a large body of willing givers, and a model of party development needs to explain why those givers were available at that particular time. Organizational and technological changes may have helped locate these donors, but it was less responsible for creating the incentives to contribute than were the events in the political economy. In this vein, one might say that the difference between Barry Goldwater in 1964 and Ronald Reagan in 1980 was not that the Republican Party organization had become so much more proficient, but that Goldwater was running in 1964 and Reagan in 1980—years that were worlds apart politically and economically.

Second, while political scientists have learned a significant amount by analyzing the components of political parties in isolation from each other, in a period of transition such as the present this tripartite model of parties obscures our understanding (Baer and Bositis 1988:chs. 1-2; ch. 6). We cannot understand what has happened with party organizations or, more importantly, the significance of any changes that have occurred, unless we demonstrate concretely how party activity affects citizens, public officials, and elections.

The final point is that in a democratic polity the status of political parties ultimately boils down to the public. Despite the enthusiasm in the party organization literature, *party* decline does not end until the voters return to party. The public's beliefs and behavior regarding the salience and relevance of party has to be the ultimate standard of party decline or resurgence. Not just changes in party activities, but also changes in the state—the structural settings of parties—are required before the voters return. Voters (and nonvoters) must believe parties control policy areas, that these policy areas are important, and that the parties differ in significant ways before we can expect any resurgence at the voter level. Short of this change, the plausibility of parties as grassroots, representative institutions comes under serious strain. The meaningfulness of party organizational "resurgence" in such a system is dubious.

Notes

1. The literature is enormous. A representative sample includes Burnham 1982; Clubb and Traugott 1977; Cooper and Hurley 1977; Brady, Cooper, and Hurley 1979; Collie and Brady 1985; Brady 1990; Nie, Verba, and Petrocik 1979; Lipset and Schneider 1987; Crotty 1984; Fiorina 1980, 1987, 1990; Kirkpatrick 1979; Ranney 1975; Polsby 1983; Shefter 1978; Silbey 1990.

2. Cotter and Bibby 1980; Bibby, Gibson, Cotter, and Huckshorn 1983; Gibson, Cotter, Bibby, and Huckshorn 1983; Cotter, Gibson, Bibby, and Huckshorn 1984; Gibson, Cotter, Bibby, and Huckshorn 1985; Reichley 1985; Huckshorn, Gibson, Cotter, and Bibby 1986; Kayden and Mahe 1985; Sabato 1988; Gibson, Frendreis, and Vertz 1989; Bibby 1990; Frendreis, Gibson, and Vertz 1990; Frantzich 1989; Crotty 1991b; Longley 1992; Jackson 1992; and Frendreis, Gitelson, Flemming, and Layzell 1993.

3. Herrnson 1986, 1988, 1990; Jacobson 1985-86; Wilcox 1989; Sorauf and Wilson 1990; and Dwyre 1992.

4. "When levels of trust in government plummet, our finest students of public opinion say, 'it does not matter.' When divided government becomes the norm on every level of government and threatens civic accountability, our wisest scholars show us why it does not matter. When discontent with politics causes party identification to crumble, participation to fall, and younger Americans to disengage from public affairs, political scientists just repeat, 'it does not matter.' And when a remarkable mobilization of middle America is aborted by Ross Perot's personal idiosyncrasies, we sigh with relief. It didn't really matter after all . . . [The] discussion can be summarized in three aphorisms: There is nothing wrong. If there is, we don't know how to fix it. If we do, it's politically impractical, anyway" (Putnam 1993).

5. Two-party dominance is not in fact a compelling measure of party strength. One can have three parties competing because people have indeed *greater* faith in the potentialities of political parties; i.e., it's worth the effort to create and support a third party. Such an interpretation of the People's Party, for example, would not do great violence to history (Goodwyn 1978). But this observation does not get us far with Perot because his was so strongly an antiparty appeal.

6. Interestingly, McGlennon (1993) finds that there is no clear relationship between the extent of activities performed by a state political party in the South and the perception of the party's organizational strength held by grassroots party activists. Note also that for reasons of space I focus here on activities as a measure of strength rather than devote attention to changing organizational complexity, i.e., bureaucratization. Cotter, Gibson, Bibby, and Huckshorn (1984: 44-45) point out that one should not dismiss party significance simply because of the lack of organizational complexity.

7. Caldeira, Patterson, and Markko 1985; Lawson, Pomper, and Moakley 1986; Bledsoe and Welch 1987; Caldeira, Clausen, and Patterson 1990; Frendreis, Gibson, and Vertz 1990;

The Resurgence of Party Organization?

Rosenstone and Hansen 1993; and Huckfeldt and Sprague 1992. In some cases, however, party activities and campaign activities are lumped together. See, for example, Caldeira, Clausen, and Patterson (1990). This study also provides a unique measure of turnout as the number of offices for which a voter recalls voting. While the recall of this information might be questioned, this is a novel attempt to view voting as a continuum rather than a dichotomous variable and deserves testing elsewhere.

8. Lawson's (1980) elegant essay acknowledges the difficulties inherent in such a seemingly simple statement.

9. To avert misunderstanding, I will simply state here that I also believe that parties can and have made important contributions to American democracy and that they are crucial agents of representation. For an elegant discussion of the strengths and weaknesses of party organizations in pursuit of these functions, see Pomper (1992:20-34).

10. On the other side, one might suggest that the improvement in Democratic fortunes in the late 1980s and 1992 were a result of organizational efforts, but one would need to contend with the argument that a fundamental fissure in the Democratic Party organization exploited by the Democratic Leadership Council was as responsible for this renewed party success (see Rae 1991 and Hale (chapter 16) for overviews of the development of the DLC).

11. The notion of a "few" political machines is particularly misleading. Brown and Halaby (1987) show that from 1870 to 1945 at least 50 percent of all middle and major sized U.S. cities featured machine politics, from the mid-1870s to the mid-1930s the figures were above 60 percent, and in the early 1890s the figures were at least 80 percent of all cities.

12. Baer and Bositis's (1988) excellent study of how social movements revitalized party organizations runs into similar difficulties, especially when attempting to explain low voter turnout (118-19). This is an important problem for their approach because it is never very clear why, if social movements infused the political parties with new life and new representativeness, the impact in the public was rather muted. If social movements were sweeping through party organizations, as the authors argue, then where were the followers of these movements? Why did movement elites fail to bring their adherents into the party system? Why is voting turnout stagnant or declining during most of the period they study?

13. Though with a different interpretation than that suggested here, Cotter and Bibby (1980) also link changing national party organization to the evolution of the New Deal political settlement.

21

Confusions in the Analysis of American Political Parties

Tim Hames

Many, if not most, discussions on the state of modern American political parties open with what would appear to be relatively straightforward and simple questions: "Is the party system reviving?" and "Are party organizations getting stronger?" Yet despite the seemingly simple nature of these questions, it is one of the few topics that one can predict will generate controversy. Many scholars believe the party system is still declining, while others point to organizational innovations as evidence of revival. I will address two issues concerning the assessment of changes in American party strength. First, why is it that political scientists, operating on the basis of very substantial research, cannot reach agreement on this issue? Second, is the conventional "tripod" model of American political parties still a valuable way of looking at parties?

On the first count, I will advance three conceptual reasons why political scientists do not agree on party strength. To begin with, there is confusion over the functions political parties are supposed to perform, and thus the frame of reference for improvement or decline. Next, it is unclear against which yardstick changes in party strength are to be assessed. And finally, there is disagreement over which aspects of party are most important and, hence, whether changes in them matter. I will attempt to convince the reader that many of the differences among political scientists on the state of the parties derive, explicitly or implicitly, from these conceptual disagreements.

On the second count, I will focus on the last part of the previous point, namely how parties are defined, particularly the tripod model of American political parties. Deriving principally from V. O. Key (1947), this model identifies a three-fold division of parties: party-in-the-electorate, party-as-organization, and party-in-government. I will attempt to persuade the reader that this model fails to address some critical matters. For instance, are the three components equally important or does one matter more than the others? How does change in one aspect of party affect the others? What exactly is the relationship between these components and the political party as an institution overall?

Taken together, these points produce criteria to assess whether significant revival of "party-as-institution" can be achieved through organizational innovation. Is there revival across all components of party, and if not, why does the nonrevival or even decline of certain components not matter? Has the alleged revival of party organization had a beneficial transmission effect on the party-in-the-electorate? And has the alleged revival of party organization had a beneficial transmission effect on the actions of the party-in-government?

I will argue that party organizational revival which does not produce a sizable transmission effect on party-in-the-electorate and party-in-government is not worth a great deal; is an interesting phenomenon, no doubt, but hardly institutional revitalization. In fact, the evidence we have is that the organization-based renewal has stern limits with regard to party-as-institution in the wider sense of the term.

The Parties: Declining, Reviving, or What?

An enormous research effort covering virtually every aspect of American political parties has not, it seems, helped political science achieve a consensus on the seemingly straightforward question of the direction American political parties are travelling in. Confusion and disagreement have marked a roller-coaster debate over the last half century. Joseph Schlesinger sums this up by asking:

> What then do we make of parties that win all the elections yet do not control their nominations, parties that take distinct policy positions yet whose leaders have little influence over their members, parties whose organizations have decomposed or atrophied yet whose personnel and payroll have blossomed, parties whose support by the electorate has declined yet which win more and more of the elections? (1984:371).

What makes the discussion over party status especially complex is that scholarly argument rarely consists of individual pieces of evidence being scrutinised and debated. Instead, different forms of evidence (about say ticket-splitting or the activities of the Republican National Committee) are offered. All of this goes to support Jack Dennis' observation: "Despite there being a quite voluminous literature on partisanship as of the 1980s, one looks in vain for any comprehensive statement on the theoretical meaning or purpose of the construct" (1988:78). In other words, because there is no agreement on what constitutes party strength, it is not possible to say whether they are ascending or descending.

There appear to be three major areas of academic dispute that underpin the division between party "declinists" and "revivalists": what are the functions of American political parties as institutions; what yardstick is used to measure the strength of American political parties; and what aspects of the American political party are being described. Revivalists may well benefit from answers to the first two questions, but do much more poorly with answers to the third.

1. What are the functions of political parties? Perhaps the central issue to address in this regard is whether political scientists can produce a set of functions expected of all party systems in all industrialized democracies. If such a checklist could be created, then it would presumably be possible to determine how well a particular party system performs and whether it is getting better or worse.

In fact, this is precisely the approach of many contributors in the field of comparative party systems, such as Duverger (1954). Some Americans, including Neumann (1956) and Schattschneider (1942, 1960), have followed this lead and advocated a version of "responsible" parties. A good contemporary example is Mileur (1989), who, in offering a model party statute on behalf of the Committee on Party Renewal, laid down ten principles of strong party organization in hope of encouraging the developments along this line. These scholars tend to find that American parties perform poorly, and are getting worse. But other scholars, such as Epstein (1986), have advanced an opposite view, claiming that the special circumstances of the United States have produced a unique set of party institutions. Drawing on this insight, Schlesinger confidently charges that "there is one standard, a party's ability to win office" (1984:1153), thus endorsing a version of the "rational-efficient" party model (Downs 1957).[1] Declinists have tended to favor the former view, while revivalists like the latter.

Given the enormously different aspirations that commentators have for American political parties, it is hardly surprising that they come to vastly different conclusions about the state of American political parties at any point in time. Even assuming that a common goal could be found, the next task—that of measuring decline or revival in the performance of these functions—will prove equally taxing.

2. What is meant by decline or revival? If something has allegedly changed, no matter in what direction, it must have changed relative to some sort of yardstick. Nevertheless, it is not always obvious what American political parties are being compared to when participants in the party debate claim that parties have declined or revived.

For example, one could measure American parties in comparison to the actual functioning of party systems in other countries. And indeed, the vast majority of research on American political parties proceeds on the implicit assumption that American parties can be found lacking by comparison to European systems (see Epstein 1980). This point of view is a particular favorite of declinists. However, comparisons to other countries are quite facile in this regard. International comparison has value only when one compares like with like, and very few countries have similar constitutions, political arrangements, and demography to make a useful standard for the United States. Observers of U.S. political parties have to look to their own history and circumstances to evaluate the performance their parties. Revivalists draw on these arguments to a considerable degree.

This leads to another approach, loaded with common sense, which is to make a historical comparison. This is not as easy as it sounds because that first requires agreement on the past strength of the American party system, and even then a suitable time frame must be chosen. Should we be comparing the parties of the 1990s with the 1870s or 1970s? Most academics accept that parties were strong in the period between the Civil War and the Progressive Era (Silby 1991). That assertion is made because the loyalty of voters and officeholders to the party appears to have been strong and the level of party activity high. Declinists most often compare contemporary parties to their late-nineteenth-century ancestors. On the other hand, the post- Second World War era appears to have been marked by the decline of machines, patronage, voter partisanship, and officeholder regularity (Ware 1985). Revivalists most often compare today's parties to their immediate predecessors (see for example, Sabato 1988:ch. 1). These differences are compounded by further uncertainty over what part of the parties one is supposed to pass judgement on.

3. Which aspect of the political party? For most of the last four decades American political parties have been analyzed according to the formula devised by V. O. Key. He argued that:

> There are other senses in which the term "party" is used. Often it refers to an entity which rolls into one the party-in-the-electorate, the professional political group, the party-in-the-legislature, and the party-in-the-government . . . In truth, this all-encompassing usage has its legitimate application, for all types of group called "party" interact more or less closely and at times maybe as one (1947:156)[2]

At some point the party-in-the-legislature and the party-in-the-government merged so that the standard division bequeathed by Key to American political science included three subsections: the electorate, government, and organization.

As a number of observers have pointed out, the core of the dispute between those favoring party decline or revival has come through employing different parts of Key's tripod. The party decline school initially came to dominance based on evidence about the decomposition of party-in-the-electorate. The party revival school has been based on evidence about party-as-organization. Even those strongly committed to one school or the other have been known to concede that their opponent's views on their particular leg of Key's tripod may be valid. The reaction of most outside observers has been to recognize two different trends and either declare the contest a draw or award victory on points to whichever side they believe has displayed the greater degree of change. Very few have categorically rejected the view that the party-in-the-electorate has declined or that party-as-organization has revived. Even fewer have asked whether Key's model is sufficient to base such judgements on.

Unanswered Questions in the Analysis of Parties

The gridlock that exists in the debate over the plight of the American political party is thus strongly related to the Key tripod. Conventional wisdom seems to accept that there are different trends evident in the electorate and organization, while no clear view has been established on the party-in-government.

In my opinion, use of the conventional tripod model produces a more complex analysis still. For there appear to be opposite trends within the electorate, government, and organization as well as across them. Although there has been a general decomposition in the party-in-the-electorate, as witnessed by the rising numbers of independents, greater ticket-splitting, and lower voter participation (Wattenberg 1990), this has coincided with a process whereby the most politically interested members of the electorate have been sorting themselves out along a liberal-conservative spectrum. In other words, at exactly the same time that the great mass of voters have disengaged from the parties, Democrats and Republicans have displayed greater philosophical consistency.

Similarly, although national and state party organizations have clearly shown a resurgence over the past two decades (Cotter et al. 1984), there is very little evidence that this change has translated into stronger vitality in party-in-the-electorate. Likewise, within the party-in-government there is also the paradox that most research indicates that individual members of Congress are more independent from their party, yet at the same time the proportion of all roll-call votes that can be described as party-based has increased (Davidson 1992).

The Key tripod, if employed in its usual form, is thus likely to leave political observers in deeper confusion about what the present tendencies really are. There are three very important questions that the conventional formulation does not explore which seem quite fundamental to the question of party strength. Do all elements of the tripod have equal value? What is the relationship between changes in one component to the others? And is party-as-institution more than the combined effect of the three components?

1. Do all the elements of party have equal value? Key provided no ranking to his three components of party. Should we therefore assume that the three are equal? Are we to assume that the three components of party are all influenced by similar external phenomena, or can they exist quite independently of each other? If external factors have an impact on any one component of party, should it be assumed that there will also be a strong effect on the other elements, only a weak effect, or no such effect at all?

In my view, it is possible to rank the three components of party in a meaningful manner, and a rough ranking is implicit in the literature. If given a choice, many if not most scholars would give priority to party-in-the-electorate or party-in-government over party-as-organization. A choice between the first two would depend on whether one preferred an integrated public or government accomplishment. It is unlikely, however, that such an observer would believe that enhancing party organization was equally worthy. Put differently, if with a stroke of a pen the United States could be given party loyalty from its the voters or party government from its politicians at the price of weakened party organization, there are few revivalists who would not accept the bargain.

2. Do changes in one component produce changes in the others? The role of party organization would be significantly more flattering if it was believed that through invigorated organization there also emerged—by some form of transmission mechanism—greater prospects for citizen loyalty to the party or greater probability of allegiance to the party among officials. Which brings in the second question left unanswered by Key: the relationship *among* the party components. If improvement in party organization produced a strong positive impact on the party-in-the-electorate and/or party-in-government then, then it would have a meaningful role in reviving the overall party as an institution. If it does not, then its value is much diminished. If the Republican National Committee's budget doubles and its payroll triples, increasing the scale of support services it can provide to candidates—but without effecting the electorate or elected—then it might be of interest to candidates, campaign managers, and consultants, but it would be of only marginal consequence to those hoping for a stronger party institution. It is barely more significant than if a conservative-inclined interest group doubled its budget, tripled its payroll, and boosted its support services to (predominantly) Republican candidates.

The questions of "Is the party system reviving?" and "Are party organizations getting stronger?" are, therefore, not two ways of saying the same thing. Unilateral improvements in (especially national) party organization that have no transmission effect on the electorate or elected are not particularly important. The emergence of the national Republican and Democratic party organizations as "super PACs" could in this sense be regarded as a sign of weakness in that it is the only role left to them because the really important ones of motivating voters and politicians have been lost.

3. Is party-as-institution more than the combined effects of its components?
In this author's view, political parties, even in the American setting, could and should be more than just bodies that stand political candidates under their label. After all, nearly every conception of party contains the core notion

that the value of such institutions comes from the linkage they provide between the governed and the government. The importance of this linkage in the relationship between organizational activity and the other components of the tripod is implicitly recognized in much of the organizational revival literature: "Thus the strengthening of the party organizations, and especially national party organizations, may lead to the development of a more party-orientated electorate and a more cohesive set of government parties" (Herrnson 1986:590).

Yet there is a bit of a contradiction here. Those who accept the rational-efficient model as the limit of reasonable aspirations for American parties must acknowledge that this model is indifferent to party-in-government and party-in-the-electorate. This view of parties (Downs 1957) makes the capture of reliable political support the ultimate goal; notions of articulating and implementing policy demands, aggregating interests, educating the pubic, and providing avenues for the fulfillment of perceived civic duties are by-products of electoral activity—that is, if they occur at all. Party revivalists, many of whom would be happy to endorse the rational-efficient model, have conceded the demise of party-in-the-electorate and party-in-government, but want to argue that this is counteracted, perhaps overcome, by an increase in party-as-organization. This seems a major inconsistency on their behalf. If they chose to espouse a rational-efficient view of parties, nonorganizational components would be of little consequence. On the other hand, if they hold a more responsible view, as much of the literature seems to suggest, how might they, in all good conscious, speak of revitalized parties when the in-government and in-electorate components lag far behind?

If political parties can no longer fulfill at least some responsible functions in the electorate, as well as help over come, in V. O. Key's terms, "constitutional obstruction" in the government, why then do we persist in suggesting that "the party goes on" (Kayden and Mahe 1985), instead of "the party being over" (Broder 1971)? As Kay Lawson put it when discussing organizational improvements at the Republican National Committee: "Such steps are commendable and should be continued, but by themselves do not...suffice to renew parties. The parties need to undertake changes that expand their role, not merely those that make them better at doing the little that presently remains for them do to" (1987:257).

The Limits of Party Organization-Based Revival

The challenge for those who want to demonstrate the overall revival of party-as-institution through organizational improvement is thus stronger than merely showing that national party organizations are carrying out more activities. Real institutional revival requires three things:

1. It should be shown that there is significant organizational revival across all levels of party organization in the United States—or it should be explained why revival in one or more levels is sufficient.
2. It should be shown that as a consequence of party organizational change voters are casting more party-based ballots than previously.
3. It should be shown that as the result of party organizational change, practicing political figures are acting in a more party-oriented manner.

Unless positive answers can be given to these questions, why should political scientists be any more interested in the precise activities of the Republican National Committee than the American Medical Association PAC? Indeed, unless linkage relationships are present, it is perfectly possible that in any given year party organizations may raise more money, hire more employees, finance more programs, and give more money to the candidates without any significant effect on the political system.

Overall, there is no substantial and convincing evidence that any of the three criteria for genuine party organization-based revival have been met. Even at the height of the Republican National Committee's fundraising success in the mid-1980s, Kayden and Mahe (1985) conceded that local political parties were in a state of collapse. Although some evidence has been presented that state parties were developing their own bureaucracies, that process seems to have stopped once the peak in national committee fundraising was passed.

Likewise, no major evidence has been outlined to show that national party organizational activity has transformed unattached citizens into partisans. Although donations from the major parties may assist a candidate in advancing their message in a particular contest, it is unclear if such activities have persuaded voters not just to vote for a particular candidate, but also to vote for another candidate from that party in a future election.

Until now, there has also been no overwhelming evidence that party activities have produced party-oriented legislators. This should not be surprising, given that party donations to candidates are still small compared to gifts from individuals and PACs. In addition, those candidates most aided by parties were invariably in the most competitive districts and are thus most likely to represent their district's interests at the expense of party unity. Indeed, most evidence suggests that major party candidates in danger of defeat will receive funding from their parties regardless of their record of party loyalty in office.

Conclusion

The first section of this chapter noted three reasons why there is such disagreement among political scientists on the present strength of the

American party system, namely, the lack of an agreed set of functions for American political parties, the uncertainty over the yardstick with which to assess decline or revival, and disagreement over which component of party is most important. I noted that many of the unfavorable comparisons that have been made involving American parties involve—implicitly or explicitly—a universal set of objectives for all party systems regardless of the wider political system in which they operate. I also noted that many of the unfavorable historical comparisons that have been made about the modern parties might also be criticized. In the sense that these comments lower the threshold that the American party system has to meet to be thought of as performing satisfactorily, they are obviously of more help to the revivalists than their declinist opponents.

From there, though, the chapter noted that much of the current discussion about the parties performance was cast in terms of Key's division of the American party into three distinct components. In recent years, party observers have reached broad agreement that the party-in-the-electorate has continued to decompose, but that party-as-organization has been strengthened. The attitude of many has been to see the two movements as canceling each other out. This chapter strongly disagrees. Changes in party organization that cannot trigger development in party-in-the-electorate or party-in-government have little if any impact on the wider party-as-institution. In this sense, the correct answer to the question of "Are party organizations getting stronger?" is "Who cares?" And the question of "Is the party system reviving?" cannot be yet answered in the affirmative.

Notes

1. For a concise review of both the responsible and rational-efficient models of political parties, see Wright (1971).

2. It should be stressed that Key borrowed this formula from Ralph Goldman, "Party Chairmen and Party Factions 1789–1900" (University of Chicago, doctoral diss, 1951).

22

Voters, Governmental Officials, and Party Organizations: Connections and Distinctions

John Frendreis

This chapter provides a response to the chapters by Coleman and Hames in this volume (chapters 20 and 21). The two authors essentially address the same issue: Are American political parties of genuine relevance to the outcomes of American electoral politics? The answers provided by these two authors are guarded, but negative. In particular, both take aim at what Coleman describes as "the new orthodoxy in party scholarship," which he feels has declared American political parties to be resurgent. Both of these authors feel this conclusion is overstated, arising from a misplaced emphasis upon party organizations and a failure of contemporary party scholars to take into account evidence of continued party decline among voters and in government. Since I was asked to respond in part because I am a contributor to the new orthodoxy (e.g., Gibson, Frendreis, and Vertz 1989; Frendreis, Gibson, and Vertz 1990; Frendreis and Gitelson, 1993), I will not disappoint either the editors or readers by failing to disagree with both Coleman and Hames.[1]

In the grand tradition of such responses, I agree with much that both of these authors say, but I also disagree with both on a fundamental point. My agreement is with what they identify as weaknesses in our current state of knowledge, particularly with regard to the relationship between party organizational activity and what happens in the electorate and in government. My disagreement, however, is over what constitutes party activity, or, more precisely, what constitutes our objects of inquiry—American political parties. With apologies to Frank Sorauf, V. O. Key, and Ralph Goldman, I will suggest that it is time to bid farewell to the idea that parties have three components—parties-as-organizations, parties-in-the-electorate, and parties-in-government— whose joint condition define the form and function of American political parties. I will argue instead that it is only the first of these that comprises "political parties" and that recognition of this offers the best hope for the advancement of our knowledge about the place of parties in American politics. Before presenting this model of American political parties, however, I will first directly address the arguments advanced by Coleman and Hames.

The State of Research on Political Parties

Both of these scholars offer similar accounts of recent work on political parties. They note that a steady stream of work over the past fifteen years has found party organizations as being active, and to the extent that trends are apparent, they appear to becoming more, rather than less, active (see Cotter et al. 1984; Gibson, Frendreis, and Vertz 1989; Frendreis et al. 1993). This is especially true of national (Longley 1992; Herrnson 1990; Bibby 1986) and state (Bibby 1990; Patterson 1989) party organizations, but also extends to local parties (Gibson et al. 1985). Increasing levels of activity are found in a variety of areas, including the bureaucratization of party organizations, the variety and level of campaign activities performed, and the amounts of campaign money raised and distributed (Herrnson 1993; Dwyre 1993).

Neither Hames nor Coleman dispute the substance of these studies; rather, they argue that the implications which are drawn from them are flawed. In Coleman's view, "the party organization literature has leapt too quickly to words like 'resurgence' and 'revitalization.' Increased activity should only be the *start* of a conception of resurgent parties" (ch. 20:xx, emphasis in original). Coleman goes on to argue that the behavior of the party-in-the-electorate is key to assessing the vibrancy of American parties and that the new orthodoxy has failed to uncover evidence of resurgence or revitalization in this area. In a similar vein, Hames contends that a correct understanding of contemporary American parties must focus on the interrelationships between the three components of parties. Since he finds little evidence of "transmission effects" between active organizations and either the party-in-the-electorate or the party-in-government, he dismisses the increasingly bureaucratized and active party organizations as being little different from PACs. He concludes: "Changes in party organization that cannot trigger developments in the party-in-the-electorate or the party-in-government have little if any impact on the wider party-as-institution. In this sense, the correct answer to the question of 'Are party organizations getting stronger?' is 'Who cares?'" (chapter 21:xxx).

It is here that I part company with both scholars. I believe their accounts of recent scholarship are accurate. Beyond this, their identification of a key problem—the apparent lack of parallel trends in party activity, mass partisanship, and party government—accurately identifies what should be the target of the next wave of party research. My main problem with both authors' arguments, however, lies in the implications of Hames's phrase, "the wider party-as-institution." In the remainder of this chapter I will argue that there is no "wider" party beyond the party-as-organization, and I will suggest how the acceptance of this perspective will define how research aimed at understanding the problems Coleman and Hames have identified should be oriented. Before turning to this task, however, I must respectfully disagree with a few of the specific positions advanced by the authors, particularly Coleman.

While I am flattered to be listed among the creators of a new orthodoxy, I must confess that such an orthodoxy is based upon a fairly small amount of research. Particularly with respect to state and local party organizations, there has been one major study, the Party Transformation Study (Cotter et al. 1984), two partial follow-up studies (Gibson et al. 1989; and Frendreis et al. 1993), and an unrelated comparative analysis of party organizations in several major American cities (Crotty 1986). Aside from this, there have been only scattered studies of organizations at one point in time in a few locales (e.g., Lawson, Pomper, and Moakley 1986; Pomper 1990). Alan Gitelson and I have discussed this problem at length elsewhere (Frendreis and Gitelson 1993); I will simply note briefly that—despite the presumed importance of political parties to the American polity—we have relatively little contemporary data on parties, compared with other political phenomena, such as the behavior of voters, legislators, or candidates. This is especially true with regard to the functioning of state and local parties in state and local politics and government. While I agree that the central focus for our research should shift from documenting what parties do toward understanding what difference parties make, we should recognize that there continues to be an urgent need for more complete cross-sectional and longitudinal data on party activity.

In a similar vein, I would also disagree that this research suffers from a mindset based upon "fighting the last battle." The original Party Transformation Study was conceived at a time when Broder's view that *The Party's Over* (1971) really *was* orthodox. The research I did with Gibson and Vertz followed fast upon Wattenberg's documentation of what he felt was *The Decline of American Political Parties 1952-1980* (1984). In our 1990 article (Frendreis, Gibson, and Vertz 1990), we described the lack of correspondence between organizational and mass partisanship trends as paradoxical, an observation which still holds true. Rather than being consumed by a desire to further dispute Broder's twenty-year-old position, however, I see this work as an ongoing attempt to make sense of what *continues* to be a paradox.

Finally, I would dispute that this research suffers from a misplaced emphasis upon party organizations, rather than the really important things like governance or mass political behavior. First, it should be evident from my comments thus far that I believe we still lack a clear understanding of what *contemporary* parties actually do. Second, it is not exactly the case that research has ignored the relationship between party activity and other electoral phenomena. In addition to my own work cited above, this question has attracted the attention of a number of other scholars, including Herrnson (1986, 1988), Gibson and Smith (1984), and Huckfeldt and Sprague (1992). (For an extension of this work to a comparative setting, see Whitely and Seyd

1994). Indeed, this represents the latest wave in a line of research that stretches back to Eldersveld (1956), Katz and Eldersveld (1961), Cutright (1963), Kramer (1970-71), and Crotty (1971). To me, the problem is not that previous research suffers from a misplaced emphasis upon uninteresting or well-worn organizational phenomena; rather, it is that there has been too little research to confidently describe contemporary parties in very much detail. Our lack of understanding of the electoral relevance of contemporary parties is merely one symptom of this broader problem.

A Model of American Political Parties

My basic disagreement with both Coleman and Hames is with the model of political parties implied by Hames's phrase, "the wider party-as-institution." Following Schlesinger (1984), I would argue that the party should be conceived as consisting of those individuals and institutions whose manifest purpose is the contesting of elections with a goal of winning the elections. Obviously, this is hardly a novel conception of party. It corresponds closely to the "minimal definition" presented by Sartori: "A party is any political group identified by an official label that presents at elections, and is capable of placing through election (free or nonfree), candidates for public office" (1976:63). Even Key, it should be noted, stressed the importance of focusing on those who "carry on the routine work in the winning and maintenance of power," a group termed the "party organization" or "inner core" (Key 1947:247, quoting Gosnell's entry in Volume XI of the *Encyclopedia of the Social Sciences*). Key concludes: "Nevertheless, in the examination of political party activities it is well to concentrate attention on the inner core or the organization, for that really is 'the party'" (Key 1947:247).

Beyond this, party scholars need to take seriously the word "organization" in the phrase "party organization." Organizational theory is well-developed, yet insights from this field are only beginning to be adapted to the study of party organizations. Identifying the degree of bureaucratization of state and local parties and assessing its connection with programmatic activity (e.g., Cotter et al. 1984; Gibson, Frendreis, and Vertz 1989) represents one step in this direction. Another recent example is Baer's (1993) discussion of the role of the "integrative community life" of parties, a concept she draws from March and Olsen (1988).

Although analogies are imperfect, I would link organizational theory with the definition of party I have set forth above as follows. In the electoral setting, the Democratic and Republican parties in the United States can be considered to be two firms, competing for customers in such a way that a vote for the party's candidates represents a purchase of the firm's product. Currently, the two parties collectively dominate the market, essentially because of the high cost of entry into the market. For a number of reasons, particularly favorable state laws and the absence of proportional representation, it is difficult for a new firm (i.e., a new party) to successfully enter the market. As a result, the two parties operate as a duopoly, dominating the market, as Schlesinger (1991) has noted.

Furthermore, these two firms operate in an atmosphere of declining brand loyalty, i.e., a weakening of partisanship. This means that the reliability of consumers' purchasing decisions is declining, as is apparent in the increase in independence, split-ticket voting, and defection by party voters. However, this decline in partisanship should be seen for what it is—a change in the marketplace in which the firms compete rather than a direct symptom of organizational decline by the firm. As I note in the next section, a methodological decision not to view mass partisanship as a component of the political party has important consequences in a search for connections between party activity and mass political behavior.

At the same time, while the structure of the electoral market has insulated the two parties from ready competition, the declining brand loyalty means that the system is potentially unstable. This has a number of implications. First, it would suggest that, ceteris paribus, greater than average swings in outcomes from election to election are possible. (Of course, not all things *are* equal, e.g., trends of increasing incumbency advantages.) Second, there should be a drop-off in purchases based solely upon brand loyalty, e.g., an increase over time in ballot roll-off for minor offices. Third, if a new firm *is* capable of absorbing the costs of entry into the market, it has the potential for significant market penetration. From this perspective, the 1992 presidential campaign of Ross Perot is less a sign of the further decline of the two parties than it is the exception that proves the rule: a "third party" candidate threatens the recent dominance of the two parties described by Schlesinger (1991) only when he or she is backed by the considerable resources necessary to overcome the high costs of market entry.

In the next two sections, I describe the implications for further research of this model of American parties as firms operating in an electoral marketplace. In particular, I discuss how this might guide our research into the two critical linkages highlighted by Coleman and Hames: the linkages between parties and voters, and between parties and government officeholders.

Parties and Voters

Coleman's essay identifies two central questions that must be answered about voters: "What has caused decreased partisanship?" "What has caused declines in voter trust of political parties as institutions?" At first glance, it would seem that these two questions are linked and, moreover, that the answers must focus at least in part upon the behavior of parties themselves.

Wattenberg's decision to title his studies of declining voter loyalty as portraits of declining political *parties* rather than declining political *partisanship* clearly implies this (Wattenberg 1984, 1990).

The methodological peril of trying to consider trends in mass political behavior as an attribute of parties becomes readily apparent when one adopts the perspective that parties and voters are as distinct as firms and their customers. What causes changes in consumer tastes? To be sure, the experience of U.S. automakers in the last twenty years suggests that brand loyalty may break down in the face of poor product quality or bad service. Yet economic history is full of examples of firms losing customer support because of exogenous factors, such as technological change or changes in customer needs and wants.

Considered in this light, the behavior of the parties becomes only one of several possible causal agents which might influence trends in partisanship. An example of another potential culprit is the rising level of education and middle-class sensibilities among the American electorate. Coleman notes the breakdown in the apparently strong linkage between party machines and voters that existed in the late nineteenth century. Accounts of this breakdown generally stress the role of rising education and the bureaucratization of the welfare function as causes. Neither of these factors could be regarded as evidence of poor performance on the part of the parties, behavior which might induce a turning away on the part of voters.

If we only take the period for which we have reliable time series data on mass political attitudes and behaviors—roughly the last 50 years—it is difficult to identify any long term trend in the behavior of parties which correlates with the decline in mass partisanship. Consider the products that the parties have to offer to the voters: candidates and party platforms. With the possible exception of presidential nominees, any analysis of today's candidates with those of the 1950s would show today's to be better educated and more knowledgeable about policy problems and the powers of the offices they are seeking (Ehrenhalt 1991). One of the effects of the decline in political machines was the elimination of offices awarded to party regulars who were unprepared for and uninterested in them. Similarly, it is not at all clear that the quality of party platforms has declined over this period. On the other hand, it is certain that other trends, many of them long-term, underlying demographic changes, can be discerned over the same time period, and some of these may be substantially correlated with changes in mass partisanship.

None of this is meant to indicate that there is no connection between party activity and the attitudes of voters. Yet, it is a very different proposition to regard party activity as one of many potential factors which might influence consumer preferences rather than to see these preferences as direct reflections of party failure or irrelevance. Coleman is correct in asserting that we do not understand the decline in partisanship, but this assertion cuts both ways. Coleman's skepticism of a "counteracting party model," in which party organizational strength may be offsetting the effects of these broader social trends, is equally unwarranted. If it turns out that the widespread and well-documented decline in partisanship during the 1960s and 1970s slowed or even stopped during the 1980s, it may yet support the view that party activity has altered an otherwise exogenously determined decline in partisanship. Coleman's dismissal of what was never more than a hypothesis is premature; more appropriately, the "counteracting party model" needs to be tested.

Parties and Government Officials

The view of American political parties as two firms competing in a duopolistic electoral marketplace marked by declining brand loyalty addresses most directly the relationship between the parties and the voters. However, with some modifications, this can be extended to address the relationship between the parties and government office-holders. Before directly addressing this linkage, it is necessary to briefly discuss the relationship between parties and public policy.

The conception of political party I am arguing for does not make direct reference to parties as agents of policy formation and enactment. If one focuses on parties as purely electoral actors, policy is relevant only to the extent that it enhances or retards the ability of the parties to attract voters. Clearly, this is neither how voters nor normative treatments of democracy view public policy. For example, it is likely that at least some of the current voter distrust of political parties is part of a general lack of regard for government institutions, a sentiment based at least partially upon the performance of these institutions in enacting policy.

At the same time, to consider the behavior of Congress as a manifestation of the activities of the political parties—of the parties-in-government—just as surely does violence to the truth. Congress and the parties are separate institutions; as a result, they must be kept analytically and methodologically distinct. However, members of Congress are part of both of these institutions. How is their behavior to be understood? Using the market model I have proposed, they are either the product being marketed, or the sales force, or both; perhaps the best corporate analogy is that they operate as independent franchise holders.

The logic of this argument is that the behavior of legislators and political executives should not be seen as the behavior of parties, but as a function of the behavior of parties. Legislatures and executive agencies are not a component of the parties, but are institutions which the parties seek to control. Considered from this perspective, two questions emerge as being critical. In what way do parties control the behavior of governmental office holders? What is the relationship between the behavior of governmental office holders and the linkage between parties and the voters?

The first of these two questions is the most accessible and is indirectly the subject of a substantial body of recent research, especially with respect to Congress (e.g., Little and Patterson 1993; Rohde 1991; Huitt 1990; Sinclair, 1983; Jones 1970; Ripley 1969). However, in general this work approaches the relationship of party to Congress from the congressional perspective. As a result, it focuses less on the means by which the parties control legislators and more on the mechanisms of partisan influence that exist internal to the legislature.

From the perspective of the party organizations, a somewhat different set of questions emerges. To the extent that the organization (the party) has a set of institutional goals regarding the behavior of legislators, (e.g., that the legislators seek to enact a specific set of policies), the problem for the party is insuring that the individuals making up the organization (i.e., party members) behave properly, that is, in concert with the organizational goals. The problem of American parties is immediately apparent: unlike many other organizations, American parties cannot usually replace recalcitrant members, at least the members who hold elective office. The direct primary, more than any other factor, is responsible for the weak hold of American parties over government institutions. Although this is fundamental to understanding the operation of American parties in a comparative perspective, the diffusion of the direct primary is essentially a historical fact. The question for scholars now is how the party exerts control over its office-holders in the absence of the ability to readily replace them.

Here, organizational theory offers some clues. Perrow (1979) observes that the surest means of organizational control is the inculcation of the organization's norms in its members. Baer's (1993) discussion of the integrative community life of parties suggests that parties do indeed attempt to do this. In addition, like all organizations, parties seeking to structure their members' attitudes should utilize recruitment and socialization as means to this end. Finally, even though parties cannot definitively eliminate deviant members, they still can seek to influence these members via the offering of selective incentives, such as funding and support by other group members.

Seen in this light, many of the party organizational development activities over the last two decades documented by party scholars may be seen as manifestations of the efforts of parties to achieve greater control over their office holders—assuming they wish to do so. Still unclear is the relationship between achieving such control and the manifest purpose of parties, to contest and win elections. More important, however, is the fact that in this area of party life, too, we actually possess little systematic evidence assessing the linkage between party activities and manifestations of partisan control over their office holders. It is clear that parties are weaker in this area than a century ago; however, there is no real data to support Hames's and Coleman's assertions that recent efforts toward strengthening party organizations bear no relationship toward *recent* trends in parties' influence over office holders.

Party Organizations, Governmental Officials, and Voters

It is easy for someone whose vision is narrowed by their own research agenda to construct a party-centered vision of American political life. Coleman and Hames raise the question: Is such a perspective justified? This question might be approached in two ways, normatively and empirically. From a normative perspective, the answer is surely yes. Although the U.S. Constitution is silent on the subject of political parties, it is virtually impossible to discuss the operation of the U.S. polity as a democracy without reference to parties. Technological change may eventually foster the creation of governing mechanisms embodying direct democracy, but for the near future, it is likely that most of our vehicles for self-governance will embody representative democracy. Given this, it seems likely that political parties—even weakened ones—will remain central components of discussions of the linkage between voters and governmental officials, between the public will and public policy.

The empirical basis for seeing political parties as central to the workings of a democratic American polity are less clear. Both Coleman and Hames are skeptical of the relevance of parties to either voters or government, although they temper their concerns with a desire for more research. Obviously, on this latter point we are in agreement. A general theme throughout this essay is that we actually know very little about the relationships among parties, voters, and government. To say that parties are not moribund—as might be expected if trends in mass partisanship were closely tied to the internal vitality of the parties—is not to say that we are certain that they exert a powerful hold over both voters and office-holders. The new orthodoxy that Coleman claims to see is based on a few summary speculations rather than upon the main substance of what party organizational scholars have said.

Throughout this essay I have identified a number of significant questions which should be the target of the next generation of party scholarship. What has caused decreased partisanship? What has caused the declines in voter trust of political parties? In what way do parties control the behavior of governmental office holders? What is the relationship between the behavior of government office-holders and the linkage between parties and the voters?

That these questions could be deduced from the old three component model of American parties does not mean that this is simply "old wine in new wineskins." The conceptualization of parties as having three components confuses the objects of party activity with the party itself. This is more readily apparent with regard to the voters, but is true nonetheless for government as well. That parties seek to control government does not mean that party members within the government are acting upon the shared organizational norms that define the party when they exercise their authority as office holders. Conceiving of the office-holders as a "party-in-government" has diverted attention away from the very real question of how the institution of the party seeks to influence and control the institutions of government.

Perhaps it seems unexceptional to argue for a continued and expanded research agenda for the study of American political parties. To avoid appearing pedestrian, I will offer a somewhat bolder suggestion. I believe that it is time for scholars of American politics to come together to support a substantial data collection effort, which will provide a basis for extensive analysis of American political parties in the same way that the National Election Studies surveys have created a foundation for work in electoral behavior. At a minimum, the scholarly community should systematically collect data on party activity, electoral behavior, and governmental policy making for a broad cross-section of political systems and over an extended period of time. An obvious setting for such research would be the states, which would permit some variation in significant social, political, and legal variables to be manifested in the data. Even focusing on the states, though, we know that data on both local and national party activity (and probably electoral and governmental activity) also need to be incorporated into such a research effort. As Alan Gitelson and I have suggested elsewhere, such an effort argues strongly for the development of a consortium of scholars who will bring diverse concerns and perspectives to a common effort to raise our understanding of parties to the level already enjoyed by other key aspects of American politics, such as voting or the operation of Congress (Frendreis and Gitelson 1993).

Throughout this essay I have argued for the adoption of a perspective that sees the party organizations *as* the party. A specific formulation that I have offered is to conceive of the Democratic and Republican parties as two firms competing in a duopolistic marketplace marked in recent years by declining brand loyalty among consumers. Further, these firms can be seen to face unique problems of internal cohesion in that some of their key members, candidates/office-holders, cannot be controlled via replacement. I have tried to indicate how adoption of this perspective might focus subsequent scholarship on the beckoning research frontier. Whatever perspective is adopted, however, one thing is clear: without additional research, future volumes on the "state of the parties" will continue to substitute discussions based upon a clear understanding of the actual relationships among parties, voters, and office-holders with ones driven by speculation, skepticism, and hope.

Notes

1. I wish to thank Laura Vertz and Alan Gitelson for their comments on this chapter.

23

Understanding Organizational Innovation and Party-Building

Andrew M. Appleton
Daniel S. Ward

This chapter reports early results of a project examining patterns of innovation in party organizations. The question we address is: why and how do parties introduce innovations in organizational structures and behavior? For example, to which forces do parties respond when they employ new methods, install new structures, or involve new personnel? Equally so, what forces push parties to abandon certain practices, to dismantle parts of their structure, and to distance themselves from particular people? It is perhaps axiomatic that organizations have a built in resistance to change. Yet ecological theories of organizations emphasize an environmental imperative: either organizations adapt to new conditions in the environment or they perish. As we will argue below, one pole of the continuum of adaptation is represented by *innovation*. At a time when the American political system is in a state of flux, many are attempting to predict the future of the political parties. To a measurable degree, that future is inextricably linked to the capacity and willingness of parties to innovate. Although this chapter will concentrate on the recent past of state party organizations, the goal is to help us better understand the impact of certain events on those organizations and, in doing so, increase our predictive ability.

The *State Party Archive Project*, of which this study is part, has as its goal the collection of observed, as opposed to reported, data on party organization and behavior. Although not critical of previous attempts to open up the "black box" of party organization through the use of survey-based measures (eg., the Party Transformation Study [PTS] of Cotter et al. 1984), we have argued that the continuing neglect of observed measures of party organization limit our ability to test hypotheses regarding organizational practice and behavior. Our work is intended to demonstrate that such measures are in fact available, primarily through the records kept by many party units; records which have been dramatically under-exploited by the recently revitalized study of party organization. As party scholars heed continued calls to incorporate the organizational dimension into the study of party development, we hope that the *State Party Archive Project* can contribute a rich source of data to complement the existing survey-based information already generating much lively scholarly interest and debate.

In the first stage of this project, we sought to demonstrate the utility of exploiting party records to generate observed measures of organizational practices and behavior (Appleton and Ward 1993b). Our approach was to select a small number of state parties and to gain access to any records they might have produced over a limited period; we then examined the feasibility of generating standardized measures that ultimately could be used in the construction of a longitudinal dataset. Our interest in sound longitudinal indicators is derived from our broader theoretical interests in party organizational adaptation, laid out in earlier work (Appleton and Ward 1993a). Using this limited case strategy, we hoped to provide a focused comparison of one feature of party organizational adaptation, namely the propensity of parties to respond to unanticipated electoral events. For reasons of time and access, this chapter concerns only two state parties, both of which had experienced unexpected electoral breakthroughs in the early 1960s. However, the long-term consequences of these victories were rather different; the use of party documents allowed us to conclude that a significant factor in the ability of a state party organization to build around previous success was the absence of factionalism in the party elite. This in turn, we argued, was linked to the ability of the party to maintain a distinction between organizational and electoral efforts (Appleton and Ward 1994). While this distinction is not always perfect even at the conceptual level, it corresponds to that which organizational theorists have made between activities that are either of an organization-maintenance nature or of a goal-directed variety

During the course of this examination of party records, we also became interested in distinguishing between different kinds of change in party organizations. One of the advantages of our observed measures of party behavior is that they permit us to make relatively precise recordings of the introduction of new forms of organization. Not only can we account for the extent and timing of such changes, it is also possible in the majority of cases to trace the stimulus for them. On the basis of the information that we have collected from our pilot study, and building upon the intellectual and theoretical foundations of organizational literature, we will outline a scheme by which innovation in party organization may be classified and suggest a model by which this phenomenon may be better understood at the state level. Before we do so, however, we will briefly report the location and extent of the data gathered in the course of our study.

The Republican Party Archives of Texas and Arkansas

Our pilot study of party organizational development was undertaken in Arkansas and Texas and has served several purposes.[1] First, it has allowed us to explore the implications of our more general model of party development. Thus in our previous case study, we examined the hypothesis that party organizations would respond to unexpected electoral victories by implementing a program of organizational development, independent from the campaign activities of the party (Appleton and Ward 1994). The use of party records enabled us to provide an explanation of the relative success of the Texas Republicans in their efforts to capitalize on John Tower's 1961 Senate election victory, and compare it to the relative failure of the Arkansas Republican Party to build a durable winning coalition in the wake of Winthrop Rockefeller's tenure as governor.

The second benefit of the pilot study has been our ability to evaluate the utility of archival data sources for students of party organization and development. Below, we will briefly describe the extent and location of the party records that were available in our research. In a follow-up to this work, we conducted two surveys—one of state parties, the other of state archives (see Appleton and Ward 1993b for the detailed results) which have shown that these two states are not atypical in the party records that they have to offer the scholarly community. Thus we feel confident that our pilot project has demonstrated the feasibility of constructing valid observed measures of party organization.

Third, this pilot study has convinced us of the need to refine our notions of organizational adaptation and change. Just as we believe that there are qualitatively and quantitatively different orders of change manifested in party organizations, we are also convinced that it is possible to distinguish between the forces that drive organizational change. In the second part of this chapter, we will offer a framework by which one kind of radical change—innovation—may be illuminated through the use of observed data derived from party archives of the Republican state parties in Texas and Arkansas.[2]

Texas Republicans

The records of the Republican Party of Texas consist of bound copies of all state committee and executive committee meetings, from 1957 through the present. The minutes are comprehensive and reliable documents that track every important development in state party history for the period covered. Issues of staffing, budgeting, candidate recruitment, party leadership, and relations between the state and local parties and the state and national parties are covered in detail. Transcripts of speeches made at committee meetings by prominent candidates, office holders, or party leaders normally are included as well.

The minutes are particularly informative on the topic of party programs. In other words, debates about party building and organizational structure are prominent. Efforts at candidate recruitment are another frequent topic at committee meetings, as are discussions about voter mobilization. Finally, reports of finance committees and chairs provide systematic accounting of party budgets and fundraising efforts. One deficiency with the Texas Republican archive is the absence of original reports and documents referred to in the minutes. Party staffers were unable to locate these other materials. By themselves, however, we believe the committee minutes may serve as a road map for archival research. Because they are internal documents, they are likely to avoid the biases that public records often display.

Arkansas Republicans

The records of the Arkansas Republican party are stored, uncatalogued and largely unidentified, in a commercial storage facility along with spare office furniture, convention banners, and other political memorabilia. The task of sifting through unmarked boxes dating from the mid-1960s to the mid-1980s was the most challenging of our efforts, but in many ways the most rewarding. Because we had complete access and freedom to photocopy any document of our choosing we were able to "sample" from a wider array of materials.[3] The downside is that we can say more about the type of material contained in the archive and less about its consistency or temporal coverage. While we came across many copies of executive committee minutes, the lack of cataloguing prevented us from determining whether a complete set of minutes is available, as in the case of the Texas Republicans. Likewise, a substantial number of reports, polls, and pamphlets were encountered, but we are less certain of the proportion of such material contained in the archives.

We can report that all of the same types of material referred to in the Texas Republican minutes were discovered in original form in the Arkansas Republican records. In addition to executive committee minutes, we found rules, daily schedules, correspondence with county, national, and other state parties, records of party functions, and virtually a complete set of budgetary data. Each of these categories of information serves some useful purpose for understanding party organization and change. In the following section, we hope to demonstrate this point more concretely. One important caveat with regard to the Arkansas Republican Party records is in order. A fair portion of the party's records for the period 1967–1970, Winthrop Rockefeller's governorship, are contained in Rockefeller's own papers, housed at the University of Arkansas, Little Rock. Our surveys of state party archives and state archives indicate that this situation is not uncommon (Appleton and Ward 1993b).

Patterns of Organizational Innovation

Elsewhere we have discussed the organizational experiences of intermediate level political parties in the wake of important electoral victories using the terms "adaptation" and "change" (Appleton and Ward 1993a; 1994). However, as Harmel and Janda point out:

> *Party change* (in the broadest sense) is any variation, alteration, or modification in how parties are organized, what human and material resources they can draw upon, what they stand for, and what they do. But this usage is so broad that it raises unrealistic expectations about the scope of a theory of party change (1992:14-5).

While we concur with their point, our earlier work has been intended to establish a key fact, namely that parties *do* change and, furthermore, that such change cannot be understood independently of the environment within which parties operate. As we have shown, there are good theoretical and empirical grounds for believing that state parties have responded to certain events through change in their organizational structure and practices.

Here we wish to focus on one specific form of change which we have chosen to label *organizational innovation*. We are most interested in exploring two related questions. First, what exactly is organizational innovation? And second, if parties innovate, from where do they get their ideas?

What do we mean by organizational innovation? Innovation is defined in *Webster's Dictionary* as "the change made by innovating; any custom, manner, etc. newly introduced." Innovation should be understood as a subset of change, which encompasses the notions of variation, modification, or alteration in existing forms. Organizational change may be quantitative (doing more of what is already done) or qualitative (improving what is already done). These kinds of change are differentiated from innovation in that they do not replace or supplement past practices with completely new ones. Thus organizational innovation may be seen as the attempt to introduce new organizational forms and practices without precedent. It should be noted that innovation does not necessarily entail replacing old forms and practices; in some cases, it merely supplements what already exists.

The literature on party organization does not always make this distinction clear. For example, Pannebianco draws a line between "continual change" and "fundamental change" (1988:243). Further on, he refers to the latter as "considerable alteration" and then "innovation." But the empirical examples that he provides of such processes (the British Conservatives, the PCI in Italy in 1956, the SPD in 1958-60, and the CDU in the 1960s and 1970s in Germany) do not really display innovation as we have defined it above. Some have considered the place of innovation in the study of party organization in the U.S., particularly in the move by the Democrats and Republicans towards a service-vendor model (Frantzich 1989). The Republican Party has generally been found to be more innovative than the Democrats, at least in the period of the 1960s and 1970s (Sabato 1981; Sorauf 1980; Cotter and Bibby 1980). While many of the changes identified by these authors do conform to our definition of innovation, others do not.

Theorists have argued that innovations in organizations are likely to occur when an equilibrium has been disrupted from the outside (Scott 1961). The quest for innovation is often one to respond to a negative change in the environment. Party specialists have emphasized this particular condition, which might be called *performance innovation*. Thus Harmel and Janda propose (1992) and test (1993) the hypothesis that, "For vote-seeking parties . . . the more pronounced their electoral failures, the more likely their organizational modification" (1992:19). Frantzich argues that party decision makers "clearly indicate that they credit election defeats as the stimulus for innovation"; obversely, "As a basic rule, winners seldom innovate" (1989:91). Yet the organizational theory literature argues two further cases where innovation may occur. The first may be called *periodic innovation*, where organizations may seek to innovate even if their performance trend is upwards but they feel that the possibility exists for a quantum shift in their behavior. The second case is that where organizations undertake *accidental innovation* when opportunities to innovate present themselves unexpectedly (March and Simon 1959).

The data from the Texas and Arkansas Republican parties reflect these different cases of innovation. While we find evidence to support the proposition that parties innovate when they are not meeting their performance goals, there is also much that points to innovation of the periodic and accidental varieties. Cotter et al. (1984) conceive of the institutionalization of party organization (i.e. "positive" change) as a strengthening of two components, organizational complexity and programmatic capacity. Using their measures for each, we can classify innovations by type (performance, periodic, or accidental) and by the particular facet of party organization that they alter (organizational complexity and programmatic capacity). This framework for understanding party organizational innovation is shown below in Table 23.1.

From where does innovation come? At the outset, a distinction must be drawn between *invention* and *innovation*. The former may be defined as "the discovery of a new process or form," while the latter is better understood as "the widespread adoption of a new process or form" (McNutt 1990:156). Students of technological changes provided two theories which explain these phenomena. One may be labelled *diffusionist*, the main argument being that innovation is an invention that is gradually diffused throughout a social group. This theory of innovation makes two assumptions; first, that inventions can occur only at one time and place, exogenous to the locus of innovation; and second, that they are diffused relatively rapidly by *infection* (exposure to knowledge of the invention). Others have criticized these assumptions and

Table 23.1 Classification of Party Organizational Innovation

Measures of Institutionalization	Innovation		
	Performance	Periodic	Accidental
Organizational Complexity: - Party HQ - Division of Labor - Budgets - Leadership			
Programmatic Capacity: - Institutional Support - Candidate-Directed			

proposed an alternative *innovation choice* model, in which it is assumed that inventions may reoccur without infection and that the application of inventions (i.e., innovation) does not necessarily follow automatically, but depends on social and political factors.

Furthermore, March and Simon (1959) argue that innovation may result from either exogenous or endogenous stimuli. Exogenous stimuli are environment-dependent; that is, they occur as a result of changes in the environment and may diffuse from the top of the organization, from the bottom, or horizontally across units. Endogenous sources of innovation come from within the organization and may be divided into two categories. First, there are those stimuli that result from internal dissatisfaction with the organization's own goals (even though external evaluations of performance may be positive). Second, innovation may be "programmed"; that is, organizations may have components whose mission is to seek innovation (for example, research and development units). Table 23.2 offers a classification of the types of innovation by the source of stimuli.

In this classification, *diffused inventions* are those that come from outside either the state party organization or its immediate environment. Diffusion may occur from the top-down (i.e. from the federal to the state level), from the bottom-up (i.e. from the county/district to the state level), or horizontally (that is, across states). *Nondiffused* inventions are those that occur within the state party organization or its immediate environment. These inventions may be either of the performance variety (that is, generated by internal dissatisfaction with the state party's own goals) or of the programmed kind (from a component of the state party charged with seeking to innovate).

Table 23.2 Classification of Stimuli for State Party Organizational Innovation

	Source of Contact	
Type of Invention	Exogenous (environmental)	Endogenous (intra-organizational)
Diffused: - Top-down - Horizontal - Bottom-up		
Nondiffused: - performance - programmed		

Whether the invention is diffused or nondiffused, the stimulus to innovate may come from environmental pressures (exogenous) or from intra-organizational processes (endogenous).

While it may be hard to conceptualize nondiffused, exogenous invention leading to innovation at the state-party level, it is not too difficult to find empirical cases. For example, in 1971 the Arkansas Republican Party commissioned a study of their strengths and weaknesses from a private organization. One major weakness identified was the lack of communication between state and county parties. The criteria used for such an evaluation were imported from the business world. This report was discussed at a State Executive Committee meeting on February 14, 1972. As a result of the discussion, five changes were proposed and adopted relating to the size and composition of the Executive Committee. The value of using data garnered from party records is that we have a relatively unbiased source for classifying and quantifying innovational stimuli; in the above case, we see the import of organizational techniques from the immediate environment (the Arkansas business community).

In the rest of this section, we will give examples of such stimuli that conform to the schema proposed above. This discussion will be confined to examples of endogenous (intraparty) stimuli. While we came across many examples of new organizational behaviors and practices that had seemingly been imported from nonparty sources, we are not presently in a position to undertake the detailed examination of such cases in order to verify their point of origin. There is little doubt that party records by themselves are more revealing of intraparty processes, whereas contacts between parties and their environments are harder to quantify from party records alone without independent validation. Since access to these other data sources is far more difficult and time consuming, we have hitherto only considered innovations that have been imported through contacts with other party units.

Cases of Diffused Innovation

Top-down Innovation

The 1960s and 1970s were decades of innovation for the Republican Party. At the national level, "chairmen Ray Bliss (1965-69) and Bill Brock (1975-80) deserve much of the credit for redirecting party efforts" (Frantzich 1989:91). In particular, "Under Bliss, the Republican Party as a national force would become much more professional, prepared to win those marginal races that would be crucial to the party's comeback hopes for 1966" (Knaggs 1986:64). In Texas, the Republicans looked to the RNC as a source of learning, picking up on the seminars organized by the national chairman. "Operatives for Tower and the state GOP attended such seminars, learning new techniques." (Knaggs 1983:64). The opportunities for innovation opened up by the appointment of Bliss were discussed early on at the state level; for example, Texas chairman O'Donnell, "made an estimate of the way in which Ray Bliss would handle the job of national chairman. Although Mr. Bliss has personally stated that he was more conservative than Barry Goldwater, he saw his job as primarily one dealing with finances and organization with the objective of electing Republicans of every persuasion to office" (RSEC, 1/16/65). The records of the party from this period offer a unique perspective upon the adoption or rejection of the RNC's steady stream of proposals.

In Arkansas, the party appears to have been rather less driven by proposals for innovation from the RNC in the 1960s, with Rockefeller's operatives and money underpinning the party's development strategy. Yet, with the passing of the Rockefeller era, the Arkansas Republicans appear to have turned to outside help in their efforts to revitalize the organization. One of the important arms of the State party, the Candidate Services Bureau (CSB) decided in 1972 to remodel their training seminars for Republican candidates for statewide office. As part of this effort, they produced a new campaign manual for all prospective candidates (3/31/72). This manual included a first for the Arkansas party in the form of a twenty-six-page section on opposition research. The manual aims to demonstrate how to proceed so that:

> if proper information is collected regarding a Democratic candidate's personality, family life, business career, political career, attitudes, and voting record, a complete picture of the candidate can be developed. His strengths and weaknesses can be assessed and, if handled properly, those weaknesses can be exploited.

The manual was not, however, unique to the CSB or indeed to Arkansas, but was a generic model developed by the RNC. At the campaign seminar on June 24, 1972, we find that one session (lead by Gene Wirges, not a member of the State Party committee at this juncture) is devoted to opposition research (Letter, 6/17/72). Thus the innovation of systematic research is introduced into the battery of organizational techniques employed by the Arkansas Republican Party in a top-down fashion.

In 1977, the Arkansas Republican party decided to set up a Black Council (part of the long-term effort to reach out to the African-American community in the state; the experience was typical of Republican parties in the South). Once again the innovation is top-down; the Black Council was to be modeled after that of the national group. Jim Cummings, chair of the Republican National Black Council, visited Arkansas to hold talks with Elijah Coleman, a long-time black Republican activist in the state. The records make it clear that Cummings' visit and the talks are intended to help Coleman organize the venture. Thus a proposal was presented to the State Executive Committee on September 17, 1977 to establish the Arkansas Republican Black Council. The records also include a subsequent letter from Brock congratulating the party on this innovation.

These are just two examples chosen from many contained in the Arkansas records. Others that show the range of innovations diffused in a top-down manner include the hiring of two organizational directors in 1978 (paid by the national GOP); the effort in 1977 to set up an Arkansas Republican Political Action Committee (ARPAC) patterned after the RNPAC; preelection studies conducted in 1980 by trained personnel of the RNC; the introduction of a precinct leader's manual in 1969, and the introduction of state-party direct mail in the early 1970s. In each of these cases, the choice to innovate followed contact with the national party organization. At times efforts to import innovations from above verged on the comic; thus the party's efforts to develop its own direct-mail operation appears to have initially ended in failure when the firm hired to treat and store the data accidentally (and irretrievably) merged the state party's list with that of the national party. Attempts to recover either the data or the money paid or both from the data management firm appear to have met with little success.

Horizontal Innovation

When we first considered the question of innovational stimuli, our assumption was that diffused innovation was either top-down or bottom-up. Much as Frantzich does, we assumed that where innovation takes place at the state level and is then diffused throughout the party organization this process would operate through the national party organization. However, once we

The Patterns of Organizational Innovation 359

began to look at the data it became clear that this is not always the case and that horizontal contact between state party organizations has an important role in the diffusion of innovation.

Such contacts have been institutionalized in the form of (a) the national association of state party chairs, (b) various regional association of state party chairs, and (c) other meetings and seminars bringing together organizations from the state parties. Furthermore, while the national party may serve as the conduit through which information about new techniques and practices flows (coverage in the party newspaper, newsletters, brochures, other circulars), that does not preclude direct contact between state party organizations. The party archives showed that all of these mechanisms were influential in the horizontal diffusion of innovation.

Documents from the Workshop on Political Organization hosted by the Southern Association of Republican State Chairmen in Atlanta, September 24–25, 1965, illustrate the process well. The meeting was introduced by Raymond Humphreys, Director of Education and Training of the RNC. In his remarks, Humphreys referred to the recent appointment of Ray Bliss. "We have a new national chairman, a great national chairman, a man who understands the importance of bringing people together and utilizing the strength that they can contribute. He also feels that it is necessary to evaluate our progress" (WOP manual, 2). No doubt such contacts helped foster a climate receptive to innovation within state party organizations throughout this period.

Humphreys was succeeded by Dr. Thomas Brigham, Chair of the Republican State Executive Committee of Alabama, speaking on the topic of "What is Party Organization?" Brigham outlined many of the activities and publications of the Alabama state party, examples of which he had brought with him to give to the other participants. Among other items, Brigham noted that organizations should:

> Give your party leaders a feeling of importance by using *proven techniques*. I am speaking now of awards in the form of pins, or keys, or certificates. I'm wearing here a gold key which has been a very successful little gimmick to stimulate fundraising activities. *We got the idea, of course, from Texas*. We have just instituted the program in Alabama, and it is going very well (emphasis added).

The representative from Texas, Barbara Man, emphasized the importance of horizontal pathways to innovation in her talk on "Improving Organization Efficiency." Man notes that, "Following the 1964 campaign, we took a long hard look at what we were doing in Texas *plus what we have learned from our friends in other Southern states* and have introduced some new concepts . . ." (18, emphasis added).

Man stressed the need not to accept the response "that won't work here" to innovational diffusion. One of the key features of the "innovation choice" model is that it allows for inventions to be rejected by potentials innovators, often on the grounds of unsuitability. In 1979, the State Executive Committee in Arkansas invited George Despot, State Chairman of Louisiana, to be the guest speaker. Despot outlined the steps that the Republican Party had taken in Louisiana to build a strong organization, and made several suggestions for innovations that could be introduced in Arkansas (RSEC, 4/6/79). Chairman Lowe thanked Mr. Despot for his "tell it like it is" comments. At a breakfast meeting of the committee the following day (with Mr. Despot no longer present), Congressman John-Paul Hammerschidt "told the group that Louisiana politics is very different from Arkansas. He commented that Arkansas was a much more difficult state in which to build a party because Arkansans are less interested in philosophical issues" (RESC, 4/7/79).

A third example of innovation through horizontal stimuli can be seen in the exploration by the Arkansas Republican Party of internships for college students to work on party campaigns. In May 1976, the Executive Director, Bob Luther, sent out a letter to all heads of journalism and political science departments of Arkansas colleges and universities. In the letter, Luther stated that, "It was recently announced that students from Ball State University and Indiana State University will work as interns on the staff of the Indiana Republican State Headquarters. The Arkansas Republican Party is considering the adaptability of such a plan" (4/6/76). Attached to the letter is a copy of an article from an unidentified newspaper (probably the *Republican News* of Indiana, although this is not certain). As emphasized above, the innovation choice model stresses the role of social and political factors in the adoption (or nonadoption) of new processes. In this case, Luther's willingness to pursue college internships with the state GOP may have been facilitated by his background as an academic and former dean of the College of the Ozarks.

The last example that we will present also involves horizontal contact with the Indiana Republican Party. Again in 1976, we find Bob Luther writing to Thomas Milligan at the Indiana Republican State Central Committee. The purpose of this letter is to request information concerning a slide presentation that had been put together by the Indiana Republicans. Luther does not mention from where knowledge of the slide presentation came, but he writes that, "Lynn Lowe, our State Chairman, indicated to me that it has been a successful project for the Party in Indiana." Continuing, he says, "If you agree, our plans are to duplicate it. This would mean that we need some way of photographing your slides" (3/1/76). One of the implications of the innovation choice model is that leadership change often signals a change in the potential for innovation. The tandem of Lynn Lowe (State Chair) and Robert Luther (Executive Director) appear from the records we have examined to have been especially favorable to the import of innovative techniques from outside the state party organization.

Bottom-up Innovation

If we had under-estimated the importance of horizontal pathways to innovation, we also over-estimated the potential for innovation from below. Several factors may account for the lack of evidence pointing to such a process. First, the two states which we chose for the pilot study were both struggling to create viable country-level party units. The preceding discussion of the decades following the Tower victory in Texas and the Rockefeller win in Arkansas has shown that these were periods in which party-building was a "top-down" process; hence, party organization at the local level was in a position of relative weakness. As a rule, "weak" party units tend not to be exporters of inventions. Second, the nature of county parties (less professionalized, less bureaucratized) means that the *types* of inventions that they may produce are generally less adaptable to a state-wide context. Innovation at the local level is more likely to be *low-level* innovation. Third, related to the last point, even where state parties pick up innovation from local units, the party records may be much less likely to detail the process. Finally, in the light of all of the above factors, it may be necessary to review the data that we have used for this study to pick up examples of bottom-up innovation that we may have overlooked.

Those examples that we do have of bottom-up innovation strain the definitions that we have introduced. We have cases where new financial relationships were introduced between state and county parties in Arkansas in the wake of persistent criticism of the quota system in place from the counties and their perennial inability to meet these quotas. Under pressure, the State Committee first introduced a 20 percent rebate scheme for counties who met their quotas early, and then allowed counties to set their own quotas. While these mechanisms were installed by the State Committee, it must be remembered that the predominant portion of the membership of this body was composed of county leaders. We may also cite the example of the Pulaski County (the largest county in Arkansas, which includes Little Rock) organization allowing the media access to its executive committee meetings, a practice that was subsequently adopted by the State Executive Committee. However, we admit that, for the time being, we do not have much evidence of a strong stimulus from county to state level.[4]

Cases of Nondiffused Innovation

Nondiffused innovation, it will be recalled, takes place (endogenously) within the particular organizational unit under study—in this case, the state party—or (exogenously) within the immediate environment of that organizational unit. In our data search, we identified a very high number of such innovations. However, a note of caution should be inserted before we present examples. This category is residual, in the sense that any innovation for which we have not identified an external stimulus will revert to it. Without a detailed and exhaustive analysis of each case, it is likely that cases will be accorded this classification even though in reality there were external stimuli that we have failed to identify. Our present nonquantitative approach reflects our reluctance to introduce a masked error in the data before we have conducted the required analyses.

In 1970, the Arkansas Republicans introduced the GOP roster (see above) that gave a full listing of all state and county officials, as well as campaign materials available, filing dates and fees, and other information of use to party organizers in the state. In the forward, then-Executive Director Neal Sox Johnson writes that this is "an innovation for the Republican Party in this state" (4/6/70). A second example occurred in 1973 when the party decided to set up a committee to report on patronage recommendations (RSEC, 1/16/73).[5] For the next four years, we have complete records of the committee's report for each recommendation, as well as correspondence with the office to which the recommendation is addressed. A whole range of nondiffused innovations are included in a plan passed by the State Executive Committee on January 26th, 1974, entitled "A comprehensive statement of what will be done, who will do it, when it will be done, and how much it will cost in the Arkansas Republican Party." Among others, one proposed innovation is the creation of a Media Relations Committee.

Many of the organizational efforts of the Arkansas Republicans covered in the previous discussion were home-grown products, examples of non-diffused innovation. What is interesting is that there does not appear to be a trade-off between diffused and nondiffused innovation. Rather the party appears to go through periods of high levels of inventions, searching simultaneously for innovations from the outside, from other parts of the Republican party, and from its own internal groupings. In part, this is a product of the search for ways to institutionalize the party following the Rockefeller years; in part (and not unconnected to the first point) these periods of innovative activity correspond to the tenure of particular individuals. Thus the Lowe-Luther tandem may not have been solely responsible for innovatory activity within the Arkansas Republican Party in the mid-1970s, but it proved particularly favorable for the adoption of many new ideas and practices at this juncture in the party's development.

The correlation of endogenous, nondiffused innovation with periods of leadership needs to be emphasized. Two important points should be highlighted; first, some leadership combinations are demonstrably more disposed towards the search for innovation that others (e.g. the Luther-Lowe partnership in Arkansas); and second, all things being equal, leaders seem to be more likely to innovate during the initial period of their tenure than at other times. Both of these observations are in keeping with the more general assumptions about the role of leaders in influencing the rate of the diffusion of new practices, behaviors, techniques, and technologies throughout organizations that are built into our model. Although this discussion has been strictly qualitative, we are confident that a systematic coding of party records can and will enable a quantitative test of the class of hypotheses that may be derived from our framework approach. In so doing, we will contribute to the growing understanding of the ecology of party organization.

Conclusions

In the introduction of this chapter we argued that "innovation" is just one of many *types* of change that can overtake a party organizations. Innovation represents an adaptive strategy that allows an organization to survive despite changing environmental conditions. As the cases of the Texas and Arkansas Republican parties show, innovation itself comes in many forms, and can be more or less successful. Texas Republicans were able to institutionalize their innovations and forge a long-term competitive political system. Their Arkansas brethren were not so fortunate. For reasons we discuss briefly above and more extensively elsewhere (Appleton and Ward 1994), Arkansas Republican fortunes were linked so inextricably to their patron, Winthrop Rockefeller, that efforts to innovate often were unsustainable. The party did not, however, return to its previous level of futility following Rockefeller's defeat and death, and in fact succeeded in electing another governor in 1980. More recently, Republicans won two of the state's four U.S. House seats in the 1992 election and the 1993 special election for Lieutenant Governor. Although the party is still not a fully competitive force in the state, it has experienced episodes of competitiveness subsequent to the era of innovation discussed above.

It would be wrong to overstate our capacity to test models of innovation through the kind of qualitative treatment used here. However, the evidence that we have gathered has tended to indicate the determinant effects of leadership upon the capacity and willingness of parties to innovate, whether the innovation be exogenous or endogenous in origin, diffused or nondiffused. In fact, we would argue that according to our preliminary analyses, the *innovation-choice* model is superior in its ability to capture observed sequences of organizational innovation than the alternative *diffusionist* model. We would argue that party units are constantly faced with opportunities to innovate, through contacts with both the immediate and the proximate environment, with the continual reception of both intra-organizational and external stimuli. Yet clearly some parties innovate more than others, some innovate more at certain periods than others, and the success rates of innovations are variable. Our hypothesis for future research, based on this preliminary study, is that leadership is a key variable in explaining this dynamic.

One purpose of this study was to demonstrate the utility of innovation as a concept for understanding the actions taken by parties and for categorizing those actions in a coherent framework that may lead to more complete explanatory models in future work. Important questions remain to be considered, however, before such a model can be proposed. Are formally dominant parties (eg., Texas Democrats) likely to choose similar or different strategies of adaptation compared to their nascent competitors? How and why does organizational innovation emerge in stable partisan systems? Do patterns of organizational change apparent at the state level suggest parallel patterns at the local level?

A second purpose of this study has been to propose a research strategy to bring together the rich theoretical and empirical worlds of party research. By turning to new sources of data, i.e., party archives, the development of finely tuned measures of party organization necessary for sophisticated quantitative analysis may be within reach. At that time, comparative and longitudinal analyses of party change in a variety of political environments will be possible. The evidence presented here is among the first steps toward that goal. We hope that it will encourage other scholars to explore party change in the context of innovation choice and to begin the work of mining party archives for vital, but previously obscured, data on party organization.

Notes

1. Arkansas and Texas were chosen for several reasons. First, our earlier study (Appleton and Ward 1993a) focused on partisan electoral response to exogenous shocks to the system, which have been concentrated in the South most recently. In the follow-up study (Appleton and Ward 1993b) we sought cases where parties had an opportunity to respond organizationally to electoral change. Both states fit this criterion. Second, archival data were available and accessible in three of the four parties in Arkansas and Texas. Third, for practical reasons, the two states were chosen because they are closest to the home base of one of the coauthors.

2. Records of the Texas Democratic party were examined *in situ* at the State Archive in Austin, Texas, where they had been deposited. No access was permitted by the Democratic Party of Arkansas. Although the Texas Democratic records were extensive (perhaps the most rich of all three sets of records examined), we have not used examples in this chapter for the sake of symmetry and brevity.

3. The only restriction on our use of materials was on documents referring to a likely future candidate for governor.

4. In contrast, we have much evidence of the efforts of the state parties to induce innovation at the county level.

5. The need for patronage recommendations increased in particular as a result of the election of John Paul Hammerschmidt to Congress.

References

Abramowitz, Alan I., John McGlennon, and Ronald B. Rapoport. 1983. "An Analysis of State Party Activists," in Ronald B. Rapoport et al., eds., *The Life of the Parties*. Pp. 44–58. Lexington, KY: Kentucky University Press.

Abramson, Jeffrey, Arterton, F. Christopher, and Orren, Gary R. 1988. *The Electronic Commonwealth: The Impact of New Media Technologies on Democratic Politics*. New York: Basic Books.

Abramson, Paul R., John H. Aldrich, and David W. Rohde. 1994. *Change and Continuity in the 1992 Elections*. Washington, DC: CQ Press.

Adamany, David. 1984. "Political Parties in the 1980s," in Michael J. Malbin, ed., *Money and Politics in the United States: Financing Elections in the 1980's*. Pp. 70–121. Chatham, NJ: Chatham House.

Advisory Commission on Intergovernmental Relations. 1984. "State Parties in the 1980s." *Intergovernmental Perspective*. Washington, DC: Advisory Commission on Intergovernmental Relations.

———. 1986. *The Transformation of American Politics: Implications for Federalism*. Washington, DC: Advisory Commission on Intergovernmental Relations.

Alexander, Herbert E. 1992. *Financing Politics*. 4th ed. Washington, DC: CQ Press.

———, Herbert, and Monica Bauer. 1991. *Financing the 1988 Election*. Boulder, CO: Westview Press.

American Political Science Association Committee on Political Parties. 1950. "Toward a More Responsible Two-Party System." *American Political Science Review* 44:Supplement.

Anderson, Jack, and Michael Binstein. 1993. "Democrats: Playing Not to Lose." *The Washington Post* July 11.

Appleton, Andrew, and Daniel S. Ward. 1994. "Party Organizational Response to Electoral Change: Texas and Arkansas." *American Review of Politics*. Forthcoming.

———. 1993a. "Party Transformation in France and the United States: The Hierarchical Effects of System Change in Comparative Perspective." *Comparative Politics* 26:1.

———. 1993b. "The State of the Data: The State Party Archive Project." Paper presented at the 1993 Annual Meeting of the Southern Political Science Association, Washington, DC.

Arden, Caroline. 1988. *Getting the Donkey Out of the Ditch*. New York: Greenwood Press.

Atkeson, Lonna Rae, James A. McCann, Ronald B. Rapoport, and Walter J. Stone. 1994. "Citizens for Perot: Activists and Voters in the 1992 Presidential Campaign," in Stephen C. Craig, ed., *Broken Contract? Changing Relationships between Citizens and their Government in the United States*. Boulder: Westview Press.

Ayres, B. Drummond. 1992. "Man Behind Convention Emerges as Major Force." *The New York Times* July 20.

Barber, James David. 1992. *The Presidential Character*. Englewood Cliffs, NJ: Prentice Hall.

Barbour, Haley. 1993a. "RNC Chairmanship Campaign Manifesto." Republican National Committee. January.

———. 1993b. "The Barbour Plan." Washington, DC: Republican National Committee.

Bachrach, Peter. 1967. *The Theory of Democratic Elitism*. Boston: Little, Brown.

Bader, John, and Charles O. Jones. 1993. "The Republican Parties in Congress: Bicameral Differences," in Lawrence Dodd and Bruce Oppenheimer, eds., *Congress Reconsidered*. Pp. 291–314. 5th ed. Washington, DC: CQ Press.

Baer, Donald. 1992. "The Race." *U.S. News & World Report* August 31.
Baer, Denise L. 1993. "Who Has the Body? Party Institutionalization and Theories of Party Organization." *American Review of Politics* 14:1–38.
———, and David Bositis. 1988. *Elite Cadres and Party Coalitions*. Westport, CT: Greenwood Press.
———. 1993. *Politics and Linkage in a Democratic Society*. Englewood Cliffs, NJ: Prentice-Hall.
Balz, Dan. 1991. "Democrats' Perennial Rising Star Wants to Put New Face on Party." *The Washington Post* June 25.
———. 1993. "Clinton, Centrist Democrats Avoid Rift on Overhaul of Health Care." *The Washington Post* December 4.
———, and Helen Dewar. 1992. "Contrasting Shows of Support for Clinton." *The Washington Post* February 28.
Barner-Barry, Carol, and Robert Rosenwein. 1985. *Psychological Perspectives on Politics*. Englewood Cliffs, NJ: Prentice Hall.
Barnes, Fred. 1986. "Flying Nunn." *The New Republic* April 28.
Barnes, James A. 1989a. "Reinventing the RNC." *National Journal* January 14.
———. 1989b. "Ron Brown's Fast Start." *National Journal* May 5.
———. 1993a. "Regrouping." *National Journal* June 12.
———. 1993b. "Double Identity." *National Journal* November 11.
Barney, Jay. 1986. "Organizational Culture: Can It Be a Source of Sustained Competitive Advantage?" *Academy of Management Review* 11:656–65.
Beaudry, Ann and Bob Schaeffer. 1986. *Winning Local and State Elections*. New York: Free Press.
Beck, Paul Allen. 1974a. "A Socialization Theory of Partisan Realignment," in Richard G. Niemi, ed., *The Politics of Future Citizens*. Pp. 199–219. San Francisco: Josey-Bass.
———. 1974b. "Environment and Party: The Impact of Political and Demographic County Characteristics on Party Behavior." *American Political Science Review* 68:1229–44.
———, and M. Kent Jennings. 1982. "Pathways to Participation." *American Political Science Review* 76:94–108.
———, and Frank J. Sorauf. 1993. *Party Politics in America*. 7th ed. New York: Harper-Collins Publishers, Inc.
Bennett, W. Lance. 1992. *The Governing Crisis: Media, Money, and Marketing in American Elections* New York: St. Martin's Press.
Berke, Richard L. 1992. "After Party Rebuke, Brown Says Leadership is Protecting Clinton." *The New York Times* March 28.
———. 1993. "Shades of Perot: Parties go for the Grass Roots." *The New York Times* June 21.
Berkman, Michael. 1993. "Former State Legislators in the U.S. House of Representatives: Institutional and Policy Mastery." *Legislative Studies Quarterly* 18:77–101.
Bibby, John F. 1986. "Political Party Trends in 1985: The Continuing but Constrained Advance of the National Party." *Publius* 16:90.
———. 1990. "Party Organization at the State Level," in L. Sandy Maisel, ed., *The Parties Respond*. Pp. 21–40. Boulder, CO: Westview Press.
———. 1992. *Politics, Parties, and Elections in America*, 2nd ed. Chicago: Nelson-Hall.
———, James L. Gibson, Cornelius P. Cotter, and Robert J. Huckshorn. 1983. "Trends in Party Organizational Strength, 1960–1980." *International Political Science Review* 4:21–7.
———. 1994. "Party Leadership, The Bliss Model, and the Development of the Republican National Committee," in John C. Green, ed., *Politics, Professionalism, and Power*. Pp. 19–33. Lanham, MD: University Press of America.
Biersack, Robert. 1994. Introduction to Robert Biersack, Paul S. Herrnson, and Clyde Wilcox, eds., *PAC Decision Making and Strategy in Congressional Elections*. Armonk, NY: M. E. Sharpe.

———, and Paul S. Herrnson. 1994. "Helping to Put Women in Their Places--the House and the Senate: Political Parties and the 1992 Congressional Elections," in Elizabeth Adell Cook, Sue Thomas, and Clyde Wilcox, eds., *The Year of the Woman: Myth or Reality*. Pp. 61–80. Boulder, CO: Westview Press.

———, Paul Herrnson, and Clyde Wilcox. 1993. "Seeds for Success: Early Money in Congressional Elections." *Legislative Studies Quarterly* 18:535–51.

———, and Clyde Wilcox. 1990. "Financing National Campaigns: A Research Agenda." *American Politics Quarterly* 18:215–241.

Bird, Caroline. 1977. *What Women Want*. New York: Simon and Schuster.

Bledsoe, Timothy, and Susan Welch. 1987. "Patterns of Political Party Activity among U.S. Cities." *Urban Affairs Quarterly* 23:249–69.

Blumenthal, Sidney. 1990. *Pledging Allegiance: The Last Campaign of the Cold War*. New York: HarperCollins.

Bolingbroke, Henry St. John. 1982. *Contributions to the Craftsman*. Simon Versey, ed. New York: Oxford University Press.

Bone, Hugh. 1958. *Party Committees and National Politics*. Seattle: University of Washington Press.

Box-Steffensmeier, Janet M. 1993. "Candidates, Contributors, and Campaign Strategy." Ph.D. diss. University of Texas at Austin.

———, and Tse-Min Lin. 1992. "A Dynamic Model of Campaign Spending in Congressional Elections." Paper presented at the 1992 Annual Meeting of the Political Methodology Society, Cambridge, MA.

Brady, David W. 1990. "Coalitions in the U.S. Congress," in L. Sandy Maisel, ed., *The Parties Respond: Changes in the American Party System*. Pp. 249–66. Boulder, CO: Westview Press.

———, Joseph Cooper, and Patricia A. Hurley. 1979. "The Decline of Party in the U.S. House of Representatives, 1887-1968." *Legislative Studies Quarterly* 4:381-407.

Bridges, Amy. 1986. "Becoming American: The Working Classes in the United States before the Civil War," in Ira Katznelson and Aristide R. Zolberg, eds., *Working-Class Formation*. Pp. 157–96. Princeton: Princeton University Press.

Broder, David S. 1971. *The Party's Over: The Failure of American Parties*. New York: Harper and Row.

———. 1992. "The Decline of Jesse Jackson." *The Washington Post* July 14.

———. 1993. "Politics Without Parties." *The Washington Post* January 5.

Brown, M. Craig, and Charles N. Halaby. 1987. "Machine Politics in America, 1870–1945." *Journal of Interdisciplinary History* 17:587–612.

Brown, Lynne, and Robert Peabody. 1987. "Patterns of Succession in House Democratic Leadership: The Choices of Wright, Foley, Coelho, 1986." Paper presented at the Annual Meeting of the American Political Science Association, Chicago.

Buell, Emmett H., Jr. 1986. "Divisive Primaries and Participation in Fall Presidential Campaigns: A Study of 1984 New Hampshire Primary Activists." *American Politics Quarterly* 14:376-390.

Burnham, Walter Dean. 1970. *Critical Elections and the Mainsprings of American Politics*. New York: Norton.

———. 1982. *The Current Crisis in American Politics*. New York: Oxford University Press.

———. 1989. "The Reagan Heritage," in Gerald M. Pomper, ed., *The Election of 1988*. Pp. 1–32. Chatham, NJ: Chatham House.

Burrell, Barbara. 1993. "John Bailey's Legacy: Political Parties and Women's Candidacies for Public Office," in Lois Duke Lovelace, ed., *Women in Politics*. Pp. 123–34. Englewood Cliffs, NJ: Prentice Hall.

———. 1994. *A Woman's Place Is in the House: Campaigning for Congress in the Feminist Era.* Ann Arbor: University of Michigan Press.
Calhoun, Jim. 1993. "OKI Plan Rapped." *Cincinnati Enquirer* September 15.
Caldeira, Gregory A., Aage R. Clausen, and Samuel C. Patterson. 1990. "Partisan Mobilization and Electoral Participation." *Electoral Studies* 9:191-204.
———, Samuel C. Patterson, and Gregory A. Markus. 1985. "The Mobilization of Voters in Congressional Elections." *Journal of Politics* 47:490-509.
Canfield, James Lewis. 1984. *A Case of Third Party Activism: The George Wallace Campaign Worker and the American Independent Party.* Lanham, MD: University Press of America.
Canon, David. 1989. "The Institutionalization of Leadership in the U.S. Congress." *Legislative Studies Quarterly* 14:415-43.
Carlson, Jody. 1981. *George C. Wallace and the Politics of Powerlessness.* New Brunswick, NJ: Transaction Books.
Ceasar, James. 1982. *Reforming the Reforms.* Cambridge, MA: Ballinger.
———, and Andrew Busch. 1993. *Upside Down and Inside Out: The 1992 Elections and American Politics.* Lanham, MD: Rowman and Littlefield.
Center for Party Development. 1993. *Former Members of Congress View the Role of Political Parties in the U.S. Congress.* Washington, DC: Center for Party Development.
Chafe, William. 1972. *The American Woman: Her Changing Social, Economic, and Political Roles, 1920-1970.* New York: Oxford University Press.
Charter Committee. 1988. "Draft 4/88." Mimeo: Charter Committee of Greater Cincinnati.
Charter Research Institute. 1991. *Queen City Almanac: A Practical Guide to Cincinnati Government and Services.* Cincinnati, OH: Charter Research Institute.
Cheney, Richard B. 1980. "The Law's Impact on Presidential and Congressional Election Campaigns," in Michael J. Malbin, ed., *Parties, Interest Groups, and Campaign Finance Laws.* Pp. 238-248. Washington, DC: American Enterprise Institute.
Cincinnati Enquirer. 1993. "Queen City at a Crossroads," an eight part series, July 25-August 1.
Clubb, Jerome M., and Santa A. Traugott. 1977. "Partisan Cleavage and Cohesion in the House of Representatives, 1861-1974." *Journal of Interdisciplinary History* 7:375-401.
Cohen, Richard. 1986. "Democratic Leadership Council Sees Party Void and Is Ready to Fill It." *National Journal* February 1.
Cole, Richard L. 1974. "The Urban Policy Process: A Note on Structural and Regional Influences," in Samuel A. Kirkpatrick ed., *Quantitative Analysis of Political Data.* Columbus, OH: Charles E. Merrill.
Coleman, John J. 1993. "Constraints on Party Responses to Recession: The Role of the State and Policy." Paper presented at the Annual Meeting of the American Political Science Association, Washington, DC.
———. 1994. "State Formation and the Decline of Political Parties: American Parties in the Fiscal State." *Studies in American Political Development.* New Haven: Yale University press. Forthcoming.
Collie, Melissa P., and David W. Brady. 1985. "The Decline of Partisan Voting Coalitions in the House of Representatives," in Lawrence C. Dodd and Bruce I. Oppenheimer, eds., *Congress Reconsidered.* 3rd ed. Pp. 272-87. Washington, DC: CQ Press.
Committee on Party Effectiveness. 1982. *Rebuilding the Road to Opportunity: A Democratic Direction for the 1980s.* Washington, DC: Government Printing Office.
Congressional Quarterly Weekly Report. 1992. "Democratic Endorsements." 50:485.
Converse, Philip E., Warren E. Miller, Jerrold G. Rusk, and Arthur C. Wolfe. 1989. "Continuity and Change in American Politics: Parties and Issues in the 1968 Election." *American Political Science Review* 63:1083-105.

Conway, M. Margaret. 1983. "Republican Political Party Nationalization, Campaign Activities, and Their Implications for the Political System." *Publius* 13:1-17.
Cooper, Joseph, and Patricia Hurley. 1977. "The Electoral Basis of Party Voting: Patterns and Trends in the U.S. House of Representatives, 1887-1969," in Louis Maisel and Joseph Cooper, eds., *The Impact of the Electoral Process*. Pp. 133-65. Beverly Hills, CA: Sage Publications.
Costain, Anne, and W. Douglas Costain. 1987. "Strategy and Tactics of the Women's Movement in the United States: The Role of Political Parties," in Mary Katzenstein and Carol McClurg Mueller, eds., *The Women's Movements of the United States and Western Europe*. Pp. 196-214. Philadelphia: Temple University Press.
Cook, Rhodes. 1991. "Cuomo Says 'No' to Candidacy at Last Possible Moment." *Congressional Quarterly Weekly Report* 49:3734-36.
———. 1992. "Candidate Field Shapes Up as Primaries Approach." *Congressional Quarterly Weekly Report* 50:28.
———. 1993. "DNC Under Wilhelm: Seeking a New Role." *Congressional Quarterly Weekly Report* 50:939.
Corrado, Anthony. 1991. "Party Rules Reform and Candidate Nomination Strategies: Consequences for the 1990s." Presented at the annual meeting of the American Political Science Association, Washington, DC.
———. 1993. *Paying for Presidents*. New York: Twentieth Century Fund Press.
Cornelius P., and John F. Bibby. 1980. "Institutional Development of the Parties and the Thesis of Party Decline." *Political Science Quarterly* 95:1-27
———, James L. Gibson, John F. Bibby, and Robert J. Huckshorn. 1984. *Party Organizations in American Politics*. New York: Praeger.
———, and Bernard C. Hennessey. 1964. *Politics Without Power: The National Party Committees*. New York: Atherton Press.
Crotty, William J. 1971. "Party Effort and Its Impact on the Vote. *American Political Science Review* 65:439-50.
———. 1978. *Decision for the Democrats*. Baltimore: Johns Hopkins University Press.
———. 1983. *Party Reform*. New York: Longman.
———. 1984. *American Parties in Decline*. Boston: Little, Brown.
———, ed. 1986. *Political Parties in Local Areas*. Knoxville, TN: University of Tennessee Press.
———. 1991a. "Urban Political Machines," in L. Sandy Maisel, ed., *Political Parties & Elections in the United States: An Encyclopedia*. Vol. 2. Pp. 1154-163. New York: Garland Press.
———. 1991b. "Political Parties: Issues and Trends," in William Crotty, ed., *Political Science: Looking to the Future*. Vol. 4. Pp. 137-201. Evanston, IL: Northwestern University Press.
Cutler, Lynn. 1993." Comments," in Michael Margolis and John C. Green eds., *Machine Politics, Sound Bites and Nostalgia: On Studying Political Parties*. Pp. 52-54. Lanham, Md: University Press of America.
Cutright, Phillips. 1963. "Measuring the Impact of Local Party Activity on the General Election Vote." *Public Opinion Quarterly* 27:372-86.
———. 1964. "Activities of Precinct Committeemen in Partisan and Non-Partisan Communities." *Western Political Quarterly* 17:93-108.
Cutright, Phillips, and Peter Rossi. 1958. "Grass Roots Politicians and the Vote." *American Sociological Review* 63:171-179.
Dahl, Robert A. 1967. "The City in the Future of Democracy." *American Political Science Review* 61:953-70.
Daley, Steve. 1991a. "Democratic Chief Sets Up Meeting Between Donors, '92 Hopefuls." *The Chicago Tribune* May 18.
———. 1991b. "Democrats Plan Early, United Fight for '92." *The Chicago Tribune* June 14.
Davidson, Roger, ed. 1992. *The Post Reform Congress*. New York: St. Martin's.

Davis, James W. 1983. *National Conventions in an Age of Party Reform*. Westport, CT: Greenwood Press.
———. 1992. *The President as Party Leader*. New York: Praeger.
Democratic Congressional Campaign Committee. 1992. DCCC Mid-Year Report. Washington, DC: Democratic Congressional Campaign Committee.
Democratic Leadership Council. 1988. "The Democratic Leadership Council. Pamphlet.
———. 1990. "The New Orleans Declaration." Pamphlet.
———. 1991a. "Convention Program." Pamphlet.
———. 1991b. "The New Choice Resolutions." Mimeo.
———. 1992. "The New Choice: Draft for a Democratic Platform." Mimeo.
Dennis, Jack. 1988. "Political Independence in the United States." *British Journal of Political Science* 18:77–110.
Dillin, John. 1991. "Democrats Unite to Map Presidential Strategy." *Christian Science Monitor* May 21.
Dionne, E. J., Jr. 1991. *Why Americans Hate Politics*. New York: Simon and Schuster.
———. 1993. "The Politics of Nastiness." *The Washington Post* July 22.
———, and Ann Devroy. 1992. "Bush-Buchanan Clash Could Soften in Tone." *The Washington Post* March 15.
Dole, Robert. 1992. "Is America Ignoring GOP Women?" *The Washington Post* May 31.
Dorsey, Robert W. 1993. "The Last True Government." *Cincinnati Magazine* August.
Downs, Anthony. 1957. *An Economic Theory of Democracy*. New York: Harper and Row.
Duffy, Michael, and Dan Goodgame. 1992. *Marching in Place: The Status Quo Presidency of George Bush*. New York: Simon and Schuster.
Duverger, Maurice. 1954. *Political Parties*. New York: Wiley.
Drew, Elizabeth. 1983. *Politics and Money: The New Road to Corruption*. New York: Macmillan.
———. 1993. "Watch Them Squirm." *The New York Times Magazine* March 14.
Dwyre, Diana. 1992. "Is Winning Everything? Party Strategies for the U.S. House of Representatives." Presented at the annual meeting of the American Political Science Association, Chicago.
———. 1993. "The Complete Congressional Party, Governing and Electing: The Congressional Campaign Committees and Responsible Party Government During Realignments." Paper presented at the annual meeting of the American Political Science Association, Washington, DC.
———, and Jeffrey M. Stonecash. 1992. "Where's the Party? Changing State Party Organizations." *American Politics Quarterly* 20:326–44.
Easterbrook, Gregg. 1986. "The Business of Politics." *The Atlantic Monthly* October.
Edelman, Murray. 1964. *The Symbolic Uses of Politics*. Urbana:University of Illinois Press.
———. 1971. *Politics and Symbolic Action: Mass Arousal and Quiescence*. New York: Academic Press.
Elder, Charles D., and Roger W. Cobb. 1983. *The Political Uses of Symbols*. New York: Longman.
Edsall, Thomas Byrne. 1984. *The New Politics of Inequality*. New York: Norton.
——— with Mary Edsall. 1991. *Chain Reaction*. Boston: Norton.
———, and Maralee Schwartz. 1989. "For Democrat Brown, Warmth Turns to Chills." *The Washington Post* March 12.
———, and Dan Balz. 1991. "DNC Poised to Play Role in Late-Starting Campaign." *The Washington Post* September 23.
Ehrenhalt, Alan. 1991. *The United States of Ambition*. New York: Random House.
Eismeier, Theodore J. and Phillip Pollock. 1986. "Strategy and Choice in Congressional Elections: The Role of Political Action Committees. *American Journal of Political Science* 30:197–213.

Eldersveld, Samuel J. 1956. "Experimental Propaganda Techniques and Voting Behavior." *American Political Science Review* 50:154–165.

———. 1964. *Political Parties: A Behavioral Analysis*. Chicago: Rand McNally.

Elving, Ronald. 1988. "Debating Length, Language, Democrats Ponder Platform." *Congressional Quarterly Weekly Report* 46:1583–4.

Elazar, Daniel J. 1984. *American Federalism: A View from the States*. New York: Harper and Row.

Epstein, Leon D. 1980. "Whatever Happened to the British Party Model?" *American Political Science Review* 54:406–27.

———. 1986. *Political Parties in the American Mold*. Madison: University of Wisconsin Press.

———. 1989. "Will American Political Parties Be Privatized?" *Journal of Law and Politics* 5:239.

Federal Election Commission. 1980–1988. *Reports on Financial Activity*. Washington, DC: Federal Election Commission.

Federal Election Commission. 1992a. "Spending Jumped to $504 Million by '92 Congressional Candidates: FEC Finds Spending in House Races Grew 41 Percent." Press Release. December 30.

———. 1992b. *Federal Elections 92: Election Results for the U.S. President, the U.S. Senate and the U.S. House of Representatives*. Washington, DC: Federal Election Commission.

———. 1993a. "1992 Congressional Spending Jumps 52 percent to $678 Million." Press Release. March 4.

———. 1993b. "Democrats Narrow Financial Gap in 1991-92." Press Release. March 11.

Feit, Rona. 1979. "Organizing for Political Power: The National Women's Political Caucus," in Bernice Cummings and Victoria Schuck eds., *Women Organizing*. Pp. 184–208. Metuchen, NJ: The Scarecrow Press, Inc.

Fenno, Richard. 1973. *Congressmen in Committees*. Boston: Little Brown.

———. 1975. "If, as Ralph Nader says, Congress is 'the Broken Branch,' How Come We Love or Congressmen so Much?," in Norman J. Ornstein, ed., *Congress in Change: Evolution and Reform*. Pp. 277-87. New York: Praeger Publishers.

———. 1978. *Home Style*. Boston: Little, Brown.

Ferguson, Thomas, and Joel Rogers. 1986. *Right Turn: The Decline of the Democrats and the Future of American Politics*. New York: Hill and Wang.

Fiorina, Morris P. 1980. "The Decline of Collective Responsibility in American Politics." *Daedalus* 109:25–45.

———. 1987. "Party Government in the United States: Diagnosis and Prognosis," in Richard S. Katz, ed., *Party Governments: European and American Experiences*. Pp. 270–300. New York: Walter de Gruyter.

———. 1990. "The Electorate in the Voting Booth," in L. Sandy Maisel, ed., *The Parties Respond: Changes in the American Party System*. Pp. 116–36. Boulder, CO: Westview Press.

———. 1994. "Is Divided Government in the American Sates a Byproduct of Legislative Professionalism?" *American Political Science Review* 88:304–16.

Firth, Raymond. 1973. *Symbols: Public and Private*. Ithaca: Cornell University Press.

Fishman, Robert. 1992. "Megalopolis Unbound: America's New City," in *The Best of the Wilson Quarterly*. Pp. 9–25. Washington, D.C.: Woodrow Wilson International Center.

Frankovic, Kathleen A. 1993. "Public Opinion in the 1992 Campaign," in Gerald M. Pomper, ed., *The Elections of 1992*. Pp. 74–109. Chatham, NJ: Chatham House.

Frantzich, Stephen E. 1989. *Political Parties in the Technological Age*. New York: Longman.

Freeman, Jo. 1986. "The Political Culture of Democratic and Republican Parties." *Political Science Quarterly* 101:327–56.

———. 1987. "Whom You Know versus Whom You Represent: Feminist Influence in the Democratic and Republican Parties," in Mary Katzenstein and Carol McClurg Mueller eds., *The Women's Movements of the United States and Western Europe*. Pp. 215–44. Philadelphia: Temple University Press.

———. 1988. "Women at the 1988 Democratic Convention." *PS* 21:875–81.

———. 1988. "Feminist Activities at the 1988 Republican Convention." *PS* 22:39–46.

———. 1993. "Feminism vs. Family Values: Women at the 1992 Democratic and Republican Conventions." *PS* 26:21–27.

Frendreis, John P., James L. Gibson, and Laura L. Vertz. 1990. "The Electoral Relevance of Local Party Organizations." *American Political Science Review* 84:226–35.

———, and Alan R. Gitelson. 1993. "Local Parties in an Age of Change." *American Review of Politics* 14:533–547.

———, Alan R. Gitelson, Gregory Flemming, and Anne Layzell. 1993. "Local Political Parties and the 1992 Campaign for the State Legislature." Paper presented at the annual meeting of the American Political Science Association, Washington, DC.

Frisby, Michael K. 1992. "A Spending Problem for the GOP." *The Boston Globe* November 2.

From, Al and Will Marshall. 1993a. "The First 100 Days." *The New Democrat* May.

———. 1993b. "The Road to Realignment: Democrats and the Perot Voters. Pamphlet.

Gailey, Phil. 1985. "Dissidents Defy Top Democrats; Council Formed." *The New York Times* March 1.

Galston, William, and Elaine Kamarck. 1989. *The Politics of Evasion: Democrats and the Presidency*. Washington, DC: Progressive Policy Institute.

Garand, James, and Kathleen Clayton. 1986. "Socialization to Partisanship in the U.S. House: The Speaker's Task Force." *Legislative Studies Quarterly* 11:409–28.

Germond, Jack W., and Jules Witcover. 1985. *Wake Us When It's Over*. New York: Macmillan.

———. 1993. *Mad as Hell: Revolt at the Ballot Box, 1992*. New York: Warner Books.

Gibson, James L., Cornelius P. Cotter, John F. Bibby, and Robert J. Huckshorn. 1983. "Assessing Party Organizational Strength." *American Journal of Political Science* 27:193–222.

———., Cornelius P. Cotter, John F. Bibby, and Robert J. Huckshorn. 1985. "Whither the Local Parties? A Cross-Sectional and Longitudinal Analysis of the Strength of Party Organizations." *American Journal of Political Science* 29:139–60

———., John P. Frendreis, and Laura L. Vertz. 1989. "Party Dynamics in the 1980s: Change in County Party Organizational Strength, 1980–1984." *American Journal of Political Science* 33:67–90.

———, and Susan E. Scarrow. 1993. "State and Local Party Organizations in American Politics," in Eric M. Uslaner, ed., *American Political Parties*. Pp. 232–262. Itasca,IL: Peacock.

———, and Gregg Smith. 1984. "Local Party Organizations and Electoral Outcomes: Linkages Between Parties and Elections." Paper presented at the annual meeting of the American Political Science Association, Washington, DC.

Gierzynski, Anthony. 1992. *Legislative Party Campaign Committees in The American States*. Lexington, KY: University Press of Kentucky.

———, and David Breaux. 1991. "Money and Votes in State Legislative Elections." *Legislative Studies Quarterly* 16:203–17.

Giles, Michael W., and Anita Pritchard. 1985. "Campaign Expenditures and Legislative Elections in Florida." *Legislative Studies Quarterly* 10:71-88.

Gillespie, J. David. 1993. *Politics at the Periphery: Third Parties in Two-Party America*. Columbia: University of South Carolina Press.

Ginsberg, Benjamin. 1986. *The Captive Public: How Mass Opinion Promotes State Power*. New York: Basic Books.

References

Gitelson, Alan R., M. Margaret Conway, and Frank B. Feigert. 1984. *American Political Parties: Stability and Change*. Boston: Houghton Mifflin.
Goldenberg, Edie N., and Michael W. Traugott. 1984. *Campaigning for Congress*. Washington, DC: CQ Press.
Goldman, Ralph M. 1990. *From Warfare to Party Politics*. Syracuse: Syracuse University Press.
Goldman, Peter, and Tom Mathews. 1992a. "How He Won." *Newsweek Special Election Issue* November/December. New York: M. Evans Co.
———. 1992b. "America Changes the Guard." *Newsweek Special Election Edition.* November/December.
Goldstein, Joshua. 1991. *The $43 Million Loophole: Soft Money in the 1990 Congressional Elections*. Washington, DC: Center for Responsive Politics.
Goodwyn, Lawrence. 1978. *The Populist Moment*. New York: Oxford University Press.
Green, Donald, and Jonathan Krasno. 1988. "Salvation for the Spendthrift Incumbent: Reestimating the Effects of Campaign Spending in House Elections." *American Journal of Political Science* 32:884–907.
———. 1990. "Rebuttal to Jacobson's 'New Evidence for Old Arguments.'" *American Journal of Political Science* 34:363–72.
Green, Donald P., James Robins, and Jonathan Krasno. 1991. "Using Polls to Estimate the Effects of Campaign Spending by U.S. House Incumbents." Paper presented at the 1991 Annual Meeting of the American Political Science Association, Washington, DC.
Gross, Bertram M. 1980. *Friendly Fascism: The New Face of Power in America*. New York: M. Evans Co.
Grove, Lloyd. 1992. "Lobbyists Thermidor." *The Washington Post* December 9.
———. 1994. "Man on a Tightrope." *The Washington Post* April 20.
Grumm, John G. 1970. "Structural Determinants of Legislative Output," in Allan Kornberg and Lloyd Musolf, eds., *Legislatures in Developmental Perspective*. Durham, NC: Duke University Press.
Hale, Jon F. 1993. "Shaping the Conventional Wisdom." *Political Communication*. Fall:285–302.
Hammer, Michael, and James Champy. 1993. *Reengineering the Corporation: A Manifesto for Business Revolution*. New York: Harper Business.
Hames, Tim. 1994. "Strengths and Limitations: The Republican Committee From Bliss to Brock to Barbour," in John C. Green, ed., *Politics, Professionalism and Power*. Pp. 149–66. Lanham: University Press of America.
Hamilton, Alexander. 1851. "Letter to Bayard, April 1802," in John C. Hamilton, ed., *The Works of Alexander Hamilton*. Vol. 6. Pp. 540–43. New York: John F. Trow.
Hargrove, Erwin, and Michael Nelson. 1983. *Presidents, Politics, and Policy*. New York: Knopf.
Harmel, Robert, and Kenneth Janda. 1992. "An Integrated Theory of Party Goals and Party Change." Paper prepared for the 1992 annual meeting of the American Political Science Association, Chicago.
———. 1993. "Leadership, Factions, and Change in Party Organizations and Identity." Paper presented at the 1993 annual meeting of the American Political Science Association, Washington DC.
Heatherly, Charles, ed. 1981. *Mandate for Leadership*. Washington, DC: The Heritage Foundation.
Herson, Lawrence J.R., and Boland, John. M. 1990. *The Urban Web: Politics, Policy and Theory*. Chicago: Nelson-Hall.
Herring, E. Pendleton. 1940. *The Politics of Democracy: American Parties in Action*. New York: Norton.
Herrnson, Paul S. 1986. "Do Parties Make a Difference? The Role of Party Organizations in Congressional Elections." *Journal of Politics* 48:589–615.
———. 1988. *Party Campaigning in the 1980s*. Cambridge: Harvard University Press.

———. 1989. "National Party Decision Making, Strategies, and Resource Distribution in Congressional Elections." *Western Political Quarterly* 42:301-23.
———. 1990. "Reemergent National Party Organizations," in L. Sandy Maisel, ed., *The Parties Respond: Changes in the American Party System.* Pp. 41–66. Boulder, CO: Westview Press.
———. 1992. "National Party Organizations and the Postreform Congress," in Roger H. Davidson, ed., *The Postreform Congress.* Pp. 48–70. New York: St. Martin's Press.
———. 1993. "Political Parties and Congressional Elections: Out of the Eighties and Into the Nineties," in Michael Margolis and John C. Green, eds., *Machine Politics, Sound Bites, and Nostalgia: On Studying Political Parties.* Pp. 7–19. Lanham, MD: University Press of America.
———. 1994a. "The Revitalization of National Party Organizations," in L. Sandy Maisel, ed., *The Parties Respond.* 2nd ed. Pp. 45–68. Boulder, CO: Westview Press.
———. 1994b. "The National Committee for an Effective Congress: Ideology, Partisanship, and Electoral Innovation," in Robert Biersack, Paul S. Herrnson, and Clyde Wilcox, eds., *PAC Decision Making and Strategy in Congressional Elections.* Armonk, NY: M. E. Sharpe.
———. Forthcoming. *Congressional Elections: Campaigning at Home and in Washington.* Washington DC: CQ Press.
———, and David Menefee-Libey. 1990. "The Dynamics of Party Organizational Development." *Midsouth Political Science Journal* 11:3-30.
Hershey, Marjorie Randon. 1989. *Running for Office.* Chatham, NJ: Chatham House.
Hess, Robert D., and Judith V. Torney. 1967. *The Development of Political Attitudes in Children.* Chicago: Aldine.
Hewitt, Don. 1992. "How About We Chuck the Parties?" *The Washington Post* November 12.
Hibbling, John. 1991. *Congressional Careers.* Chapel Hill: University of North Carolina Press.
Huckfeldt, Robert, and John Sprague. 1992. "Political Parties and Electoral Mobilization: Political Structure, Social Structure, and the Party Canvass." *American Political Science Review* 86:70–86.
Huckshorn, Robert J. 1976. *Party Leadership in the States.* Amherst: University of Massachusetts Press.
———, James L. Gibson, Cornelius P. Cotter, and John F. Bibby. 1986. "Party Integration and Party Organizational Strength." *Journal of Politics* 48:976-91.
Huitt, Ralph K. 1990. "Democratic Party Leadership in the U. S. Senate," in R. Huitt, ed., *Working Within the System.* Berkeley, CA: Institute of Governmental Studies Press.
Ifill, Gwen. 1992a. "At Jackson's Behest, Clinton Kicks Off Voter Drive." *The New York Times* September 13.
———. 1992b. "Keeper of Democratic Flame Applies Heat as Necessary." *The New York Times* April 19.
Isikoff, Michael. 1992. "Democrats Hire Firms to Investigate Bush." *The Washington Post* July 2.
Jackson, Brooks. 1988. *Honest Graft.* New York: Knopf.
Jackson, John S. 1992. "The Party-as-Organization: Party elites and Party Reforms in Presidential Nominations and Conventions," in John Kenneth White and Jerome M. Mileur, eds., *Challengers to Party Government.* Pp. 63–83. Carbondale: Southern Illinois University Press.
Jacobson, Gary C. 1980. *Money in Congressional Elections.* New Haven: Yale University Press.
———. 1985-1986. "Party Organization and Campaign Resources in 1982." *Political Science Quarterly* 100:604-25.
———. 1985. "The Republican Advantage in Campaign Finance," in John Chubb and Paul Peterson, eds., *The New Direction in American Politics.* Pp. 143–73. Washington, DC: Brookings Institution.
———. 1990. *The Electoral Origins of Divided Government.* Boulder: Westview Press.

———. 1992. *The Politics of Congressional Elections*. New York: HarperCollins.
———. 1993. "The Misallocation of Resources in House Campaigns," in Lawrence Dodd and Bruce Oppenheimer eds. *Congress Reconsidered*. 5th ed. Pp. 115–39. Washington, DC: CQ Press.
———, and Samuel Kernell. 1983. *Strategy and Choice in Congressional Elections*. New Haven: Yale University Press.
Jehl, Douglas. 1992. "Buchanan Seeks GOP Chairman's Ouster." *The Los Angeles Times* March 11.
Jewell, Malcolm E. 1986. "A Survey of Campaign Fund Raising by Legislative Parties." *Comparative State Politics Newsletter* 7:9–13.
———, and David Olson. 1988. *Political Parties and Elections in American States*. 3rd ed. Chicago: Dorsey Press.
Johnson, Richard R. 1987. "Partisan Legislative Campaign Committees: New Power, New Problems." *Illinois Issues* July:16–8.
Johnston, Michael. 1979. "Patrons and Clients, Jobs and Machines: A Case Study of the Uses of Patronage." *American Political Science Review* 73:385–98.
Jones, Charles O. 1970. *The Minority Party in Congress*. Boston: Little, Brown.
Kamarck, Elaine Ciulla. 1990. "Structure as Strategy: Presidential Nominating Politics in the Post-Reform Era," in L. Sandy Maisel, ed., *The Parties Respond*. Pp. 160–86. Boulder, CO: Westview Press.
Katz, Daniel, and Samuel Eldersveld. 1961. "The Impact of Local Party Activity upon the Electorate." *Public Opinion Quarterly* 25:1–24.
Kayden, Xandra, and Eddie Mahe, Jr. 1985. *The Party Goes On*. New York: Basic Books.
Kazee, Thomas A., and Mary C. Thornberry. 1990. "Where's the Party? Congressional Candidate Recruitment and American Party Organizations." *Western Political Quarterly* 43:61–80.
Keith, Bruce E., David B. Magleby, Candice J. Nelson, Elizabeth Orr, Mark C. Westyle, and Raymond E. Wolfinger. 1992. *The Myth of the Independent Voter*. Berkeley: University of California Press.
Kelly, Michael. 1992. "The Making of a First Family: A Blueprint." *The New York Times* November 14.
Kesaris, Paul L., ed. 1987. *Papers of the Republican Party, Part I: Meetings of the Republican National Committee, 1911–1980; Series B: 1960–1980*. Frederick, MD: University Publications of America.
Key, V. O., Jr. 1947. *Politics, Parties, and Pressure Groups*. New York: Thomas Y. Crowell Company.
———. 1955. "A Theory of Critical Elections." *Journal of Politics* 18:3–18.
———. 1956. *American State Politics: An Introduction*. New York: Knopf.
Kirkpatrick, Jeane J. 1979. *Dismantling the Parties*. Washington, DC: American Enterprise Institute.
Klinkner, Philip A. 1992. "The Response of Political Parties to Presidential Election Defeats: A Study in Organizational Culture." Ph.D. diss. Yale University.
———. 1994. *The Losing Parties: Out-Party National Committees, 1956–1993* New Haven: Yale University Press.
Kondratieff, Nikolai. 1984. *The Long Wave Cycle*. New York: Richardson and Snyder.
Kosova, Weston. 1994. "Party Pooper." *The New Republic* June 20.
Knaggs, John R. 1986. *Two-Party Texas*. 2nd ed. New York: Oxford University Press.
Kramer, Gerald. 1971. "The Effects of Precinct-level Canvassing on Voter Behavior." *Public Opinion Quarterly* 34:560–72.
Kurtz, Karl T. 1992. "The 1992 State Legislative Elections in Perspective." *APSA Legislative Studies Section Newsletter* 16:10–14.

Labaton, Stephen. 1992. "Despite Economy, Clinton Sets Record for Funds." *The New York Times* October 24.
Ladd, Everett Carl. 1991. "On the Uselessness of 'Realignment' for Understanding Changes in American Politics," in Byron E. Shafer, ed., *The End of Realignment?* Pp. 24-36. Madison, WI: University of Wisconsin Press.
Lambrecht, William. 1994. "It Is the Future: GOP Marshals 3 New Television Ventures." *The St. Louis Post-Dispatch* January 30.
Lambro, Donald. 1994. "President's Team on the Lookout for Potential Primary Challengers." *The Washington Times* May 10.
Lamis, Alexander P. 1990. *The Two-Party South.* New York: Oxford University Press.
Lawson, Kay. 1980. "Political Parties and Linkage," in Kay Lawson, ed., *Political Parties and Linkage: A Comparative Perspective.* Pp. 3-24. New Haven: Yale University Press.
―――. 1987."How State Laws Undermine Parties," in A. James Reichley, ed., *Elections American Style.* Pp. 240-260. Washington, DC: Brookings.
―――, and Peter Merkl. 1989. *When Parties Fail.* Princeton, NJ: Princeton University Press.
―――, Gerald Pomper, and Maureen Moakley. 1986. "Local Party Activists and Electoral Linkage: Middlesex County, NJ." *American Politics Quarterly* 14:345-75.
Leyden, Kevin M. and Stephen A. Borrelli. 1990. "Party Contributions and Party Unity: Can Loyalty Be Bought?" *Western Political Quarterly* 43:343-65.
Lipset, Seymour Martin, and William Schneider. 1987. "The Confidence Gap during the Reagan Years, 1981-1987." *Political Science Quarterly* 102:1-23.
Little, Thomas H., and Samuel C. Patterson. 1993. "The Organizational Life of the Congressional Parties." *American Review of Politics* 14:39-70.
Loftus, Tom. 1985. "The New 'Political Parties' in State Legislatures." *State Government* 58:108.
Longley, Lawrence D. 1992. "The Institutionalization of the National Democratic Party: A Process Stymied, Then Revitalized." *Wisconsin Political Scientist* 7:9-15.
Loomis, Burdett. 1984. "Congressional Careers and Party Leadership in the Contemporary House of Representatives." *American Journal of Political Science* 28:180-202.
―――. 1982. "Congressional Caucuses and the Politics of Representation," in Lawrence C. Dodd and Bruce I. Oppenheimer, eds., *Congress Reconsidered.* 2nd ed. Washington, DC: CQ Press.
―――. 1988. *The New American Politician.* New York: Basic Books.
Lowi, Theodore J. 1975. "Party, Policy, and Constitution in America," in William N. Chambers and Walter Dean Burnham, eds., *The American Party Systems: Stages of Political Development.* 2nd ed. Pp. 238-76. New York: Oxford University Press.
―――. 1979. *The End of Liberalism.* 2nd. ed. New York: Norton.
―――. 1992a. "The Party Crasher." *The New York Times Magazine* August 2-3.
―――. 1992b. "The Time is Ripe for teh Creation of a Genuine Three-Party System." *The Chronicle of Higher Education.* December 16.
―――. 1994. "It Is Time for a Third Major Party in America," in Gary L. Rose, ed., *Controversial Issues in Presidential Selection.* Albany: State University of New York Press.
Lugar, Richard. 1983. "A Plan to Elect More GOP Women." *The Washington Post* August 21.
Maisel, L Sandy. 1992. "Quality Candidates in House and Senate Elections from 1982 to 1990," in Allen D. Hertzke and Ronald M. Peters, Jr., eds., *The Atomistic Congress.* Pp. 141-71. Armonk, NY: M. E. Sharpe.
―――. 1994. "The Platform-Writing Process: Candidate-Centered Platforms in 1992." *Political Science Quarterly* 108:671-98.
―――, Linda L. Fowler, Ruth S. Jones, and Walter J. Stone. 1990. "The Naming of Candidates: Recruitment or Emergence?," in L. Sandy Maisel, ed., *The Parties Respond: Changes in the American Party System.* Pp. 137-59. Boulder, CO: Westview Press.
March, James G, and Herbert Simon. 1959. *Organizations.* New York: Wiley.

——, and Johan P. Olsen. 1984. "The New Institutionalism: Organizational Factors in Political Life." *American Political Science Review* 78:334–49.

——, and Johan P. Olsen. 1989. *Rediscovering Institutions: The Organizational Basis of Politics.* New York: Free Press.

Margolis, Michael, and John C. Green, eds. 1992. *Machine Politics, Sound Bites, and Nostalgia.* Lanham, MD: University Press of America.

——. 1993. "The Importance of Local Parties for Democratic Governance," in Michael Margolis and John C. Green, eds., *Machine Politics, Sound Bites, and Nostalgia.* Pp. 29–37. Lanham, MD: University Press of America.

——, Burtt, Robert, and McLaughlin, Jeffrey. 1986. "The Impact of Industrial Decline: Braddock, North Braddock, and Rankin," in Jim Cunningham and Pamela Martz, eds., *Steel People: Survival and Resilience in Pittsburgh's Mon Valley.* Pp. 9–32. Pittsburgh: River Communities Project, University of Pittsburgh, School of Social Work.

——, and Raymond E. Owen. 1985. "From Organization to Personalism: A Note on the Transmogrification of the Local Party Organization." *Polity* 18:313–28.

Marshall, Will, and Martin Schram, eds. 1993. *Mandate for Change.* New York: Berkeley Books.

May, A. L., and Joe Drape. 1991. "Democrats Make Pitch to Middle America, Seek to Blame Bush for Economic Squeeze." *The Atlanta Constitution* June 23.

Mayhew, David R. 1991. *Divided We Govern: Party Control, Lawmaking, and Investigations, 1946–1990.* New Haven: Yale Press.

Mazmanian, Daniel A. 1974. *Third Parties in Presidential Elections.* Washington, DC: Brookings.

McGlennon, John. 1993. "Party Activity and Party Success: Southern Precinct Leaders and the Evaluation of Party Strength." Paper presented at the Annual Meeting of the American Political Science Association, Washiongton, DC.

McGeer, Michael E. 1986. *The Decline of Popular Politics: The American North, 1865–1928.* New York: Oxford University Press.

McNutt, Paula. 1990. *The Forging of Israel.* Sheffield: The Almond Press.

Menefee-Libey, David. 1994. "Embracing Campaign-Centered Politics at the Democratic Headquaters: Charles Manatt and Paul Kirk," in John C. Green, ed., *Politics, Professionalism, and Power.* Pp.167–85. Lanham, MD: University Press of America.

Mileur, Jerome M. 1989. "In the Polity." *Polity* 22:1–3.

Milkis, Sidney M. 1993. "The New Deal, Party Politics, and the Administrative State," in Peter W. Schramm and Bradford P. Wilson, eds., *American Political Parties and Constitutional Politics.* Pp. 141–80. Lanham, MD: Rowman and Littlefield.

Miller, Zane L. 1993. "The Rules of the Game (Changing) at City Hall, 1893–1993," in *Cincinnati: Rededication of City Hall, May 13, 1993.* Cincinnati: Berman Printing Company.

Morin, Richard, and E.J.Dionne, Jr. 1992. "Public Takes Dim View of Political Parties." *The Washington Post* July 8.

Nagourney, Adam. 1991. "Select Democrats Try to Regroup at '92 'Summit'." *USA Today* June 13.

National-House Democratic Caucus. 1984. *Renewing America's Promise: A Democratic Blueprint for Our Nation's Future.* Washington, DC: National-House Democratic Caucus.

National Republican Congressional Committee. 1991. "Rules of the National Republican Congressional Committee."

National Republican Congressional Committee. 1992. *NRCC Report '92: A Report Outlining Services and Activities of 1992.* Washington, DC: National Republican Congressional Committee.

Neumann, Sigmund. 1956. "Toward a Comparative Study of Political Parties," in Sigmund Newmann, ed., *Modern Political Parties.* Chicago: University of Chicago Press.

Nie, Norman H., Sidney Verba, and John R. Petrocik. 1979. *The Changing American Voter.* 2nd ed. Cambridge: Harvard University Press.

Nimmo, Dan, and J.E. Coombs. 1980. *Subliminal Politics: Myth and Mythmakers in America.* Englewood Cliffs, NJ: Prentice-Hall.
OKI Regional Council of Governments. 1993. *State of the Region: Committee Report on Transportation, the Economy and the Environment.* Cincinnati: OKI Regional Council of Governments.
Oldfield, Duane M. 1992. "The Christian Right in the 1992 Campaign." Paper presented at the annual meeting of the Northeastern Political Science Association, Providence, RI.
Ornstein, Norman J., Thomas E. Mann, and Michael J. Malbin. 1992. *Vital Statistics on Congress, 1991-1992.* Washington, DC: CQ Press.
Ott, J. Steven. 1989. *The Organizational Culture Perspective.* Pacific Grove, CA: Brooks/Cole.
Paddock, Joel. 1990. "Beyond the New Deal: Ideological Differences Between 11 State Democratic Parties, 1956-1980." *Western Political Quarterly* 43:181-90.
Pannebianco, Angelo. 1988. *Political Parties: Organization and Power.* Cambridge: Cambridge University Press.
Patterson, Samuel C. 1989. "The Persistence of State Parties," in C. Van Horn, ed., *The State of the States.* Pp. 153-74. Washington, DC: CQ Press.
———. 1990. "State Legislators and the Legislatures," in Virgina Gray, Herbert Jacob, and Robert Albitton, eds., *Politics in the American States.* 5th ed. Glenview, Il: Scott, Foresman/Little.
Peabody, Robert. 1976. *Leadership in Congress: Stability, Succession, and Change.* Boston: Little Brown.
Pennar, Karen. 1992. "The Economists' Ouija Boards Spell 'George'." *Business Week* August 3.
Perrow, Charles. 1979. *Complex Organizations.* 2nd ed. Glenview, IL: Scott, Foresman.
Peters, Ronald M. 1990. *The American Speakership.* Baltimore: Johns Hopkins University Press.
Phillips, Kevin P. 1993. *Post-Conservative America.* New York: Vintage.
Pitney, John. 1993. "Comments," in Michael Margolis and John C. Green, eds., *Machine Politics, Sound Bites and Nostalgia.* Pp. 49-52. Lanham, MD: University Press of America.
Piven, Frances Fox, and Richard A. Cloward. 1989. *Why Americans Don't Vote.* New York: Pantheon Books.
Polsby, Nelson W. 1963. "Two Strategies of Influence: Choosing a Majority Leader 1962," in Robert Peabody and Nelson Polsby, eds., *New Perspectives on the House of Representatives.* Pp. 237-70. Chicago: Rand McNally.
———. 1968. "The Institutionalization of the U.S. House of Representatives." *American Political Science Review* 62:144-68.
———. 1983. *Consequences of Party Reform.* New York: Oxford University Press.
———, and Aaron Wildavsky. 1984. *Presidential Elections.* 6th ed. New York: Scribner
Popkin, Samuel L. 1991. *The Reasoning Voter.* Chicago: University of Chicago Press.
Porter, Stephen. 1993. "Allocation Strategies of Congressional Campaign Committees." Paper presented at the annual meeting of the Midwest Political Science Association, Chicago.
Pressman, Jeffrey L. 1977-1978. "Groups and Group Caucuses." *Political Science Quarterly* 92:673-82.
Price, David E. 1984. *Bringing Back the Parties.* Washington, DC: CQ Press.
———. 1992. "The Party Connection," in Jerome Milieur, ed., *Challenges to Party Government.* Pp. 133-53. Carbondale: Southern Illinois University Press.
Pridham, Geoffrey. 1988. "The Social Democratic Party in Britain: Protest or New Political Tendency?" in Kay Lawson and Peter Merkl, eds., *When Parties Fail.* Pp. 229-56. Princeton, NJ: Princeton Press.
Pomper, Gerald M. 1970. *Elections in America.* New York: Dodd, Mead.
———. ed. 1981. *Party Renewal in America.* New York: Praeger.

———. 1985. "The Nominations," in Gerald Pomper, ed., *The Election of 1984*. Pp. 1–34. Chatham, NJ: Chatham House.
———. 1990. "Party Organization and Electoral Success." *Polity* 23:187–206.
———. 1992. *Passions and Interests: Political Party Concepts of American Democracy*. Lawrence, KS: University Press of Kansas.
Putnam, Robert. 1992–93. "Celebrators of the Status Quo: Reflections on the Study of Politics in the 1990s." *Clio Newsletter of Politics and History* 3:1ff.
Pyle, Arthur. 1993. "Big Help Wanted." *Cincinnati Magazine* August.
Quirk, Paul J., and Jon K. Dalager. 1993. "The Election: A 'New Democrat'," in Michael Nelson, ed., *The Elections of 1992* Pp. 57–88. Washington, DC: CQ Press.
Rae, Nicol C. 1991. "The Problem of Centrist Politics in an Ideological Age: The Case of the DLC." Paper presented at the annual meeting of the American Political Science Association, Washington, DC.
Ranney, Austin. 1975. *Curing the Mischiefs of Faction*. Berkeley: University of California Press.
Rapoport, Ronald B., Walter J. Stone, Randall W. Partin, and James A. McCann. 1992. "Spillover and Carryover: Nomination Involvement and General Election Success." Presented at the annual meeting of the American Political Science Association, Chicago.
Redfield, Kent D. and Jack Van Der Slik. 1992. "The Circulation of Political Money in Illinois Elections." Paper delivered at the 1992 Midwest Political Science Association, Chicago.
Reich, Robert B. 1987. *Tales of a New America*. New York: Times Books.
Reichley, A. James. 1985. "The Rise of National Parties," in John Chubb and Paul Peterson, eds., *The New Direction in American Politics*. Pp. 175–200. Washington, DC: Brookings Institution.
———. 1992. *The Life of the Parties: A History of American Political Parties*. New York: Free Press.
Riker, William H. 1982. *Liberalism Against Populism*. New York: W. H. Freeman.
Ripley, Randall B. 1969. *Majority Party Leadership in Congress*. Boston: Little, Brown.
Roberts, George C. 1994. "Paul Bulter and the Democratic Party: Leadership and New Directions in Party Building," in John C. Green, ed., *Politics, Professionalism, and Power*. Pp. 93–104. Lanham, MD: University Press of America.
Rohde, David W. 1991. *Parties and Leaders in the Postreform House*. Chicago: University of Chicago Press.
Romney, Ronna, and Beppie Harrison. 1987. *Momentum: Women in American Politics Now*. New York: Crown Publishers.
Rosenstone, Steven J., Roy L. Behr, and Edward H. Lazarus. 1984. *Third Parties in America: Citizen Response to Major Party Failure*. Princeton, NJ: Princeton University Press.
Rosenstone, Steven J., and John Mark Hanson. 1993. *Mobilization, Participation, and Democracy in America*. New York: Macmillan.
Rosenthal, Alan. 1990. *Governors and Legislatures: Contending Powers*. Washington, DC: CQ Press.
Rule, Wilma, and Pippa Norris. 1992. "Anglo and Minority Women's Underrepresentation in the Congress: Is the Electoral System the Culprit?" in Joseph F. Zimmerman and Wilma Rule, eds., *United States Electoral Systems: Their Impact of U.S. Electoral Systems on Minorities and Women*. Pp. 41–54. Westport, CT: Greenwood Press.
Rusk, David. 1993. *Cities Without Suburbs*. Washington, DC: Woodrow Wilson Center.
Sabato, Larry J. 1981. *The Rise of the Political Consultants*. New York: Basic Books.
———. 1984. *PAC Power: Inside the World of Political Action Committees*. New York: W. W. Norton.
———. 1988. *The Party's Just Begun*. Glenview, IL: Scott, Foresman.
———. 1989. *Paying for Elections: The Campaign Finance Thicket*. New York: Priority Press.

Salmore, Barbara G., and Stephen A. Salmore. 1989. *Candidates, Parties, and Campaigns: Electoral Politics in America*. Washington, DC: CQ Press.
Sapir, Edward. 1934. "Symbolism." *Encyclopedia of the Social Sciences* 14:492–95.
Sartori, Giovanni. 1976. *Parties and Party Systems: A Framework for Analysis*. Cambridge: Cambridge University Press.
Schattschneider, E. E. 1942. *Party Government*. New York: Rinehart.
———. 1960. *The Semi-Sovereign People*. New York: Holt, Rinehart, and Winston.
Schlesinger, Arthur M. 1986. *The Cycles of American History*. Boston: Houghton Mifflin.
Schlesinger, Joseph A. 1984. "On the Theory of Party Organization." *Journal of Politics* 46:369–400.
———. 1985. "The New American Political Party." *American Political Science Review* 79:1152-69.
———. 1991. *Political Parties and the Winning of Office*. Ann Arbor: University of Michigan Press.
Schein, Edgar. 1985. *Organizational Culture and Leadership*. San Francisco: Jossey-Bass.
———. 1990. "Organizational Culture." *American Psychologist* 45:109–19.
Schwartz, Maralee. 1992. "GOP Women Complain About Role in Shadows." *The Washington Post* August 19.
Scott, William. 1961. "Organization Theory: An Overview and Appraisal." *Journal of the Academy of Management* 4:1.
Seasongood, Murray. 1954. "The Triumph of Good Government in Cincinnati," in Robert Loren Morlan, ed., *Capitol, Courthouse, and City Hall*. Boston: Houghton-Mifflin.
Seib, Gerald F. 1994. "Modem Operandi." *The Wall Street Journal* March 16.
Shafer, Byron E. 1983. *Quiet Revolution: The Struggle for the Democratic Party and the Shaping of Post-Reform Politics*. New York: Russell Sage.
———. 1988. *Bifurcated Politics: Evolution and Reform in the National Nominating Convention*. Cambridge: Harvard University Press.
———. 1991. "The Nature of an Electoral Order," in Byron E. Shafer, ed., *The End of Realignment?* Pp. 37–84. Madison: University of Wisconsin Press.
Shafritz, Jay M., and J. Steven Ott, eds. 1992. *Classics of Organizational Theory*. 3rd ed. Pacific Grove, CA: Brooks/Cole.
Shea, Daniel M. Forthcoming. *Transforming Democracy: State Legislative Campaign Committees and Political Parties*. Albany, NY: SUNY Press.
Shefter, Martin. 1976. "The Emergence of the Political Machine: An Alternative View," in Willis Hawley, ed., *Theoretical Perspectives on Urban Politics*. Pp. 14–44. Englewood Cliffs, NJ: Prentice-Hall.
———. 1978. "Party, Bureaucracy, and Political Change in the United States," in Louis Maisel and Joseph Cooper, eds., *Political Parties: Development and Decay*. Pp. 211–265. Beverly Hills, CA: Sage Publications.
———. 1984. "Political Parties, Political Mobilization, and Political Demobilization," in Thomas Ferguson and Joel Rogers, eds., *The Political Economy: Readings in the Politics and Economics of American Public Policy*. Pp. 140–48. Armonk, NY: M. E. Sharpe.
———. 1986. "Trade Unions and Political Machines: The Organization and Disorganization of the American Working Class in the Late Nineteenth Century," in Ira Katznelson and Aristide R. Zolberg, eds., *Working-Class Formation*. Pp. 197–276. Princeton: Princeton University Press.
Shepsle, Kenneth. 1978. *The Giant Jigsaw Puzzle*. Chicago: University of Chicago Press.
Shogan, Robert. 1991. "Democrats Map a Strategy for '92 Comeback." *The Los Angeles Times* March 24.

Silbey, Joel H. 1990. "The Rise and Fall of American Political Parties, 1790-1990," in L. Sandy Maisel, ed., *The Parties Respond: Changes in the American Party System*. Pp. 3-20. Boulder, CO: Westview Press.
Sinclair, Barbara. 1981. "The Speaker's Task Force in the Postreform House of Representatives." *American Political Science Review* 75:397-410.
———. 1983. *Majority Leadership in the U. S. House*. Baltimore: Johns Hopkins University Press.
———. 1990. "Congressional Leadership: A Review Essay and a Research Agenda," in John Kornacki, ed., *Leading Congress*. Pp. 97-162. Washington, DC: CQ Press.
———. 1992. "The Emergence of Strong Leadership in the 1980s House of Representatives." *Journal of Politics* 54:657-84.
Smallwood, Frank. 1983. *The Other Candidates*. Hanover, NH: University Press of New England.
Smith, Ben. 1991. "GOP Working to Keep Duke Off State Ballots." *The Atlanta Constitution* December 21.
Smith, Larry David, and Dan Nimmo. 1991. *Cordial Concurrence: Orchestrating National Party Conventions in the Telepolitical Age*. New York: Praeger.
Smith, M.L. 1993. "Alexander, the New Mr. Rogers in GOP Neighborhood." *The Nashville Banner* May 11.
Smith, Steven, and Christopher Deering. 1984. *Committees in Congress*. Washington, DC: CQ Press.
Sorauf, Frank J. 1980. "Political Parties and Political Action Committees: Two Life Cycles." *Arizona Law Review* 22:445-464.
———. 1988. *Money in American Elections*. Glenview: Scott, Foresman/Little, Brown.
———. 1992. *Inside Campaign Finance: Myths and Realities*. New Haven: Yale University Press.
———, and Scott A. Wilson. 1990. "Campaigns and Money: A Changing Role for the Political Parties?," in L. Sandy Maisel, ed., *The Parties Respond: Changes in the American Party System*. Pp. 187-203. Boulder: Westview Press.
Squire, Peverill. 1988. "Career Opportunities and Membership Stability in Legislatures." *Legislative Studies Quarterly* 13:65-83.
———. 1989. "Competition and Uncontested Seats in U.S. House Elections." *Legislative Studies Quarterly* 14:281-95.
Stengel, Richard. 1986. "Rising Stars from the Sunbelt." *Time* March 31.
Stone, Walter J. 1984. "Prenomination Candidate Choice and General Election Behavior: Iowa Presidential Activists in 1980." *American Journal of Political Science* 28:361-78.
———, Alan Abramowitz, and Ronald B. Rapoport. 1989. "How Representative Are the Iowa Caucuses?," in Peverill Squire, ed., *The Iowa Caucuses and the Presidential Nominating Process*. Pp. 19-49. Boulder: Westview Press.
———, Lonna Rae Atkeson, and Ronald B. Rapoport. 1992. "Turning On or Turning Off? Mobilization and Demobilization Effects of Participation in Presidential Nomination Campaigns." *American Journal of Political Science* 36:665-91.
Sturrock, David E., Michael Margolis, John C. Green, and Dick Kimmins. 1994. "Ohio Political Parties and Elections in the 1990s," in Alexander P. Lamis and Mary Anne Sharkey, eds., *Ohio Politics*. Kent, OH: Kent State University Press. Forthcoming.
Sullivan, Denis G., Jeffrey L. Pressman, and F. Christopher Arterton. 1976. *Explorations in Convention Decision Making: The Democratic Party in the 1970s*. San Francisco: Freeman.
Sundquist, James L. 1982. "Party Decay and the Capacity to Govern," in Joel Fleishman, ed., *The Future of American Political Parties*. Englewood Cliffs, NJ: Prentice Hall.
———. 1983. *Dynamics of the Party System*. Rev. ed. Washington, DC: Brookings.
Tashjian v. Republican Party of Connecticut. 479 U.S. 209 [1986] 210-11.
Tisinger, Russell. 1993. "Keeping Clinton Politically Correct." *National Journal* December 4.

Toner, Robin. 1991a. "Democrat Session Previews '92 Race." *The New York Times* May 8.
———. 1991b. "Despite Bleak Polls, Democrats Insist They Aren't a War Casualty." *The New York Times* March 23.
———. 1991c. "Democrats Review Presidential Bids, Vowing to Avoid the Losers' Mistakes." *The New York Times* September 23.
———. 1991d. "Arkansas' Clinton Enters the '92 Race for President." *New York Times* October 4.
U.S. Department of Commerce. 1992. *1990 Census of Population: General Characteristics of Ohio*. Washington, DC: U.S. Government Printing Office.
Van Buren, Martin. 1967. *Inquiry into the Origins and Course of Political Parties in the United States*. New York: Kelley.
———, and Norman H. Nie. 1972. *Participation in America*. New York: Harper.
Verba, Sidney, Kay Lehman Schlozman, Henry Brady, and Norman H. Nie. 1993. "Citizen Activity: Who Participates? What Do They Say?" *American Political Science Review* 87:303–18.
The Washington Post. 1989. "Democrats Face Fundraising Woes." June 22.
———. 1992. "RNC Chairman Scores Buchanan." April 16.
Ware, Alan. 1985, 1988. *The Breakdown of Democratic Party Organization, 1940–1980*. New York: Oxford University Press.
Watson, Tom. 1986. "A Year of Little Turmoil in House Elections." *Congressional Quarterly Weekly Report*. November 8:2841–55.
Wattenberg, Martin P. 1990. *The Decline of American Political Parties: 1952–1988*. Cambridge, MA: Harvard University Press.
———. 1991a. *The Rise of Candidate-Centered Politics*. Cambridge, MA: Harvard University Press.
———. 1991b. "The Republican Presidential Advantage in the Age of Party Disunity," in Gary W. Cox and Samuel Kernell, eds., *The Politics of Divided Government*. Boulder, CO: Westview Press.
Wekkin, Gary D. 1984. "National-State Party Relations: The Democrats' New Federal Structure." *Political Science Quarterly* 99:45–72.
Whitely, Paul F., and Patrick Seyd. 1994. "Local Party Campaigning and Electoral Mobilization in Britain." *Journal of Politics* 56:242–52.
Wickham, DeWayne. 1992. "If Clinton Wins, Credit Brown." *USA Today* October 14.
Wilcox, Clyde. 1989. "Share the Wealth: Contributions by Congressional Incumbents to the Campaigns of Other Candidates." *American Politics Quarterly* 17:386–408.
Wilhite, Al, and John Theilmann. 1989. "Campaign Contributions By Political Parties: Ideology vs. Winning." *Atlantic Economic Journal* 17:11–20.
Will, George F. 1993. "Selling Out the First Amendment." *The Washington Post* May 27.
Wines, Michael. 1992. "Crippled by Chaos and Lack of Strategy, Bush Campaign Stumbled to Defeat." *The New York Times* November 29.
The Wisconsin State Journal. 1992. "GOP Video Town Meeting." September 24.
Wolfinger, Raymond E. 1963. "The Influence of Precinct Work on Voting Behavior." *Public Opinion Quarterly* 27:387–98.
Wright, Quincy. 1942. *A Study of War*. Chicago: University of Chicago Press.
Wright, William E. 1971. "Comparative Party Models: Rational Efficient and Party Democracy," in William E. Wright *A Comparative Study of Party Organizations*. (Columbus, OH: Charles E. Merrill).
Zaldivar, R.A. 1992. "Moderates Form Group to Shift GOP." *The Dallas Morning News* December 16.

Russian army no longer controls
Grozny, Chechnya.
 - Dec 94 Yeltsin sent troops South
to "preserve democracy in & from the
Communist-nationalist onslaught"

149.31
48.87
70.44

Index

Abortion, 72-80
Adams, John, 21
Adams, John Quincy, 21
Activists, party, 149-164
"Adaptive brokerage model of parties," 144
"Agency agreements," 89, 185; See also Coordinated expenditures
Alexander, Lamar, 242
Allen, George, 241
Alsop, Stewart, 278
American Medical Association PAC, 336
American Political Science Association Committee on Political Parties, 238, 311
Anthony, Beryl, 177
Arkansas Republican Political Action Committee (ARPAC), 358
Atwater, Lee, 71, 81
Austen, Jeanie, 171
Australia, 14,

Babbit, Bruce, 251
Baer, Denise, 342, 346
Barbour, Haley, 240-242, 279, 287
Beck, Paul Allen, 302
Behr, Roy, 130
Bibby, John, 117-119, 220, 279, 283, 312-325, 339-341
Biddle, Nicholas, 22
Biersack, Robert, 175, 190
"Bill of Rights for Parties," 39-42
Black, Charles, 76
Blacks
  and Democratic party, 67, 69
  as part of Democratic coalition, 281, 286
  as part of Republican party in Arkansas, 358
Blackwell, Morton, 246
Bliss, Ray C. 33, 280-281, 285, 287, 357, 359
Bolingbroke, Viscount Henry St. John, 28
Bond, Richard, 71-72, 81
Bone, Hugh, 278
Borrelli, Stephen, 192
Boxer, Barbara, 93, 170

Braun, Carol Moseley, 170, 172
Breaux, John, 261
Brigham, Thomas, 359
Britain, 14, 15, 17, 24
British party system, 28
Brock, William, 237, 239, 281, 285, 287, 357
Broder, David, 33
Brown, Jerry, 68, 72
Brown, Ronald, 64-69, 255-256
Bryan, William Jennings, 22
Buchanan, Patrick, 71-72, 74-76, 80
Burnham, Walter Dean, 20, 233
Bush, Barbara, 171
Bush, George, 5, 18, 64, 70-72, 83, 254, 260, 271
  economic plan, 74
  as seen by Perot supporters, 156-160
  '88 campaign, 315
Business-Industry Political Action Committee (BIPAC), 101
Butler, Paul, 262

Campaign Conference for Democratic Women, 168
Campaign consultants, 14, 35, 72, 85, 90, 94-103
Campaign finance 312
  congressional elections, 89-94, 176-188
  law, 108-110
  reform, 61, 81,
  See also Congressional campaign committees
Campaigns
  congressional finance, 89-94, 176-188
  contributions, 191-197
  incumbent advantages, 176-179, 192
  quality of, 318
Campaigns & Elections, 167
Candidates,
  for Congress, 55; for governor, 55
  See also congressional elections
Candidate-centered politics, 3, 85, 298
Carter, Jimmy, 18, 270-271
Catt, Carrie Chapman, 166

Chiles, Lawton, 251
Christian Constitutional Society, 28
Christian Democratic Party, 41
Christian right and Christian Coalition, 74-75
Cincinnati, 291-305
Civil War, 13, 15, 18, 22, 24
Cleveland, Grover, 19
Clinton, Bill, 5, 7, 25, 170, 284
  administration of, 27, 50,
  and Democratic Leadership Council, 259-262
  as presidential candidate, 68, 71, 77
  as seen by Perot supporters, 156-160
  role of women in campaign, 167
Clinton, Hillary Rodham, 52, 243
Coalition for Democratic Values, 262
Coelho, Tony, 100, 181
Cole, Tom, 89, 177
Coleman, Elijah, 358
College Republicans, 241
Committee on Political Education, of AFL-CIO, 101
Commonsense, 244
Congress,
  party control, 18-19, 48-49,
  party unity, 14, 345
  leaders in, 31
  members of, 34
  See also "Party-in-government," House of Representatives
Congressional campaign committees, 14, 16, 83-106, 175-186
  association with PACs, 99-102, 194
  campaign communications, 97-98
  campaign spending in '92, 89-94
  campaign services, 89-98
  nationalization of American politics, 98
  distribution of resources, 177-187, 191-199
  efforts to strengthen state party committees, 85-86, 94-97
  fundraising, 99-102, 177-180, 194
  help on gubernatorial elections, 85, 95-96
  impact on campaign services, 102-103
  in-government cohesion, 177
  issue and opposition research, 96-97
  party differences, 103-104
  policy concerns, 176-177
  seat maximization goal, 86-89, 177-188, 194-199

  See also Democratic Congressional Campaign Committee (DCCC); National Republican Congressional Committee (NRCC); Democratic Senatorial Campaign Committee (DSCC); National Senatorial Campaign Committee (NSCC).
Congressional elections,
  '92, 83-106
  cost of, 36,
  open seats in '92, 84
  See also Congressional campaign committees
Congressional Research Service, 97
Conservatism, 20
Constitution, United States, 39
  Bill of Rights, 39
  First Amendment, 39, 52
  on presidential selection, 52-53
Conte, Sylvio, 99
Conventions, national party, 72-76,
  women during '92, 170-173
Cook Political Report and Charlie Cook, 101
Cooper, Jim, 261
Coordinated expenditures, 67, 77, 89-94, 99, 196, 206
Cotter, Cornelius, 134-136, 221-222, 312-326, 340-342
"Counteracting" party model, 323, 345
County party committees, 133-144, 312-313, 318, 321
  aid to state legislative candidates, 142-143
  activities in '92 election, 136-143,
  basic functions, 133
  candidates' view of county committee aid, 142-143
  relationship to state legislative candidates, 138-143
  structural strength, 137-138,
  well being, 133-136
  See also Local party organizations
Crawford, Mary, 240,
Critical elections, 3, 20, 25
Crotty, William, 134, 275, 342
Cutler, Lynn, 170
Cuomo, Mario, 68, 73, 80, 259

Daley, Richard, 36
Democratic Advisory Council, 239, 262
Democratic Congressional Campaign Committee (DCCC), 83-106, 175-188

campaign services, 94-103
distribution of resources, 177-188
finances in '92, 89-94, 110-132
linkages with PACs, 99-102
staffing levels and organization of, 86
targeting strategies, 87-89
timing of contributions, 191-199
See also Congressional campaign committees
Democratic Leadership Council (DLC), 7, 65, 73
activities in '88 campaign, 255
activities in '92 campaign, 257-262
and Bill Clinton, 257-259
and Clinton Administration, 259-262
benefits of association with, 252-253
Cleveland Convention, 255-257
DLC Network, 255
formation of, 249-253
long term impact on Democratic party, 262-263
Mandate For Change, 261
New Choices Resolution, 251-258
"New Democrats," 255-262
Progressive Policy Institute, 255-257
relationship to Democratic party, 253-254
the institutionalization of, 254-257
Democratic National Committee (DNC)
advertisements in '92 general election, 79
Asian-American Group, 243
Committee on Party Effectiveness (CPE), 250
Constituency Division, 243
delegate selection process, 63
drafting committee, 73
efforts to mobilize black voters, 67
finances in '92 election, 77, 110-132
intra-organizational improvements, 66
leaders, 64, 67
platform in '92, 267-273
Policy Commission, 253
policy initiatives since 1992, 237-240, 242-247
relationship to the DLC, 249-263
role in 1992 election, 71-81
role in presidential nomination process, 62-64
relations with state party committees, 65-66
rules reforms, 66
strategy in '92 general election, 76-79
Woman's Caucus of, 170

Youth Division, 243
See also Democratic Leadership Council; Democratic Congressional Campaign Committee; Democratic Senatorial Campaign Committee
Democratic party
views on government, 50-51
core constituencies, 69
culture of, 281-285
in Arkansas, 349-352
in Texas, 349-352
See also Democratic National Committee (DNC); Democratic Congressional Campaign Committee (DCCC); Democratic Senatorial Campaign Committee (DSCC)
Democratic Senatorial Campaign Committee, 175-188
campaign services, 94-103
distribution of resources, 177-188,
finances in '92, 89-94, 110-132
linkages with PACs, 87-89
staffing levels and organization, 86
Woman's Council, 170
Dealignment, 13, 26
Delegates. See Conventions
Dennis, Jack, 330
Direct mail
by hill committees, 101
by national committees, 241
by Republicans, 278
Divided government, 3, 25, 46
Dixicrats, 54
Dixon, Alan, 83
Dole, Robert, 169, 242
Dukakis, Michael, 64, 155, 254
Duke, David, 71
Dunn, Jennifer, 242
Duverger, Maurice, 14, 221, 331
Dwyre, Diana, 220

Ehrenhalt, Alan, 231
Eisenhower, Dwight, 18, 279
El Salvador, 30
Eldersveld, Samuel, 134, 342
Electoral college, 15, 16
Electorate. See Voters and political behavior
EMILY's List, 170
Emmanuel, Rahm, 77
Empower America, 6
Engel, Rob, 95, 104

Epstein, Leon, 331
Espy, Mike, 184
Estrich, Susan, 167
European party system, 331

Farley, Jim 33
Farmer-Labor Party, 17, 54
Fazio, Vic, 99
Federal Election Campaign Act (FECA), 89-90, 108, 179, 185-188
Federal Election Commission (FEC), 70, 89-90, 106-110, 175, 179
    regulatory system before 1991, 108-109
    regulatory system after 1991, 109-111
Federalists, 28, 31
Federation of Independent Parties, 55
Feinstein, Dianne, 170, 172
Fenno, Richard, 205
"First-past-the-post" 14-15, 45-46
Flavin, Deborah, 88
Foley, Thomas, 246
Ford, Gerald, 20, 63
Francis, Les, 180
Frantizich, Steve, 358
Freeman, Jo, 280
Frendreis, John 134-144, 321
From, Al, 250, 260

Gay and lesbians, 70, 281
General Accounting Office (GAO), 97
Gender gap, 162
Gephardt, Richard, 250-251, 255
Gibson, James, 131-144, 312-325, 340-342
Gierzynski, Anthony, 220, 232
Ginrich, Newt, 99
Gitelson, Alan, 321, 341, 348
Goldman, Ralph, 339
Goldwater, Barry, 22, 239, 325, 357
Goodling, Bill, 87
Gore, Albert, 254, 259
Gorton, Slade, 242
Gramm-Rudman Act, 56
Grassroots activities, 5, 286, 318
    See also, Local party organizations
Great Depression, 17, 18, 22, 24
Green Party, 41
Greenberg, Stanley, 78, 261
Greener, Chuck, 241
Guiliani, Rudy, 241
Guinier, Lani 261

Hamilton, Alexander, 15, 28
Hamilton County, 297-305
Hammerschidt, John-Paul, 360
"Hard money," 110-117
Harkin, Tom, 258
Harmel, Robert, 353
Harriman Communications Center, 98
Harris, Lou, 16
Herchensohn, Bruce, 93
Heritage Foundation, 261
Herring, Pendleton, 211-311
Herrnson, Paul, 62, 80, 135, 176, 192-193, 312-325, 341
Hibbing, John, 208
Hill, Anita, 34, 83
Hill committees, 5, 85, 191-199
    See also Democratic Congressional Campaign Committee (DCCC); National Republican Congressional Committee (NRCC); Democratic Senatorial Campaign Committee (DSCC); National Senatorial Campaign Committee (NSCC).
Hill, Kenneth, 245
Hoover, Herbert, 25,
House banking scandal, 87
House of Representatives, 28, 51-52, 175
    party leadership of, 201-215
    See also Congress
Huckshorn, Robert, 134-136, 312-325, 340-342
Huddleson, Walter "Dee," 251
Humphrey, Hebert, 36
Humphreys, Raymond, 359
Hunt, James, 251
Hutchinson, Kay Bailey, 171
Houston Woman's Rights Convention, 166

Ideology, 14
Incumbency advantage 19
Independence Party, 55,
Independents, 13
Interest groups, 13, 26, 49, 85, 294
    activists and Perot supporters, 160, 313, 317

Jackson, Andrew, 20-21, 48
Jackson, Jesse, 65, 68, 73, 81, 253
Jacobson, Gary, 177-179, 165, 192
Janda, Kenneth, 353
Jefferson, Thomas, 15, 20-21, 28, 48, 273

Index

Jewell, Malcolm, 220
Johnson, Lyndon, 22, 270
Johnson, Neal Sox, 362
Jones, James, 251

Kayden, Xandra, 176, 336
Kemp, Jack, 99
Kennedy, Edward, 65
Kennedy, John F., 23-24, 36, 271-272
Kenwood Towne Center, 292-293
Kernell, Samuel, 184
Kerry, Robert, 258
Key, V. O., 20, 329-337, 339, 342
Keynesian economics, 324
Kirk, Paul, 253, 283
Kissinger, Henry, 18
Kondratieff, Nikolai, 24-25
Kramer, Gerald, 342
Kurtz, Karl, 230

Labor party, in Britain, 16
Ladd, Everett Carll, 21
La Follette, Robert, 54
Lawson, Kay, 118, 316, 335
Lazarus, Edward, 150
Legislative campaign committees, 320
  See also, State legislative campaign committees;
  Congressional campaign committees; Hill committees
Legislative professionalization, 219, 227-233, 297-298
Lewis, John, 258
Leyden, Kevin, 192
Liberalism, 20
Likud party, 262
Lincoln, Abraham, 20, 271
Local party organizations, 134-144, 289-305, 341
  activities in '92 election, 136-142
  leadership, 116-127, 299-305
  structural strength, 137-138
  and women candidates, 173
  also see County party committees; Grassroots activities
Long, Gillis, 250-252
Loomis, Alan, 202
Lowe, Lynn, 360
Lowi, Theodore, 16
Lugar, Richard, 168
Luther, Robert, 360
Lynch, John, 184

Madison, James, 28
Mahe, Eddie, 157, 336
Maisel, L. Sandy, 75
Man, Barbara, 359
Manatt, Charles, 63, 239
March, James, 355
Marvroules, Nick, 87
Marshall, William, 250, 255
Martin, Lynn, 171
Mass media, 14, 31, 36-37,
  coverage of women candidates in '92 election, 169
  impact on perceptions of party, 28-30
Matalin, Mary, 76, 167
Mayhew, David, 19
McCarthy, Eugene, 284
McGovern/Fraser Reform Commission, 249
McKinley, William, 20-21
Metzger, Leigh Ann, 241
Mexico, 19
Mileur, Jerome, 24, 331
Miller, Zell, 258
Milligan, Thomas, 360
Minor party candidates, 16
  See also Third parties
Mondale, Walter, 250
Moore, Catherine, 244
Multi-party system, 16
  See also Third parties
Muckrakers, 29
Mondale, Walter, 63

National Committee for an Effective Congress (NCEC), 96
National Conservative Political Action Committee (NCPAC), 319
National Federation of Republican Women, 171
National party committees
  "brokerage role," 107
  campaign services, 61
  finances in '92, 107-132
  financial relationship with state party committees, 117-123
  financial role of, 107-108
  fundraising by in '92, 65-72
  policy initiatives since 1992, 237-247
  relations with state and local parties, 61
  renewal, 61
  role in the '92 election, 61-73

National party presidential nominating conventions
  delegate selection rules, 61
National Policy Forum, 240, 245
National Republican Congressional Committee (NRCC), 209
  campaign services, 94-103
  distribution of resources, 177-188
  finances in '92 campaign, 89-94, 111-117
  linkages with PACs, 87-89
  staffing levels and organization 86
  targeting strategies, 87-89,
  timing of contributions, 191-199
National Republican Senatorial Committee (NRSC)
  campaign services, 94-103
  distribution of resources, 177-188
  finances in '92 campaign, 89-94, 111-117
  linkages with PACs, 87-89
  staffing levels and organization, 86
  and women candidates, 168
National Woman's Political Caucus (NWPC), 166
New Alliance Party, 55
New Deal, 25, 34, 49
New Democrat, 255
"New orthodoxy of party resurgence," 311, 339
New York State Democratic Committee, 244
News Media. See Mass media.
Neumann, Sigmond, 331
Nickles, Don, 74
Niemeyer, Matt, 100
Nixon, Richard, 20, 21, 71, 272
Nonpartisan elections, 29, 31
Norris, Genie, 178
North Atlantic Free Trade Agreement (NAFT), 261
Nunn, Sam, 251, 255

Oakar, Mary Rose, 87
Olson, David, 219
Olver, John, 99

PACs. See Political Action Committees.
Partisan identification, See "Party-in-the-electorate," Voters and voter behavior
Partisan press, 29

Party culture, 274-287
  theories of organizational culture, 276-277
  and political behavior, 285-287
Party leadership, 46, 50, 61-65, 72-76, 201-214, 299
"Party-as-organization" and party organization, 2, 315-316, 339-340, 332-334, 349, 347-349
"Party-in-government," 2-3, 201-214, 290, 316, 324, 329-330, 333-335, 349, 338, 347-349
"Party-in-the-electorate," 2, 35, 290, 324, 329-330, 333-335, 339, 344
Party platforms, 35, 63, 72-75, 81, 294, 344
  statements regarding women, 169
  the use of symbols in, 265-273
  as tools of political persuasion, 267-273
Party system, 2, 3, 311-312
Party Transformation Study (PTS) 134-136, 312, 341, 349
Patriot Party, 55
Patronage, 14
Perot, Ross 1, 5, 13, 15, 16, 33, 36, 45, 50, 55, 74, 167, 237, 247, 314, 343
  activists for, 159-164
  characteristic of, 152-156
  ideology, 154
  pre and post convention activity, 161
  view toward two major parties, 158
Penny, Tim, 261
Perez-Ferguson, Anita, 242
Pierce, Steven, 99
Platforms. See Party platforms
Political Action Committees (PACs), 19, 36, 84-85, 194
  working with the hill committees, 87-89, 177-188, 191, 194
Political consultants. See Campaign consultants.
Political elites, 4
  See also Party leadership
Political machines, 14, 34, 134
Political parties
  as agents of change, 27-43, 46-47;
  as corrupt and undemocratic, 27-29;
  as resistant to change, 49;
  as linkage mechanisms and tools of popular sovereignty, 27-43, 47-48
  as alternatives to war, 30-31
  as recruiters of public servants, 31

as civic educators 31
as agenda makers, 31-32
as public utility cooperations, 32
as serving a constituent function, 46-49
cycles of party control, 19-26
decline, 1, 6, 26, 311, 319-325
decline versus revival debate, 1-9, 13-14, 32, 133-136, 19-220, 311-313, 319-325, 349-364
functions of 27-43, 46-49, 313-317
innovation, 349-366
leaders and elites, 48, 50, 59-63, 72-76
local party leaders, 134-144
machines, 34, 134
perceptions of, 33
role in metropolitan areas, 291-296
the impact of economics on, 22
the study of 1-9, 311-326, 329-337, 339-349, 349-364
Political science and scientists, 1, 16, 24, 45-46, 55-56, 275, 291, 298, 301, 314, 325
Polls and polling, 56, 67, 78, 95-96, 180-181
Pomper, Gerald, 20, 118, 250, 263, 316
Popular sovereignty, 30
Populists, 16
Presidential elections,
public funding of, 17
'92, 2, 13, 62-81, 149-163, 258-262
Price, David, 260
Primary elections, 41
Progressives, 16, 29
Progressive Movement and Party; 54, 172, 332
Public financing of elections, 27, 36-41
Public opinion 49, 95-96, 316, 323-324
Public opinion polling, 35
See also Polls and polling

Qualye, Dan, 75-76
Qualye, Marilyn, 171

Ranney, Austin, 228, 320
"Rational-efficient" model of party, 3, 47, 335
Reagan, Ronald, 18, 24, 63, 184, 271-272, 325
economic principles of, 76
Realignment, 20
periods of, 21
generational change, 24
Reconstruction, 22, 29
Redistricting, effects of, 84, 87

Reed, Bruce, 252
Reforms, 27, 282
Regional (Ohio-Kentucky-Indiana) Council of Governments (OKI), 300
RENEW, 171
Republican Campaign Academy, 95
Republican Committee on Committees, 208
Republican Exchange Satellite Network, 242
Republican Neighborhood Meeting, 242
Republican National Black Council, 358
Republican National Committee (RNC),
Committee on Resolutions, 74
convention strategy, 74
finances in '92, 69, 78, 111-117,
platform in '92, 74, 267-273
policy initiatives since '92, 237-242, 245-247
reliance on family values theme in '92, 72-76,
role in the 1992 election, 62-81,
role in the presidential nomination process, 62-81,
delegate selection process, 63
strategy in '92 general election, 76
women in, 165-173
Woman's Political Caucus, 171
Republican Policy Committee, 209
Republican Party
views on government, 50
culture, 277-281
in Arkansas, 349-352
in Texas, 349-352
See also, Republican National Committee (RNC); National Republican Congressional Committee (NRCC); National Republican Senatorial Committee (NRSC)
Republican Women's Task Force of 1976, 282
"Responsible" party model, 2, 34, 47, 143, 291-296, 300-302, 321-322, 335
Republican Coordinating Committee, 239
Republican Research Committee, 209
"Responsible three-party system," 4, 45-57
Richardson, Bill, 73
Riker, William, 24
Rising Tide, 241
Robb, Chuck, 251, 255
Rockefeller, Jay, 245
Rockefeller, Winthrop, 351-352, 363
Rook, Susan, 167

Roosevelt, Franklin D., 20, 270
Roosevelt, Theodore, 18, 20, 271
Rosenstone, Steven, 150, 318
Rothenberg Political Report and Stuart Rothenberg, 101

St. Petersburg, Florida, 295
Sartori, Giovanni, 342
Scandal, as alternatives to issues, 50,
Schattschneider, E.E., 317, 331
Schein, Edgar, 276, 284
Schlesinger, Arthur, Jr., 20, 22, 24,
Schlesinger, Joseph, 314, 330, 342-343
Senate, United States. See Congress
Shafer, Byron, 19-20
Simon, Herbert, 355
Sinclair, Barbara, 175, 191
Single-issue interest groups, 54
60 Minutes, 38
Smith, Craig, 242
Smith, Lee, 242
Smith, Mary Louise, 168
Social Security Administration, 34, 110-117
"Soft money," 5, 70, 77-79, 81, 110-117, 317
Sohn, Adam, 243-244
Sorauf, Frank, 304, 320, 339
South Africa, 30
South, politics in, 29, 195, 207
Southern Association of Republican State Chairmen, 359
Southern Democrats, 68
Soviet Union, 17
State legislative campaigns, 138-144, 321
State legislative campaign committees (LCCs), 6, 70, 78, 219-233
    fit with traditional party organizations, 221-233
    services provided by, 219
    financial interdependence with parties, 224-226
State legislative leaders, 228-233
    See also Party leadership
State legislators, 203
State Party Archive Project, 349-366
State party organizations
    finances in '92 congressional races, 89
    finances in '92, 117-123
    innovation and change, 349-366
    the study of, 341
"Stratarchy," 134
Steering and Policy Committee, 209
Stonecash, Jeffrey, 220

Suburban governments, 296
Sundquist, James, 20
"Super cycles," 4, 21-23,
"Super PAC," parties as, 334
Supreme Court, 41
Survey research. See Political polls; Public opinion polling
Sweeden, 14
Switzer, Don, 246
Sycamore Township, 292
Symbols, to convey a party message, 265-273
    condensational symbols, 266-267, 270-273
    identity symbols, 266
    oppositional symbols, 266
    See also Party Platforms

Tammany Hall, 29,
Term limits, 34, 36
Thurmond, Strom, 15
Third parties
    sources of activism, 149-151
    candidates, 16-18
    the need for and benefits of, 51-55
    financing of, 52
    policy development, 53-56
    See also Minor party candidates
Thornburg v. Gingles, 84, 87
Thomas, Clarence 33, 84
Toledo, 295
Tower, John, 351, 361
Travis, Alice, 243
Tripod view of parties, 2-9, 329-337
    relationship between components, 333-335
Truman, Harry, 270
"Truncated" view of party, 315
Tsongas, Paul, 74, 258
Tully, Paul, 67
Turnout, See Voter mobilization and turnout
Tutwiler, Margaret, 167
Two-party system
    reasons for, 13-19
    failures of, 45-52

United We Stand America, 55

Van Buren, Martin, 21, 27, 42, 48
Van Rest, Judith, 241
Vertz, Laura, 134-144
Voter mobilization and turnout, 312-325

Voters and voter behavior, 14, 314
Voter preferences, 2

Walker, Robert, 76
Wallace, George, 15, 28
Ware, Alan, 320
Washington, George, 28
Watergate affair, 202
Wattenberg, Martin, 62, 344
Weber, Vince, 75-76
Welch, Susan, 321
Welfare state, 34, 47
Whigs, 30
White House,
   control of, 18
Whitman, Christine Todd, 171
Wilcox, Clyde, 175, 191
Wilhelm, David, 243-245
Will, George, 38
Wilson, James Q., 320
Wilson, Woodrow, 19, 22

Wirth, Tim, 250
WISH List, 171
Wolfe, Kristine, 100
Wolfinger, Raymond, 134
Women
   in party politics, 88, 165-173
   and party organizations, 166-168
   as candidates, 88, 168-171
   as candidates in '92 election, 169-171
   as part of Democratic coalition, 284
   role in '92 presidential campaign, 167-168
   See also "Year of the Woman"
Woods, Harriet, 170
Wright, Betsy, 167
Wright, Quincy, 24

Yeakel, Lynn, 170, 172
Yeutter, Clayton, 71,
"Year of the Women," 88, 165
   See also Women in party politics
Young Republicans, 241

About the Contributors

Andrew Appleton is Assistant Professor of Political Science at Washington State University. He has published on party organization and behavior.

Laura Berkowitz is a graduate student in political science at the University of Akron.

Robert Biersack is Supervisory Statistician at the Federal Election Commission. He has written on congressional elections and campaign finance.

Stephen A. Borrelli is Assistant Professor of Political Science at the University of Alabama. He has coauthored articles on political parties, interest groups, and public opinion.

Janet M. Box-Steffensmeier is Assistant Professor of Political Science at Ohio State University. She has written on elections, Congress, and methodology.

Barbara Burrell is a Researcher with the Wisconsin Research Laboratory at the University of Wisconsin—Madison. She has published extensively on parties and elections, and women and politics.

John J. Coleman is Assistant Professor of Political Science at the University of Wisconsin—Madison. He has written on party organizations, elections, and political economy.

Anthony Corrado is Associate Professor of Government at Colby College in Waterville, Maine. Most recently, he wrote *Paying for Presidents: Public Financing in National Elections* (1993).

Diana F. Dwyre is Assistant Professor of Political Science at the University of Maryland at Baltimore. Her research interests include party organizations, elections, and Congress.

Terri Susan Fine is Assistant Professor of Political Science at the University of Central Florida. She has written on party platforms, party organizations, and women and politics.

Gregory Fleming is a graduate student in political science at the University of Wisconsin-Madison.

John P. Frendreis is Professor of Political Science at Loyola University of Chicago. He has published extensively on political parties, elections, and urban politics.

Alan R. Gitelson is Professor of Political Science at Loyola University of Chicago. He has published many articles and is coauthor of *American Political Parties: Stability and Change* (1984).

Ralph M. Goldman is President of the Center for Party Development, Washington D.C. Among his most recent books is *From Warfare to Party Politics* (1990).

John C. Green is Professor of Political Science and the Director of the Ray C. Bliss Institute of Applied Politics at the University of Akron. His most recent publication is the edited volume *Politics, Professionalism, and Power* (1994).

Jon F. Hale is Assistant Professor of Political Science at the University of Oklahoma. His research interests include mass media, political campaigns, and political parties.

Tim Hames is Lecturer in Politics at Pembroke College, Oxford where he specializes in contemporary American parties and elections.

Paul S. Herrnson is Associate Professor of Government and Politics at the University of Maryland at College Park. His most recent book is *Campaigning for Congress* (forthcoming).

Philip A. Klinkner is Assistant Professor of Political Science at Loyola Marymount University. He authored *Losing Parties: Out-Party National Committees, 1956-1993* (1994).

Anne Layzell is a graduate student in political science at Loyola University of Chicago.

Kevin M. Leyden is Assistant Professor of Political Science at West Virginia University. He has coauthored articles on political parties, interest groups, and public opinion.

Steve Lillenthal is Director of State Policy fro the Free Congress Foundation. He has written of campaigns, elections, and parties.

Theodore J. Lowi is the John L. Senior Professor of American Institutions at Cornell University.

Michael Margolis, Professor of Political Science at the University of Cincinnati. His publications include *Manipulating Public Opinion* (1989).

Randall W. Partin is a Ph.D. candidate in political science at the University of Colorado.

Ronald B. Rapoport is the John Marshall Professor of Government at the College of William & Mary. He is coeditor of *The Life of the Parties: A Study of Presidential Activists* (1993).

A. James Reichley is a Visiting Senior Fellow in the Graduate Public Policy Program at Georgetown University. His most recent book is *The Life of the Parties* (1992).

David Resnick is Associate Professor of Political Science and Director of the Center for the Study of Democratic Citizenship at the University of Cincinnati. He has written on democratic theory and political philosophy.

Daniel M. Shea is Assistant Professor of Political Science and Bliss Institute Fellow at the University of Akron. He is the author of *Transforming Democracy* (forthcoming).

Walter J. Stone is Professor of Political Science at the University of Colorado. He is the author of *Republic at Risk: Self Interest in American Politics* (1992).

Daniel S. Ward is Assistant Professor of Political Science at Rice University. He has published on party cohesion in Congress and party organizations.

Lori M. Weber is a graduate student in political science at the University of Colorado.